Financial Advisor Series

FOUNDATIONS OF FINANCIAL PLANNING: AN OVERVIEW

Allen McLellan, Editor

FA262.03.2

This publication is designed to provide accurate and authoritative information about the subject covered. While every precaution has been taken in the preparation of this material, the authors, and The American College assume no liability for damages resulting from the use of the information contained in this publication. The American College is not engaged in rendering legal, accounting, or other professional advice. If legal or other expert advice is required, the services of an appropriate professional should be sought.

© 2014 The American College Press
All rights reserved
ISBN-10: 1-58293-147-x
ISBN-13:978-1-58293-147-0
Library of Congress Control No.: 2012934702
270 S. Bryn Mawr Avenue
Bryn Mawr, PA 19010
(888) AMERCOL (263–7265)
theamericancollege.edu
Printed in the United States of America

FINANCIAL ADVISOR SERIES

Sales Skills Techniques
Techniques for Exploring Personal Markets
Techniques for Meeting Client Needs
Techniques for Prospecting: Prospect or Perish
Women and Money—Matters of Trust

Product Essentials
Essentials of Annuities
Essentials of Business Insurance
Essentials of Disability Income Insurance
Essentials of Life Insurance Products
Essentials of Long-Term Care Insurance
Essentials of Multiline Insurance Products

Planning Foundations
Foundations of Estate Planning
Foundations of Retirement Planning
Foundations of Financial Planning: An Overview
Foundations of Financial Planning: The Process
Foundations of Investment Planning

THE AMERICAN COLLEGE

The American College® is an independent, nonprofit, accredited institution founded in 1927 that offers professional certification and graduate-degree distance education to men and women seeking career growth in financial services.

The Solomon S. Huebner School® of The American College administers the Chartered Life Underwriter (CLU®); the Chartered Financial Consultant (ChFC®); the Chartered Advisor for Senior Living (CASL®); the Registered Health Underwriter (RHU®); the Registered Employee Benefits Consultant (REBC®); the Chartered Healthcare Consultant™, the Chartered Leadership Fellow® (CLF®); and the Retirement Income Certified Professional (RICP®) professional designation programs. In addition, The College offers prep programs for the CFP® and CFA® certifications.

The Richard D. Irwin Graduate School® of The American College offers a Master of Science in Financial Services (MSFS) degree, a Master of Science in Management (MSM), a one-year program with an emphasis in leadership, and a PhD in Financial and Retirement Planning. Additionally, it offers the Chartered Advisor in Philanthropy® (CAP®) and several graduate-level certificates that concentrate on specific subject areas.

The American College is accredited by **The Middle States Commission on Higher Education**, 3624 Market Street, Philadelphia, PA 19104 at telephone number 267.284.5000.

The Middle States Commission on Higher Education is a regional accrediting agency recognized by the U.S. of Education and the Commission on Recognition of Postsecondary Accreditation. Middle States accreditation is an expression of confidence in an institution's mission and goals, performance, and resources. It attests that in the judgment of the Commission on Higher Education, based on the results of an internal institutional self-study and an evaluation by a team of outside peer observers assigned by the Commission, an institution is guided by well-defined and appropriate goals; that it has established conditions and procedures under which its goals can be realized; that it is accomplishing them substantially; that it is so organized, staffed, and supported that it can be expected to continue to do so; and that it meets the standards of the Middle States Association. The American College has been accredited since 1978.

The American College does not discriminate on the basis of race, religion, sex, handicap, or national and ethnic origin in its admissions policies, educational programs and activities, or employment policies.

The American College is located at 270 S. Bryn Mawr Avenue, Bryn Mawr, PA 19010. The toll-free number of the Office of Professional Education is (888) 263-7265; the fax number is (610) 526-1465; and the home page address is theamericancollege.edu.

Certified Financial Planner Board of Standards, Inc., owns the certification marks CFP®, CERTIFIED FINANCIAL PLANNER™, and CFP (with flame logo)®, which it awards to individuals who successfully complete initial and ongoing certification requirements.

CONTENTS

Financial Advisor Series iii
The American College v
Table of Contents vii
Acknowledgments xxi
About the Author xxiii
Special Notes to Advisors xxv
Overview of the Book xxvii

1 The Financial Planning Process 1.1

Emergence of a New Profession 1.1
What Is Financial Planning? 1.3
    Financial Planning Is a Process 1.4
    Steps in the Financial Planning Process: The Eight
    Financial Planning Domains 1.6
        Step 1: Establishing and Defining the Client-Planner
        Relationship 1.6
        Step 2: Gathering Information Necessary to Fulfill the
        Engagement 1.9
        Step 3: Analyzing and Evaluating the Client's Current
        Financial Status 1.13
        Step 4: Developing the Recommendation(s) 1.16
        Step 5: Communicating the Recommendation(s) 1.18
        Step 6: Implementing the Recommendation(s) 1.19
        Step 7: Monitoring the Recommendation(s) 1.20
        Step 8: Practicing Within Professional and Regulatory
        Standards 1.21
    How Is Financial Planning Conducted? 1.22
        Single-Purpose Approach 1.23
        Multiple-Purpose Approach 1.23
        Comprehensive Approach 1.24
    Financial Planning Areas of Specialization 1.25
    Content of a Comprehensive Financial Plan 1.26
        Life-Cycle Financial Planning 1.28
        Format of a Comprehensive Financial Plan 1.30
    Trends Creating Opportunities for Financial Planning
    Advisors 1.33
    Consumer Needs for Financial Planning 1.36
        Obstacles Confronting Consumers 1.39
        Role of Financial Planning Advisors 1.40

Financial Planning Umbrella 1.40
Chapter Review 1.41
    Review Questions 1.41

2 Insurance Planning and Risk Management 2.1

Importance of Protection Objectives 2.1
Risk 2.2
Types of Pure Risks 2.4
Planning for Pure Risks: Insurance and Other Techniques 2.6
    Establishing and Defining the Client-Advisor Relationship
    .... 2.8
    Gathering Information Necessary to Fulfill the
        Engagement 2.8
    Analyzing and Evaluating the Client's Current Financial
        Status 2.12
        Risk Measurement 2.12
            Property Risks 2.12
            Liability Risks 2.15
            Personal Risks 2.15
        Risk Evaluation 2.18
    Developing the Recommendations 2.18
        Alternative Risk Treatment Devices 2.19
            Risk Avoidance 2.20
            Loss Prevention 2.20
            Loss Reduction 2.21
            Retention 2.21
            Insurance 2.22
        Selecting Techniques for Handling a Client's Pure
            Risks 2.25
        A Plan Using the Selected Techniques 2.28
    Communicating the Recommendations and Implementing
        the Recommendations 2.29
    Monitoring the Recommendations 2.29
A Survey of Personal Insurance Coverages 2.30
    Meeting Personal Risks 2.30
        Life Insurance 2.30
            Term Life Insurance 2.31
            Whole Life Insurance 2.33
            Universal Life (UL) Insurance 2.36
        Annuities 2.38
        Individual Health Insurance 2.40
            Medical Expense Insurance 2.41

    Disability Income Insurance.. 2.41
    Long-Term Care Insurance... 2.45
  Meeting Property and Liability Risks 2.52
    Homeowners Insurance 2.52
      Coverage A Dwelling 2.54
      Coverage B Other Structures 2.54
      Coverage C Personal Property 2.55
      Coverage D Loss of Use 2.56
      Coverage E Personal Liability 2.56
      Coverage F Medical Payments to Others 2.57
    Personal Auto Insurance.. 2.57
      Part A Liability Coverage 2.58
      Part B Medical Payments Coverage 2.59
      Part C Uninsured Motorists Coverage 2.59
      Part D Coverage for Damage to Your Auto 2.60
      No-Fault Benefits 2.60
    Umbrella Liability Insurance.. 2.61
  A Concluding Comment 2.62
Chapter Review... 2.63
  Review Questions 2.63

3 Employee Benefits Planning 3.1

Scope and Significance of Employee Benefits............................. 3.1
  Meaning of Employee Benefits.. 3.1
  Significance of Employee Benefits 3.2
  Growth of Employee Benefits 3.3
    Industrialization 3.3
    Organized Labor 3.4
    Wage Controls 3.4
    Cost Advantages 3.5
    Inflation 3.5
    Legislation 3.5
Importance of Benefit Planning 3.5
  Benefit-Planning for the Employer.. 3.6
  Advisor Awareness of Employee Benefits 3.7
    The Basis of a Financial Plan 3.8
    The Purchase of Additional Insurance and Retirement
      Benefits.. 3.8
    A Source for Negotiating a Compensation Package 3.9
Eligibility for Benefits 3.9
  Covered Classifications 3.9
  Full-Time Employment 3.10

Foundations of Financial Planning: An Overview

    Probationary Periods 3.10
    Insurability 3.10
    Premium Contributions 3.10
    Termination of Coverage 3.10
  Types of Employee Benefits 3.11
    Medical Expense Insurance 3.12
      Types of Plans 3.12
        HMOs 3.15
        PPOs 3.17
        POS Plans 3.17
        A Comparison of Plan Types 3.18
      Plan Provisions 3.19
        Eligibility 3.19
        Covered Expenses 3.19
        Coordination of Benefits 3.21
        Cost Sharing 3.22
      Additional Benefits for Executives 3.23
      Taxation 3.23
      Coverage after Termination of Employment 3.24
        COBRA 3.24
        Conversion 3.25
        Portability 3.26
        Postretirement Coverage 3.26
    Life Insurance 3.27
      Benefit Schedule 3.27
        Multiple-of-Earnings Schedules 3.28
        Specified-Dollar-Amount Schedules 3.28
        Reduction in Benefits 3.28
      Termination of Coverage 3.28
        Conversion 3.28
        Portability of Term Coverage 3.29
      Added Coverages 3.29
        Supplemental Life Insurance 3.29
        Accidental Death and Dismemberment
          Insurance 3.30
        Dependent Life Insurance 3.31
      Taxation 3.32
        General Tax Rules 3.32
        Nondiscrimination Rules 3.33
        Taxation of Proceeds 3.34
        Treatment of Added Coverages 3.34
      Group Universal Life Insurance 3.35
        Coverage Available 3.35

Foundations of Financial Planning: An Overview

    Options at Retirement and Termination 3.35
    Taxation 3.35
  Disability Income Insurance 3.36
   Short-Term Plans 3.36
   Long-Term Plans 3.36
    Benefits 3.37
    Supplemental Benefits 3.38
   Taxation 3.38
  Dental Insurance 3.38
   Benefits 3.39
    Scheduled Plans 3.40
    Nonscheduled Plans 3.40
    Combination Plans 3.41
   Taxation 3.41
  Vision Insurance 3.41
  Voluntary Insurance Benefits 3.42
   Legal Expense Insurance 3.43
    Taxation 3.43
  Long-Term Care Insurance 3.43
   Taxation 3.44
  Supplemental Medical Expense Insurance 3.44
  Property and Liability Insurance 3.45
   Taxation 3.45
  Miscellaneous Fringe Benefits 3.45
   Education Assistance 3.45
   Adoption Assistance 3.46
   Dependent Care Assistance 3.46
    Child-Care Plans 3.47
    Eldercare Benefits 3.47
    Taxation of Benefits 3.47
   Personal Time Off Without Pay (Family Leave) 3.48
    State Laws 3.48
    Federal Law 3.48
   Other Benefits 3.49
 Cafeteria Plans 3.50
  Nature 3.50
  Types 3.51
 Chapter Review 3.53
  Review Questions 3.54

4 Investment Planning 4.1

 The Meaning of Investment 4.1

Investment versus Speculation 4.2
Expected Return and Risk.. 4.3
Basic Investment Theorems 4.5
Service to the Client 4.6
Determining Risk Tolerance 4.7
Asset Allocation Models 4.9
Categories of Investment Assets 4.10
Cash Equivalents 4.10
Bank Deposits 4.11
Money Market Instruments 4.11
Treasury Bills 4.12
Long-Term Debt Instruments 4.13
Governmental Debt Securities 4.13
Corporate Debt Securities 4.14
Equity Securities 4.15
Common Stock 4.15
Preferred Stock 4.16
American Depositary Receipts (ADRs) 4.16
Investment Companies 4.16
Real Estate and Other Investments 4.20
Real Estate 4.20
Other Investments 4.21
Sources of Investment Risk 4.22
Purchasing Power Risk 4.22
Interest Rate Risk 4.23
Business Risk 4.24
Special Portfolio Considerations 4.25
Liquidity 4.25
Marketability 4.27
Taxation 4.27
Diversification 4.30
Investment Returns 4.31
Current Yield 4.31
Holding-Period Return (HPR) 4.33
Approximate Yield 4.34
Historical Before-Tax Returns 4.35
Investment Principles, Strategies, and Techniques 4.37
Meeting Emergency and Protection Needs First 4.37
Matching Investment Instruments with Investment
  Goals 4.37
Holding Periods for Equity Investments 4.38
Tax-Saving Rationale 4.38
Understanding the Investment 4.39

Using a Consistent Pattern of Investing 4.39
The Power of Compounding 4.40
High-Pressure Sales Tactics 4.40
Avoiding Discretionary Power 4.41
Applying Control through the Financial Planning
  Process 4.42
Investment Markets and Regulation 4.42
Investment Markets 4.42
  True-Auction Markets 4.42
  Negotiated Markets 4.43
  Dealer Markets 4.44
  Organized Securities Markets 4.44
Regulation of the Markets 4.45
  Securities Act of 1933 .... 4.45
  Securities Exchange Act of 1934 .... 4.45
  The Investment Advisors Act of 1940 .... 4.46
  Investment Company Act of 1940 .... 4.46
  Securities Investor Protection Act of 1970 .... 4.46
A Final Word 4.47
Chapter Review 4.48
Review Questions 4.48

5 Income Tax Planning 5.1

The Purpose of Income Tax Planning 5.1
The Principle of Gross Income 5.2
Exclusions from Gross Income 5.3
Deductions 5.4
  Adjusted Gross Income 5.4
  Taxable Income 5.5
  The Standard Deduction or Itemized Deductions 5.6
  Categories of Deductions 5.7
  Depreciation: A Special Type of Deduction 5.8
Personal and Dependency Exemptions 5.11
Tax Rates and Brackets 5.12
Tax Credits 5.14
The Alternative Minimum Tax (AMT) 5.15
Tax Periods and Accounting Methods 5.16
Three Important Issues 5.17
  The "What" Issue: The Economic Benefit Doctrine 5.18
  The "To Whom" Issue: The Fruit and Tree Doctrine 5.18
  The "When" Issue: The Constructive Receipt Doctrine .. 5.19
Basic Income-Tax-Planning Concepts 5.20

Income and Deduction Shifting 5.21
Avoiding Limitations on Deductions 5.22
Deferral and Acceleration Techniques................................. 5.23
The Passive-Loss Rules.. 5.24
Tax-Exempt Transactions... 5.25
Nonrecognition Transactions.. 5.25
    Computation of Gain or Loss 5.26
    How Nonrecognition Transactions Differ from Taxable
      Transactions 5.27
Transactions That Result in a Taxable Loss........................ 5.28
Ordinary versus Capital Gain and Loss............................... 5.28
    Capital Gain versus Ordinary Income 5.28
    Tax Treatment of Dividends as Capital Gains............. 5.30
    Tax Treatment of Capital Losses 5.30
    Sec. 1231 Assets: Depreciable Property and Real
      Property Used in a Trade or Business...................... 5.31
Taxable Entities 5.32
Conclusion 5.32
Chapter Review.. 5.33
    Review Questions 5.33

6 Retirement Planning...6.1

Starting Retirement Planning When Young................................ 6.2
The Role of the Retirement Advisor 6.3
    Holistic Retirement Planning 6.3
    Responsibilities of the Retirement Advisor........................ 6.6
    Retirement Planning and the Financial Planning
      Process 6.7
      Step 1: Establishing and Defining the Client-Planner
        Relationship... 6.7
      Step 2: Gathering Information Necessary to Fulfill the
        Engagement 6.8
      Step 3: Analyzing and Evaluating the Client's Current
        Financial Status 6.8
      Step 4: Developing the Recommendation(s)...................... 6.9
      Step 5: Communicating the Recommendation(s)............... 6.9
      Step 6: Implementing the Recommendation(s) 6.10
The Art of Financial Planning for Retirement 6.10
    Older Clients Still Need to Plan for Retirement 6.12
    Overcoming Roadblocks to Retirement Saving..................... 6.14
Developing a Retirement Plan 6.17
    Replacement Ratio Method... 6.19

        Reduced Taxes 6.20
        Reduced Living Expenses 6.21
        Additional Factors 6.21
    Expense Method 6.21
    The Effects of Inflation.. 6.22
Potential Sources of Retirement Income.. 6.24
    Tax-Advantaged Qualified Plans 6.25
        Defined-Benefit versus Defined-Contribution
            Plans.. 6.26
        Pension versus Profit-Sharing Plans 6.29
        Types of Tax-Advantaged Qualified Plans 6.30
            Defined-Benefit Pension Plans............................... 6.30
            Cash-Balance Pension Plans 6.32
            Money-Purchase Pension Plans 6.33
            Target-Benefit Pension Plans 6.33
            Profit-Sharing Plans.. 6.34
            401(k) Plans 6.34
            Stock Bonus Plans and ESOPs............................. 6.36
    Other Tax-Advantaged Plans 6.38
        Simplified Employee Pension (SEP)............................... 6.38
        SIMPLEs.. 6.38
            Salary Deferral Contributions 6.39
        403(b) Plans... 6.40
    Nonqualified Plans 6.40
    IRAs.. 6.42
        Traditional IRAs 6.43
            Active Participant 6.43
            Monetary Limits 6.44
            Special Spousal Rule 6.45
            Distributions.. 6.46
        Roth IRAs.. 6.46
Overcoming Inadequate Retirement Resources 6.48
    Trading Down to a Less Expensive Home 6.48
    Obtaining a Reverse Mortgage 6.49
    Postretirement Employment 6.50
    Pension Maximization 6.52
Chapter Review.. 6.53
    Review Questions 6.54

7 Estate Planning.. 7.1

The Goals of Estate Planning 7.1
Starting the Process... 7.3

- Types of Property Interest 7.5
  - Individual Ownership of Property 7.5
    - Fee Simple Estate 7.5
    - Life Estate 7.6
    - Estate for Term of Years 7.6
    - Future Interest 7.7
  - Joint Concurrent Ownership of Property 7.8
    - Tenancy in Common 7.8
    - Joint Tenancy with Right of Survivorship 7.8
    - Tenancy by the Entirety 7.9
    - Community Property 7.10
  - Other Property Rights 7.11
    - Beneficial Interests 7.11
    - Powers 7.11
      - Power of Appointment 7.11
      - Power of Attorney 7.12
- Estate Planning Documents 7.12
  - Wills 7.13
    - Requirements for a Valid Will 7.13
    - What Can a Valid Will Accomplish? 7.13
  - Trusts 7.14
    - Living *(Inter Vivos)* Trust 7.15
    - Testamentary Trust 7.17
  - Durable Powers of Attorney 7.17
  - Advance Medical Directives 7.20
- Transfers at Death 7.21
  - The Probate Estate 7.22
    - Transfers through Will Provisions 7.22
    - Transfers by Intestacy 7.23
  - The Nonprobate Estate 7.24
    - Transfers by Operation of Law 7.24
    - Transfers by Operation of Contract 7.25
- Taxes Imposed on Transfers of Wealth 7.26
  - Federal Transfer Taxes 7.27
    - Federal Gift Tax 7.31
      - Exempt Transfers 7.31
      - Gift Tax Annual Exclusion 7.32
      - Deductions from the Gift Tax Base 7.33
      - Applicable Credit Amount 7.33
    - Federal Estate Tax 7.34
      - The Gross Estate 7.34
      - Items Deductible from the Gross Estate 7.35
      - Marital Deduction 7.35

- Charitable Deduction 7.35
- Applicable Exclusion Amount 7.35
  - State Death Tax Credit 7.36
- Generation-Skipping Transfer Tax (GST Tax) 7.36
  - Types of Transfers 7.36
  - Lifetime Exemption and Annual Exclusion 7.38
- State Death Taxes 7.38
  - State Inheritance Tax 7.39
  - State Estate Tax 7.39
  - Credit Estate Tax 7.39
  - Planning for State Death Taxes 7.40
- Preserving the Client's Wealth 7.41
  - The Advantages of Lifetime Gifts 7.41
    - Nontax Advantages of Lifetime Gifts 7.41
    - Tax Advantages of Lifetime Gifts 7.42
    - Opportunities Created by the Gift Tax Annual
      Exclusion 7.42
    - Gifts to Minors 7.43
      - Uniform Gifts to Minors Act (UGMA) or Uniform
        Transfers to Minors Act (UTMA) 7.43
      - Sec. 2503(b) Trust 7.44
      - Sec. 2503(c) Trust 7.44
      - Irrevocable Trust with Current Withdrawal
        Powers 7.44
    - Federal Estate Tax Planning 7.45
      - Planning for the Marital Deduction 7.45
        - Portability Under the New Estate Tax Law 7.46
        - Outright Transfers 7.47
        - Estate Trust 7.48
        - Power-of-Appointment Trust 7.48
        - QTIP Marital-Deduction Trust 7.48
      - Planning for the Gift and Estate Tax Applicable
        Credit Amount 7.49
      - Coordination of the Marital Deduction and the
        Applicable Credit Amount 7.50
      - Planning Charitable Contributions 7.52
        - Advantages of Gifts to Charity 7.52
        - Gifts of Remainder Interests to Charity 7.52
        - Donating Income Interests to Charity 7.53
    - Life Insurance in the Estate and/or Financial Plan 7.53
      - Life Insurance for Estate Enhancement 7.54
      - Life Insurance for Estate Liquidity 7.54
      - Life Insurance Trusts 7.55

    Revocable Life Insurance Trusts............................7.55
    Irrevocable Life Insurance Trusts..........................7.55
 Conclusion 7.56
 Chapter Review...7.57
  Review Questions 7.58

8 Social Security, Medicare, and Medicare Supplements...................8.1

 Social Security and Medicare..8.1
  The Importance, Coverage, and Financing of Social
   Security and Medicare 8.2
   Importance of Programs 8.2
   Extent of Coverage 8.2
   Tax Rates and Wage Bases...8.2
  Eligibility for Social Security 8.4
   Fully Insured 8.4
   Currently Insured 8.4
   Disability Insured...8.5
  Social Security Benefits..8.5
   Retirement Benefits 8.5
   Survivors Benefits 8.7
   Disability Benefits..8.8
   Eligibility for Dual Benefits 8.8
   Termination of Benefits 8.9
  Social Security Benefit Amounts 8.10
   Calculating Benefits 8.10
   Other Factors Affecting Benefits 8.11
    Benefits Taken Early... 8.11
    Delayed Retirement..8.12
    Earnings Test..8.14
    Cost-of-Living Adjustments...................................8.15
    Offset for Other Benefits 8.15
   Requesting Benefit Information...................................8.16
  Eligibility for Medicare 8.16
  Medicare Part A: Hospital Benefits.......................................8.18
   Hospital Benefits 8.18
   Skilled-Nursing Facility Benefits..................................8.20
   Home Health Care Benefits 8.21
   Hospice Benefits 8.21
   Exclusions...8.22
  Medicare Part B Benefits..8.23
   Benefits 8.23
   Exclusions...8.24

> Amount of Benefits 8.24
> Medicare Part C 8.26
> Medicare Part D Prescription Drug Plans 8.27
> Coverage to Supplement Medicare 8.30
> > Employer Plans to Supplement Medicare 8.30
> > Individual Medigap Policies to Supplement Medicare 8.30
> > > Basic Benefits 8.31
> > > Changes in Medigap Benefits 8.32
> > > > Additional Medicare Supplement Plan Benefits 8.32
> > > Eligibility 8.34
> Postscript 8.34
> Chapter Review 8.35
> > Review Questions 8.35

APPENDICES

Answers to Questions A.1

Bibliography B.1

Risk Identification Questionnaire C.1

Glossary Glossary.1

Index Index.1

ACKNOWLEDGMENTS

Publication of this book required the collaborative efforts of the author as well as many other individuals. I am especially grateful to Todd Denton and Jane Hassinger for their outstanding production assistance. I also want to acknowledge Emily Schu's enthusiastic and competent technical help. I appreciate the following individuals who contributed so much in the past while authoring or editing portions of the content of this book:

- Dr. Walt Woerheide, ChFC®, CFP®, Vice President of Academic Affairs, Dean, Professor of Investments, and holder of the Frank M. Engle Distinguished Chair in Economic Research at The American College.

- Theodore T. (Ted) Kurlowicz, JD, LLM, CAP®, ChFC®, CLU®, AEP, Charles E. Drimal Professor in Estate Planning, Professor of Taxation at The American College.

- Connie Fontaine, JD, LLM, ChFC®, CLU®, Larry R. Pike Chair in Insurance and Investments, Associate Professor of Taxation at The American College.

- Christopher P. Woehrle, JD, LLM, Assistant Professor of Taxation at The American College.

Other past faculty members at The American College also contributed significantly, especially C. Bruce Worsham, JD, and Burton T. (Tom) Beam, ChFC®, CLU®, CPCU, CASL®. I am in debt to all who went before me.

It is foolish to believe that any book is perfect. Please take some time to give me your constructive comments on how to improve future editions. As a motivation, remember that readers may someday be advising you and your family about financial planning!

Allen McLellan, The American College, Bryn Mawr, PA.

ABOUT THE AUTHOR

Allen C. McLellan, LUTCF, CLU, ChFC, CASL, CFP, is an Assistant Professor of Insurance at The American College. Allen graduated from the United States Air Force Academy with a BS in aeronautical engineering. As an Air Force officer, Allen served as a navigator on several types of aircraft and completed three professional development programs in residence: Squadron Officer School, Air Command and Staff College, and The Air War College. In 1984, he was awarded the Secretary of the Air Force Leadership Award as the top graduate in his Air Command and Staff College. Allen completed a MS in Aeronautics at the Air Force Institute of Technology and taught mathematics at the Air Force Academy for four years, where he also served as an instructor in the Academy's navigation program. After Allen retired from the Air Force, he entered the financial services field and worked nearly 16 years as an agent, registered representative, and financial planner. Much of his practice was focused on senior issues such as Medicare, Medicaid, and long-term care needs.

Allen was active in the Life Underwriters Association (now the National Association of Insurance and Financial Advisors) and served as president of his local association in Montgomery, AL. He was named the "Life Underwriter of the Year" by the Montgomery association in 1999. At The American College, Allen is principal editor of *Foundations of Financial Planning: An Overview, Foundations of Financial Planning: The Process, Foundations of Investment Planning,* and *Health and Long-Term Care for Seniors.* Allen is a member of NAIFA, the Air Force Association, and the Military Officers Association of America.

SPECIAL NOTES TO ADVISORS

This publication is designed to provide accurate and authoritative information about the subject covered. While every precaution has been taken in the preparation of this material to insure that it is both accurate and up-to-date, it is still possible that some errors eluded detection. Moreover, some material may become inaccurate and/or outdated either because it is time sensitive or because new legislation will make it so. Still other material may be viewed as inaccurate because your company's products and procedures are different from those described in the book. Therefore, the editor, authors, and The American College assume no liability for damages resulting from the use of the information contained in this book. The American College is not engaged in rendering legal, accounting, or other professional advice. If legal or other expert advice is required, the services of an appropriate professional should be sought.

Caution Regarding Use of Text Materials: Any illustrations, fact finders, techniques, and/or approaches contained in this book are not to be used with the public unless you have obtained approval from your company. Your company's general support of The American College's educational programs and publications does not constitute blanket approval of any illustrations, fact finders, techniques, and/or approaches presented in this book, unless so communicated in writing by your company.

Use of the term "Financial Advisor" as it appears in this book is intended as the generic reference to professional members of our reading audience. It is used interchangeably with the term "Advisor" so as to avoid unnecessary redundancy. Financial Advisor takes the place of the following terms:

Account Executive	Financial Planning Professional	Practitioner
Agent		Producer
Associate	Financial Services Professional	Property & Casualty Agent
Broker (stock or insurance)	Health Underwriter	Registered Investment Adviser
Employee Benefit Specialist	Insurance Professional	Registered Representative
Estate Planner	Life Insurance Agent	Retirement Planner
Financial Consultant	Life Underwriter	Senior Advisor
Financial Planner	Planner	Tax Advisor

OVERVIEW OF THE BOOK

Foundations of Financial Planning: An Overview is designed to be an overview of the major planning components that make up a comprehensive financial plan. Although each of these components is covered in more depth in other American College publications, this is the one College text where all these components are brought together to show what needs to be covered in a truly comprehensive financial plan.

Chapter 1 begins the discussion by explaining that financial planning is an eight-step process that can involve a single-purpose, multiple-purpose, or comprehensive approach, with the focus being on the later. The content of a comprehensive financial plan should include a discussion of each of the major planning areas. Priority given to a client's goals in financial planning is strongly influenced by which phase of the life cycle the client is experiencing. Financial planning is a process that should be ongoing throughout the client's financial life.

Chapters 2 through 7 introduce the major planning components that make up comprehensive financial planning. Chapter 2 discusses insurance planning, including the risk management process and insurance coverages. Chapter 3 examines employee benefits planning, since many of the financial needs of a client and her family may be met—or at least partially met—with benefits provided by and/or through an employer. Chapter 4 is an introduction to investment planning. It describes basic risk/return concepts, financial risk tolerance, asset allocation models, categories of investments, and several portfolio considerations. In chapter 5, basic concepts of income taxation are presented with an emphasis on tax planning. In chapter 6, retirement planning concepts are addressed, including retirement income needs and the types of retirement plans available. Chapter 7 covers estate planning, the final major planning area. The chapter 7 discussion focuses on preserving the client's wealth for his family.

Although the Social Security and Medicare programs could have been covered in earlier chapters as subparts of one of the major planning areas, they are dealt with separately in chapter 8 because of their importance as the foundation upon which the client's comprehensive financial plan should be built. The last part of chapter 8 is devoted to explaining the various types of coverages designed to supplement Medicare.

Just a word on the author's writing style. Throughout the text, I will alternate between using "he/him/his" and "she/her/hers." In my view, this eliminates the awkward style of referring to "his or her," "him or her," and "his or hers," and allows the text to flow more naturally.

It is certainly our hope that this course will motivate students to seek more education from The American College or elsewhere. Financial planning is a complicated and ever-changing discipline. To serve well as a financial advisor will require your dedication toward life-long learning to stay current and help your clients survive and thrive in a complex environment.

THE FINANCIAL PLANNING PROCESS   1

Learning Objectives

An understanding of the material in this chapter should enable the student to

1. Explain the eight steps in the financial planning process.
2. Describe three different approaches to financial planning, and identify areas of specialization in which advisors concentrate their activities.
3. Identify the subjects that should be included in a comprehensive financial plan.
4. Describe what is meant by a person's financial life cycle, and explain how it relates to life-cycle financial planning.
5. Describe how a financial plan could be organized around the steps in the financial planning process.
6. Describe the trends that helped develop financial planning as a profession.
7. Explain the trends that are creating opportunities in the financial planning marketplace.
8. Identify the principal financial goals and concerns of most consumers, and describe three major obstacles that prevent them from achieving these goals.

Financial planning is a client-focused process for helping the client achieve his or her financial goals. While a client's financial goals may involve business as well as personal objectives, this course focuses primarily on planning to meet the personal financial goals of individuals and families.

EMERGENCE OF A NEW PROFESSION

Although providing financial planning advice and services to clients is a relatively new and still-emerging field of professional endeavor, very affluent individuals have had access to such help for many years. Moreover, some financial advisors, such as accountants and life insurance agents, argue that they have been practicing financial planning all their professional lives. However, it is generally recognized that financial planning services that cover a spectrum of client concerns have become available to most Americans in the middle- and upper-middle-income brackets only in the past 40 to 45 years.

Financial advisors claiming to be practicing financial planning first appeared in numbers in the late 1960s, a period of rising inflation and interest rates. The financial planning movement grew rapidly during the 1970s as the general trend of prices continued upward. By the late 1970s and into the early 1980s, inflation and interest rates were virtually out of control. Confronted with very high income tax rates along with spiraling inflation and interest rates, American consumers clamored for help. The growth of the financial planning movement was explosive. Often, however, what advisors labeled as financial planning consisted mostly of selling "get rich quick" products and elaborate income tax dodges, usually accompanied by an abundance of "hype." A few advisors, sometimes with great zeal, preached the message of comprehensive financial planning as the financial salvation of the American household.

By the mid-1980s, much of the turbulence in economic conditions began to settle down. In addition, when income tax reform eliminated the most extreme types of tax shelters from the marketplace, many so-called financial planning advisors disappeared from the scene. Many advocates of a comprehensive approach to financial planning realized that this type of financial planning was practical for only a small, affluent clientele, especially on a fee-for-service basis. Also, with the oldest members of the "baby boom" generation entering their 40s, retirement planning became an increasingly important component of financial planning practices.

In the 1990s, the financial planning profession gained some stability and maturity. Today, it is possible to describe more realistically what financial planning is and what client needs it can fulfill.

In the second decade of the 21st century, financial planning is more widely accepted and many specialized planning areas have developed. Today, financial planners specialize in education planning, divorce planning, income distribution and a number of other specialties. While this course does not prepare you to take the exam for the CFP® designation, we include the descriptions of financial planning and the steps in the financial planning process followed by Certified Financial Planner® professionals. Our belief is

WHAT IS FINANCIAL PLANNING?

financial planning

One factor that has hampered the development of *financial planning* as a discipline and profession is that there has been very little agreement among advisors as to what defines it. Indeed, there are as many definitions of financial planning as there are people who believe they are engaged in it. This debate, which continues among financial advisors even today,[1] is not merely an exercise in semantics. The discussion becomes intensely practical when questions are raised about such issues as who shall regulate those advisors engaged in financial planning, who shall set standards for the financial planning profession and how those advisors should be regulated and compensated.

The Securities and Exchange Commission (SEC) defines financial planning by outcome: "Financial planning can help assess every aspect of your financial life—including saving, investments, insurance, taxes, retirement, and estate planning."[2] The Financial Planning Association (FPA), one of financial planning's largest member and advocate groups, defines financial planning as "the long-term process of wisely managing your finances so you can achieve your goals and dreams."[3] Definitions of financial planning vary across the industry, yet common themes emerge. Financial planning is a process performed by professionals with training and expertise. Financial planners span compensation models (some are fee-based, some paid on the sale of products, and some receive both fees and commissions), backgrounds (traditional college track or a career-changing professional), and specializations.

---

1. Shelley A. Lee, "What Is Financial Planning, Anyway?" *Journal of Financial Planning,* December 2001, pp. 36–46.
2. www.sec.gov/answers/finplan.htm.
3. Financial Planning Association — What is Financial Planning? accessed on www.fpanet.org/Whatisfinancialplanning.

Financial Planning Is a Process

Despite conversations about compensation and business model preferences, financial planning can be defined conceptually as a process that accomplishes both of the following:

- ascertaining the client's financial goals and objectives
- developing a plan for achieving the client's goals and objectives

financial planning process

Whether a single financial problem is being addressed or a comprehensive financial plan is being developed, the *financial planning process* has eight distinct steps, also referred to as domains. Historically the planning process contained only six steps. As planning has evolved into a profession, the six-step process did not accurately reflect the challenges in communicating recommendations to a client or working in today's advanced legal environment. Using eight domains better captures the sophisticated nature of planning, and those domains are derived from the College for Financial Planning® Board's job analysis survey, completed in 2009. The planning domains are outlined and summarized on the following chart.

Table 1-1 Domains of Financial Planning: The Eight-Step Planning Process

Domains of Financial Planning	Description
Establishing and Defining the Client-Planner Relationship	The financial planner outlines the responsibilities of the planner and the responsibilities of the client. The planner should disclose the length and scope of the relationship as well as the method and magnitude of planner compensation. Establishing the relationship helps guide the decision-making process.
Gathering Information Necessary to Fulfill the Engagement	The financial planner should gather client data, including broad and specific goals and objectives. Ask the client about risk tolerance measures. Documents such as tax returns, wills, trusts, account statements and pay stubs may need to be collected to truly establish constructive outcomes.
Analyzing and Evaluating the Client's Current Financial Status	Data gathered in the second step must be analyzed and synthesized within the context of meeting goals. This step of the planning process accounts for significant variations among planners. Planners without expertise in a specific planning area may need to employ a technical staff or teammates when analyzing and evaluating client goals.

Domains of Financial Planning	Description
Developing the Recommendations	The financial planner develops recommendations based on evaluation (Step 3) of data collected (Step 2). Planners will present recommendations and alternatives that address client goals and concerns. Presenting more than one recommendation to a client provides alternative courses of action, and may result in additional fact finding and discovery on the part of the planner. After making recommendations, the client may provide or revise their goals (Step 2) which will require additional analysis (Step 3).
Communicating the Recommendation(s)	The financial planner ensures recommendations are communicated and understood by the client. The client gives acceptance of recommendations, and the planner and client both are cognizant of direct and indirect consequences of actions taken. When presenting recommendations to a client, planners often need to revisit previous steps in the planning process. Communications may be live, virtual, or over the phone, and multiple communication sessions are often needed before the planning process moves to implementation. Financial professionals should take particular care when working with vulnerable populations to ensure they understand the communications.
Implementing the Recommendation(s)	After agreement is reached between the client and planner on a course of action, the planner outlines how implementation will occur. If implementation results in additional planner compensation, the form and magnitude of compensation needs to be disclosed to the client. Depending on the business model of the planner, the client may implement his or her own recommendations or the planner may implement recommendations on behalf of the client. Any conflict of interest of the planner through the implementation of a product should be disclosed to the client.
Monitoring the Recommendation(s)	This step of the planning process is limited by the first. The client and planner need to agree on monitoring responsibilities when establishing the relationship. Planners who entered into a long term relationship with their clients have an obligation of following up and updating the plan. Monitoring may occur on a time basis, such as monthly or annually, or monitoring may occur on a strategic basis, such as when asset allocations become misaligned.
Practicing within Professional and Regulatory Standards	Financial planners, insurance agents, stock brokers and other financial service professionals must be constantly vigilant of their dynamic regulatory environments. Today's regulatory environment changes quickly; standards of care due to clients require exploration and are undergoing significant regulatory challenges.

Advisors who primarily sell financial products generally view the financial planning process as a selling/planning process that has ten steps, that is, the eight domains of the financial planning process identified above preceded by two additional steps: (1) identify the prospect, and (2) approach the prospect.

Steps in the Financial Planning Process: The Eight Financial Planning Domains

For advisors, this process for helping clients achieve their financial goals can be applied to the full range of client goals on a comprehensive basis. The process can also be applied on a narrower basis to only a subset of those goals or even to a client's single financial goal. It is not the number or range of client goals addressed that determines whether an advisor is engaged in financial planning. Rather, the determining factor is the process used by the advisor in addressing client goals. The following sections briefly discuss the eight domains involved in the financial planning process.

Financial Planning Domains

1. Establishing and Defining the Client-Planner Relationship
2. Gathering Information Necessary to Fulfill the Engagement
3. Analyzing and Evaluating the Client's Current Financial Status
4. Developing the Recommendation(s)
5. Communicating the Recommendation(s)
6. Implementing the Recommendation(s)
7. Monitoring the Recommendation(s)
8. Practicing within Professional and Regulatory Standards

Step 1: Establishing and Defining the Client-Planner Relationship

The first step in the financial planning process is to establish and define the advisor-client relationship. This normally begins at the first client meeting, although it can start prior to this meeting through telephone interactions or other contacts with the client. The first client meeting is essential for establishing the framework for a successful advisor-client relationship. This meeting is where you begin to build trust with the client and create a relationship with the client that (it is hoped) will span the client's entire financial life.

Establishing the advisor-client relationship when the client is a couple is a more complex challenge because you must build trust and rapport with both parties. Covering the goals of both parties in one financial plan requires you to completely understand the goals that both have in common and how the partners' needs may differ. Couples often have significantly different goals, priorities, risk tolerance or basic planning objectives. You must learn how to help couples negotiate through the planning process as a team, and in some situations refer couples with vastly different interests to outside specialists.

> **EXAMPLE**
>
> Kirk is a financial planner in Philadelphia, PA. He recently met with Rick and Carol Marks, a married couple both age 42, who were referred to Kirk by another client. In Kirk's first meeting with Rick and Carol, they completed an extensive fact-finder and Kirk discovered the following:
>
> - Rick has a very high financial risk tolerance and prefers investments, such as small-cap stocks and emerging markets, which have the potential for highest returns but are generally very volatile. Rick's 401(k) suffered a 40 percent decline in 2008–2009, but it has gained back most of that loss in 2010–2011.
> - Carol's father lost a small fortune in the stock market in 2001 when the "dot-com" market imploded. As a result, Carol is extremely fearful of investing in any asset in which she can "lose her principal." Carol's entire 401(k) is invested in a "stable value fund" that has averaged a 3.0 percent return over the last three years.
> - Rick's primary objective is rapid accumulation of funds so that they both can retire by age 58 and buy a condo in Florida.
> - Carol's top concern is to fund the education of their twins, Eric and Shelley, age 12. Carol wants to send both children to an Ivy League university, if they can qualify. She is willing to work much longer, if necessary, to provide a top education for the children.
>
> Note that with such widely different objectives and risk tolerances, Kirk's job is complicated in building a financial plan that harmonizes the interests and attitudes of both Rick and Carol.

structuring

In any kind of planned and purposeful communication setting, the first element that needs attention is *structuring*. Structuring determines both the format and subject matter of the interaction—in our case, between you and the client(s). Your task in structuring is to make the purpose of the initial meeting and those that follow clear to the client at the outset of the relationship. Structuring includes the inevitable introductions, an explanation of the financial planning process, a discussion of forms used (for example, a fact-finder form, risk tolerance questionnaire and a disclosure form) and the time required to complete them. There must also be a discussion of the confidential nature of the relationship, and some prediction of outcomes the client might reasonably expect. This structuring need not be lengthy and cumbersome; in fact, you should structure the communication in a clear, straightforward, and succinct fashion. A word of advice here: do not "wing it" in your initial communications with your prospects. Ad libs are for amateurs. Prepare an agenda, and make sure you cover all areas in a professional manner.

Structuring for the financial planning process requires you to explain how you work and the types of products and/or services you can provide. You should explain the financial planning process and how you use that process to develop financial plans for your clients. Some advisors show examples of how their products and/or services have helped other clients meet their financial goals and objectives. Of course, you must preserve the confidential nature of your work with others.

At the first meeting with a prospect, you also need to disclose your background, philosophy, and method of compensation, such as fee-only, commission, or a fee and commission. The financial planning process does not vary by compensation type. The Certified Financial Planner® Board of Standards Code of Ethics and Professional Responsibility requires CFP® professionals to provide written disclosure to clients (prior to the engagement) of the methods and sources of their compensation, their educational background, experience, conflicts of interest, and practice philosophy. (Note: be sure to have all forms approved by your compliance department before you use the forms!) This domain may better be described with the following activities, taken from the CFP® Certification Examination Job Task Domains:

1. Identify the client (e.g., individual, family, business, organization).
2. Discuss financial planning needs and expectations of the client.
3. Discuss the financial planning process with the client.
4. Explain scope of services offered by the CFP® professional and his/her firm.
5. Assess and communicate the CFP® professional's ability to meet the client's needs and expectations.
6. Identify and resolve apparent and potential conflicts of interest in client relationships.
7. Discuss the client's responsibilities and those of the CFP® professional.
8. Define and document the scope of the engagement with the client.

9. Provide client disclosures:
    a. Regulatory disclosures
    b. Compensation arrangements and associated potential conflicts of interest

Step 2: Gathering Information Necessary to Fulfill the Engagement

financial goals

After you have established and defined the advisor-client relationship, you are ready to move to the second domain in the financial planning process. This step can begin during the initial meeting or in a unique meeting later in the planning process. Occasionally, you may interview the client remotely (over the phone and Internet), or through a series of correspondences to gather client data and discuss *financial goals*.

While few people begin a vacation without a specific destination in mind, millions of people make significant financial decisions without a specific financial destination in mind. Determining a specific financial destination—that is, goal setting—is critical to any successful financial plan. Few people actually set clearly defined goals. By leading the client through the goal-setting exercise, you help your client establish reasonable, achievable goals and set the tone for the entire financial planning engagement.

Clients typically express concern about a whole host of topics including retirement income, education funding, premature death, disability, taxation, and qualified plan distributions. Clients may sometimes enumerate specific, prioritized goals, but they are more likely to present a vague list of worries that suggest anxiety and frustration rather than direction. Your task is to help your client transform these feelings into goals.

You should question clients to learn what they are trying to accomplish. Usually the response is couched in general terms such as, "Well, we want to have a comfortable standard of living when we retire." At first glance this seems to be a reasonable goal, but a closer evaluation reveals that it is far too vague.

[Goal but should be simpler]

- When do they want to retire?
- What is meant by "comfortable"?
- How should inflation be addressed?
- Do they want to retire on "interest only" or draw down their accumulated portfolio over their expected lives?

[Instead ask about current cash flows and what they want to get through retirement.]

Skillful and thoughtful questioning may reveal a more precise goal such as, "We want to retire in 20 years with an after-tax income of $60,000 per year in current dollars inflating at 3 percent annually, and we want the income to continue as long as we live without depleting the principal." Helping the client quantify specific goals is one of the most valuable services a financial advisor can provide.

Another important service you can provide is goal prioritization. Clients usually mention competing goals such as saving for retirement and saving for education. Good advisors help clients rank these competing goals. Quite often, clients have multiple goals such as college savings, retirement planning, and asset accumulation. A competent financial planner must be able to help their client sort through their goals and develop a clear sense of priorities. One good technique is simply to ask: "Rick, which is more important to you: saving for your children's education or saving for your own retirement?"

After you and the client discuss goals, objectives, and concerns, you must then gather all the information about the client relevant to the problem(s) to be solved and/or the type of plan to be prepared. The more complex the client's situation and the more varied the number of goals, the greater the information-gathering task. We should stress again the importance of agreeing on the client's goals before you take any further steps in the financial planning process. Remember, the goals are the client's goals; if you do a great job otherwise but you do not sufficiently solve the client's problems and help meet his goals, your planning is ineffective.

Two broad types of information will need to be gathered: objective and subjective. Some examples of objective (factual) information include a list of the client's securities holdings, inventory of assets and liabilities, a description of the present arrangement for distribution of the client's (and spouse's) assets at death, a list of annual income and expenditures, and a summary of present insurance coverages. Objective goals are typically quantitative in nature. Equally important is the subjective information about the client. You will need to gather information about the hopes, fears, values, preferences, attitudes, and nonfinancial goals of the client (and the client's spouse).

> **EXAMPLE**
>
> In further discussions with Rick and Carol Marks, Kirk learned that Rick had been married previously, and he had a 20 year-old son Michael from his first marriage. Michael has some learning disabilities and probably will never be able to live independently as an adult. Michael currently lives with his mother Annette, Rick's first wife. Rick does not feel he has any further financial responsibilities toward Michael; however, Annette has indicated she may go to court to force Rick to contribute financially to Michael's support. In addition, Rick's current wife Carol is adamantly opposed to providing any support to Michael, as that would decrease any funds available for her twins' education.

This example, a very "real world" one, illustrates the complexity found in many financial planning situations. It shows the importance of your learning as much as possible about the clients' relationships, attitudes, and financial responsibilities before you make your recommendations.

financial risk tolerance

One piece of information worthy of special attention is the client's *financial risk tolerance*. You must determine your client's (and spouse's) attitude toward risk before making your recommendations, preferably with the help of a scientific risk tolerance questionnaire developed by a third party. The American College's *Survey of Financial Risk Tolerance* is just such a questionnaire. It provides the type of analysis that helps you suggest financial strategies and investment alternatives that are truly appropriate for the client. Such information offers the additional benefit of helping avoid (or at least defend) lawsuits from a dissatisfied client. Such a fact-finder documents your discussions and information provided by the client, in case you are called upon to explain and justify your recommendations and actions with the client. Make such documentation a required part of any engagement with your clients.

Before you begin the information-gathering process, you should discuss a couple of concerns with the client. First, the client should understand that she will have to invest time, perhaps a significant amount of time, in the information-gathering stage of financial planning. Even though part of your responsibility is to avoid consuming the client's time unnecessarily, this commitment of the client's time is essential. The time commitment will depend on the scope and complexity of the client's goals and circumstances, but producing even a narrowly focused and fairly uncomplicated plan requires information only the client can provide.

fact-finder form

Second, the client should understand that he probably will have to provide you with some highly confidential information, perhaps even sensitive or painful for the client to reveal. Again, the scope and complexity of the client's goals will influence this matter. The creation of even straightforward plans, however, may require clients to disclose such things as their income and spending patterns, their attitudes toward other family members, or the extent of their own financial responsibilities to others. Effective gathering of client information requires a systematic approach to the task. One common way to systematize the gathering of information is using a structured *fact-finder form*. Some fact finders are only a few pages long and ask for basic information, while others are thick booklets that seek very detailed data on each asset and amount. Most fact finders are designed for specific financial planning software to simplify data entry. For many client situations, a formal fact finder elicits considerably more information than needed. The sections that should be completed depend on the particular areas of concern addressed in each client's financial plan.

Information gathering involves more than asking the client a series of questions during an interview to fill out a fact-finder form. Usually information gathering also requires examination and analysis of documents—such as wills, tax returns, employee benefit plan coverage, and insurance policies—supplied by the client or the client's other financial advisors. Gathering information typically requires counseling, advising, and listening during face-to-face meetings with the client(s). These skills are especially important because you need to help the client(s) identify and articulate clearly what they really want to accomplish and what financial risks they are willing to take. Regardless of how the information is gathered, it must be accurate, complete, up-to-date, relevant to the client's goals, and well organized. Otherwise, financial plans based on the information will be deficient—perhaps erroneous, inappropriate, and inconsistent with the client's other goals, or even dangerous to the client's financial well-being.

Financial planning is targeted to the unique goals and preferences of clients. Gathering data provides the necessary context for planning to take place. Client goals are moving targets, and gathering data gives you a way to aim.

This domain can be expanded, specifically addressing what types of information advisers should seek, using the CFP® Board Job Task Domains:

Identify the client's values and attitudes:

1. Explore with the client his or her personal and financial needs, priorities and goals.
2. Explore the client's time horizon for each goal.
3. Assess the client's level of knowledge and experience with financial matters.
4. Assess the client's risk exposures and tolerances (longevity, investment, liability and health care).

Gather data:

1. Summary of assets (for example, cost basis information, beneficiary designations and titling)
2. Summary of liabilities (for example, balances, terms, interest rates).
3. Summary of income and expenses
4. Estate planning documents
5. Education plan and resources
6. Retirement plan information
7. Employee benefits
8. Government benefits (for example, Social Security, Medicare)
9. Special circumstances (for example, legal documents and agreements, family situations)
10. Tax documents
11. Investment statements
12. Insurance policies and documents (for example, life, health, disability, liability, long-term care)
13. Closely held business documents (for example, shareholder agreements)
14. Inheritances, windfalls, and other

Recognize the need for additional information.

Step 3: Analyzing and Evaluating the Client's Current Financial Status

Once the client's goals have been determined and data has been gathered, organized, and checked for accuracy, consistency, and completeness, your next task is to analyze and evaluate the data to determine the client's present financial status.

Thorough analysis may reveal certain strengths in the client's present position relative to those goals. For example, the client may be living well within his means, and resources are available to meet some wealth accumulation goals within a reasonable time period. Maybe the client has excellent health and disability insurance coverages through his employer, thereby adequately covering the risks associated with serious disability. Perhaps the client's will has been reviewed recently by his attorney and brought up-to-date to reflect the client's desired estate plan.

Sometimes, your analysis of a client's financial position will disclose a number of weaknesses or conditions that are hindering achievement of the client's goals. For example, the client may be paying unnecessarily high federal income taxes or using debt unwisely. The client's portfolio of investments may be inconsistent with his financial risk tolerance. Maybe the client's business interest is not being used efficiently to achieve his personal insurance protection goals, or important risks have been overlooked, such as the client's exposure to huge lawsuits from the possible negligent use of an automobile by someone other than the client.

One conclusion from your analysis may be that the client cannot attain the goals established in Step 2. For example, the client's resources, savings rates, and investment returns may preclude reaching a specified retirement income goal. Considering an unfunded retirement, you can coach the client and show what changes the client must make to achieve the goal. Postponing retirement, saving more money, seeking higher returns, and deciding to deplete principal during retirement are four ways to help achieve the goal. Presented with alternatives, the client may need to restate the original goal by either lowering it or revising restrictive criteria to make it achievable.

> **EXAMPLE**
>
> As Kirk analyzed the data obtained from his extensive interviews with Rick and Carol Marks, he found that with their present savings rates and probable investment returns, it was extremely unlikely that Rick and Carol could retire at the desired age of 58. In addition, it is highly improbable that Rick and Carol could afford a condo in FL, even at today's depressed real estate values. Kirk will meet again with the Marks to redefine their retirement goals. Possible actions are (1) for both Rick and Carol to contribute more to their respective 401(k) plans and possibly to Roth IRAs, for which they are both eligible; (2) delay retirement for 5 or more years; (3) lower their spending goals in retirement; (4) invest for more long-term growth in their assets, especially in Carol's 401(k); and (5) combinations of these actions.

Additional clarification of the expectations in this domain can be found in the 2011 CFP® Board Job Task Force report:

The Financial Planning Process

1. Evaluate and document the strengths and vulnerabilities of the client's current financial situation.
   - Financial status
   - Statement of financial position/balance sheet
   - Cash flow statement
   - Budget
   - Capital needs analysis (for example, insurance, retirement, major purchases)
2. Risk management and insurance evaluation
   - Insurance coverage
   - Retained risks
   - Asset protection (for example, titling, trusts, business form)
   - Client liquidity (for example, emergency fund)
3. Benefits evaluation
   - Government benefits (for example, Social Security, Medicare)
   - Employee benefits
4. Investment evaluation
   - Asset allocation
   - Investment strategies
   - Investment types
5. Tax evaluation
   - Current, deferred and future tax liabilities
   - Income types
   - Special situations (for example, stock options, international tax issues)
6. Retirement evaluation
   - Retirement plans and strategies (for example, pension options, annuitization)
   - Accumulation planning
   - Distribution planning
7. Estate planning evaluation
   - Estate documents

- Estate tax liabilities
- Ownership of assets
- Beneficiary designations
- Gifting strategies

8. Business ownership
    - Business form
    - Employer benefits
    - Succession planning and exit strategy
    - Risk management

9. Education planning evaluation
    - Sources of financing
    - Tax considerations

10. Other considerations
    - Special circumstances (for example, divorce, disabilities, family dynamics)
    - Inheritances, windfalls, and other large lump sums
    - Charitable planning
    - Eldercare (for example, CCRCs, long-term care needs, nursing home)

11. Identify and use appropriate tools and techniques to conduct analyses (for example, financial calculators, financial planning software, simulators, research services)

Step 4: Developing the Recommendation(s)

financial plan

After you have analyzed the information about the client and, if necessary, helped the client revise his goals, your next job is to devise a realistic *financial plan* for bringing the client from his present financial position to attainment of his goals. Since no two clients are alike, an effective financial plan must be tailored to the individual with all your recommended strategies designed toward each particular client's concerns, abilities, and goals. The plan must address the needs of your client, and not be colored by your compensation model, product offerings, or bias.

It is unlikely that any individual advisor can maintain familiarity and currency with all the strategies that might be appropriate for her clients. Based on your education and professional specialization, you are likely to rely on a limited number of "tried and true" strategies for treating the most frequently encountered planning problems. When you need additional expertise, such as estate planning, you should consult with a specialist in the field for help in designing the client's overall plan.

There is usually more than one way to achieve a client's financial goals. When this is the case, you should present alternative strategies for the client to consider and should explain the advantages and disadvantages of each strategy. Strategies that will help achieve multiple goals should be highlighted.

The financial plan you develop should be specific. It should detail exactly who is to do what (the advisor, the client, other professionals or family members), when, and with what resources. Financial plans are only worthwhile if they are implemented by a client. Without specific implementation schedules, the best of plans are unlikely to be fulfilled.

EXAMPLE
As Kirk developed recommendations for Rick and Carol Marks, he decided on three alternatives, each of which would meet Rick's and Carol's retirement goals, under the assumptions of inflation, rates of return, and longevity. They were as follows: <ul><li>Continue their current investments, under their assumed rates of return, and continue working until age 68 before retiring and claiming their Social Security benefits.</li><li>Increase their current savings by $700 per month (total for both Rick's and Carol's contributions), using the same investment portfolios, and retire at age 64.</li><li>Increase their current savings by $400 per month (total for both Rick's and Carol's contributions), increase the savings by 4 percent per year, reallocate both 401(k) plans to a moderate growth portfolio, and retire at age 62.</li></ul>

Implicit in plan development is the importance of obtaining client approval. It follows that the plan must not only be reasonable, it must also be acceptable to the client. Usually interaction between advisor and client continues during plan development, providing constant feedback to increase the likelihood that the client will approve the plan.

Additional clarification of the expectations in this domain can be found in the 2011 CFP® Board Job Task Force report:

1. Synthesize findings from analysis of the client's financial status.

2. Consider alternatives to meet the client's goals and objectives.
   - Conduct scenario analysis with changing lifestyle variables.
   - Conduct sensitivity analysis with changing assumptions such as interest rate, rates of return, and time horizon.
3. Consult with other professionals on technical issues outside of the planner's expertise.
4. Develop recommendations.
   - Consider client attitudes, values and beliefs.
   - Consider behavioral finance issues (for example, market-timing, overconfidence, recency).
   - Consider interrelationships among financial planning recommendations.
5. Document recommendations.

Step 5: Communicating the Recommendation(s)

Normally, the report containing the financial plan should be in writing (although plans developed for achieving single goals are often not expressed in a formal written report). Recently, more financial planners have begun presenting plans using online and multimedia presentations such as laptop computer presentations. Since the objective of the financial planning report is to communicate, its format should be one the client can easily understand and evaluate what is being proposed. Some financial advisors take pride in the length of their reports, although long reports are often filled with standardized or "boilerplate" passages. Many of those reports are never read in detail by the client. In general, the simpler the report, the easier it will be for the client to understand and possibly adopt. Careful use of graphs, diagrams, summaries, and other visual aids can help clarify important points of the plan.

After you have presented and reviewed the plan with the client, the moment of truth arrives. At this time, you must ask the client to approve the plan and alternative recommendations. You and the client must agree on your next steps together.

Effective communication requires financial professionals to ensure clients understand what actions should be taken, what the cost (in both capital and time) those actions will take, and the consequences of inaction. Communication must be tailored to the communication style of the client.

Additional clarification of the expectations in this domain can be found in the 2011 CFP® Board Job Task Force report:

1. Present financial plan to the client and provide education.
    - Client goals review
    - Assumptions
    - Observations and findings
    - Alternatives
    - Recommendations
2. Obtain feedback from the client and revise the recommendations as appropriate.
3. Provide documentation of plan recommendations and any required product disclosures to the client.
4. Verify client acceptance of recommendations.

Step 6: Implementing the Recommendation(s)

No matter how solid its foundation, the mere giving of financial advice does not constitute financial planning. A financial plan is useful to the client only if the plan is put into action. Therefore, part of your responsibility is to make sure that plan implementation occurs according to the schedule agreed on with the client.

Financial plans of limited scope and limited complexity may be implemented for the client entirely by the advisor. For other plans, however, additional specialized professional expertise will be needed. For example, such legal instruments as wills and trust documents must be obtained, insurance policies may have to be purchased, or investment securities may have to be acquired. Part of your responsibility is to motivate and assist the client in completing each of the steps to implement the entire financial plan.

Implementation requires a clear statement of duties by the advisor and the client. Duties will vary based on the advisor's business model. Some advisors offering fee-only consulting will outsource product acquisition decisions; advisors working in a commission environment will typically provide products to clients directly.

Additional clarification of the expectations in this domain can be found in the 2011 CFP® Board Job Task Force report:

1. Create a prioritized implementation plan with timeline.

2. Assign responsibilities (for example, professional, client or other family member duties).
3. Support the client directly or indirectly with implementing the recommendations.
4. Coordinate and share information, after being granted authorization, with others.
5. Define monitoring responsibilities with the client.

Step 7: Monitoring the Recommendation(s)

The relationship between you and your client should be an ongoing one that spans the client's entire financial life, and that goes through all the stages of the lifecycle process. Therefore, the next step in the financial planning process is monitoring the recommendations. Normally, an advisor meets with the client at least once each year (more frequently if changing circumstances warrant it) to review the plan. The frequency of meetings is determined during the first stage and emphasized during the implementation stage. The review process should involve measuring the performance of the implementation vehicles, such as investments and insurance contracts. Second, updates should be obtained if changes in the client's personal and financial situation have occurred. Third, changes in the economic, tax, or financial environment should be reviewed with the client.

In dynamic and changing times, clients need to hear from their advisors more frequently. Phone calls, informal visits, and structured meetings are all valuable pieces of the monitoring process. You should contact your clients at least as frequently as the client's other professional relationships. If this periodic review of the plan indicates satisfactory performance in light of the client's current financial goals and circumstances, no action needs to be taken. However, if performance is not acceptable or if there is a significant change in the client's personal or financial circumstances or goals or in the economic, tax, or financial environment, you and your client should revise the plan to fit the new situation. This revision process should follow the same steps used to develop the original plan, though the time and effort needed to complete many of the steps will be less than in the original planning engagement.

The monitoring domain will likely involve revisiting other financial planning domains. As a client grows older, their needs will change and even the most comprehensive and detailed financial plan will eventually require changes. Any significant changes will result in making new recommendations and communicating those recommendations to the client, potentially using different communication techniques than in prior years.

> **EXAMPLE**
>
> Kirk, the financial planner in Philadelphia, had two other clients, Wilber and Margaret Downs, who have been Kirk's clients for over 15 years. Wilber was the primary wage earner, and he purchased large amounts of life insurance on himself to provide for Margaret if Wilber died before her. Last week, Kirk learned that Margaret had died unexpectedly at age 65. Kirk called Wilber to express his sympathy. Several weeks from now, Kirk will meet with Wilber to review his financial plan, especially the life insurance policies on Wilber. Wilber may want to change the beneficiary on his policies to his adult children, or Wilber may gift the policies to his children or to a favorite charity.

Additional clarification of the expectations in this domain can be found in the 2011 CFP® Board Job Task Force report:

1. Discuss and evaluate changes in the client's personal circumstances (aging issues, births, deaths, matriculating through the lifecycle process).
2. Review the performance and progress of the plan with the client.
3. Review and evaluate changes in the legal, tax and economic environments.
4. Make recommendations to accommodate changed circumstances.
5. Review scope of work and redefine the engagement as appropriate.
6. Provide client ongoing support as needed.

Step 8: Practicing Within Professional and Regulatory Standards

Financial service professionals from all walks of life (insurance, brokerage or registered investment advisers) are required to follow federal and state rules and regulations, and company procedures applicable to their industry and their particular financial practice. Specific rules for the financial service industry are available on numerous websites such as:

- www.sec.gov
- www.finra.org
- www.cfpboard.net
- www.naic.org
- www.aicpa.org
- www.theamericancollege.edu

- www.thewealthchannel.com

Financial plans must be implemented in a correct legal framework, and the legal framework of financial planning is constantly in flux. Comprehensive financial planners must contend with securities law, investment advisory laws, insurance regulation, banking and consumer advocacy provisions. As the financial services environment becomes more complicated, the need for effective compliance leadership becomes imperative. Financial advisers who hold professional designations are responsible for maintaining the rules, ethical codes and standards attached to their respective designations.

Additional clarification of the expectations in this domain can be found in the 2011 CFP® Board Job Task Force report; the following standards only apply to financial service professionals who hold the CFP® mark.

1. Adhere to CFP® Board's Code of Ethics and Professional Responsibility and Rules of Conduct.
2. Understand CFP® Board's Disciplinary Rules and Procedures.
3. Work within CFP® Board's Financial Planning Practice Standards.
4. Manage practice risk and compliance considerations.
5. Maintain awareness of and comply with regulatory and legal guidelines.

HOW IS FINANCIAL PLANNING CONDUCTED?

The ongoing debate over what financial planning is and who is engaged in financial planning has often centered on the breadth of services provided to clients. Some contend that the financial advisor who focuses on solving a single type of financial problem with a single financial product or service is engaged in financial planning. Others argue that true financial planning involves consideration of all of the client's financial goals and all the products and services available to achieve those goals. What if the advisor's focus is somewhere in between these two extremes?

Once financial planning is recognized as being a process, the traditional debate is relatively easy to resolve. Regardless of the breadth of services provided, an advisor is engaged in financial planning if she uses the financial planning process in working with a client to develop a plan (not necessarily written) for achieving that client's financial goals. Thus, true financial planning can involve a single-purpose, multiple-purpose, or comprehensive approach to meeting a client's financial goals as long as the advisor uses the financial planning process in doing so.

Single-Purpose Approach

Some advisors take the position that the simple selling of a single financial product or service to a client to solve a single financial problem constitutes financial planning. Clearly, if an advisor does not use the financial planning process to determine whether their product or service solves the client's specific financial problem, then the engagement is not financial planning. In addition, if the advisor does not consider alternatives and whether the recommended product or service is the most appropriate product or service for solving that client's problem, then the engagement is not financial planning. In such cases, the advisor would be involved in product sales, not financial planning.

However, if you recommend and then sell a client a product while using the financial planning process, and the recommendation is approved by the client, then you are engaged in financial planning. According to this specialist or *single-purpose approach,* all the following individuals are engaged in financial planning if they use the financial planning process in working with their clients:

- a stockbroker who advises a customer to buy shares of common stock of a particular company
- a salesperson who sells to a client shares in a real estate investment trust (REIT)
- a preparer of income tax returns who suggests that a client establish an IRA
- a banker who opens a trust account for the benefit of a customer's handicapped child
- a life insurance agent who sells key person life insurance to the owner of a small business

Multiple-Purpose Approach

Client financial needs and financial products and services are often seen as falling into one of the following major planning categories: insurance planning, tax planning, and investment planning. Rather than taking a single-purpose approach of just solving a single financial problem with a single financial product or service, many financial advisors take a *multiple-purpose approach* by dealing with at least a large part of one of these categories, and perhaps some aspects of a second category. According to the multiple-purpose approach, the following individuals would be engaged in financial planning as long as they use the financial planning process in working with their clients:

- a multiline insurance agent who sells all lines of life, health, property, and liability insurance
- a tax attorney who assists clients with their income, estate, and gift tax planning
- a life insurance agent who also sells a family of mutual funds to meet both the protection and wealth accumulation needs of clients

Comprehensive Approach

A few advisors take a *comprehensive approach* to providing financial planning services. Comprehensive financial planning considers all aspects of a client's financial position. Such planning includes all the client's financial needs and objectives, and utilizes several integrated and coordinated planning strategies for fulfilling those needs and objectives. The two key characteristics of comprehensive financial planning are

- that it encompasses all the personal and financial situations of clients to the extent these can be uncovered, clarified, and addressed through information gathering and counseling, and
- it employs all the techniques and expertise used in more narrowly focused approaches to solving client financial problems.

Because of the wide range of expertise required to engage in comprehensive financial planning, effective performance commonly requires a team of specialists. The tasks of the advisor managing the team are to coordinate the efforts of the team and to contribute expertise in his own field of specialization.

In its purest form, comprehensive financial planning is a service provided by the managing advisor on a fee-only basis. No part of the managing advisor's compensation comes from the sale of financial products, thus helping to enhance objectivity in all aspects of the plan. Some team specialists also are compensated through fees, while others might receive commissions from the sale of products, while still others might receive both fees and commissions. In its less pure—but often more practical form—comprehensive financial planning compensates the managing advisor with some combination of fees for service and commissions from the sale of financial products. Again, other members of the team might receive fees, commissions, or both.

It is interesting to compare the methods of compensation by practicing Certified Financial Planner® practitioners as reported in the 2011 Survey of Trends in the Financial Planning Industry.[4] In the survey of 345 practitioners, 60 percent received a combination of fees and commissions; 17 percent were fee-only, and 7 percent were commission-only. The remaining 13 percent received either salary only, salary and fee, or salary and commissions.

Furthermore, in its purest form, comprehensive financial planning is performed for a client all at once. A single planning engagement by the managing advisor and her team of specialists creates one plan that addresses all the clients concerns and utilizes all the needed financial strategies. This plan is then updated with the client periodically and modified as appropriate. In its less pure form, comprehensive financial planning occurs incrementally during several engagements with the client. For example, you might prepare a plan this year to treat the client's tax concerns and insurance planning problems. Next year, you might focus on the client's investment concerns and coordinate the strategies for dealing with them with the previously developed tax and insurance strategies. In a third engagement, you might address any remaining issues in the tax, insurance, and investment planning areas and coordinate all the recommended strategies and previously developed plans. Again, each incremental part, as well as the overall plan, is reviewed periodically and revised as appropriate.

FINANCIAL PLANNING AREAS OF SPECIALIZATION

Regardless of the breadth of the approach to financial planning—single-purpose, multiple-purpose, or comprehensive—employed by a particular advisor in working with clients, financial advisors tend to have areas of specialization in which they concentrate their activities. The following areas of specialization are common today and give us a good indication of the types of services provided by advisors to clients:

- investment planning/advice
- pension/retirement planning
- comprehensive planning
- estate planning

---

4. *2011 Survey of Trends in the Financial Planning Industry*, College for Financial Planning. Denver, CO, 2011, p. 6.

- portfolio management
- income tax planning
- insurance planning
- education planning
- elder/long-term care planning
- closely-held business planning
- financial planning employee education
- income tax preparation
- divorce planning

CONTENT OF A COMPREHENSIVE FINANCIAL PLAN

As indicated in the previous section, many financial advisors see comprehensive financial planning as one of their areas of specialization. In practice, however, it is the least frequently encountered type of financial planning engagement for most advisors for several reasons. First, not many clients are willing to invest as much of their own time in the undertaking as comprehensive financial planning requires. Second, usually only affluent clients are willing and able to pay for all the time of the advisor and her staff that is needed in developing a comprehensive financial plan. Third, not many clients can easily deal with the totality of their financial goals, capabilities, and difficulties all at one time. Instead, most prefer to concentrate on only one or a few related issues at a time. (As has been mentioned, however, even clients in the last group can have a comprehensive plan developed and implemented for them in incremental stages.)

For those cases in which you are called upon to prepare a comprehensive financial plan for a client, whether entirely in one engagement or incrementally over a period of time, what should the plan contain? Clearly, comprehensive financial planning is such an ambitious and complex undertaking that it must cover numerous subjects. At a minimum, these subjects should include the major planning areas identified by the Certified Financial Planner Board of Standards in its Topic List for CFP® Certification Examinations. These areas are

- general principles of financial planning (for example, personal financial statements, client attitudes and behavioral characteristics, and so forth)

- insurance planning and risk management
- employee benefits planning
- investment planning
- income tax planning
- retirement planning
- estate planning

> **FOCUS ON ETHICS**
>
> **Beginning a Dialogue on Ethics**
>
> Ethics should be implicit in any discussion of financial planning and the role of the financial advisor. This box addresses a question that many advisors have asked: "Is the highly ethical advisor financially rewarded for being ethical?" The answer is that he or she may be, but there is no guarantee. There are certainly some instances of the shady advisor reaping significant financial gains. Disciplined ethical conduct, by itself, does not guarantee financial success.
>
> Perhaps the question should be addressed from a different perspective. Do clients want to do business with someone who really understands financial planning but who has questionable morals? Do clients want to do business with someone whose integrity is unassailable but whose financial planning skills are marginal? *The answer to both questions is no!*
>
> The skilled financial advisor who is client-centered and ethically well disciplined clearly has the attributes that clients desire and deserve. Again, ethical practice provides no guarantees of financial success. It is clear, however, that clients want to do business with financial advisors who have earned their trust and are technically competent. They will give such an advisor their loyalty, their referrals, and their lasting appreciation.

A comprehensive financial plan should address **all** of these major planning areas as they relate to the client. If you do not have the expertise to personally address each of the major planning areas in the development of the plan, you should form a team of specialists and serve as its manager. Your role would be to coordinate the efforts of the team and contribute expertise in your own field of specialization. If, for some reason, one of the major planning areas does not apply to the client, the plan should spell out this fact. This will indicate that an important planning area was not overlooked in developing the plan but it simply did not apply to the client at this time.

In addition to the major planning areas that pertain to almost every client, there are a number of more specialized areas relevant to many clients. These specialized areas are mostly subsets of the major planning areas and may involve several areas such as investment and tax planning. However, because all of these specialized areas are unique, they merit separate treatment. They should be part of a client's comprehensive financial plan only if he is affected by them. Typically, a single-purpose or multiple-purpose financial plan focused on the particular planning need deals with these specialized areas.

Educational planning is the most important of these specialized areas in terms of the number of people it affects. Most clients understand the need to save for college and are aware that college costs have risen at a significantly higher rate than the *Consumer Price Index (CPI)*. Still, the vast majority of families accumulate far too little money for college by the matriculation date. They usually have to cut back on living expenses, borrow money, tap into retirement assets, or seek additional employment to meet the funding need. Graduating students are often saddled with very high loans that must be paid off over time. Often, students must lower their sights and target a school that is less expensive, rather than the one best suited to their needs. Consequently, planning to meet the costs of higher education has become a necessity for most people who have children.

The other specialized areas worthy of mention can be categorized as financial planning for special circumstances. These areas typically include planning for

- divorce
- terminal illness
- nontraditional families
- job change and job loss, including severance packages
- dependents with special needs

As previously mentioned, these specialized planning areas are subsets of one or more major planning areas. For example, divorce planning could affect every major planning area; nevertheless, divorce planning should not be part of a comprehensive financial plan unless the client is contemplating divorce. Even then, divorce planning would be better handled under a single-purpose or multiple-purpose financial plan because of its unique aspects and shorter planning horizon than the major planning areas.

Life-Cycle Financial Planning

life-cycle financial planning

There are five distinct phases in an individual's *financial life cycle*. Starting at a relatively young age (that is, age 25 or younger), a career-minded person typically will pass through four phases en route to phase 5—retirement. These five phases and their corresponding age ranges are

1. early career (age 25 or younger to age 35)
2. career development (age 35 to age 50)
3. peak accumulation (age 50 to ages 58–62)
4. preretirement (3 to 6 years prior to planned retirement)
5. retirement (ages 62–66 and older)

Together, these five phases span a person's entire financial life. While some people will not experience all of the phases or may spend little time in a phase, the vast majority of career-minded people will go through all five phases.

Your first step in creating a comprehensive financial plan is to lead the client through the goal-setting process. Goal setting requires clients to recognize the various phases in their financial life; for young clients, the early career phase is the beginning of that life. The goals that young clients set while in this phase typically reflect this fact. For example, a client in the early career phase often is newly married and has young children, and the client and spouse are establishing employment patterns. The client probably is concerned about accumulating funds for a home purchase if he has not already done so. As the children grow older, the client begins to think about saving for college. Protecting the family from a potential financial disaster due to death or disability is also important, as is building a cash reserve or emergency fund to meet unexpected contingencies. However, the client's goals that pertain to retirement and estate planning generally will not have a very high priority in the first few years of the early career phase, but those areas still need to be considered if the financial plan is to be a truly comprehensive one.

Once the client has a comprehensive financial plan, it is incumbent for you as the advisor to monitor the plan. As the client moves into the career development phase of her financial life cycle, some goals may need revision. This phase is often a time of career enhancement, upward mobility, and rapid growth in income. The phase usually includes additional accumulation and then expenditure of funds for children's college educations. Moreover, you should recommend coordinating the employee benefits of the client and her spouse and integrating them with insurance and investment planning goals.

As the client moves into the peak accumulation phase, the ever-vigilant advisor should monitor the plan for any needed changes. In this phase, the client is usually moving toward maximum earnings and has the greatest opportunity for wealth accumulation. The phase may include accumulating funds for special purposes, but it is usually a continuation of trying to meet the goals set for the major planning areas, especially education and retirement goals.

The preretirement phase often involves winding down both the career and income potential, restructuring investment assets to reduce risk and enhance income, and greater emphasis is placed on tax planning and evaluating retirement plan distribution options relative to income needs and tax consequences. Throughout this phase, you should be actively involved in keeping your client's financial plan on target to meet all the client's goals.

The final phase in the client's financial life cycle is retirement. If you have kept your client's financial plan fine-tuned, then this phase should be a time of enjoyment with a comfortable retirement income and sufficient assets to preserve purchasing power. While all of the major planning areas should have received attention throughout the client's financial life cycle, now is the time for you to make certain your client's estate plan is in order.

The advisor who monitors a client's financial plan throughout the client's financial life cycle is practicing *life-cycle financial planning*. A comprehensive financial plan developed for a relatively young client needs to be reviewed and revised frequently as the client ages and passes through the phases of his financial life cycle. Many financial goals will need adjusting as life's circumstances change; having the right goals is always critical to maintaining a successful financial plan. Your role in setting goals is to help the client establish reasonable, achievable goals and to set a positive tone for the entire financial planning process. The successful process encompasses not only developing the client's first financial plan but also any future revisions and modifications to that plan.

The content of a comprehensive financial plan should, as we mentioned earlier, include a discussion of each major planning area. The current phase of the client's financial life cycle strongly influences the priority given to the goals for each planning area. Financial planning is a process that should be ongoing throughout the client's financial life. That is why financial planning over the client's financial life is called life-cycle financial planning.

Format of a Comprehensive Financial Plan

A financial plan, whether comprehensive or not, is essentially a report to the client regarding your findings and recommendations. This report results from applying the financial planning process to the client's present situation to assist the client in meeting his financial goals. Although there are as many different formats for a comprehensive financial plan as there are financial advisors, every comprehensive financial plan should include certain types of information. For example, every comprehensive plan should cover all major planning areas.

Every plan should be based on reasonable, achievable goals set by the client, and every plan should be structured around strategies for achieving the client's goals. In addition, in the process of formulating strategies, all assumptions should be spelled out in the plan documents. Typical assumptions include the interest rate, the rate of inflation, and the client's financial risk tolerance, to name a few. Finally, every plan is developed around information gathered during a fact-finding process. Much of this information, such as financial statements, should also be included in the plan. Recognizing the many possible variations for organizing all of this information into a cohesive plan, one approach is to structure the plan to parallel the steps in the financial planning process as described below.

First (paralleling Step 1, establishing and defining the advisor-client relationship), a comprehensive financial plan should start by specifying the responsibilities of each party for implementing the plan and taking it to completion. The plan also should clarify how you are compensated for your work in planning. Covering these all-important ground rules at the beginning of the plan helps define the advisor-client relationship and set the tone for the relationship as well.

Second (paralleling Step 2, determining goals and gathering data), a comprehensive plan should specify the client's stated goals and indicate the priority of each goal and the time frame to achieve it. Each goal should be stated as specifically as possible. Since there are likely to be several goals in a comprehensive financial plan, it helps for the client to list them in relevant categories, such as protection, accumulation, liquidation, and so on. Keep in mind that the best solution for a specific goal may involve a combination of major planning areas. Regardless of the approach used to categorize the goals, the plan should avoid confusing the client!

In addition to specifying the client's goals, the plan should describe the client's present situation based on the personal and financial data gathered from the client. For the personal situation, include basic information about the client and family, such as names, addresses, phone numbers, e-mail addresses, dates of birth, and Social Security numbers. In addition, include other relevant personal information that helps define the client's total situation and will affect the plan. For example, information about a child's serious disability, a client's intention to care for aging parents, previous marriages, child-support obligations, expected inheritances, and history of bankruptcies are all useful in financial planning.

pro forma statement

The plan should include a description of the client's present financial situation. This is most commonly done by including a copy of the client's financial position statement, listing his assets and liabilities and showing net worth; a cash-flow statement that identifies all the client's income and expenses and indicates net cash flow for the latest period; and a copy of the client's most recent federal income tax return and an analysis of it. The information presented should also include *pro forma statements,* that is, projections of future financial position relevant to understanding the client's current position. The client's current investment portfolio should also be documented with assessments about its liquidity, diversification, and risk characteristics.

Next, for each goal, at least three critical areas of information should be presented:

- (paralleling Step 3, analyzing and evaluating the data) the problem(s) you have identified that the client would encounter in attempting to accomplish the goal
- (paralleling Step 4, developing and presenting a plan) the recommended financial and tax services, products, and strategies for overcoming the identified problem(s) (including any underlying assumptions you made in formulating the recommendation) so the client can achieve the goal
- (paralleling Step 5, implementing the plan) your recommendations (and alternatives) for implementing the proposed solution for achieving the goal

Regardless of the format you adopt to organize a comprehensive financial plan, it is important that the plan be communicated to the client in the form of a written report. The format of this financial planning report should make it easy for the client to understand and evaluate what is being proposed. In general, the simpler the report, the easier it will be for the client to understand and adopt. Careful organization, as well as the use of graphs, diagrams, and other visual aids, can help a great deal!

TRENDS CREATING OPPORTUNITIES FOR FINANCIAL PLANNING ADVISORS

baby boom generation

A number of trends with important implications for advisors engaged in financial planning emerged in the United States in recent years. These trends all point to enormous opportunities for advisors to render valuable service to clients and earn substantial compensation from their advisory services.

> **Trends Creating Opportunities for Financial Planning Advisors**
> 1. Rising median age
> 2. Increased impact of dual-income families
> 3. Volatility of financial conditions
> 4. Technological change

One of the most important trends is that the population is aging rapidly. The median age of Americans has risen more than seven years in the past three decades, which means a larger proportion of the population has moved into the period of highest earnings. In addition, as people get older, they tend to devote a smaller share of their income to current consumption and more toward savings and investments.

One cause of the rising median age of Americans is that members of the *baby boom generation* are no longer babies. The children born after World War II from 1946 to 1964 now range in age from their mid-40s to their mid-60s and constitute almost 30 percent of the U.S. population. Another factor that drives up the median age is the increased life expectancies of Americans. Approximately 13 percent of Americans are now age 65 or over, compared to 9.2 percent in 1960. This trend is referred to as the "graying of America." In 2012, an estimated 10,000 baby boomers reach age 65 every day! By the year 2030, the population of Americans over 65 is estimated to reach nearly 20 percent, resulting in tremendous social changes to government support programs, health care, and housing.

Clearly, the aging American population means that more consumers need retirement planning assistance during their remaining years of active work and their retirement period. In addition, the "echo boomers," who are the children of baby boomers, represent a huge proportion of Americans and will need help with insurance, investments, and education planning. Opportunities abound for knowledgeable, competent, and ethical financial advisors!

Another extremely important trend in the financial planning marketplace is that dual-income families are increasingly common. This trend results from an increasing percentage of women entering (and reentering) the labor force, even while they have young children. Dual-income families typically have higher total incomes, pay higher income and Social Security taxes, and have less time to manage their own finances. Again, this represents many opportunities for financial advisors.

A third broad trend is the increasing volatility of financial conditions in the American economy. Two deep bear markets in the first decade of this century depleted many investors' retirement savings, and the tremendous volatility remains an obstacle for many clients who need equity investing to survive a long retirement period. The "great recession" of 2008–09 resulted in millions of Americans out of work, depleted savings, and a deeply depressed real estate market. As this text is written, interest rates remain very low which hurts clients who depend on CDs or bonds for income.

Inflation rates have been volatile as measured over the last 30–40 years. During the 1970s, inflation (as measured by the Consumer Price Index, or CPI) exceeded 11 percent in two years. In the 1980s and 1990s, inflation declined significantly and remains in the 2 to 3 percent range annually in this decade.

In addition to volatility of inflation rates, interest rates, and stock market prices, another destabilizing factor for American consumers has been a series of important U.S. income tax laws—including the 1986 Tax Reform Act, the Economic Growth and Tax Reform Reconciliation Act of 2001, and the Pension Protection Act of 2006, among others. With these tax acts, the landscape for personal and estate taxes changed dramatically, and this increases the demand for capable financial advisors.

With the possible exception of the great bull market during the late 1990s, where many investors felt they could "do it themselves" with no professional advice or consideration of the risks, volatile economic conditions generally create a greater demand for financial planning services. The volatile conditions also increase the importance of advisors monitoring their clients' financial situations and adjusting their plans accordingly. A very critical consideration is the client's risk tolerance, which may change in the face of deep market sell-offs and gloomy media projections. Some of the advisor's best work consists of "hand holding" for the client during turbulent economic times.

Table 1-2 Consumer Price Index Changes (Urban Consumers), the Prime Rate, and the Standard & Poor's 500 Stock Index: 1965-2010

Year	Percentage Change in CPI	Average Prime Rate %	Average S & P 500 Index
1965	1.6%	4.54%	88.2
1970	5.7	7.91	83.2
1971	4.4	5.72	98.3
1972	3.2	5.25	109.2
1973	6.2	8.03	107.4
1974	11.0	10.81	82.8
1975	9.1	7.86	87.1
1976	5.8	6.84	102.0
1977	6.5	6.82	98.2
1978	7.6	9.06	96.0
1979	11.3	12.67	102.8
1980	13.5	15.27	118.7
1981	10.3	18.87	128.0
1982	6.2	14.86	119.7
1983	3.2	10.79	160.4
1984	4.3	12.04	180.5
1985	3.6	9.93	186.8
1986	1.9	8.33	236.3
1987	3.6	8.21	268.8
1988	4.1	9.32	265.9
1989	4.8	10.87	323.1
1990	5.4	10.01	335.01
1991	4.2	8.46	376.20
1992	3.0	6.25	415.75
1993	3.0	6.00	451.63
1994	2.6	7.15	460.42
1995	2.8	8.83	541.72
1996	3.0	8.27	670.49
1997	2.3	8.44	873.43
1998	1.6	8.35	1085.50
1999	2.2	8.00	1327.33
2000	3.4	9.23	1427.22
2001	2.8	6.91	1194.18
2002	1.6	4.67	989.38
2003	2.3	4.12	967.93
2004	2.7	4.34	1132.60
2005	3.4	6.19	1207.75
2006	3.2	7.96	1318.31
2007	2.8	8.05	1478.10
2008	3.8	5.10	832.14
2009	−0.4	3.25	948.52
2010	1.6	3.25	1130.66

Source: *Statistical Abstract of the United States*; "Selected Interest Rates: Historical Data," *Statistics: Releases and Historical Data*, The Federal Reserve Board, updated weekly, available at http://www.federalreserve.gov/releases/; and *Federal Reserve Bulletin*, various issues.

A fourth major trend in financial planning is the technological revolution that has occurred in the industry. This revolution has made possible the creation of many new financial products, and technology has made it easier to tailor products to individual client needs. In addition, the technology has enabled improved analyses of the performance of financial products by advisors with the right analysis skills.

CONSUMER NEEDS FOR FINANCIAL PLANNING

A basic and inescapable principle of economics is the law of scarcity—in every society, human wants are unlimited whereas the resources available to fill those wants are limited. The available resources must be somehow rationed among the wants. This rationing problem creates the need for financial planning even in affluent societies, such as the United States, and even among the most affluent members of such societies. To put it colloquially, there is just never enough money to go around.

What are the main financial concerns of American consumers? Are they able to handle those concerns on their own or do they need professional help? In short, do U.S. consumers have a significant need and effective demand for professional financial planning services in the 21st century?

A national consumer survey conducted by the CFP Board of Standards identified the following top 10 reasons people begin financial planning:[5]

- building a retirement fund (82 percent of those surveyed)
- purchasing or renovating a home (41 percent)
- building an "emergency fund" (40 percent)
- managing or reducing current debt (34 percent)
- vacation or travel (34 percent)
- building a college fund (32 percent)
- accumulating capital (31 percent)
- providing insurance protection (29 percent)
- sheltering income from taxes (26 percent)
- generating current income (25 percent)

---

5. *2004 Consumer Survey*, Certified Financial Planner Board of Standards, Denver, CO. This was a survey of 1,112 upper-quartile households of all ages (income ranged from $60,000+ depending on the householders' ages).

The Financial Planning Process

In reporting the results of its 2008 Consumer Survey, the CFP Board of Standards also broke the findings down according to three key groups of respondents—"up and coming," "mid-life," and "retirement cusp." The following table shows the financial planning focus of each of the groups and highlights the relative importance of retirement planning to all three consumer groups.

Table 1-3 Financial Planning Needs

Consumer Group	Who Are They?	Financial Planning Focus
Up and Coming • 39% of respondents	• Ages: 20–39 • 28% have a written financial plan • 52% completed plan within the last 3 years • Most tolerant of risk • More likely to use the Internet for financial purposes • Most likely to have financial software	• Prepare for retirement • Manage/reduce debt • Build an emergency fund • Build a college fund • Save for a home purchase/renovation
Mid-Life • 36% of respondents	• Ages: 40–54 • 39% have a written financial plan • 56% completed plan at least 4 years ago • More likely to use a financial professional to develop a plan • Highest amount of household income • Have low to moderate risk tolerance	• Prepare for retirement (strongest focus of all three consumer groups) • Build an emergency fund • Vacation/travel • Finance college education • Manage/reduce debt • Shelter income from taxes

Consumer Group	Who Are They?	Financial Planning Focus
Retirement Cusp • 25% of respondents	• Ages: 55–69 • 47% have a written financial plan • 62% completed plan at least 5 years ago • Higher net worth and lower risk tolerance • Most likely to have a financial professional as a primary advisor	• Prepare for retirement • Vacation/travel • Accumulate capital • Generate income • Shelter income from taxes • Provide for future medical needs • Build an emergency fund

Source: *2008 Consumer Survey,* Copyright © 2009, Certified Financial Planner Board of Standards, Inc., Denver, CO. All rights reserved. Used with permission.

The Employee Benefits Research Institute (EBRI) is an outstanding source of information about consumer issues. For years, they have conducted a nationwide survey of Americans to determine their feelings and confidence in retiring comfortably. The 2011 survey results revealed the following:[6]

- Americans' confidence in their ability to afford a comfortable retirement has plunged to a new low as the percentage of workers "not at all confident" grew from 22 percent in 2010 to 27 percent in 2011—the highest level in the 21 years of the Retirement Confidence Survey.
- Only 42 percent of workers report they and/or their spouse have tried to calculate how much money they need to live comfortably in retirement.
- A sizable percentage of workers report they have virtually no savings or investments. Twenty-nine (29) percent say they have less than $1,000. More than half (56 percent) say that the total of savings and investments, excluding the value of their home and any primary defined benefit plans, is less than $25,000.
- More workers expect to work for pay in retirement. Seventy-four percent report they plan to work in retirement, three times the percentage of retirees who say they actually worked for pay in retirement (23 percent).

---

6. *The 2011 Retirement Confidence Survey,* Employee Benefit Research Institute, Washington, DC, March 2011.

These and other findings of the EBRI Retirement Confidence Survey and other mounting evidence show conclusively that a huge percentage of Americans need professional guidance as they move toward, and live in, their retirement years.

A study of baby boomers conducted by The Allstate Corporation in 2001 predicted that many baby boomers were likely to encounter a retirement that is quite different in financial terms from the past.[7] Now, in 2012, we see Allstate's predictions coming true. Americans are retiring later and continuing to work in some capacity during retirement (more than 70 percent). Among other things, the survey revealed that during retirement, more than one in three baby boomers will be financially responsible for parents or children. That obviously creates intense generational strains for many families. The survey showed that about one in five American retirees will pay college tuition for one or more children. Survey respondents had saved only an average of 12 percent of the total they will need to meet even basic living expenses in retirement. Furthermore, they have grossly underestimated the predicted increase in cost of living (that is, effects of inflation) over the next 20 years.

The baby boom generation has also become known as the *sandwiched generation* because many of its members are pressed between competing priorities. They are faced with helping finance their children's education and aiding their aging parents while they should be saving for their own retirement. Retirement, college funding, and long-term care are important to everyone, but especially to sandwiched baby boomers.

Obstacles Confronting Consumers

The results of the surveys discussed above and similar studies make it clear that many American households still have not gained control of their financial destinies. Certainly, there are many reasons why they have not developed effective financial plans. Three of the most important obstacles they face are the following:

- the natural human tendency to procrastinate—Among the reasons for putting off the task of establishing a financial plan may be a lack of time due to a hectic lifestyle, the seeming enormity of the task of

---

7. *Retirement Reality Check,* The Allstate Corporation, Northbrook, IL, December 2001. Harris Interactive polled 1,004 people born between 1946 and 1961, with household incomes ranging from $35,000 to $100,000. An update of this survey has been released annually since the original survey in 2006.

getting one's finances under control, and the belief that there is still plenty of time to prepare for achieving financial goals.
- the very common tendency for Americans to live up to or beyond their current income—The pressure in households to overspend for current consumption is enormous, and many families have no funds left to implement plans to meet future goals.
- the lack of financial knowledge among consumers—Although in recent years there has undoubtedly been some growth in the financial sophistication of Americans, there is still widespread ignorance about how to formulate financial objectives and how to identify and properly evaluate possible strategies to achieve them.

Role of Financial Planning Advisors

A basic inference that can be drawn from the results of consumer surveys is that Americans need help in managing their personal finances to achieve their financial goals. Moreover, many Americans seem to realize that they would benefit from professional help, and with better education, most others would reach the same conclusion. A major part of the challenge facing advisors who are doing financial planning is to help clients overcome obstacles by educating them and motivating them to gain control of their own finances.

FINANCIAL PLANNING UMBRELLA

The major planning areas that follow the General Principles of Financial Planning are

- Insurance Planning and Risk Management
- Employee Benefits Planning
- Investment Planning
- Income Tax Planning
- Retirement Planning
- Estate Planning

These areas are viewed as the major planning areas under the financial planning umbrella. Even though each one of these planning areas is a specialty unto itself, together they make up elements of comprehensive financial planning. The order in which these planning areas are covered in this book is identical to their order on the Topic List for CFP® Certification Examinations.

Even though the government and quasi-government programs stemming from Social Security, Medicare, and Medicare supplements could just as easily be discussed under insurance planning, employee benefits planning, and retirement planning, they are dealt with separately because of their importance in providing a minimum floor of protection. They are viewed by most advisors as the foundation for comprehensive financial planning.

CHAPTER REVIEW

Key Terms and Concepts are explained in the Glossary. Answers to the Review Questions are found in the back of the book in the Answers to Questions section.

Key Terms and Concepts

financial planning
financial planning process
structuring
financial goals
financial risk tolerance

fact-finder form
financial plan
life-cycle financial planning
pro forma statement
baby boom generation

Review Questions

1. Identify the eight steps in the financial planning process and briefly indicate the kinds of activities involved in each step. [1]

2. Describe each of the following approaches to financial planning: (a.) single-purpose approach, (b.) multiple-purpose approach, and (c.) comprehensive approach. [2]

3. At a minimum, what subjects should be included in a comprehensive financial plan? [3]

4. Explain what is meant by life-cycle financial planning. [4]

5. Summarize the major events occurring from the late 1960s to the present in the evolution of financial planning as a profession. [6]

6. Describe the opportunities in the financial planning marketplace resulting from each of the following trends: (a.) rising median age, (b.) increasing number of dual-income families, (c.) volatility of financial conditions, (d.) increasing use of sophisticated technology by the financial services industry. [7]

7. What are the top 10 reasons why people begin financial planning? [8]

8. Describe three important obstacles preventing households from gaining control of their own financial destinies. [8]

INSURANCE PLANNING AND RISK MANAGEMENT

> **Learning Objectives**
>
> *An understanding of the material in this chapter should enable the student to*
>
> 1. Define risk and explain its two categories: pure risk and speculative risk.
> 2. Describe the various types of pure risks faced by individuals and families.
> 3. Explain how the financial planning process can be used to deal with the possibility of financial loss associated with pure risks.
> 4. Describe the various types of insurance coverages available for meeting personal risks.
> 5. Describe the various types of insurance coverages available for meeting property and liability risks.

Risk can be divided into two categories: pure risk and speculative risk. Insurance is a technique for dealing primarily with pure risks that can be categorized as personal risks, property risks, and liability risks. The similarity of the financial planning process to risk management and needs analysis is then explained, with the financial planning process used to discuss how to help individuals and families deal with the possibility of financial loss associated with pure risks.

IMPORTANCE OF PROTECTION OBJECTIVES

Financial planning represents an integrated approach to developing and implementing plans to achieve individual or family financial objectives. Although financial objectives may differ in terms of individual circumstances, goals, attitudes, and needs, all integrated plans should include an analysis and recommendations that satisfy the client's protection objectives.

While planning for the accumulation of wealth may be more exciting, the protection of that accumulated wealth cannot be overlooked. Most people work to acquire assets (wealth) such as homes, automobiles, savings, and investments, but the pleasure associated with this wealth is sometimes interrupted by the chilling thought that some event they cannot control could cause assets to be damaged or destroyed. Protecting assets and preserving the wealth represented by those assets against the possibility of loss is a challenge nearly all people face. Efforts by individuals and families to meet this challenge are aimed at dealing with the problem of risk.

RISK

risk

Because risk is the basic problem with which insurance deals, we must fully understand what risk is to deal with it efficiently through the use of insurance and/or other risk handling techniques. For insurance and financial planning purposes, the term *risk* means the possibility of financial loss. In applying this definition of risk, recognize that there are two ways a financial loss can occur. The most common notion of a loss involves a reduction in the value of something that an individual already possesses—for example, the value of a family's home can be reduced by a fire, or the value of one's income-earning ability can be reduced by death or disability. In addition to a reduction in the value of something someone already possesses, a loss can arise from a reduction in the value of something that he does not currently possess but expects to receive in the future. For example, an investor incurs a risk of earning only a 5 percent return on an investment that he expected would yield 10 percent. An individual has a risk of receiving a smaller inheritance than she had expected because the deceased's financial advisor did a poor job of minimizing taxes and estate settlement costs in the deceased's estate plan. Recognizing that a loss can arise from a reduction in either the value of something someone already possesses, or in the value of something one expects to receive in the future, risk involves the possibility of a financial loss. Defined in this way, risk falls into two categories:

pure risk

speculative risk

- *pure risk*—involves only the possibility of financial loss

- *speculative risk*—involves both the possibility of financial loss and the possibility of financial gain

Both pure and speculative risks involve the possibility of financial loss. However, with pure risk the possibility of gain is essentially absent, and all that remains is the alternative of loss or no loss (no change).

The difference between pure and speculative risk can be illustrated by the situation of a client who owns a home. The possibility of damage or destruction to the home due to fire is a pure risk. What are the possible outcomes? Either a fire occurs and causes damage that results in a loss, or no fire occurs and there is no change or loss. In contrast, the risk that the home could appreciate or depreciate in market value is a speculative risk. In this case, the client may realize either a gain or a loss from the sale of the home. With few exceptions, insurance is a technique for dealing with pure, rather than speculative, risk.

Two additional points are important in fully understanding what risk is:

- Risk and uncertainty are not the same.
- Risk is not the probability of loss.

Although risk can give rise to uncertainty, risk is not the same as uncertainty. Unlike uncertainty, which is a state of mind characterized by doubt, risk exists all around us as a condition in the world. As a result of this difference, the following may occur:

- A client can be uncertain in a situation in which no risk exists.
- Risk can exist when a client lacks knowledge of the risk and, thus, does not experience uncertainty.
- Two clients facing the same risk can experience different degrees of uncertainty (for example, two passengers on the same airplane, one confident and the other fearful).

Recognizing this difference between risk and uncertainty enables you to prepare your clients to view and deal with risk objectively. Effective handling of a client's risk from a particular cause of loss (a *peril*) can reduce the client's uncertainty about incurring a financial loss from that peril. However, mere reduction of uncertainty does not reduce the risk—the possibility of a financial loss—that exists as a condition in the world. Consider the situation of a client who is a 25-year-old single mother with two young dependent children. Transferring the risk associated with the client's death to an insurance company by purchasing life insurance would reduce the client's uncertainty about her dependent children suffering a severe financial loss upon her death. However, suppose instead the client merely reasoned that, since she was young and not likely to die in the near future, there was really no good reason to buy life insurance at that time. While the client may have succeeded in reducing her own uncertainty, her low level of uncertainty had no effect on the risk—possibility of financial loss—faced by her children. The risk remained, regardless of her knowledge or attitudes about the risk. If she is one of the relatively few females aged 25 who die in the next year, her dependent children will lose all the financial support her income would have provided.

A second point important to understanding risk is that while risk may be measurable in terms of probabilities, it need not be measurable to exist. That is the reason risk is defined as the *possibility,* not the probability, of financial loss. For risk to be measurable in terms of probabilities, there must be a considerable number of similar exposures to which the probability can be applied in estimating the outcome. An insurance company that insures many similar houses in an area (many similar exposures) can use probabilities to measure its risk of loss—that is, the chance that the ratio of houses that burn to houses insured in the next year will exceed the ratio of houses expected to burn during that year.

However, even knowing the probability that a house of a particular type in an area will burn within the next year does not help a client measure the risk he faces. With only one house (one exposure), the client will either have a loss or no loss. In this case, risk—the possibility of financial loss—exists; the client just cannot measure the risk he faces with probabilities because there is only a single exposure to loss. For insurance companies who insure houses, the law of large numbers is employed to estimate the rate at which their insured properties will incur losses.

TYPES OF PURE RISKS

personal risk
property risk
liability risk

As mentioned earlier, insurance is a technique for dealing primarily with pure risks—risks involving a chance of loss or no loss. Pure risks can be categorized as *personal risks, property risks* and *liability risks*. These three types of pure risks can be described briefly as follows:

1. personal risks—involve the possibility of

    a. loss of income-earning ability because of

    (1) premature death

    (2) disability

    (3) unemployment or

(4) retirement

    b. extra expenses associated with accidental injuries, periods of sickness, or the inability to perform safely some of the activities of daily living (ADLs) (that is, bathing, dressing, transferring from bed to chair, and so on)

2. property risks—involve the possibility of

    a. direct losses associated with the need to replace or repair damaged or missing property

    b. indirect (consequential) losses, such as additional living expenses that are required due to a direct loss

3. liability risks—involve the possibility of

    a. loss from damaging or destroying the property of others

    b. loss from causing physical or personal injuries to others

Examples of personal risks include the possibility of a loss of income to family members upon a client's premature death, disability or retirement. In addition, the possibility of incurring increased expenses associated with medical and long-term care is a type of personal risk.

Clients are exposed to property risks through the ownership of real and personal property. Real property includes the client's dwelling and associated buildings, and personal property includes such items as household goods, clothing, and automobiles. *Direct losses* to one's real or personal property can be the result of many perils (causes of loss) including, among others, fire, windstorm, theft, flood, earthquake, and automobile collisions. *Indirect losses* are associated with the loss of use of property following the occurrence of a direct loss. In addition to the indirect loss referred to as additional living expenses, other types of consequential losses include debris removal costs, rental income losses, and demolition losses. Of these, additional living expenses and debris removal are the more common indirect losses for individuals and families.

> **EXAMPLE**
>
> Mark and Sheila Brown suffered a serious fire with extensive smoke damage to their residence in March 2012. They also incurred water damage throughout the home from the efforts of fire fighters to extinguish the fire. While the fire did not cause a total loss of the home, the estimates to repair the home exceed $150,000. They also incurred an estimated $50,000 in losses to their furniture and other household items. The damages to the home and furnishings represent direct losses resulting from the fire. In addition, the Browns and their two children had to live in a local short-term rental hotel for two months while their home was being repaired and cleaned. The total cost of the temporary housing was $8,000. Mark Brown also incurred a loss of income because he suffered some smoke inhalation injuries that made him unable to work for a week. The costs of living in the rental hotel and the loss of income are examples of indirect losses from the fire.

The ownership, maintenance, or use of an automobile is the best known source of liability risk. However, individuals should realize that potential liabilities also arise from ownership, maintenance, or use of real property and out of personal activities. In addition, workers' compensation statutes can create an exposure in certain states when a client has household employees.

PLANNING FOR PURE RISKS: INSURANCE AND OTHER TECHNIQUES

risk management

needs analysis

How should you approach your clients' pure-risk situations? The process used for dealing with pure risks has traditionally been called different names depending upon the type of risk situation faced. When dealing with pure risks involving possible damage or destruction of property or legal liability, financial advisors have tended to use a process called *risk management*. On the other hand, when dealing with pure risks involving the loss of income earning ability due to death, disability, or old age, they have tended to use a process called *needs analysis*. However, the risk management and *needs analysis* processes not only contain the same steps, but they also involve the similar steps to the financial planning process. This should not really be surprising, since all three processes are simply different statements of a professional approach to identify and solve a client's financial problem(s). Given the similarity of the steps in the risk management, needs analysis, and financial planning processes, the financial planning process will be used in discussing the steps involved in helping individuals and families deal with the possibility of financial loss associated with pure risks.

Table 2-1 Processes for Dealing with Pure Risks			
Step	Risk Management	Needs Analysis	Financial Planning
1	Determination of objectives	Identify the client's needs in the event of death, disability, and/or retirement*	Establishing and defining the client-planner relationship
2	Risk identification	Collect information on the client's current financial situation	Gathering information necessary to fulfill the engagement
3	Risk analysis	Determine the types and amounts of resources required to meet the client's needs Determine the types and amounts of resources currently available to meet the client's needs Subtract the resources currently available from the resources required to meet the client's needs to determine the gaps to be filled by additional resources	Analyzing and evaluating the client's current financial status
4	Consider alternative risk treatment devices and select the method(s) and products believed to be the best for treating the risk(s)	Develop a plan and recommendation(s) for filling the resource gaps with proceeds from additional insurance coverage(s) or resources from other relevant risk treatment devices	Developing the recommendation(s)
5			Communicating the recommendations
6	Implement the decision	Buy additional life and/or disability income insurance; increase savings for retirement*	Implementing the recommendations
7	Monitor periodically	Monitor periodically for changes in the client's needs and/or external factors (inflation rate, rate of return that can be earned on investments, and so on)	Monitoring the recommendations
8			Practicing within professional and regulatory standards

*While loss of income earning ability due to retirement is a type of pure risk and some life insurance and annuity products provide savings vehicles for dealing with this risk, retirement planning for a client primarily involves investment and tax considerations rather than planning for insurance product acquisitions.

Establishing and Defining the Client-Advisor Relationship

When helping a client plan for handling the pure risks he faces, the first step is establishing and defining the client-advisor relationship. For the advisor, this generally involves building trust with the client, ensuring client satisfaction, and creating a relationship with the client that will, it is hoped, span the client's entire life. To do this, you need to explain how you work and the types of products and services you can provide. You should also provide examples of how your products and services help clients handle the pure risks they incur.

Gathering Information Necessary to Fulfill the Engagement

In this step, you will typically complete a fact-finder to help determine the client's current situation and to identify the most important risks the client is incurring. The client's concerns regarding various pure risks can be identified in a number of ways. For example, in discussing the client's general financial concerns or the concerns that specifically caused the client to seek financial planning assistance, you should listen for references to potential losses or other financial problems related to various types of pure risks.

Alternatively, you might present the client with an outline of various types of pure risks and ask the client to indicate her degree of concern with each type and the reasons why. In addition to helping you identify the client's key concerns related to pure risks, the latter approach also may help identify certain pure risks with which the client should consider despite her apparent lack of concern at the beginning of the financial planning engagement. You can then evaluate the need for greater concern about these pure risks in the process of gathering and analyzing relevant data.

Once the client's concerns about dealing with various pure risks have been identified, you should query the client to learn what goals he has with respect to dealing with each of these concerns. For example, what is the client's goal concerning the risk of loss due to his premature death? Perhaps it is to ensure that his children are fed, clothed, and sheltered until they reach a certain age when they presumably will no longer be dependent. This goal may also include ensuring adequate resources for each child to attend college at the state university and/or for the spouse to return to school to update her job skills. In discussing the client's goal for dealing with each pure risk he faces, you should help the client, through skillful questioning, to be as specific as possible in quantifying the goals.

Finally, where goals for dealing with various pure risks are competing, you should help the client rank these goals. For example, for a family with young children and limited resources, protecting the dependent children against the financial consequences of a working parent's death until they graduate from high school might be more important than funding the children's college educations, which in turn may have a higher priority than having only a $100 deductible for property damage covered by the family's auto and homeowners policies. Likewise, with a little education from the financial advisor, carrying adequate insurance to protect against liability risks is likely to be viewed as more important than maintaining low deductibles on insurance for property risks and personal health risk.

After the client's goals for dealing with various types of pure risks have been established, you will need to gather information from the client to identify the specific pure risks to which he is exposed. At a minimum, you should gather the following types of objective and subjective information from the client:

- an inventory of assets and liabilities
- a description of the present arrangement for distributing the client's (and spouse's) assets at death
- a list of annual income and expenditures
- a summary of present insurance coverages
- the client's preferences regarding such things as
    - the amount of income the family should have during various periods following the client's death (for example, when dependent children are still at home versus after they have left home)
    - the amount of income the family will need during various periods following a long-term disability suffered by the client
    - the colleges the client would like the children to attend following his death or disability
    - who should be responsible for managing the income and assets provided to the family and its members following the client's death
    - the spouse's role (working versus staying home to raise young children) following the client's death or disability

After you gather this information from the client, you can use a checklist of property and activities (that give rise to the various pure risks encountered by individuals and families as shown on the form in Appendix C) to identify the pure risks specifically faced by the client. This provides you with a systematic approach to discovering a particular client's loss exposures.

> **FOCUS ON ETHICS**
>
> **When Responsibility Exceeds Knowledge**
>
> When financial advisors address a client's financial security, they often emphasize future income production and protection. The goal is to produce a level of wealth that will generate a sufficient stream of income that will prepare the client for retirement or will ensure a chosen lifestyle should there be an interruption in income production.
>
> Commission-based financial advisors are often not licensed to sell property and liability insurance, and they frequently overlook threats posed by property destruction or major liability claims. An underinsured home destroyed by fire or natural disaster can destroy the best financial plan. The same can happen if the client is underinsured and loses a major liability suit resulting from an accident, professional negligence, or other reason.
>
> The financial advisor must sensitize the client to these needs as well. Insurance can minimize the client's property and liability losses. Protecting the client's assets is an essential part of financial planning. Just because the advisor is less knowledgeable in these areas does not reduce the need or the responsibility.

To illustrate how risk identification might be done, assume that the information gathered from the client, Burt Beamer, indicates the following: Burt Beamer, age 45, has a wife, age 43, a son, age 18, and a daughter, age 16. Burt is a manager for a local firm and currently earns $78,000 annually. The Beamers purchased a home 5 years ago for $225,000. Last year they purchased a small cabin in the mountains for $45,000. They plan to use this cabin as much as possible during the summer months and occasionally on weekends during the balance of the year. They are also thinking about renting the cabin out periodically during the summer season. The Beamers own two automobiles, a 3-year-old station wagon and a one-year-old foreign compact.

Although this is a simplified example, a partial listing of risks the Beamer family faces is shown in the table below. In actual practice you should seek additional information from the Beamer family to complete the list of their exposures to pure risk. You should include other assets or property that might be owned or used by the Beamers. You should consider expanding the liability exposure to include any business pursuits and the use of nonowned autos. In this illustration, personal risks are limited to the premature death of Burt. In practice this area would be expanded to include premature death of Burt's spouse, risks associated with the loss of earning power because of periods of disability, incurring additional expenses for medical and long-term care, and the need for income at retirement. Even the needs under the premature death category might be expanded beyond those shown in this illustration.

Table 2-2 Risk Identification (Type of Risk)

Property risks
- Direct losses
  - Dwelling
  - Cabin
  - Furniture, clothing, etc. (dwelling)
  - Furniture, clothing, etc. (cabin)
  - Automobiles
- Indirect losses
  - Additional living expenses
  - Debris removal

Liability risks
- Owned premises (dwelling, cabin)
- Owned automobiles
- Personal activities

Personal risks
- Premature death (of Burt)
  - Education fund
  - Mortgage redemption fund
  - Lifetime income for spouse

The risk-identification process may appear to be a relatively simple task. Some financial advisors and clients may feel it is a waste of time to formalize the risk-identification process. They need only be reminded that forgetting or neglecting an existing risk could have disastrous financial consequences.

In addition to risk identification, the data gathered provides you with a basis to identify potential problems the client's current situation may present for achieving the client's goals. For example, the types and amounts of the client's present insurance coverages may be either not appropriate or not efficient for meeting the client's goals. In analyzing the client's exposures to pure risk in the next step of the financial planning process, your review of the present insurance coverages may reveal that the client's liability insurance limits are too low, the type of life insurance coverage currently held is too costly to enable the client to purchase an adequate amount of insurance to protect his dependents, or your client could handle higher deductibles in his property insurance policies.

Analyzing and Evaluating the Client's Current Financial Status

Once the relevant information about the client has been gathered, organized, and checked for accuracy, consistency, and completeness, your next task is to analyze the client's present financial condition with respect to the pure risks she faces. The objective here is to determine the weaknesses or conditions in the client's current financial situation that hinder achieving the client's goals. In the case of pure risks, data analysis requires at least two important activities:

- measuring the potential losses associated with the identified pure risks
- evaluating these risks from the standpoint of their potential financial impact on the client

Risk Measurement

Theoretically, risk measurement should include information on both the frequency (probability of occurrence) and severity of loss. As mentioned earlier, for risk to be measurable in terms of probabilities, there must be a considerable number of similar exposures to which the probability can be applied in estimating the outcome. However, in most cases, the pure risk situations faced by a particular individual or family involve only one or a few exposures to loss. Therefore, statistical probabilities of loss do not help measure the pure risks faced by a single person or family. As a result, the major emphasis in risk measurement must be on the severity of the loss. When dealing with pure risks faced by individuals and families, it is safest to assume total loss and identify this as the maximum possible loss. Then ask: "What would be the impact of a total loss on the individual's (or family's) financial situation?"

actual cash value

replacement cost

depreciation

Property Risks. The easiest asset to measure for loss purposes is cash; each one dollar bill is worth one dollar (except, of course, when it is numismatic property or when problems of foreign exchange enter the picture). For property other than cash, however, risk measurement problems begin to emerge. Three key terms of the measurement process are (1) actual cash value, (2) replacement cost, and (3) depreciation.

Actual cash value is an insurance term used in many property insurance contracts. These contracts often limit the insurer's liability for damaged property to its actual cash value at the time of loss. Actual cash value has generally been defined as replacement cost less a reduction resulting from depreciation and obsolescence. This is normally expressed simply as

> Actual Cash Value = Replacement Cost minus Depreciation

Actual cash value is sometimes a difficult measurement to understand, primarily because of confusion that arises from the interpretations of *replacement cost* and *depreciation*. Although useful life is frequently used as a guideline in measuring depreciation, depreciation as a factor in measuring actual cash value differs from depreciation in an accounting sense. Depreciation depends on the age of the asset, its use, its condition at the time of loss, and any other factor causing deterioration. In addition, anything that causes the property to become obsolete in any fashion is also included in the depreciation determination of actual cash value.

Replacement cost is simply that cost to replace or repair the damaged asset. For personal property, this is replacement with a comparable asset at the current price. In the calculation of actual cash value, replacement cost would be reduced for the comparable age of the damaged property. For example, assume an auto purchased new 3 years ago for $11,995 was completely destroyed in an accident. The same auto purchased today would cost $15,000, which would be its replacement cost. The actual cash value is an amount sufficient to replace the destroyed auto with one of like age and condition. Note, however, that depreciation is deducted from the current price, not the original price. It is immaterial that the damaged auto cost $11,995 new 3 years ago. The actual cash value is $15,000 (replacement cost) less an allowance for depreciation.

When replacement cost is used for real property, such as a dwelling, it is normally interpreted to mean the cost to rebuild the same type dwelling on the same site for the same type of occupancy and with materials of like kind and quality. If the replacement cost for the dwelling is determined to be $160,000 and depreciation is $17,200, the actual cash value will be

Actual cash value = Replacement cost − Depreciation
= $160,000 − $17,200
= $142,800

Replacement cost has become the more practical measure of the maximum possible loss associated with a client's real property in pure-risk situations, especially when insurance is the most appropriate technique to treat the particular risk. Sometimes there is a temptation to use market value as the measurement of loss for real property. While this is the value most familiar to consumers and owners of real estate, market value is closely linked to supply and demand conditions and includes the value of land. The land, however, is not likely to be lost, destroyed, or severely damaged by a property risk. Thus, exercise caution in using market value as the measurement of maximum possible loss for pure-risk situations. Remember that pure risk is the possibility of loss or no loss; the concern is for the damage or destruction of property, not its transfer of ownership.

For insurance purposes, the measurement of loss for personal property such as furniture, clothing, and automobiles has traditionally been the item's actual cash value. Actually, however, the maximum possible loss is the replacement cost of the particular item. For an extra premium, most insurance companies will provide replacement cost coverage on personal property other than automobiles. For this reason, and for the purpose of showing the value differences, the maximum possible loss for personal property (and for real property as well) is measured on both a replacement cost and actual-cash-value basis. An example of this is shown below.

Finally, for measurement purposes some loss exposures listed under the property risk category are not costs of replacing property but are indirect expenses incurred because of damage to property. The best example of this for most individuals is the category of additional living expenses. These are the costs over and above normal living expenses that would be necessary to provide living accommodations, food, and transportation if a residence could not be occupied due to damage or destruction. An estimate of these expenses should be made as the measurement of this loss exposure.

Table 2-3 Risk Identification and Measurement

Type of Risk	Maximum Possible Loss	
	Actual Cash Value	Replacement Cost
Property risks		
Direct losses		
Dwelling	$160,000	$200,000
Cabin	30,000	42,000
Furniture, clothing, etc. (dwelling)	60,000	90,000
Furniture, clothing, etc. (cabin)	4,000	7,500
Automobiles	19,000	28,000
Indirect losses		
Additional living expenses		9,600
Debris removal		3,500
Liability risks		
Owned premises (dwelling, cabin)		unlimited
Owned automobiles		unlimited
Personal activities		unlimited
Personal risks		
Premature death (of Burt)		
Cash for cleanup fund		50,000
Education fund		78,000
Mortgage redemption fund		137,000
Lifetime income for spouse		$1,100,000

Liability Risks. No perfect method has been developed for measuring the maximum possible dollar loss that individuals can suffer from the liability exposure. A client can enter into certain contractual arrangements that will limit the extent of liability, but in most cases the liability loss will depend upon the severity of the future accident and the amount the court awards to the injured parties (or amount of the out-of-court settlement agreement). Because a liability loss could range anywhere from a few dollars to $1 million or more, it is appropriate to recognize this uncertainty about the liability loss and to identify this amount as "unlimited."

human-life-value method

Personal Risks. There are several ways to measure the loss associated with personal risks. For example, *the human-life-value method* of measuring loss due to premature death is based on a calculation of the present value of a given dollar amount annually over a given number of years at some assumed interest rate. The human-life value is the capitalized present value of future net earnings that would be available to an insured's dependents if the insured remained alive and able to work. A major shortcoming of this approach is that it does not take into account the types or amounts of the dependent's needs following the client's death or the types or amounts of resources that will be available to meet those needs.

Another method to determine the loss associated with premature death is known as needs analysis. This commonly used approach (and the method used in this chapter for analyzing data related to key personal income risks) involves

1. identifying and attaching a dollar amount to the specific financial needs of the survivors
2. identifying and attaching a dollar amount to the resources currently available to meet those needs
3. determining the gaps between the survivors' needs and the resources available to meet them

These gaps must be filled with additional financial resources if the survivors' needs are to be fully met. The needs analysis approach can also be used to measure loss that would be experienced by the client and his dependents as a result of serious disability. When needs analysis is applied to disability income planning, the financial needs of the disabled client and the needs of dependent family members are substituted for the needs of survivors in the premature death estimation.

In planning for the client's premature death, you will analyze information gathered from the client in Step 2 of the financial planning process to identify and measure the survivors' financial needs and resources currently available to meet those needs. Generally, in the event of a client's death, the survivors' needs will include both lump-sum cash needs and income needs. For the Beamer family, the lump-sum cash needs are identified as a cleanup fund, education fund, and mortgage redemption fund. The income need was identified as a lifetime income for the surviving spouse. To determine the amount of additional resources needed to meet the survivors' lump-sum and income needs, the amounts of currently available resources are subtracted from the needs. For example, any proceeds of existing life insurance policies on Burt's life and the after-tax balance of Burt's 401(k) plan would be available to reduce the amount needed to provide for the lump-sum cash needs at Burt's death. Similarly, any wages and employee retirement benefits expected to be earned by Burt's spouse, along with Social Security benefits she would be entitled to at retirement, are generally considered in determining the additional resources required to meet the spouse's income needs.

The dollar amount shown for the cleanup fund is an estimate of the amount needed in addition to currently available resources for last illness expenses, funeral costs, outstanding debts, probate expenses, federal and state estate and inheritance taxes, and so forth. The dollar amount for the education fund is the present value of the projected future costs of educating the two Beamer children reduced by any resources currently available to help meet those costs. Planning for future education expenses has become a common part of the financial planning process, and the dollar amount needed for this item would most likely be provided in some other part of the total financial planning process. If not, some time should be spent in developing an estimate of these costs. The amount for the mortgage is typically the current unpaid balance shown in the amortization schedule less any resources currently available to help pay off the mortgage in the event of Burt's death.

Measuring the amount needed to fund the lifetime income for the surviving spouse requires calculations beyond the scope of this chapter. In the advisor's discussions with the client it was determined that, in the event of his premature death, Burt wanted his widow to have the equivalent purchasing power of $4,000 per month throughout her lifetime. To calculate the value of the principal sum needed presently to satisfy this objective, it is necessary to make assumptions regarding future rates of inflation and future rates of interest earnings. For this case, these assumptions were 4.5 percent and 6.5 percent, respectively. It was also assumed that upon reaching age 66 Mrs. Beamer would qualify for an inflation adjusted benefit equal to $1,000 per month from Burt's Social Security. Based on these assumptions and a projection of Mrs. Beamer's longevity of life, the current principal sum needed is calculated to be $1,100,000. This is the amount entered as the maximum possible loss associated with the spouse's income need. Since Mrs. Beamer might live beyond the age indicated by the projection of the longevity of her life, an alternative approach that would truly guarantee her a lifetime income would be to determine the current principal sum needed to meet her income need until age 70, and then also determine how much she would need to purchase a life annuity of an appropriate amount if she is still living at age 70.

At this point, the risk identification and measurement activities should have been completed for all the pure risks to which the client is exposed. The table above illustrates the maximum possible loss values determined for the partial list of risks facing the Beamer family.

Risk Evaluation

After you have identified all the pure risks and determined appropriate values to measure the maximum possible loss for each, you should evaluate these risks for their potential financial impact upon the client. You can assist in this process by having the client assess the seriousness of each potential loss on her financial status and by ranking the various risks according to their severity. One method of showing this that will be useful later in selecting the most cost-effective technique(s) for handling each of the client's pure risk situations is to categorize losses as high severity or low severity. What is high or low severity must be interpreted in terms of the client's financial ability to absorb a risk situation's maximum possible loss.

The risks listed for the Beamer family in the previous table are evaluated using this method in the Risk Impact Chart. In addition to the low severity property losses indicated below, consider other low severity losses commonly experienced by individuals and families such as the first few hundred dollars of medical expenses each year, income lost during the first few weeks of disability, and expenses during the first few weeks of long-term care.

One additional comment should be made about the evaluation of pure risks. It is a mistake to view these risks as isolated individual events; for example, the fire that causes damage to the dwelling should not be isolated from the concurrent loss due to fire damage of the furniture contained in that dwelling. All the losses that may result from a single event should be combined into one unit to obtain a true measure of the maximum possible loss. Therefore, the fire damage to the dwelling and furniture should be considered as one loss and the combined total will determine the estimated financial impact on the individual or family.

Developing the Recommendations

After you have analyzed the client's data and current situation, and, if necessary, refined the client's objectives, your next job is to devise a realistic plan with recommendations to bring the client from his present financial position to the attainment of those objectives. This truly represents the heart of the entire planning process. In planning to deal with pure risks faced by

Insurance Planning and Risk Management

the client, this step in the financial planning process involves considering the various alternative techniques to handle pure risks and selecting the most cost-effective technique(s) for each of the client's pure risk exposures. A plan containing the techniques you identify as the most appropriate is then shared with the client for his approval.

Table 2-4 Risk Impact Chart

<u>High Severity</u>
    Liability losses
        Owned premises (dwelling, cabin)
        Owned automobiles
        Personal activities
    Property losses in excess of $500 per occurrence
        Dwelling including debris removal and additional living expenses
        Cabin
        Furniture, clothing, etc. (from dwelling) including debris removal and additional living expenses
        Furniture, clothing, etc. (from cabin)
        Automobile (foreign compact)
        Automobile (station wagon)
    Personal losses
        Cash for cleanup fund
        Education fund
        Mortgage redemption fund
        Lifetime income for spouse
<u>Low Severity</u>
    Property losses of $500 or less

Alternative Risk Treatment Devices

loss control
loss financing
retention
insurance

The techniques typically available to individuals and families for handling pure risks are grouped in two categories: *loss control* and loss financing. Loss control (sometimes referred to as risk control) concerns reducing the probability that events resulting in financial loss will occur and minimizing the magnitude of those losses that do occur. Since some losses will occur regardless of any loss control activities undertaken, *loss financing* is concerned with how to fund these losses.

Both loss control and loss financing include several alternative techniques to handle pure risks. Loss control techniques typically available to individuals and families include *risk avoidance, loss prevention* and *loss reduction*. The two loss financing techniques most commonly used for handling pure risks faced by individuals and families are *retention* and *insurance*.

risk avoidance

Risk Avoidance. The objective of risk avoidance is to eliminate the activity or condition that creates the particular risk so that the possibility of a loss becomes nonexistent. For example, since certain types of animals are known to be vicious, someone practices liability risk avoidance by never owning such an animal or by selling or destroying such an animal if it is currently owned.

While risk avoidance is potentially the most powerful risk-treatment action, it is often a very difficult treatment technique for an individual or family to practice. For example, if a person is concerned about the liability loss exposure from the ownership or use of an automobile, applying risk avoidance would call for the complete elimination of the ownership and use of automobiles. In today's mobile society this could be extremely difficult to accomplish. Since it is neither possible nor practical to avoid all risks, we must consider techniques that will forestall, minimize, or finance the losses.

loss prevention

Loss Prevention. Loss prevention attempts to reduce the frequency of loss associated with unavoidable risks by preventing the loss from occurring. Loss-prevention actions tend to focus on the hazards or conditions that increase the likelihood of a loss. For example, if a client drives an auto, he can reduce the chance of being killed in a drunk-driving accident by no longer drinking before driving or by using a designated driver. While loss prevention measures reduce the likelihood of loss, they do not totally eliminate the risk associated with drunk driving. The client still faces unavoidable risk that he may be killed by another motorist who has been drinking.

While many loss prevention activities involve things that should not be done, loss prevention activities can also be positive in nature. For example, the construction of a fence around the swimming pool in the client's backyard makes it more difficult for someone to gain access to the pool and reduces the likelihood of a liability loss if someone uses the swimming pool without the client's knowledge.

Insurance Planning and Risk Management

While the goal of loss prevention activities is to eliminate the occurrence of the event, not all loss exposures can be totally prevented. Therefore, some effort must be made to minimize the magnitude and severity of the losses that do occur.

loss reduction

Loss Reduction. Loss reduction is directed at reducing the severity of losses that do occur. Loss reduction can be employed before, during, or after a loss has occurred and is designed to minimize the magnitude of the loss and its financial impact on a family or individual.

Two examples of loss reduction actions directed at the possibility of fire are (1) maintaining fire extinguishers in the home to extinguish flames before they spread and cause extensive damage to the property, and (2) installing smoke detectors to alert residents that there is a fire so that they may extinguish the fire or call the fire department. Note, however, these tools serve no loss-reduction purpose unless they are properly serviced and all household members know how to use them. Also, we include smoke detectors here as a loss-reduction action; however, they also serve as a loss-prevention action because individuals can vacate the property when the alarm sounds, thereby reducing the likelihood of death or injury due to fire.

Retention. Many individuals purchase insurance for pure risks and fail to consider other loss-financing techniques. Yet it is obvious that everyone retains some risks, either consciously or unconsciously. In many cases, voluntary risk retention is a useful tool for handling pure risks. However, involuntary or unintentional risk retention because of one's failure to identify exposures can be a serious problem.

Risk retention is the process of financing or paying one's own losses—or absorbing the loss "out-of-pocket." In cases where retention is consciously practiced, a person may set aside funds earmarked for a particular risk. For example, a client may choose to purchase only liability insurance on his personal automobile policy, especially if the vehicle is older. Then, the client may set aside personal savings earmarked to cover costs if a loss occurs. However, this formal method of employing retention is rarely practiced—most retention is practiced informally by covering losses with funds by borrowing (often on a credit card), or by paying for the loss out-of-pocket.

Retention is cost-effective for handling pure risk when the maximum possible loss is too small to cause financial hardship—few people would insure the loss that would result from theft of a single inexpensive item of personal property. Such risk is appropriately retained with deductibles in property insurance policies. In contrast, retaining risk in every case where the probability of loss is small is not necessarily a cost-effective choice. Retaining risks where the probability of loss is small—but the potential amount of loss is severe—is a dangerous practice since the application of probability is not appropriate for the single exposure unit of the individual. As mentioned earlier, while a young parent with dependent children might decide not to purchase life insurance because the probability of dying at a young age is very small, retention of the risk could have very serious consequences.

Retention is frequently practiced even when insurance is purchased for a particular risk. As mentioned above, a deductible may apply to losses covered by the insurance policy purchased, when the insured pays the first dollar amount of the loss. Similarly, the exposure to loss by causes excluded under an insurance contract is retained by the policyowner. The policyowner may have to retain these loss exposures simply because there is no alternative. Retention is also practiced when insurance policies exclude the loss to certain types of property or property at certain locations. Exclusions in insurance policies may also preclude coverage for particular types of loss. Explaining the need for this sort of retention to purchasers of insurance is an important service a financial advisor provides.

risk transfer

risk pooling

law of large numbers

Insurance. Insurance is a risk-financing technique that involves the transfer of the financial burden of risk from one party, called the insured, to another party called the insurer for a price (premium). All true insurance involves pooling together a large number of similar risks by the insurer as a method to make losses more predictable and thus reduce risk. A technique for handling pure risk must have both of these features—risk transfer and pooling of similar risks— to be true insurance.

The first part of the definition of insurance—*risk transfer*—describes how insureds view insurance, whereas the second part—pooling of similar risks—is how insurers see it. From the viewpoint of an individual insured, insurance can eliminate (or possibly reduce) a pure risk he faces by transferring it to an insurance company. The insurance company, in turn, accepts similar risks from a large number of insureds and, by pooling them together, is able to reduce the overall risk it faces.

To understand this last statement, let us review the insurance process. As insurers accept insureds, they pool those with similar loss exposures, and the combination of many similar exposure units permits the operation of the *law of large numbers*. From a statistical standpoint, as the number of exposure units increases, the deviation of actual losses (for example, deaths) from the expected experience diminishes. As the potential margin of error decreases, so also does the risk of loss faced by the insurer due to inaccurate predictions of the chance (frequency) and amount (severity) of loss. The application of the law of large numbers allows for greater predictability of probable losses and results in an overall reduction of risk for the insurer. This increased knowledge of probable loss frequency and severity also means that the insurer can determine a more suitable charge (premium) for accepting the transfer of risk from the insured. Predictability, based on accurate statistics, is the key to all forms of insurance!

EXAMPLE

If you flip a fair coin, the probability of getting a "head" is 50 percent, or 0.50. If you flipped the coin 10 times, you would not be shocked to get 7 "heads" and only 3 "tails." However, if you flipped the coin 10,000 times, you would expect the result to be "very close" to 50 percent "heads" and 50 percent "tails." This is a simple application of the law of large numbers, in that as the number of trials (that is, flips in our case) increases, the actual results get very close to predicted results. Similarly, insurance companies use the law of large numbers to predict how many insured people will die in any given year. The company does not know exactly "who" will die; however, they can use various mortality tables to predict very accurately how many will die. With that information and employing time-value-of-money techniques, insurers can calculate how much they must charge each insured to profitably run the business.

The law of large numbers actually has a dual application in insurance. When an insurer determines the premium rate for insurance it will sell in the future, it does not know the actual frequency and severity of loss for those it will insure. As a result, the insurer must use historical data for similar loss exposures it insured in the past to estimate the frequency and severity of loss it expects to actually experience in the future. If the insurer assumes that conditions affecting losses in the future will be the same as conditions affecting losses in the past, the insurer can use the past data to estimate the true underlying probability of loss in the past. Then, the insurer can use the estimate of the true underlying probability of loss in the past to estimate the expected frequency of loss in the future. Because two estimates are being made, there is a dual application of the law of large numbers:

- The larger the sample of past data used in calculating the expected frequency of loss, the more accurate the estimates of the true underlying probability of loss.
- The larger the number of exposure units insured in the future, the more accurate the estimate will be of the actual frequency of loss in the future.

Because the law of large numbers is a statistical law, there are several assumptions that must be met for the pooling of a large number of similar exposure units to reduce the insurer's risk to a desired level. Stated in insurance-related terms these assumptions include

1. the ability to accurately determine when an insured loss has occurred and to accurately measure the amount of that loss
2. an equal probability of loss for each exposure unit that is pooled by the insurer (called homogeneous exposure units)
3. the existence of a sufficiently large number of exposure units to enable risk to be reduced to the desired level (known as *mass*)
4. a loss to one exposure unit does not affect the occurrence or nonoccurrence of a loss to another exposure unit (called independence)
5. to permit the dual application of the law of large numbers in insurance, conditions affecting loss in the future are the same as conditions affecting loss in the past

In some types of risk situations, violation of one or more of these assumptions may essentially eliminate the risk-reducing effect of the law of large numbers and make the risk uninsurable, at least by privately-owned insurers. For example, violation of the assumption of independence by the risk of loss due to unemployment requires that unemployment insurance be provided by the government rather than by private insurers. However, in most insurable pure risk situations, violation of one or more of the assumptions merely reduces the effectiveness of the law of large numbers in reducing risk.

Regardless of how effectively the law of large numbers works in reducing risk for an insurer, all insurers continue to face some degree of risk that the actual frequency and/or severity of loss for insured exposures will exceed the expected frequency and/or severity computed from past experience and included in the premium rates. If this happens, an insurer may not collect enough premium to cover actual losses and expenses, and as a result, may suffer an underwriting loss.

Selecting Techniques for Handling a Client's Pure Risks

A commonly used approach to identify the most appropriate risk treatment device(s) for handling the pure risk(s) faced by a client is based on two key risk characteristics—the potential frequency (probability) of loss and the potential severity (amount) of loss. The severity of loss for each pure risk situation faced by the client—maximum possible loss—was measured and evaluated in terms of seriousness in Step 3 of the financial planning process. Thus, application of the financial planning process provides information to identify high severity and low severity risk situations. As mentioned earlier, what is high or low severity must be interpreted in terms of the client's financial ability (or capacity) to absorb a risk situation's maximum possible loss.

For reasons discussed earlier, no attempt is made to measure frequencies (probabilities) of loss in analyzing each of the pure risk situations faced by clients who are individuals or families. Thus, to select techniques for dealing with the pure risks faced by a particular client, you must categorize each of the client's pure risk situations as being high frequency or low frequency based on how the client sees each risk situation as being likely to occur in her own situation.

Several key points about the use of insurance in handling the pure risks faced by a client are indicated in the following table. First, insurance is used most efficiently in dealing with risk situations involving low frequency, high severity losses. In this case, the consequences of a severe loss are transferred to the insurer for a premium that is economical due to the risk situation's low frequency. Some examples of low frequency, high severity risk situations where insurance is an especially cost-effective risk treatment device include

- the financial loss that young dependent children would experience upon the death of a young working parent
- the financial loss an individual would experience from a large liability judgment when a friend is accidentally injured at his home
- the financial loss if a young working person were to become severely disabled and unable to work for the rest of her life
- the financial loss from medical bills in the case of an extremely serious, long-term illness
- the financial loss from huge costs of long-term care services for a chronically ill individual
- the financial loss from the total destruction of a family's home due to a fire

Second, even as loss frequency becomes higher and insurance premium rates increase significantly, insurance may still be the most effective technique for dealing with risk situations where loss severity is high. For example, although premium rates tend to be quite high for young male drivers or adult drivers with several accidents, auto liability insurance would still be the most appropriate technique for handling the risk of legal liability in a situation where the individual has no alternative form of transportation available for getting to work. Similarly, while life insurance rates increase considerably with age, life insurance would still be the most appropriate technique for handling the risk that would be encountered by young dependent children in the event of their 50-year-old father's death, if there was not enough money to meet the financial needs of the surviving family. In cases such as these, eliminating the devastating impact of a very high severity loss through the purchase of insurance far outweighs the high cost of the insurance coverage.

Third, insurance is not an efficient way to deal with low severity risk situations, regardless of the frequency involved. Retention is clearly the most appropriate technique for dealing with low frequency, low severity risk situations, because losses seldom occur and when they do they are small. Even when the frequency of a low severity risk situation is high, retention is a more efficient technique than insurance because the high frequency makes insurance costly.

For example, the probability of an individual visiting the doctor once a year is probably very close to one. If the doctor charges $75 for a single visit, buying insurance to cover the first visit would cost approximately $75 (1 X $75) plus a loading to cover the insurer's expenses, profit, and contingencies. Retaining the risk would cost only $75 when the individual goes to the doctor the first time. This shows why retention through the use of deductibles is cost-effective in dealing with high frequency, small losses even when insurance is purchased to handle severe losses from the same cause. By removing the high frequency, low severity portion of a potential loss from coverage, a deductible leaves the low frequency, high severity portion of the potential loss to be covered by insurance, precisely the pure risk situation where insurance is most cost-effective.

Finally, in low frequency, high severity pure risk situations where insurance is an appropriate risk handling device, also employing loss reduction techniques may help to make insurance even more economical by reducing loss severity. For example, insurance companies give a premium discount on homeowners insurance for proper installation of an alarm system.

Table 2-5 Risk Characteristics As Determinants of the Appropriate Risk Treatment Device(s)

	High Frequency	Low Frequency

High Severity	• Voluntary retention is not realistic
	• Insurance/transfer is too costly
	• Loss control to reduce frequency through loss prevention will be productive only if either
	    – frequency is reduced sufficiently to make insurance/transfer economical, or
	    – severity is also reduced to a manageable level through loss reduction
	• Avoidance should be used if it is not possible either to reduce severity to a manageable level (through loss reduction), or to make insurance/transfer economical
	• Involuntary retention may be unavoidable if it is not possible to avoid, reduce or transfer the risk
		• Voluntary retention is not realistic
		• Insurance/transfer and possibly also loss control through loss reduction
		    – Insurance/transfer will shift catastrophic loss at relatively low cost
		    – Loss control through loss reduction may reduce severity and thus, further reduce the cost of risk transfer
		• Loss control through loss reduction to reduce severity to a manageable level
		• Avoidance should be used if it is not possible either to reduce severity to a manageable level, or to transfer the risk
		• Involuntary retention may be unavoidable if it is not possible to avoid, reduce, or transfer the risk

Low Severity	• Retention and loss control through loss prevention
	    – Retention is appropriate since high frequency implies that transfer will be costly
	    – Loss control through loss prevention is appropriate since a reduction of frequency will reduce the aggregate amount of losses to be borne under retention
		• Retention is most appropriate since losses seldom occur and when they do, they are small

A Plan Using the Selected Techniques

Once the appropriate techniques have been identified, you must formulate a plan to use the techniques to treat the pure risks faced by your client. Where insurance is to be used, you should be concerned with matching particular insurance policies to the various risks identified and measured earlier in the financial planning process. In addition, you should identify specific opportunities to use risk retention and/or risk reduction to make the use of insurance as economical as possible. Finally, a plan to use insurance as a technique for treating risks cannot be formulated in isolation from insurance or other financial resources the client may already have. For example, it is highly probable that the client already has purchased a homeowners policy, an auto policy and life insurance, and has accumulated some personal savings. The client's employer may provide employee benefits for health care financing, life insurance, income replacement for periods of disability and retirement, and Social Security will provide income during retirement and may provide income following the client's death or disability. The client's spouse may be employed and earning a salary and also accumulating retirement benefits. Failure to consider these existing financial resources will result in a misleading picture of the types and amounts of insurance needed by the client.

The following table provides a sample of insurance policies for the Beamer family, taking into account opportunities for risk retention and consideration of resources the family already has available. The policy listing is broken down into the categories of essential, desirable, and useful insurance contracts to indicate the priority in spending the client's premium dollars.

Table 2-6 Insurance Planning for the Beamer Family

Essential

1. Personal auto policy—$300,000 liability
2. Homeowners HO Form 3—$180,000 dwelling (more than enough to satisfy the 80 percent replacement provision) with $500 deductible and $300,000 liability
3. Personal umbrella liability—$2 million
4. Dwelling form on cabin—$40,000 on cabin with $300,000 optional liability coverage
5. Life insurance policy on Burt—$50,000 for clean-up fund

> 6. Life insurance on Burt—$1,100,000 to provide lifetime income to surviving spouse
>
> Desirable
>
> 7. Dwelling form for personal property (cabin)—$4,000 with theft endorsement
> 8. Personal auto policy—ACV for physical damage to the one-year-old compact auto; $1,000 deductible
> 9. Mortgage redemption policy—$137,000
>
> Useful
>
> 10. Personal auto policy—ACV for physical damage to the 3-year-old station wagon; $1,000 deductible
> 11. Life insurance on Burt—$78,000 for education fund

Communicating the Recommendations and Implementing the Recommendations

After you have developed and refined your recommendations, it is time to communicate them to the client. Normally, your recommendations should be in writing, although they may be illustrated using a multimedia presentation on a laptop computer or other device. Once the plan has been presented to and approved by the client, it must be implemented. Your responsibility at this point is to motivate and assist the client in obtaining the insurance coverages necessary for plan implementation. If you are a licensed insurance agent, you can help the client purchase the needed insurance policies. Otherwise, you will need to work with a licensed agent in securing the necessary coverages. In either case, you should ensure that the insurance companies recommended are financially stable and provide quality service, and that the premium costs for the coverages proposed are competitive.

Monitoring the Recommendations

As an advisor, you should meet with the client at least once each year to determine whether the plan is still satisfactory in light of the client's current objectives and circumstances. With changes in the client's personal or financial situation, the client may now be faced with some new pure risk situations and no longer faced with others. Also, the relative importance of certain pure risks may have shifted over time. Changes in the economic, tax, or financial environment may have affected the types and/or amounts of insurance protection needed. As a result of these changes, you and your client may need to revise the existing insurance plan by following the same financial planning process used to develop the original plan.

A SURVEY OF PERSONAL INSURANCE COVERAGES

As mentioned earlier, insurance is often an appropriate technique to handle all or a portion of the losses associated with pure risks. The remainder of the chapter provides a brief summary of the various insurance coverages available for dealing with the pure risks typically faced by individuals and families.

Meeting Personal Risks

Personal risks are those pure risks that involve the loss of income earning ability due to premature death, disability, unemployment, and retirement. Personal risks also include the possibility of incurring extra expenses as a result of medical care for accidental injuries or sickness and long-term care for chronic illness. Since the occurrence of losses arising from unemployment lacks independence and thus, is potentially catastrophic in nature, private insurers are unable to insure the loss of income due to unemployment. Instead, only social insurance provided by the government can handle this pure risk situation. However, coverages for loss of income earning ability due to premature death, disability and retirement as well as for extra expenses incurred due to medical care are available from both private and social insurance programs. At present, long-term care coverage is available only from private insurers. The discussion that follows concentrates on products for handling personal risks that are available from private insurers.

Life Insurance

While many types of life insurance policies have cash surrender values that can be used alone or with other sources of savings and investment to meet certain client accumulation objectives, the feature that distinguishes life insurance from all other financial products is its unique ability to create an immediate large sum of money at a client's premature death. Unlike decisions regarding the timing or extent of retirement over which a client may have some control, death is total, permanent, and usually unpredictable. As shown earlier, even when currently available resources (such as those from the client's existing savings, existing life insurance policies, and Social

Security) are taken into account in Step 3 of the financial planning process, there is often a very large amount of additional resources still needed to meet the various lump-sum cash and income needs of the surviving dependent members of a client's family in the event of his premature death. If a client were to die shortly after implementing her financial plan, life insurance is the only product that could immediately generate the large amount of additional resources required to meet the needs of the surviving dependent family members. This is why protection of a client's dependents in the event of his death is the most important personal use of life insurance; protection should be the key consideration in selecting the most cost-effective life insurance products to deal with the risk of premature death.

Virtually all life insurance products that are widely marketed today are variations of the following three types of life insurance:

- term life insurance
- whole life insurance
- universal life insurance

renewability provision

conversion provision

Term Life Insurance. Term life policies provide insurance coverage for a limited period of time (the policy period), and are generally well suited to situations where there is a temporary need for protection. The policy period in term life insurance policies is expressed as a number of years (such as 1, 5, or 20), or until a certain age of the insured (such as to age 60 or 65). If the insured dies during the policy period, the specified amount (normally the face amount of the policy) will be paid to the designated recipient (beneficiary). Thus, with a $500,000 5-year term insurance policy, the beneficiary is paid $500,000 if the insured dies during the 5-year policy period. However, if the insured survives until the end of the policy period, no benefit is paid by the insurance company.

A term policy without a renewability provision would expire at the end of the policy period, and satisfactory proof of insurability would be required to purchase a new policy if continued protection is needed. To prevent the loss of insurance due to bad health or failure to meet other underwriting requirements, clients should be encouraged to include a *renewability provision* in term insurance policies, especially those with policy periods of 10 years or less. If this provision is included, the policy can be renewed while protection is still needed without having to provide evidence of insurability to the insurer at the end of each policy period. While most insurers do not permit renewals to carry coverage beyond a certain age (generally 65 or 70), a few companies now offer term insurance policies that are renewable to age 100.

The death benefit, or *face amount,* of a term life policy normally remains constant throughout the policy period. However, term life is also written on a decreasing death-benefit basis or, with some companies, on an increasing basis. A decreasing term policy may be appropriate for meeting all or at least a major portion of a client's needs that decline over time, such as the amount needed to liquidate a mortgage following the client's death. Increasing term life insurance may be used to "refund" the premiums paid on a whole life policy at the time of the insured's death or to have a policy's death benefit keep abreast of some index, such as the cost of living.

Because term life insurance provides protection for only a limited period of time, initial premium rates per $1,000 of coverage are lower for term policies than for whole life products issued at the same age. Moreover, initial premium rates per $1,000 for term policies issued at the same age are higher, the longer the policy period. For this reason, one-year term insurance permits a client to initially purchase the greatest amount of life insurance for a given outlay. The amount of insurance protection needed is generally greatest for a family with young dependent children, and the funds available to pay premiums are often quite limited. Thus, one-year or perhaps 5-year term insurance with a renewability provision may allow a client to afford a sufficient amount of life insurance to adequately protect a surviving spouse and dependent children and meet the family's protection objective in the event of premature death. The client should know that if the term coverage is to be renewed, the premium rate will increase to reflect the higher mortality charges in each successive policy period. Although these premium increases may be nominal at the younger ages, they increase rapidly at older ages. Note that few clients can afford term insurance rates beyond their 60s.

In addition to the uses of term life insurance already mentioned, it should be recognized that term insurance can be the basis for one's future permanent insurance program. For example, when a client such as a young doctor needs a large amount of life insurance but can afford only relatively small premiums today, purchasing term insurance may be the only way to provide adequate protection for her dependents. However, if permanent insurance will be needed in the future, consider including a *conversion provision* in the term policy when it is issued. This feature permits the insured to exchange the term policy for a permanent insurance contract (whole life, for example)

> **EXAMPLE**
>
> Brent Baker purchased a $300,000, 20-year level term insurance policy at age 30 to cover the potential education costs for his three young children. While Brent did not anticipate needing the insurance beyond 20 years, his agent suggested inclusion of both a renewable provision and a conversion provision into the policy at a very small increase in premium. When Brent was 48 years old, he was diagnosed with a rare form of leukemia and required several rounds of chemotherapy. While Brent is now in remission, this illness made Brent uninsurable for new life insurance coverage. Fortunately, Brent was able to convert his 20-year term policy into a participating whole life contract without having to show any evidence of insurability. This whole life policy provided the permanent coverage Brent needed for his spouse if he should die before she does.

Whole Life Insurance. All whole life policies promise to pay the face amount to the beneficiary upon the death of the insured, regardless of when death occurs. To price a whole life policy it is necessary to assume that all insureds die by a given age, such as age 100 for older policies. The few insureds who are still alive at age 100 are assumed to have died and are entitled to the face amount of their policy. Thus, unlike term insurance policies with their rather limited policy periods, whole life policies have long policy periods which end at age 100. (Note that policies sold today are based on the 2001 Commissioners Standard Ordinary (CSO) mortality table that assumes death occurs for all insureds by age 120.) Moreover, unlike term insurance policies where payment of a death benefit is an uncertainty because all insureds do not die during the policy period, payment of a death benefit is a certainty for each whole life policy (assuming premiums are paid and other policy provisions are complied with) because all insureds die (or are assumed to have died) during the policy period.

Due to their longer policy period and the certainty of a death benefit payment, initial premiums for whole life policies are higher than for term insurance policies issued at the same age for the same face amount. However, with their life-long policy periods and lower premiums in the later years of life compared to term policies issued at the same age for the same face amount, whole life policies are often well suited for situations where there is a permanent need for protection. Such situations include providing funds for estate liquidity, meeting a client's obligation under a business buy-sell agreement, or providing a client's spouse with a lifetime income following the client's death.

policy reserve

net amount at risk

Due to the certainty of a death benefit payment, premium rates for whole life policies must be set high enough so that (taking into account interest) they can not only cover a policy's share of the death claims and expenses, but also build a fund called the *policy reserve* that will grow over the policy period. The reserve must equal the face amount of the whole life policy at age 120 so that the insureds who either die or survive during the last year of the policy period can each be paid the face amount of their policy. When the amount of the reserve in a given policy year is subtracted from the policy's face amount, the difference is the insurer's *net amount at risk* and is part of the policy's death benefit that is funded by loss sharing among policyowners in that year. Since a whole life policy's reserve increases over the policy period, the part of the death benefit paid by loss sharing declines. As a result, whole life policies are often referred to as being composed of an increasing savings element (the reserve) and a decreasing protection element paid for by loss sharing among policyowners.

Figure 2-1
Whole Life Insurance Policy with a $500,000 Face Amount Purchased at Age 35

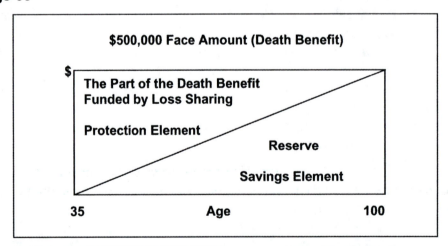

Policyowners can access part of the reserve called the cash value in several ways:

- Under the policy's *loan provision,* part of the cash value can be borrowed to provide the policyowner with cash or to be used to automatically pay premiums. In either case, the amount borrowed is charged interest at either the fixed or variable rate stated in the policy. If any part of the loan plus interest is outstanding at the time of the insured's death or at the time the policy is surrendered, the amount of the outstanding loan plus interest will be deducted from the policy's face amount or cash value, respectively.

- Under the policy's *nonforfeiture options,* when a whole life policy is terminated, the policyowner has a choice of surrendering the policy for its cash value or exchanging the policy's cash value for either

    1. a reduced amount of paid-up insurance of the same type as the original policy, or
    2. paid-up term insurance for the full face amount of the original policy and for a period calculated by the insurer that depends on the insured's age and gender, the policy reserve, and face amount

While all whole life policies promise to pay the face amount to the beneficiary when the insured dies, these policies can differ in the following ways:

- the length of the period over which premiums must be paid (the premium-paying period)
- whether they are participating or nonparticipating policies
- how and where the funds in the policy reserve (and thus, the cash value) are invested

Ordinary life policies are whole life policies where premiums are paid until the insured dies. In this case, the last annual premium might be paid at age 119. In contrast, limited-payment whole life policies require premiums to be paid only for a specified number of years or until the insured reaches a specified age at which time the policy is fully paid up. The policyowner is guaranteed that no additional premiums will be due once the policy is paid up. The shorter the premium-paying period for a whole life policy, the higher the premium rate. Thus, ordinary life policies have lower premiums than limited-payment whole life policies issued at the same age for the same face amount. However, due to their higher premiums, limited-payment whole life policies have a more rapid buildup of cash values than an ordinary life policy.

Participating (par) policies provide for, but do not guarantee, the payment of *dividends* to the policyowner. The dividends reflect the insurance company's past experience with respect to mortality, interest, and expenses. Favorable experience—lower mortality, lower expenses, and higher interest than expected—tends to increase the dividend scale, whereas unfavorable experience tends to have the opposite effect.

In contrast to par policies, *nonparticipating (nonpar) policies* do not pay policyowner dividends. Today nearly all nonpar whole life policies, often called *current assumption whole life* policies, share the company's actual or anticipated experience by either changing the policy's premium or cash value. Favorable experience tends to lead to lower premiums or higher cash values, whereas unfavorable experience tends to have the opposite effects.

Traditionally, the reserves (and thus, cash values) of whole life policies have been invested in the general assets of the insurance company where their allocation among various types of assets has been managed by the insurer. As a result, these traditional whole life policies contain a guaranteed interest rate which is the lowest interest rate with which policy funds can be credited. In contrast, some whole life policies, called *variable life insurance,* now permit the policyowner to allocate the funds generated by the policy among a variety of separate accounts each reflecting a different investment objective (similar to a family of mutual funds). Variable life policies shift the investment risk to the policyowner and provide no minimum guaranteed rate of return or guaranteed cash value. The rate of return credited to policy funds and the amount of the cash value depend upon the investment success of the policyowner.

The performance of the separate account portfolio selected by the policyowner also affects the death benefit of a variable life insurance policy. Unlike a traditional whole life policy whose death benefit is a stated face amount equal to the amount of insurance purchased, the death benefit of a variable life policy can vary up and down above a minimum death benefit (equal to the amount of insurance purchased) depending upon investment performance.

universal life (UL) insurance

Universal Life (UL) Insurance. First sold in its current form in 1979, a universal life insurance (UL) policy is a flexible-premium, adjustable death benefit life insurance contract that enables the policyowner to see how premiums are allocated to the protection and cash value elements of the policy.

Universal life policies require at least a minimum level of premium payments during the first year of coverage. After the first year, the premium on this type of policy is truly flexible. Policyowners may pay whatever amounts at whatever times they wish, or even skip premium payments, as long as the cash value is large enough to cover required policy charges, such as mortality charges and policy fees.

In addition to flexibility with regard to premium payments, universal life policyowners may also request a change in the face amount of the policy. Decreases in the policy death benefit can be made by policyowner request at any time. However, evidence of insurability may be required if an increase in the death benefit is requested.

Each year the policyowner of a universal life policy receives a report illustrating the flow of funds during the year. This report shows the amount in the cash value account at the beginning of the period which is increased by any premiums paid, reduced by mortality charges and expenses (if any), and increased by the interest earnings credited to the account. This type of detailed information is not generated for traditional whole life policyowners.

Universal life policies offer two death-benefit designs, usually labeled as options A and B. Option A provides a constant or level death benefit, like that of traditional whole life policies. However, at older ages the death benefit begins to increase because of the technical need to satisfy the Internal Revenue Code definition of life insurance. Option B provides a death benefit that at any time is equal to the sum of the original face amount of the policy and the accumulating cash value. The death benefit continues to increase as long as the cash value increases.

In addition to providing access to the policy's cash value through loans or full surrender of the contract, universal life insurance introduced a withdrawal (or partial surrender) feature which permits the policyowner to make partial withdrawals from the policy's cash value without incurring any indebtedness. Because the policy's cash value is reduced by the amount of the withdrawal, future interest earnings are also reduced. The policy death benefit is also reduced by the amount of the withdrawal.

The cash value of a universal life policy is invested in the general assets of the insurance company where the investment allocation is managed by the insurer. To provide the policyowner with the ability to direct the investment of the cash value, variable universal life (VUL) insurance was developed by modifying the universal life policy. A *variable universal life (VUL)* policy is identical to a universal life policy except that the cash value is invested by the policyowner in a variety of separate accounts rather than in the general assets of the insurance company. As with variable life insurance, variable universal life policies shift the investment risk to the policyowner and provide no minimum guaranteed rate of return. The rate of return credited to the policy's cash value depends upon the performance of the separate account(s) in which the policyowner invested the funds.

Annuities

Two important general challenges facing many clients in planning to deal with the pure risk associated with retirement are accumulating sufficient financial resources to meet their retirement objectives and distributing those resources in a manner consistent with those objectives. Annuities can be helpful in meeting both challenges.

Financial resources to meet retirement objectives can come from a number of sources, including Social Security retirement benefits, employer-sponsored retirement plans, private saving and investment for retirement, cash value life insurance owned by the client, and deferred annuities purchased by the client. For clients who wish to liquidate the financial resources accumulated for retirement without the risk of outliving their income, life annuities—both deferred and immediate—should be considered. Life annuities (and similar life income settlement options available for distributing the cash value of a life insurance policy for retirement) are the only financial products that can guarantee a client a lifetime income.

The vast majority of annuities sold by life insurance companies today are life annuities that provide a systematic liquidation of a principal sum over the lifetime of the annuitant (the recipient of the payments). *Life annuities* can be purchased either by a single premium or on an installment basis. An *immediate annuity* must be purchased with a single premium because it begins to pay periodic benefits at the end of the first payment period (such as one month) following the purchase date. The single premium used to purchase an immediate annuity can come from financial resources accumulated by the client for retirement or other purpose. In contrast, *deferred annuities* that begin to pay periodic benefits at some specified future time can be purchased with either a single premium or on an installment premium basis. Prior to the date when the periodic payments begin (the accumulation period), the premiums paid for a deferred annuity are invested either in the general assets of the insurance company or in separate accounts where the allocation of funds for investment purposes is managed by the contract owner (that is, variable annuities). Thus, while both immediate and deferred life annuities provide for liquidation of financial resources over the lifetime of the annuitant, a deferred life annuity also provides a tool for accumulating financial resources before retirement on a tax-deferred basis.

> **Application—Investing in a Deferred Variable Annuity**
>
> Susan Moore is 30-year-old attorney with a thriving practice. In 2011, after putting as much money as possible into her retirement accounts (401(k) and a traditional IRA), Susan purchased a deferred variable annuity. Her goal is to put $1,000 per month into the annuity to build additional funds for her planned retirement at age 62. At an assumed investment rate of 5 percent, Susan would have over $900,000 in her annuity at age 62. She could then choose to annuitize her contract in a fixed basis and receive a guaranteed income for life. Her payments would depend on the exact amount in the annuity, her age, gender, and the insurer's internal rates of interest and costs at the time of annuitization.

Annuities can be purchased to provide periodic payments of a guaranteed fixed amount or a variable amount. When the variable annuity is elected, the periodic payment depends on the performance of the underlying investment portfolio, typically common stocks. As deferred annuities, variable annuities may be variable (invested in separate accounts) in both the accumulation and the payout periods or may be variable in the accumulation period and provide a guaranteed fixed amount during the payout period.

At a minimum, life annuities guarantee a lifetime income for the annuitant. Under a pure life annuity, payments cease upon the death of the annuitant, with no further obligations placed on the insurance company. Most annuity purchasers dislike this contingency basis and prefer arrangements that will also guarantee payments to the annuitant's survivors on some basis if the annuitant dies shortly after payments begin. This can be accomplished through the election of guaranteed payments for a certain period of time or through the selection of a cash or installment refund arrangement. However, regardless of any guarantees of payments to the annuitant's survivors, the annuitant of a life annuity would continue to receive payments for life if she lived beyond the period required to payout the minimum guaranteed payments. An alternative to a single life annuity with payments based on the life of one annuitant, the joint-and-survivor annuity bases payments on the lives of two or more annuitants, such as a husband and wife.

> **EXAMPLE**
>
> Nora Brown purchased an immediate annuity at age 70 for $100,000. Her insurer quoted a monthly payment of $670 for a "straight life" annuity in which all payments would cease upon Nora' death. The insurer also quoted a "life with 20 years certain" annuity with a monthly payment of $610. Nora chose the second option and began receiving her monthly payments one month after the contract was issued. Nora died unexpectedly after exactly 5 years of payments had been made. The monthly payments (in the same amount of $610) continued for another 15 years to Nora's beneficiary, her daughter Shelley.

Annuities can be purchased on either a qualified or a nonqualified basis. In terms of annuity considerations received by life insurers in 2010, qualified and nonqualified annuities are both major components of the life annuity market, representing 63 percent and 37 percent of that market, respectively.[8] Many of the annuity sales in the qualified arena (for example, 401(k), IRAs) are due to the guaranteed living benefits that are now common in variable annuities. Because qualified annuities are often purchased by employers for use in employee benefit plans, knowledge of annuities is important in understanding the funding of some forms of pension plans and the distribution options commonly available to participants in many qualified retirement plans. However, you should also recognize that retirement purposes can be served through the purchase of individual life insurance policies with cash values. At some time in the future, the accumulated savings in a whole life or universal life policy can either be distributed using the life income settlement options (similar to life annuities) contained in the policy or be exchanged, typically at net cost, for an annuity to provide income to a client to supplement Social Security and other sources of retirement income.

Individual Health Insurance

As mentioned earlier, three pure risks associated with the loss of health include

- extra expenses incurred for medical care due to accident or sickness
- loss of income earning ability due to accident or sickness
- extra expenses incurred for long-term care due to the inability to perform safely some of the activities of daily living (ADLs)

---

8. LIMRA Annuity data, accessed 1/13/2012 at http://marketing.cpsinsurance.com/visionscape/2011/July/pdf/7.11.11%20LIMRA%20q1%20Annuitties.pdf.

The types of health insurance available to help deal with these personal risks are *medical expense insurance, disability income insurance* and *long-term care insurance,* respectively. Although each of these types of health insurance is available on either an individual basis (policies sold to individuals) or a group basis (policies sold most commonly to employers), the coverage in this chapter focuses on individual medical expense, disability income, and long-term care insurance. Group health insurance coverages are discussed in the next chapter on employee benefits.

Medical Expense Insurance. The popularity of the group medical insurance coverage, as opposed to individual coverage, stems from both the opportunity for cost savings due to lower costs associated with the group mechanism and favorable tax treatment of employer contributions for premiums. Unlike individual medical expense insurance premiums which are paid with after-tax dollars, employer contributions for medical expense insurance premiums are deductible by the employer and are not taxed to the employee. This last factor alone enables employer-provided medical expense coverage to be either less costly than comparable individual coverage or more comprehensive than individual coverage that costs the same amount.

The impact of health care reform legislation passed in 2010 as the Patient Protection and Affordable Care Act (PPACA) is very far-reaching in its scope. If it is fully implemented as written, many larger employers will either have to provide health coverage for employees or pay a tax. Also, the individual mandate in the PPACA will require virtually all Americans to have health coverage with certain basic benefits, or pay a penalty. A detailed study of health care reform is beyond the scope of this course. However, financial advisors need to have a good understanding of medical issues to advise their clients accordingly.

Disability Income Insurance. One of the more frequently overlooked personal risk exposures is the possible loss of wages or earnings during periods of disability. Most people seem to be aware of the medical care costs associated with accident or illness and of the total discontinuation of earnings because of premature death, but tend to overlook the seriousness of losing income because of disability. At most working ages the likelihood of a serious, long-term disability is considerably greater than the probability of death. Moreover, the severity of loss in terms of income needs is often greater in the case of serious, long-term disability than in the case of premature death, because the disabled income earner must be provided for along with other dependent family members.

You should begin the planning process for meeting the client's need for income replacement due to serious disability by examining the client's employee benefits package. In some disability income-replacement situations, the combination of Social Security disability benefits and employer-provided salary continuation or disability income benefits may provide most or all of the replacement income needed. However, individual disability income insurance is often needed in the following situations:

- self-employed individuals and high-income professionals in fields such as medicine or law who have no employer-provided disability income protection
- employees of companies, especially small private firms, that do not offer long-term disability income insurance as an employee benefit
- executives and middle-income earners who wish to supplement employer-provided disability income benefits to protect more of their earnings than are protected by their employer's plan
- businesses and their owners who require a source of funds to finance a buy-sell agreement or to provide protection against a loss of income and/or extra expenses incurred in the event of an owner's or key employee's disability

Insurance is used most efficiently in handling pure risk situations involving the possibility of low frequency, high severity losses. Thus, while coverage is available to protect against *partial disability* and *residual disability,* disability income insurance is most efficiently used in dealing with the possibility of a client experiencing a long term, total disability. In this case, the consequences of a severe loss are transferred to the insurer for a premium that is economical due to the low frequency. Also, as mentioned earlier, retention is generally the most efficient way for dealing with low severity losses. Through the use of an appropriate *elimination (waiting) period,* retention can be achieved for low severity disability income losses while insurance covers the low frequency, high severity losses. In helping a client use insurance efficiently in dealing with the risk of a serious, long term disability, you should focus primarily on five key features of individual disability income insurance—the definition of *total disability,* the elimination period, the benefit period, the benefit amount, and the terms of renewability.

Definition of Total Disability—Definitions of disability in disability income policies are based on the ability of the insured to perform certain occupational tasks. One definition, typically called the *any-occupation* definition, states that insureds are considered to be totally disabled when they cannot perform the major duties of any gainful occupation for which they are reasonably suited by education, training, or experience.

A somewhat less restrictive definition is usually referred to as the *own-occupation* definition. With a pure own-occupation definition, insureds are deemed to be totally disabled when they cannot perform the major duties of their regular occupations. For purposes of this definition, the regular occupation is the one engaged in when the disability begins. Because this definition would allow an insured to work in some other capacity and still be entitled to benefits, many insurers now use a modified own-occupation definition which also provides that benefits either will not be paid or will be reduced if the insured chooses to work in any other occupation. In virtually all definitions of disability, insurers add a provision stipulating that the disabled person must be under the care and attendance of a physician.

Due to adverse claims experience, most companies no longer issue contracts of long benefit duration that have pure own-occupation definitions of disability for the contract duration. Instead, either a modified own-occupation definition or a dual definition of total disability is typically used in long-term disability income policies. With a dual definition, an own-occupation definition applies during the first few years of the benefit period, after which it is replaced by an any-occupation definition. Typically, the insured is given a choice between two options ranging from 2 to 5 years regarding the length of time the own-occupation definition of disability will remain in force.

EXAMPLE

Robert Perez is owner and manager of his own insurance agency. He recently purchased a disability income insurance plan that will pay him $2,000 per month after an elimination period of 180 days. His contract uses a dual definition for disability. The insurer will pay Robert for up to 2 years if he is unable to perform the duties of his current occupation ("own-occupation" definition). After 2 years, the policy will pay another 3 years of benefits, but only if Robert is unable to perform any occupation for which he is reasonably suited by his education, training, and experience ("any-occupation" definition).

Elimination Period—The elimination period is the number of days that must elapse between the start of disability and the start of benefit payments. It is sometimes called the waiting period or simply the deductible stated in time rather than dollars. The intent of this provision is to avoid coverage of the short-term illness or injury that temporarily disables an insured and for which retention is a more economical solution than insurance.

Elimination periods are generally available for periods ranging from 30 days to one year. The length of time recommended to a client should depend on the availability of other funds to support a risk retention program. For example, if a client's employer provides a salary continuation plan that will compensate the employee in full for 6 months, there is little need to add an individual disability income insurance policy that will pay benefits at the end of 30 days. However, if a short-term disability would cause financial hardship, a 30-day elimination period might be very appropriate. As with any deductible, the longer the elimination period selected, the lower the premium.

Benefit Period—The benefit period is the length of time during which income benefits will be paid after the elimination period is satisfied. Although a few companies still offer lifetime benefits, benefit periods typically range anywhere from 2 years in duration to the insured's age 65 or 70. Historical data indicate that most disabilities are of short duration, but the likelihood of full productive recovery diminishes as the length of the disability increases. This means that long-term disabilities will be more devastating and that insurance is usually the best tool for dealing with this contingency. Therefore, the recommended benefit period should be of long duration. Of course, the longer the benefit period, the higher the premium, but a long elimination period might offset part of this higher cost.

Benefit Amount—Individual disability income policies specify the amount of monthly benefits payable for total disabilities continuing after the elimination period has been satisfied. At the time of policy issuance, the stated benefit amount should be in line with the client's income and provide fairly complete protection. However, over time, the stated amount is likely to become inadequate as the client's income increases because of both inflation and job promotions. Disability income policies are available with provisions to counteract such erosion in benefit levels. Prior to disability, disability income benefits can be kept in step with increased income in three ways—by purchasing new policies periodically (requires evidence of insurability), by purchasing a rider that guarantees the right to purchase additional coverage at specified future intervals up to some specified maximum age (such as 45, 50 or 55), or by purchasing a rider that automatically increases the benefit amount periodically. A cost-of-living (COLA) rider can be used to increase benefits once disability has commenced. Be aware that adding a COLA to a disability income policy increases the premium considerably.

Insurance companies limit the amount of disability income coverage they will write so that the total benefit from all sources does not exceed a given percentage of the insured's earned income—normally about 65 percent for individuals in higher income brackets. One reason for this limitation is that individually purchased disability income benefits are not taxable income to the recipient. Another reason is the potential disincentive for a disabled person to return to work if benefit payments are too high relative to pre-disability income.

Terms of Renewability—State laws specify that individually purchased disability income policies (and medical expense policies) must indicate the basis upon which the insured can continue the contract, a very important consideration to the insured.

Most disability income policies sold to individuals are issued on either a *noncancelable* or *guaranteed renewable* basis. Under a guaranteed renewable contract, the insurer reserves the right to change premium rates for all insureds of the same class but cannot cancel or refuse to renew the policy, as long as the insured pays premiums on a timely basis. Under a noncancelable policy, the insurer can neither change premium rates nor cancel the policy. A noncancelable policy is clearly more valuable and costs more than a comparable guaranteed renewable one.

Following repeated underwriting losses and resulting market contraction and consolidation from the mid-1980s to 1998, the noncancelable disability income insurance business has experienced rising profits since 1999, resulting from the more restricted contractual features, higher pricing, tighter underwriting practices and more proactive claims management. With this improved environment, more insurers are in the market and more products are available. For example, one recently developed disability income product is the disability-to-long-term care conversion policy which is initially a disability income insurance policy, that can be converted to long-term care coverage without evidence of insurability and at lower cost than purchasing a new stand-alone long-term care policy later in life.

long-term care insurance

Long-Term Care Insurance. Another personal risk faced by individuals and families is the possibility of incurring extra expenses for long-term care due to the inability to perform safely some of the activities of daily living (ADLs). As Americans live longer, both the frequency and the severity of loss associated with this personal risk increase. Longer life spans today and in the future increase the chance that a client will experience a need for some long-term care services to assist with the ADLs. For example, while only one percent of persons between ages 65 and 74 reside in nursing homes, the percentage increases to 6 percent between the ages of 75 and 84 and to approximately 25 percent at age 85 and over.

Also, because of continuing increases in the costs of nursing home care and home health care, increasing life spans result in clients experiencing the costs of long-term care services at higher and higher levels. For example, already high annual nursing home costs of $70,000 to $80,000 or more and monthly part-time home health care costs of $3,500 or more are increasing faster than inflation because of growing demand for nursing home beds and shortages of skilled medical personnel. By 2030, the annual cost of nursing home care is expected to approximate $230,000 with comparable increases in home care charges. Also, while most nursing home stays are for less than two years, the average stay remains at about 2.5 years. The average is slightly less for men and slightly longer for women.

As mentioned earlier, insurance is an efficient mechanism for handling pure risks involving the possibility of low frequency, high severity losses and retention is efficient for handling low severity losses. Since possible long-term care losses can be very severe, this risk should not be totally retained unless a client is willing to use a major portion of her retirement savings and other assets for long-term care expenses. In addition to the possibility of forcing the client and her dependents into poverty, this approach may also leave the client unable to meet the financial objective of leaving assets to heirs.

For most clients, the severity of the potential loss associated with long-term care expenses suggests that it be transferred by the purchase of long-term care insurance, especially if purchased at a younger age when the frequency of loss is relatively low. Retention can be used to efficiently handle low severity losses by choosing an appropriate elimination period.

A relatively new form of insurance coverage that was rare before the early 1980s, long-term care insurance has evolved to being an important form of insurance product carried by over 8 million persons. Significant variations (and therefore differences in cost) exist among the individual long-term care policies sold today. In recent years, a number of companies have dropped out of the long-term care insurance market and the sales of new policies are predominantly among the 5 or 6 largest carriers.

- Issue Age—While significant differences exist among insurance companies with respect to the age at which they will issue policies, a healthy client between the ages of 40 and 75 should be able to buy long-term care insurance from most companies. Most companies sell policies to persons as young as 18 and have a maximum age in the range of 84 to 89 beyond which coverage is not issued.

- **Types of Care Covered**—There are many types of care for which benefits may be provided under a long-term care policy. By broad categories, these can be categorized as nursing home care, assisted-living care, hospice care, Alzheimer's facilities, home health care, care coordination, and alternative sources of care. A long-term care policy may provide benefits for one, several, or all of these types of care.

Much of the variation among long-term care policies is related to the types of care for which benefits are provided. These benefit variations fall into three broad categories: facility-only policies, home health care only policies, and comprehensive policies. While policies providing benefits only if the insured is in a nursing home still exist, the term facility-only policy is now more commonly used to describe broader policies that provide benefits not only for nursing home care but also for care in other settings such as assisted-living facilities and hospices. A home health care only policy is designed to provide benefits for care outside an institutional setting.

Most long-term care policies written today can be described as comprehensive policies. A comprehensive long-term care insurance policy combines benefits for facility care and home health care into a single contract. However, variations exist within this type of policy with respect to what is covered as part of the standard policy and what is an optional benefit that the applicant may select. For example, some policies cover almost all care settings as part of their standard benefits; other policies provide facility-only coverage as a standard benefit with home health care covered as an option for an additional premium.

- **Benefit Amounts**—When purchasing long-term care insurance, the applicant selects the level of benefit she desires up to the maximum level the insurance company will provide. Benefits are often sold in increments of $10 per day up to frequently found limits of $300 or $350 or, in a few cases, as much as $400 or $500 per day. Some policies base benefits on a monthly (rather than daily) amount that can vary from $1,000 to $6,000 or more.

The same level of benefits is usually provided for all levels of institutional care. Most comprehensive policies that provide home health care benefits once limited the daily benefit to one-half the amount payable for institutional stays. However, many insurers now allow applicants to select home health care limits that are as high as 75 percent to 100 percent of the benefit for institutional care; a few insurers even offer limits as high as 125 percent or 150 percent. If a policy provides home health care benefits only, the daily amount of that benefit is what the applicant selects.

Policies pay benefits in one of two basic ways—reimbursement or per diem. The majority of newer policies pay benefits on a *reimbursement basis*. These contracts reimburse the insured for actual expenses up to the specified policy limit. Some policies provide benefits on a *per diem basis* once care is actually being received. This means that benefits are paid regardless of the actual cost of care. All things being equal, the per diem policy costs more than the reimbursement type.

- **Elimination Period**—The applicant must select a period of time that must pass after long-term care commences but before benefit payments begin. The majority of long-term care insurers refer to this period as an elimination period. However, some insurers call it a waiting period or a deductible period. Choices may be as low as zero days or as high as 365 days, with 90 to 100 days being most common.

- **Maximum Duration of Benefits**—The applicant selects the maximum period for which benefits are paid (often referred to as the benefit period) from several options. For example, one insurer offers durations of 2, 3, and 5 years as well as lifetime benefits Very few companies now offer lifetime coverage because of the risk it presents to the carrier. The benefit period begins from the time benefit payments start after satisfaction of the elimination period.

There are actually two ways that the benefit period is applied in the payment of benefits. Under one approach, benefit payments are made for exactly the benefit period chosen. If the applicant selects a benefit period of 4 years and collects benefits for 4 years, the benefit payments cease. The other approach, most commonly but not exclusively used with reimbursement policies, uses a *pool of money*. Under this concept, there is an amount of money that can be used to make benefit payments as long as the pool of money lasts. The applicant does not select the amount in the pool of money; it is determined by multiplying the daily benefit by the benefit period selected. For example, if the daily benefit for institutional care is $200 and the benefit period is 1,460 days (or 4 years), then the pool of money is $292,000 ($200 × 1,460). Daily benefit payments from the pool of money cannot exceed the daily policy benefits for each type of care (in this case, $200 per day for institutional care).

- Inflation Protection—Most states require that a long-term care policy offer some type of automatic inflation protection. The applicant is given the choice to select this option, decline the option, or possibly select an alternative option. The cost of an automatic-increase option is built into the initial premium, and no additional premium is levied at the time of an annual increase. The automatic option found in almost all policies is a 5 percent benefit increase compounded annually over the life of the policy. Under such a provision, the amount of a policy's benefits increases by 5 percent each year over the amount of benefits available in the prior year. A common alternative that many insurers make available is based on simple interest, with each annual automatic increase being 5 percent of the original benefit amount. Another alternative offered by some insurers is to allow the policyowner to increase benefits without evidence of insurability on a pay-as-you-go basis at specified intervals, such as every one, 2, or 3 years.

- Qualification for Favorable Tax Treatment—Long-term care policies that meet the prescribed standards of the Health Insurance Portability and Accountability Act (HIPAA) are treated as accident and health insurance for federal income tax purposes and are referred to as *tax-qualified contracts.* While most companies that write individual long-term care policies now issue only tax-qualified contracts, a few companies issue both qualified contracts and *nonqualified contracts.*

- Eligibility for Benefits—Almost all tax-qualified contracts use the same two criteria for determining benefit eligibility, with the insured being required to meet only one of the two. The first criterion is that the insured is expected to be unable, without substantial assistance from another person, to perform two of the six ADLs (eating, bathing, dressing, transferring from bed to chair, using the toilet, and maintaining continence) that are acceptable under HIPAA for a period of at least 90 days due to loss of functional capacity. The second criterion is that substantial supervision is required to protect the individual from threats to health and safety because of severe cognitive impairment.

> **Application—Qualifying for Benefits in a Qualified Long-Term Care Insurance Policy**
>
> Walter Woods is a 79 year-old man who purchased a qualified long-term care insurance policy in 2001. In 2012, Walter suffered a severe fall which left him unable to transfer from his bed, bathe without assistance, or dress himself without assistance. Thus, he is unable to do 3 of the activities of daily living as defined in his policy. His physician certifies that Walter will be disabled for at least 90 days. Walter submits a claim to his insurance company, and after the expiration of his elimination period, Walter will be paid reimbursements for care as specified in his contract.

Nonqualified contracts, on the other hand, have more liberal eligibility requirements. Many of these contracts use the same criteria that are in tax-qualified contracts, except there is no time period that applies to the inability to perform the ADLs. A small number of nonqualified contracts require only the inability to perform one ADL and/or use more than the six ADLs allowed by HIPAA. Finally, some nonqualified contracts make benefits available if a third criterion—medical necessity—is satisfied. This generally means that a physician can certify that long-term care is needed, even if neither of the other two criteria is satisfied. Note that over 99 percent of LTC insurance policies sold in recent years are qualified contracts.

- Renewability—Long-term care policies currently being sold are guaranteed renewable, which means that an individual's coverage cannot be canceled except for nonpayment of premiums. While premiums cannot be raised on the basis of a particular applicant's claim, they can (and often are) raised by class.

- Nonforfeiture Options—Most companies give an applicant for long-term care insurance the right to elect a nonforfeiture benefit, and most states require that such a benefit be offered. With a nonforfeiture benefit, the policyowner will receive some value for a policy if the policy lapses because the required premium is not paid in the future.

- Premiums—The vast majority of long-term care policies have premiums that are payable for life and determined by the age of the insured at the time of issue. A few insurers, however, offer other modes of payment. Lifetime coverage can sometimes be purchased with a single premium. Some insurers offer policies that have premium payment periods of 10 or 20 years or to age 65, after which time the premium is paid up.

Most long-term care policies have a provision that waives premiums if the insured has been receiving benefits under the policy for a specified period of time, often 60 or 90 days. Some policies offer an optional feature that waives premium on the first day of home care if the insured is eligible for benefits under the contract.

Numerous factors affect the premium that a policyowner will pay for a long-term care policy. Among these factors are the following:

- age: While age plays a significant role in the cost of long-term care insurance, coverage can be obtained at a reasonable cost if it is purchased at a young age.
- types of benefits: Most policies cover care in a long-term care facility. However, many policies also cover home health care and other benefits provided to persons who are still able to reside in their own homes. This broader coverage increases premiums by 60 to 70 percent.
- duration of benefits: The longer the maximum benefit period, the higher the premium. The longer the elimination period, the lower the premium.
- inflation protection: All other factors being equal, the addition of a 5 percent compound annual increase in benefits can raise premiums by 50 to 100 percent.
- spousal coverage: Most insurance companies offer a discount of 10 percent to 40 percent if both spouses purchase long-term care policies from the company.
- nonsmoker discount: A few insurers offer a discount, such as 10 percent, if the insured is a nonsmoker.

Even if the provisions of several policies are virtually identical, premiums will vary among companies. For example, the premiums for three similar policies from three different companies are shown below. Each policy has a daily benefit of $120 per day, a zero-day elimination period, a lifetime benefit period, and coverage for home health care.

Table 2-7 Comparison of Long-Term Care Premiums for Similar Policies			
Age	Company A	Company B	Company C
40	$ 391	$ 590	$ 590
50	641	714	832
60	1,104	1,126	1,331
70	2,550	3,157	2,736
75	4,540	5,491	4,763

Meeting Property and Liability Risks

Individuals and families face a number of pure risks involving possible property and liability losses. As mentioned earlier, property risks involve direct and indirect losses arising from the need to replace or repair damaged or missing property. Liability risks involve the possibility of loss as a result of physical or personal injuries to others, or damage to or destruction of others' property.

Low severity property losses can be handled most efficiently through retention. However, given their potentially severe impact on a client's assets, large property losses and liability losses require transfer through the purchase of insurance. While some clients require specialized forms of insurance such as yacht policies, flood insurance, and professional liability insurance, the majority of the property and liability risks faced by clients and their dependents can be handled with the following types of insurance, using deductibles where appropriate to retain small property losses:

- homeowners insurance
- personal automobile insurance
- umbrella liability insurance

Homeowners Insurance

Homeowners insurance policies are package policies designed to provide protection for the following types of losses in one contract:

- with some exceptions including automobiles, the direct and indirect property losses typically faced by individuals and families
- with some exceptions including automobiles and business or professional activities, the bodily injury and property damage liability losses and defense costs typically faced by individuals and families

- without regard to whether or not legal liability exists, medical expenses incurred by a person other than a resident of the insured household when injured at an insured location or injured because of the insured's activities away from the insured location

To accomplish this, homeowners policies are divided into two parts—Section I which provides property coverage and Section II which provides liability and medical expense coverage.

The basis for the discussion of homeowners insurance policies in this chapter is the program introduced and made available by the Insurance Services Office (ISO). The ISO format has been adopted by many insurance companies throughout the country. There are, however, insurance companies that use their own policy forms, and regional or state variations that modify the basic forms.

In most states, there are six standard homeowners forms available:

HO 00 02 - Homeowners 2 Broad Form
HO 00 03 - Homeowners 3 Special Form
HO 00 04 - Homeowners 4 Contents Broad Form
HO 00 05 - Homeowners 5 Comprehensive Form
HO 00 06 - Homeowners 6 Unit-Owners Form
HO 00 08 - Homeowners 8 Modified Coverage Form

Section II in each of the homeowners forms is identical in providing both liability and medical expense insurance. However, Section I providing property insurance differs among the forms, depending upon the types of property for which they are used and the perils (causes of loss) they are designed to cover.

Four homeowners forms are available for clients who own their dwelling—HO-2 (commonly used shorthand for HO 00 02), HO-3, HO-5 and HO-8 (used for certain types of older property). Each of these forms provides four property coverages in Section I—Coverage A for the dwelling, Coverage B for other structures separated from the dwelling, Coverage C for personal property (contents), and Coverage D for loss of use (indirect loss). HO-4 for those who live in a rented dwelling or apartment and HO-6 for condominium unit-owners and members of cooperatives provide Coverage C for personal property (contents), and Coverage D for loss of use (indirect loss). In addition, Coverage A of HO-6 provides insurance protection for several items of property including fixtures and alterations made by the unit-owner. Note that the HO-3 form is by far the most common contract used for single family homeowners.

The forms also differ as to the causes of loss—that is, the perils—for which coverage is provided. There are two general approaches for insuring property—named perils and open perils. With the *named-perils* approach, the policy lists the specific perils for which coverage is provided. Under the *open-perils* approach, losses caused by any peril are paid by the insurer unless the cause of loss is specifically excluded. Homeowners property insurance coverage is written using both approaches—the basic form provides coverage for losses caused by 10 named perils, the broad form extends the list of named perils to 16, and the special form provides coverage on an open-perils basis. The following table indicates where the basic, broad, and special forms are used to define the covered causes of losses in the homeowners program.

Coverage A Dwelling. Dwelling coverage requires the selection of a limit or dollar amount of insurance coverage. For HO-2, HO-3, HO-5 and HO-8, this is the only part of Section I for which the insured must choose a limit of coverage. The limits for all other property covered by these homeowners forms are either a fixed-dollar amount or a fixed percentage of the limit on the dwelling. However, some of these limits can be changed by the insured.

Protection against inflation can be provided in two ways. To help the insured satisfy the 80 percent *replacement-cost requirement* at the time of loss and reduce the chance of underinsurance due to increasing construction costs, the inflation guard endorsement periodically and automatically increases the limit of coverage on the dwelling by a specified percentage of the policy's original Coverage A limit. The guaranteed replacement cost coverage offered by some insurance companies guarantees the full cost of replacing the damaged dwelling even if that cost exceeds the Coverage A limit.

Coverage B Other Structures. Coverage B provides insurance on other structures located on the premises that are not attached to the dwelling. These include detached garages or tool-sheds and such things as fences, driveways, and retaining walls. Unless increased by the insured, the amount of coverage is 10 percent of the limit on the dwelling. Losses to these other structures are settled on a replacement-cost basis.

Insurance Planning and Risk Management

Table 2-8 Homeowners Forms

For Use By	Persons Who Own Their Home				Renters	Condo Owners
Forms	HO-2	HO-3	HO-5	HO-8	HO-4	HO-6
Section I - Property Coverages						
	Coverage A Dwelling	**Coverage A** Dwelling	**Coverage A** Dwelling	**Coverage A** Dwelling		**Coverage A** Unit-owner's Additions Flat $1,000
	Coverage B Other Structures	**Coverage B** Other Structures	**Coverage B** Other Structures	**Coverage B** Other Structures		
	Coverage C Personal Property	**Coverage C** Personal Property	**Coverage C** Personal Property	**Coverage C** Personal Property	**Coverage C** Personal Property	**Coverage C** Personal Property
	Coverage D Loss of Use	**Coverage D** Loss of Use	**Coverage D** Loss of Use	**Coverage D** Loss of Use	**Coverage D** Loss of Use	**Coverage D** Loss of Use
Perils Covered in Section I						
	Broad Form (16 named perils)	Coverages A & B Special Form (open perils) Coverage C Broad Form (16 named perils)	Special Form (open perils)	Basic Form (10 named perils)	Broad Form (16 named perils)	Broad Form (16 named perils)
Section II - Liability & Medical Payments Coverages						
	Coverage E Personal Liability	**Coverage E** Personal Liability	**Coverage E** Personal Liability	**Coverage E** Personal Liability	**Coverage E** Personal Liability	**Coverage E** Personal Liability
	Coverage F Medical Payments to Others	**Coverage F** Medical Payments to Others	**Coverage F** Medical Payments to Others	**Coverage F** Medical Payments to Others	**Coverage F** Medical Payments to Others	**Coverage F** Medical Payments to Others

Coverage C Personal Property. Personal property includes the items normally contained in a dwelling, such as furniture, appliances, and clothing, and property stored in a garage, other structure, or outdoors. Unless increased, the limit of coverage on personal property for HO-2, HO-3, HO-5 and HO-8 is 50 percent of the dwelling limit. For HO-4 and HO-6, the insured selects the amount of coverage on personal property.

Certain types of valuable property such as furs, jewelry, fine arts, and antiques can be covered individually on an open-perils basis using the homeowners scheduled personal property endorsement. In some cases such as large or powerful watercraft, a separate policy may be the most effective means of providing not only adequate property insurance, but also essential liability insurance coverage.

Personal property is covered on an actual-cash-value basis. Sometimes it is desirable to place this coverage on a replacement-cost basis, which can be done by endorsement for an additional premium. Because the replacement cost of personal property will be greater than its actual cash value, it makes sense to increase Coverage C when loss settlement will be based on replacement cost.

Coverage D Loss of Use. Coverage D provides insurance protection for certain indirect losses. The primary loss-of-use coverage is for additional living expenses—those increased costs necessary to maintain normal living standards when the insured's dwelling is uninhabitable because of damage caused by a covered cause of loss. The automatic limit for this coverage is a percent of the coverage (normally 30 percent) applicable to the dwelling and a percent of the coverage applicable to personal property. Payment is limited to the period required to repair or replace the damage or if the insured permanently relocates, to the period required to resettle the household.

Coverage E Personal Liability. Personal liability insurance provides protection for activities and conditions at the premises where the named insured (the person named on the policy's declarations page) maintains a covered residence and for personal activities of the named insured and members of his family anywhere in the world. All homeowners forms contain the same liability coverage.

Coverage E is similar to other liability insurance policies. Protection is provided for legal liability involving bodily injury or property damage, but not for personal injury. The latter includes such injuries as libel, slander, violation of privacy, malicious prosecution, and wrongful entry. These may be added by endorsement or covered under the umbrella liability policies discussed later in this chapter. The standard liability limit is $100,000 per occurrence, but may be increased for a relatively small additional charge. Given the potential severity of legal liability losses, clients should be advised to increase the Coverage E limit to the amount required as an underlying limit by an umbrella liability policy (commonly $300,000 for a homeowners policy).

Also, as with other liability policies, the insurer promises to defend the insured at the company's expense even if the suit is groundless, false, or fraudulent. The insurer may investigate and settle any claim that it feels is appropriate. The costs associated with investigating and defending a claim against an insured are paid in addition to the limit of liability.

Coverage F Medical Payments to Others. Coverage F provides medical benefits to persons, other than residents of the insured household, who suffer bodily injury at an insured location or who are injured because of an insured's activities away from the insured location. The basic limit for Coverage F is $1,000 per person. This amount is available for all necessary medical expenses incurred within 3 years of the date of the accident. Benefits under this coverage will be paid whether or not the insured is legally liable. While a client must carry an amount of coverage equal to the $1,000 basic limit, carrying higher limits would generally be an inefficient use of premium dollars, since an insured is protected by Coverage E if the injury was due to his negligence, and if not, the injured person should have her own medical expense insurance to cover such injuries.

Personal Auto Insurance

While there are several forms that are currently used to provide personal automobile insurance to individuals and families, ISO's Personal Auto Policy (PAP) is by far the most widely sold and will serve as the basis for discussion in this section. Since this policy is a very complicated contract, only the highlights can be covered here.

The PAP is a package policy that provides coverage for the three types of potential losses that may arise out of the ownership or operation of an automobile—legal liability, medical expenses, and damage to (or loss of) the auto. The PAP offers the following four coverages:

Part A, Liability Coverage
Part B, Medical Payments Coverage
Part C, Uninsured Motorists Coverage
Part D, Coverage for Damage to Your Auto

Unlike homeowners insurance where the insured is required to carry at least a minimum amount of insurance for each of the coverages included in the particular policy form being used, the PAP, for the most part, allows the insured to choose the coverages he desires and the amount of insurance for each coverage chosen.

Part A Liability Coverage. In addition to defending an insured at its own expense, the insurance company agrees to pay damages for bodily injury or property damage for which any insured becomes legally responsible because of an auto accident. Part A of the PAP contains either

- a *single limit of liability,* such as $300,000, which is the maximum amount that will be paid for all damages for bodily injury and property damage resulting from any one accident, or
- a *split limit of liability,* such as $100,000/$300,000/$50,000, which is the maximum that will be paid for bodily injury to each person in an accident, for all bodily injury in an accident, and for all property damage in an accident.

Because the minimum limits available for auto liability insurance reflect the financial responsibility laws of the various states, they tend be quite low, such as $50,000 or $25,000/$50,000/$10,000. Given the potential severity of legal liability losses, clients should be advised to increase the Part A limit to the amount required as an underlying limit by an umbrella liability policy (such as, $500,000 or $500,000/ $500,000/ $50,000 for an auto policy).

The PAP identifies the named insured (the person named on the declarations page), the spouse, and any other family member as insureds for the liability exposure arising from the ownership, maintenance, or use of any auto. This means that unless a situation is specifically excluded by the policy (for example, legal liability for property damage to a rented auto), an insured is protected for legal liability whether or not the auto being operated is owned by the named insured. A family member in this case is anyone who is related to the named insured by blood, marriage, or adoption and who resides in the named insured's household. Other persons are also covered by the named insured's PAP for liability arising out of the use of the insured's covered auto.

A rule to remember is "the insurance follows the vehicle." This means that if John borrows Mary's car and has an accident, then Mary's PAP is "first payer" for any damages or liability. John's PAP may be "second payer," if necessary.

A covered auto is any vehicle shown in the declarations of the policy. It also includes any trailer the named insured owns. If the insured purchases an additional vehicle during the policy period, it will be covered automatically as long as the insurance company is notified of this addition within 14 days. If the new vehicle is a replacement auto, the insurance company will provide coverage (other than coverage for Part D—Damage to Your Auto) until the end of the policy period without any notice being given. Finally, for all coverages other than Part D, a covered auto includes any auto or trailer not owned by the named insured while being used as a temporary substitute for another covered auto that is out of normal use because of breakdown, repair, servicing, loss, or destruction.

Clearly, the insuring agreement for the liability coverage portion of the PAP is broadly stated to provide coverage for a wide mix of individuals and autos. As might be expected, there are several exclusions applicable to this broad coverage. However, despite the number and complexity of the exclusions, the PAP continues to provide insureds with very broad auto liability insurance coverage.

Part B Medical Payments Coverage. Under the medical payments coverage of the PAP, the insurer will pay reasonable expenses incurred for necessary medical and funeral services because of bodily injury caused by an accident and sustained by an insured. Subject to certain exclusions, benefits are payable to the named insured and family members if injured while occupying any motor vehicle designed for public roads or if struck by a motor vehicle. This coverage differs from medical payments coverage under the homeowners policy where the named insured and members of the household are not covered, and coverage applies only to other persons injured on the premises or because of an insured's activities. In the PAP, medical expenses of other persons are also covered, but only while they are occupying a covered auto.

Part C Uninsured Motorists Coverage. Uninsured motorists coverage is a rather unique addition to the PAP. It basically provides that if an insured sustains bodily injury (some states also include property damage) in an auto accident where the other driver was operating an uninsured motor vehicle, the insured may recover from her own insurance company those sums she is legally entitled to recover from the owner or operator of the uninsured motor vehicle.

An uninsured motor vehicle includes a motor vehicle to which no bodily injury liability insurance applies at the time of the accident, a motor vehicle for which the bodily injury liability insurance limit is less than the minimum limit required by the financial responsibility law of the state where the insured's covered auto is principally garaged, a hit-and-run vehicle, and a motor vehicle to which bodily injury liability insurance applies at the time of the accident, but the insurance company denies coverage or becomes insolvent.

The limit of liability for uninsured motorists coverage is typically the required limit of the financial responsibility law in the insured's state. However, the policy can be endorsed to add underinsured motorists coverage which increases this limit. The underinsured benefit provides payment when the at-fault driver or owner has liability insurance, but its limits are less than the limits purchased for the underinsured motorists coverage.

Part D Coverage for Damage to Your Auto. The physical damage coverage of the PAP is referred to as Part D—Damage to Your Auto. The two primary coverages in this part of the policy are *collision* and *other than collision*. The latter has historically been called "comprehensive" and is still referred to in this way by many in the insurance business. Collision is defined as the upset of the covered auto or its impact with an object or another vehicle. Other than collision is every other cause of loss except collision and those causes specifically excluded by the policy. The insured has a choice of purchasing both the collision and the other-than-collision coverages, one of the coverages and not the other, or neither coverage.

The limit of liability for physical damage claims is the lesser of the actual cash value of the stolen or damaged property and the amount necessary to repair or replace the property. In addition, the damage amount is subject to a deductible that, within limits, can be selected by the named insured. A single deductible may apply to all losses or different deductibles may apply to collision losses and other-than-collision losses. An increase in the amount of the deductible can often result in a substantial premium savings.

No-Fault Benefits. Approximately half the states have adopted some form of no-fault automobile insurance plan. Under a pure no-fault plan, legal liability arising out of automobile accidents would be abolished, and anyone suffering a bodily injury loss in an automobile accident would collect from her own insurance company. None of the plans now in existence have gone to this extreme. Rather, the right to sue another party either has not been altered or has been modified to eliminate suits for which losses are below a certain dollar limit (called a threshold) or below some verbalized statement regarding the severity of the injury. No-fault benefits typically include some combination of medical expenses, lost wages, replacement of services, survivors' benefits, and funeral expenses.

In those states with no-fault laws, individuals either must be offered the coverage or are required to carry insurance to compensate themselves, their families, and possibly passengers in their autos for their own bodily injuries. This is accomplished by adding the required endorsement to the PAP.

Umbrella Liability Insurance

The homeowners and automobile insurance policies are the basic coverages for most individuals and families. With the continual increase in the severity of legal liability judgments and settlements, there is an increasing need, particularly among the affluent, for liability limits greater than those provided by these two basic policies. One policy that is becoming increasingly popular for this purpose is the *personal umbrella liability policy*.

While there is no standardized personal umbrella liability insurance policy, a few generalizations can be made. These policies provide excess liability limits over underlying liability coverage limits and, in most cases, broader coverage than the underlying policies. Umbrella liability policies typically provide a liability limit of $1 million or more per occurrence, often up to a maximum of $5 or $10 million. The insured is required to carry certain underlying liability policies and limits—for example, a homeowners policy with a liability limit of $300,000 and an automobile liability policy with a single limit of $500,000. Other coverages may also be required if the exposures exist.

With respect to the underlying coverages, the umbrella liability policy provides excess coverage. For example, if an individual has an automobile liability policy with a single limit of $500,000 and an umbrella liability policy with a limit of $2,000,000, the first $500,000 of any claim arising out of an automobile accident would be payable under the automobile policy, and the balance (up to the policy limit) would be payable under the umbrella policy. Therefore, the insured would have total coverage amounting to $2,500,000.

The umbrella policy also covers situations not covered by underlying insurance policies, such as personal injury in the form of libel, slander, and invasion of privacy; or auto liability outside the United States and Canada. When the umbrella policy does provide coverage in these cases, it drops down to provide primary coverage over the insured's retained limit. A retained limit is like a deductible that must be paid by the insured. This can be as low as $250, but is typically in the $500 to $1,000 range.

Umbrella liability policies do contain some exclusions. Some typical ones are intentional acts, amounts payable under workers' compensation laws, business pursuits, and damage to the insured's own property. Professional liability may also be excluded, but insurance companies are now offering this coverage if the insured carries an underlying professional-liability policy.

The umbrella liability policy enables an individual to have protection against very severe bodily injury, personal liability, and property damage liability losses. Moreover, due to the relatively low frequency of such losses, the coverage is available at a very reasonable cost. You should generally recommend this coverage to all your more affluent clients.

A Concluding Comment

Just as in planning for other areas of client needs, the financial planning process provides an organized approach for developing plans that help clients deal effectively with the various types of pure risks they face. While clearly not the most appropriate technique for handling all the pure risks faced by individuals and families, insurance is an efficient technique to deal with those pure risk situations that involve low frequency, high severity losses. When coupled with retention through the use of deductibles and elimination periods, insurance becomes an even more cost-effective technique for financing potentially severe losses that have a relatively small chance of occurring, but which could have a great impact on a client's overall financial plan if they do occur.

While this chapter has provided a survey of insurance coverages that are available to meet certain pure risks most commonly faced by individuals and families, the financial advisor must recognize two important points. First, the coverages discussed in this chapter are much more complex than the limited space allotted to each may suggest. A more in-depth knowledge of these coverages (or the assistance of an advisor who specializes in insurance) is essential if you use even these basic coverages properly in working with clients. Second, since each client situation presents different problems to solve, additional study or help from an insurance advisor will also be needed in planning to effectively deal with the various unique pure risk exposures faced by different clients.

CHAPTER REVIEW

Key Terms and Concepts are explained in the Glossary. Answers to the Review Questions are found in the back of the book in the Answers to Questions section.

Key Terms and Concepts

risk
pure risk
speculative risk
personal risk
property risk
liability risk
risk management
needs analysis
actual cash value
replacement cost
depreciation
human-life-value method
loss control
loss financing

retention
insurance
risk avoidance
loss prevention
loss reduction
risk transfer
risk pooling
law of large numbers
renewability provision
conversion provision
policy reserve
net amount at risk
universal life (UL) insurance
long-term care insurance

Review Questions

1. What does the term risk mean for insurance and financial planning purposes? [1]

2. Identify the two categories of risk, and explain the meaning of each. [1]

3. Identify the three types of pure risk, and briefly describe each type. [2]

4. Explain the relationship of the financial planning process to the process called risk management and the process called needs analysis. [3]

5. Distinguish between actual cash value and replacement cost as measures of loss associated with property risks. [4]

6. What is the most appropriate measure of the loss associated with liability risks? Explain. [5]

7. Describe two methods of measuring the financial loss associated with premature death. [4]

8. Identify the two categories of techniques for handling pure risks, and briefly explain each one. [2]

9. Briefly explain the operation of the law of large numbers. [2]

10. Distinguish participating whole life policies from nonparticipating whole life policies. [4]
11. Distinguish traditional whole life policies from variable whole life policies. [4]
12. Describe the various ways in which disability may be defined in a disability income insurance policy. [4]
13. What choices are typically available to a client who is considering the purchase of a long-term care insurance policy with respect to (a.) how the daily benefit amount is paid, (b.) how the benefit period is applied in the payment of benefits, (c.) the options for protecting against inflation. [4]
14. Summarize the coverage that is provided by homeowners forms HO-2 and HO-3 for damage to (a.) the dwelling, (b.) other structures, (c.) personal property. [5]
15. Describe the coverage provided in a homeowners policy for loss of use of damaged property. [5]
16. Describe the coverages provided by homeowners policies for (a.) personal liability, (b.) medical benefits [5]
17. Explain how a typical umbrella liability insurance policy works in conjunction with underlying coverages. [5]

EMPLOYEE BENEFITS PLANNING   3

> **Learning Objectives**
>
> *An understanding of the material in this chapter should enable the student to*
>
> 1. Describe the meaning of employee benefits, and explain why they have grown in significance.
> 2. Explain the importance of benefit planning
> 3. Describe the eligibility requirements for employee benefits.
> 4. Describe the various types of employee benefits that can be categorized as traditional group insurance benefits, voluntary insurance benefits, and miscellaneous fringe benefits.
> 5. Explain the nature of cafeteria plans and how they can be used in financial planning.

SCOPE AND SIGNIFICANCE OF EMPLOYEE BENEFITS

Many of the financial needs of individuals and their families are met—or at least partially met—with benefits available to them through their employment. Employee benefits include a wide variety of benefits and services. They represent a major portion—and growing percentage—of total employee compensation. Financial advisors need to understand these benefits so they can incorporate them into financial plans they develop for their clients.

Meaning of Employee Benefits

employee benefits   There is not always agreement about what constitute employee benefits. No matter what definition is used, however, the magnitude of these benefits is significant.

The narrowest definition of employee benefits includes only employer-provided benefits for situations involving death, accident, sickness, retirement, or unemployment. On the other hand, the broadest definition of *employee benefits* includes all benefits and services, other than wages for time worked, that employees receive in whole or in part from their employers. This chapter uses a broad definition and defines employee benefits as including the following five categories:

- legally required payments for government programs. These include employer contributions to such programs as Social Security, Medicare, unemployment compensation insurance, workers' compensation insurance, and temporary disability insurance.
- payments for private insurance and retirement plans. These include the cost of establishing such plans, as well as contributions for insurance premiums or payments through alternative funding arrangements. Benefits are provided under these plans to cover loss exposures from personal risks, such as old age, death, disability, long-term care expenses, medical expenses, dental expenses, and legal expenses. In addition, a few employers have plans that cover some property and liability risks that employees incur.
- payments for time not worked. These include family leave, vacations, holidays, jury duty, maternity leave, and National Guard/Reserve duty.
- extra cash payments, other than wages and bonuses based on performance, to employees. Benefits in this category include educational assistance, moving expenses, suggestion awards, and Christmas bonuses.
- cost of services to employees, such as day care, adoption assistance, financial planning programs, subsidized meals, employee discounts, wellness programs, retirement counseling, and free parking

The first category of employee benefits is usually known as social insurance, and the last four categories are commonly called group benefits.

Significance of Employee Benefits

In a 2008 study of 453 companies of various sizes, the U.S. Chamber of Commerce found that the average payment by employers for employee benefits was equal to 42.7 percent of payroll.[9] Of this figure, 9.5 percent of payroll went for the employer's share of legally required social insurance

---

9. U.S. Chamber of Commerce, The 2008 Employee Benefits Study.

payments, 10.4 percent for payments to private retirement and savings plans, and 12.1 percent for medical and medically related benefits. The remaining 10.7 percent was for all other types of benefits, with paid vacations being the single most costly item in this category. The study showed substantial variations among business firms, with 15 percent of employers having benefit costs less than 24 percent of payroll and another 15 percent having benefit costs in excess of 50 percent. Large variations were also shown by industry. Within specific industries, benefit percentages tend to be higher for firms with more than 100 employees than for firms with fewer than 100 employees, and nonmanufacturing firms have slightly higher percentages than manufacturing firms. The percentages also vary by geographic region.

Over 95 percent of the companies surveyed provide paid vacation, holiday benefits and health insurance benefits to full-time employees. The majority also provide retirement (85 percent), life insurance (79 percent), dental (74 percent), sick leave (65 percent), long-term disability (55 percent), and short-term disability (54 percent).

In addition to employer costs, employee payroll deductions for benefits were approximately 15 percent of payroll. The majority of this amount was for Social Security and Medicare taxes and employees' contributions to retirement and savings plans.

The 2008 Chamber of Commerce study also shows that employees received an average of $18,496 in benefits in 2007, a decrease from the $21,527 reported in 2006. The 2007 figures showed increases in dollar values of medical care and retirement plan contributions by employers.

Growth of Employee Benefits

It is obvious that employee benefits comprise a significant portion of overall employee compensation. This has not always been the case, and this growth over the last 75 years stems from several factors that include industrialization, the influence of organized labor, wage controls, cost advantages, inflation, and federal and state legislation.

Industrialization

During the nineteenth and early 20th centuries, the United States made the transition from an agrarian economy to one of increasing industrialization and urbanization. The economic consequences of death, sickness, accidents, and old age became more significant as individuals began to depend more on monetary wages than on self-reliance and family ties to meet their basic needs. As a result, some employers began to provide retirement, death, and medical benefits to their employees. While benevolence may have influenced the decision to provide such benefits, the principal reason was probably the employers' realization that it was in their own best interest to do so. Such benefits improved morale and productivity and reduced employee turnover and the associated expenses.

While some of the earlier benefits were self-funded directly by employers, the development of group insurance and pension contracts enabled these benefits to be funded by systematic payments to another party, usually an insurance company. However, many employers today still self-fund some of their benefit plans. For example, short-term sick pay benefits are commonly paid directly by many employers, and very large employers often self-fund most of their medical expense plans. As employee benefits became more common, employers were faced with adopting new or better plans to remain competitive in attracting and keeping employees. This competition in employee benefits continues to exist.

Industrialization also led to more government benefits, such as Social Security, Medicare, unemployment insurance, and workers' compensation insurance.

Organized Labor

Labor unions have the right to legally negotiate for employee benefits for their members. Labor unions have also affected benefits for nonunion employees, because some employers provide generous benefit plans to discourage their employees from unionizing. In addition, employers with both union and nonunion employees often provide the same benefits for the nonunion employees as those stipulated in the union contracts.

Wage Controls

Employee benefit plans grew substantially during World War II and the Korean War. Although wages were frozen, no restrictions were imposed on employee benefits, thus making them an important factor in attracting and retaining employees in tight labor markets with little unemployment. Although unemployment increased after these conflicts ended, employee benefits were not cut back.

Cost Advantages

With the economies associated with group underwriting and administration, benefits can usually be obtained at a significantly lower cost through group insurance than through separate policies purchased by individual employees. The Internal Revenue Code also provides favorable tax treatment to employer contributions for certain types of employee benefits. The employer may deduct most benefit contributions as usual business expenses, and employees often have no taxable income as a result of employer contributions in their behalf. In addition, employees may receive tax-free benefits from certain types of benefit plans, even if provided by employer contributions (for example, medical benefits). The extent of the favorable tax treatment applicable to various employee benefits is discussed later. Nevertheless, note that the types of employee benefits with the most favorable tax treatment also tend to be the most prevalent.

Inflation

Inflation also affects employee benefits. When benefit levels are related to employees' wages, the level and cost of these benefits increase as wages increase; when benefit levels are stated as fixed amounts, inflation results in employee pressure for increases. For most employers, the cost of employee benefits has been increasing at a rate much faster than wages, primarily because of the skyrocketing increase in the cost of providing medical expense benefits.

Legislation

Many states and the federal government have legislation that affects employee benefits. At the state level, benefit laws are often in the form of mandates regarding the provisions that must be included in group insurance contracts. Similar federal laws on the other hand typically apply to plans of any employer (with the possible exception of small employers), whether the plans are insured or not. These mandates include coverage for such conditions as maternity, mental illness, alcoholism, and drug abuse.

IMPORTANCE OF BENEFIT PLANNING

The significant growth in employee benefits requires increasingly complex decisions. Whether these decisions are by employers providing benefits, unions negotiating for benefits, or employees selecting benefit options, the need for proper benefit planning is crucial.

Before proceeding with a discussion of the types of benefits available to employees, we will look at the benefit-planing process for employers and the reasons why you need to understand benefits provided to and used by employees.

Benefit-Planning for the Employer

Employee benefit planning from the employer's perspective is a dynamic process that must continually be reviewed and modified if an overall benefit plan is to meet the needs of employees in a changing environment. Whether the planning is done by a team of financial advisors or the employer's own benefits department, certain steps need to be followed. Using the financial planning process introduced in chapter 1, the first step is to establish and define the client-planner relationship. You must clearly explain the responsibilities of the financial planner and the client (employer). You should disclose the scope of the relationship and the methods and magnitudes of planner compensation.

Once the client-planner relationship is established, the second step of the financial planning process is to gather information necessary to fulfill the engagement. This data must be accurate, complete, up-to-date, relevant to the employer's goals, and well organized. The data you obtain must be adequate for you to develop a good understanding of the employer's current situation, employee benefits, and the employer's history with, and satisfaction with, other benefit providers. In this step, you must help the employer to clearly define goals and objectives. You should also try to determine, if possible, the degree of employees' satisfaction with their current benefits package.

The third step in the process is to analyze and evaluate the employer's current benefits status, if there is one. The objective is to determine where the employer is now in relationship to the goals established in Step 2.

The analysis will help to determine the kind of benefits to include in a new plan.

After the data are gathered and analyzed, the next step in the process is to develop your recommendations for a new benefit plan for the employees or for changes to the existing benefits package. This often requires a comparison of the present plan's costs to those for a new plan. If the costs for the new plan are excessive, the employer's goals may need to be revised. A major determinant of a benefit plan's cost is the method of funding.

Should it be insured, self-funded from current revenues, or funded by some combination of the two approaches? How much, if any, should employees pay for the benefits? Employers are increasingly using alternatives to traditional funding arrangements in an effort to reduce costs.

The fifth step in the financial planning process is to communicate the plan to the client/employer. There are many tools today for illustrating the value of employee benefits and the tax advantages for both the employer and employee. Your objective must be to ensure that your recommendations are clearly communicated and understood by the employer. The employer needs to give an explicit acceptance of your recommendations before you proceed in the planning process.

After you obtain the employer's approval of your recommendations, it is crucial that you assist in implementing the recommendations. A vital component in implementation is properly communicating the benefits package to participating employees. Without good communication, it is often difficult for an employer's goals to be realized effectively. Communication has become more than merely describing benefits; it also involves letting employees know the value of the benefits. Many excellent employee benefit packages are unsuccessful because the employees do not truly understand the value of the benefits provided by their employers.

The final step in the process requires employers to monitor the plan's performance and make any necessary changes as needed. As new benefits or funding arrangements appear on the scene, should they be considered? Has the character of the work force changed so that a different benefit package would better meet the needs of employees? Has new federal or state legislation affected the character of the benefits (health care reform, for example)?

Advisor Awareness of Employee Benefits

Employee benefits form the basis of almost all financial plans developed by financial advisors for their clients. Moreover, many employees are able to purchase additional life insurance and/or retirement benefits from their employer-sponsored plans. In addition, some executive level employees are able to negotiate their own compensation packages, including employee benefits as part of nonqualified programs.

The Basis of a Financial Plan

As previously indicated, the second step in the financial planning process is the gathering of information necessary to fulfill the engagement. This includes the employee benefits provided to employees. These employee benefits form the basis on which any sound financial plan should be designed. For example, if an employee's goal is to have a retirement income of $70,000 per year, it is important to know the extent to which this goal is already being met by Social Security and the employee's employer-provided retirement plan. As another example, an employee who needs $500,000 in life insurance may have a substantial portion of this need met by Social Security and an employer-provided group life insurance program. The advisor's challenge is to fully understand the employee benefits package, know their advantages and limitations, and coordinate the employee benefits with personal products, such as life insurance, disability income insurance, and retirement savings.

The Purchase of Additional Insurance and Retirement Benefits

As a financial advisor, you need to be aware of employee benefits that can be obtained through an employer-sponsored plan. For example, an employee may be provided with employer-paid group life insurance equal to one and one-half times salary. In addition, employees may be able to purchase up to an additional two times salary with their own funds. This arrangement, called a *buy-up plan,* is common for life insurance and sometimes found with other types of group insurance.

Many employers are also the source *for voluntary benefit plans.* Under this type of arrangement, the employer does not share in the cost of the benefit but merely makes it available to employees who pay the entire cost of coverage if they elect the benefit. Long-term care insurance, dental insurance, and long-term disability income benefits are often offered under voluntary plans.

In the case of both buy-up plans and voluntary benefit plans, the cost of coverage may be significantly less expensive than comparable coverage in the individual marketplace. However, this is not always the case, and individual insurance outside the employment relationship may be a more cost-effective purchase. Note, however, that the election of coverage through an employer-sponsored plan is usually accompanied by the convenience of payroll deduction—a popular feature for employees. In addition, benefits can sometimes be purchased with before-tax dollars through a cafeteria plan or some other arrangement.

Finally, many retirement plans allow employees to make additional contributions to employer-provided retirement plans—often on a before-tax basis.

A Source for Negotiating a Compensation Package

Some employees are in a position to negotiate their own compensation packages, including employee benefits. These negotiations often result in the employer providing benefits to executives not available to the same degree for all employees. These benefits may take the form of supplemental retirement income, additional life insurance coverage, enhanced medical expense coverage, and similar programs. The executives may also be provided with special benefits not otherwise available to any employees, such as company cars, parking privileges, club membership, and long-term care insurance. Many of these benefits are intended to attract and retain top talent in the executive positions of a company. As a financial advisor, you may be asked to assist a client in evaluating either existing or potential executive benefits for a client.

ELIGIBILITY FOR BENEFITS

Employee benefit plans are very precise in their definition of what constitutes an eligible person for coverage purposes. In general, an employee must be in a covered classification and work full-time. In addition, any requirements concerning probationary periods, insurability, premium contributions, and termination must be satisfied.

Covered Classifications

All employee benefit plans specify that an employee must fall into one of the classifications contained in the benefit schedule. While these classifications may be broad enough to include all employees of the organization, they may also exclude many employees from coverage. In some cases, these excluded employees may have coverage through union plans or under other employee benefit plans provided by the employer. In other cases, the excluded employees may have no coverage because the employer wishes to limit benefits to certain groups of employees. For the most part, and within federal guidelines, employers have flexibility to decide which groups of employees get specific benefits. As mentioned later, however, some types of benefits are subject to nondiscrimination rules.

Full-Time Employment

Most types of employee benefits limit eligibility to full-time employees. For insurance purposes, the employee must work at least 30 hours per week, although there are special considerations for seasonal workers. Some benefits may be provided to part-time employees. When this is the case, the benefits may be smaller than those provided to full-time employees.

Probationary Periods

Employee benefit plans may contain a probationary period that must be satisfied before an employee is eligible for coverage. Such probationary periods may vary by the specific benefit but they are usually either 1 to 3 months and rarely exceed 6 months. Different employee benefits often have different probationary periods to reduce enrollment and administrative costs of employees who may have a high turnover rate.

Insurability

While most employee benefits are issued without individual evidence of insurability, in some instances underwriting practices require evidence of insurability. This commonly occurs when an employee fails to elect coverage at their first eligibility and then later wants coverage, or when an employee is eligible for a large amount of coverage. Evidence of insurability is also frequently required in voluntary benefit plans. This does not mean that no underwriting takes place, but rather that underwriting for group benefits (especially for larger groups) focuses on the characteristics of the group (average age, gender mix, nature of the work) instead of the insurability of individual members of the group.

Premium Contributions

If an employee benefit plan is contributory, an employee is not eligible for coverage until the employer receives proper authorization from the employee for payroll deductions.

Termination of Coverage

Employee benefit plans specify when coverage for an employee (or dependent) terminates. Coverage for any insured person terminates automatically (subject to any provisions for a continuation or conversion of coverage) when

- the employee terminates employment, including retirement
- the employee ceases to be eligible (for example, if the employee no longer satisfies the full-time work requirement or no longer falls into a covered classification)
- the policyowner or insurance company terminates a group insurance contract
- any required contribution by the employee has not been made (generally because the employee has notified the policyowner to cease the required payroll deduction)

However, most group insurance contracts provide that the employer may elect to continue coverage on employees during temporary interruptions of active full-time employment arising from leaves of absence, layoffs, or inability to work because of illness or injury. The employer must continue paying the premium, and the coverage may be continued only for a relatively short period of time, such as 3 months.

Employee benefit plans—particularly those providing health and life insurance coverage—normally make some provision for the continuation of coverage on employees whose active employment terminates due to disability.

TYPES OF EMPLOYEE BENEFITS

The types of employee benefits discussed here fall into three basic categories. The first is traditional group insurance plans for which the employer typically pays all or a part of the cost of an employee's coverage. These include medical expense insurance, 60 percent of which is obtained by Americans under age 65 through the workplace. For the most part, the medical expense coverage available to persons outside the workplace is similar to employer-provided coverage. However, the deductibles and copayments are often higher, and there may be somewhat more restrictive exclusions.

There is also a discussion of other types of traditional group insurance coverage—life insurance, disability income insurance, dental insurance, and vision insurance.

The second category of employee benefits is voluntary benefit plans. And finally, we will discuss selected miscellaneous fringe benefits that take the form of payments for time not worked, payments to employees, and payments to cover the cost of specific services to employees.

Our discussion of these benefits will focus on their nature and any resulting taxation to employees. As will be seen, taxation is not necessarily consistent from benefit to benefit and may or may not be affected by nondiscrimination rules that apply to many types of plans. Note that while the tax treatment of benefits varies for an employee, the cost of providing benefits is almost always tax deductible to an employer as long as the overall compensation of the employee is reasonable.

Medical Expense Insurance

Medical expense insurance is arguably the most important employee benefit to most employees. It is also the single most expensive benefit for employers to provide. The average cost of family coverage in 2011 rose to $15,073, an increase of 9.5 percent over the 2010 average of $13,770; the cost has more than doubled in the last decade.[10] It is important for you to understand a client's coverage in order to determine whether it is adequate. If not, supplemental coverages can sometimes be obtained. In addition, most employees have an option of two or more types of plans (for example, a PPO or an HMO option) from which they can select. You will need to understand the differences among these plans in order to properly advise clients. It is also important for you to know the alternatives available when a client's employment and/or insurance coverage terminates.

The Patient Protection and Affordable Care Act (PPACA) and Health Care and Education Reconciliation Act (HCERA), passed into law in 2010 and known collectively as the Affordable Care Act and as "health care reform", was a massive legislation that will eventually affect nearly all health care programs in the nation. When fully implemented, the health care industry will be entirely reshaped and have little resemblance to the system we know today. An in-depth study of health care reform is well beyond the scope of this course; however, we will point out the major effects on various employee programs as they are discussed in the text.

Types of Plans

major medical plans

Until the 1980s, most employees and their families were provided coverage under traditional *major medical plans*. These plans provide protection against catastrophic

---

10. http://articles.latimes.com/2011/sep/27/business/la-fi-employer-insurance-2011092, accessed 1/17/2012.

medical expenses, subject to some exclusions and limitations. Employees, however, must often assume part of their medical expenses through deductibles and percentage participation (sometimes called coinsurance).

EXAMPLE

Major Medical Insurance

Mary Stuart is covered under a major medical plan that has an annual deductible of $500 and a coinsurance provision that requires her to assume 20 percent of her medical expenses in excess of the deductible up to a stop-loss limit of $10,000. If Mary incurs annual medical bills of $3,000 in 2012, she will have total out-of-pocket costs of $1,000 (consisting of her $500 deductible and 20 percent of the remaining $2,500 of charges). Thus, Mary will be reimbursed for only $2,000 of the total charges.

Although the example shows a deductible and percentage participation provision that applies to all expenses, some major medical contracts waive this cost sharing for certain types of medical expense. The *stop-loss limit* is the maximum out-of-pocket amount (usually in the range of $3,000 to $10,000) that the insured is responsible for in any given year. Note that—all other factors being the same—the higher the stop-loss limit, the lower the premium.

Traditional major medical plans require insureds to file claims for reimbursement and limit the reimbursement to reasonable and customary charges. The portion of any charge that exceeds this limit is not paid by the insurer, and the medical provider can (and usually) does bill the insured for this amount. Each insurer determines which is reasonable and customary, based on the range of fees normally charged for a given procedure by medical practitioners of similar training and experience within a geographic region.

One of the main attractions of traditional major medical plans is that insureds have complete freedom to use the physician or hospital of their own choice.

Historically, traditional major medical plans did little to control medical costs, monitor quality of care, or encourage preventive care. As a result, the 1970s saw the first large scale attempts to promote managed health care. Today, it is estimated that more than 90 percent of employees with medical expense insurance are covered under managed care plans, such as HMOs and PPOs. Two reasons account for this growth, but both are related to the fact that managed care plans are less expensive than traditional major medical plans. First, many employers offer only managed health care plans to their employees. And, second, employees who elect traditional major medical coverage when it is available typically must pay a larger share of the premium cost.

Despite reports of backlash over managed care, surveys indicate that a large majority of Americans are satisfied with their own managed care plans. In many cases, this backlash is aimed at the health care system in general. In other cases, criticism is aimed primarily at the tight controls over health care imposed by health maintenance organizations.

managed care plan

gatekeeper

While variations exist, it is generally acknowledged that a true *managed care plan* should have five basic characteristics:

- controlled access to providers. It is difficult to control costs if participants have unrestricted access to physicians and hospitals. Managed care plans attempt to encourage or force participants to use predetermined providers who have agreements with the managed care organization (an HMO, for example). Because a major portion of medical expenses results from referrals to specialists, managed care plans tend to use primary care physicians as *gatekeepers* to determine the necessity and appropriateness of specialty care. By limiting the number of providers, managed care plans are better able to control costs by negotiating provider fees.
- comprehensive case management. Successful plans perform utilization review at all levels. This involves reviewing a case to determine the type of treatment necessary, monitoring ongoing care, and reviewing the appropriateness and success of treatment after it has been given. While case management may involve a single episode of inpatient care such as an automobile accident, it may also focus on conditions that are chronic, severe, and expensive to treat such as forms of cancer. In this case, the oversight is typically known as *disease management*.
- preventive care. Managed care plans encourage preventive care and healthier lifestyles. Such care often includes routine physicals for children at young ages, well-baby care, childhood immunizations, and mammograms. Other preventive programs such as weight-loss clinics, smoking cessation, and nutrition clinics are available in some managed care plans.
- risk sharing. Managed care plans are most successful if providers share in the financial consequences of medical decisions. Newer managed care plans have contractual guarantees to encourage

cost-effective care. For example, a physician who minimizes diagnostic tests may receive a bonus. Ideally, such an arrangement will help minimize unnecessary tests, not discourage tests that should be performed.

- high-quality care. A managed care plan will not be well received and selected by participants if there is a perception of inferior or inconvenient medical care. In the past, too little attention was paid to this aspect of cost containment. Newer managed care plans not only select providers more carefully but also monitor the quality of care on a continuing basis. The leading organization for accreditation appears to be the National Committee for Quality Assurance (NCQA), an independent, not-for-profit organization that has been rating and accrediting managed care plans since 1991. (See the NCQA website at ncqa.org).

HMO
PPO
POS plan

Within this framework, three general types of managed care arrangements have developed: health maintenance organizations (HMOs), preferred-provider organizations (PPOs), and point-of-service (POS) plans.

HMOs. HMOs were the first type of managed care plan to be widely used. They are generally regarded as organized systems of health care that provide a comprehensive array of medical services on a prepaid basis to voluntarily enrolled persons living within a specified geographic region. HMOs act like insurance companies in that they finance health care. However, unlike insurance companies, they also deliver medical services. HMOs can be either profit or not-for-profit organizations. They may be sponsored or owned by insurance companies, Blue Cross and Blue Shield plans, consumer groups, physicians, hospitals, or private investors.

HMOs have several characteristics that distinguish them from traditional medical expense contracts:

- comprehensive care. HMOs offer their subscribers a comprehensive package of health care services, generally including benefits for outpatient services as well as for hospitalization. Subscribers usually get these services at no cost except the periodically required premium. However, in some cases a copayment, such as $25 or $30 per physician's visit, may be imposed for certain services. HMOs emphasize preventive care and provide such services as routine physicals and immunizations.

- **delivery of medical services.** HMOs provide for the delivery of medical services, which in some cases are performed by salaried physicians and other personnel employed by the HMO who accept the HMO's reimbursement as payment in full. Providers deal directly with the HMO for reimbursement, eliminating the need for subscribers to file claims.
    - Subscribers are required to obtain their nonemergency care from providers of medical services who are affiliated with the HMO. Since HMOs may operate in a geographic region no larger than a single metropolitan area, this requirement may result in limited coverage for subscribers if treatment is received elsewhere. Most HMOs do have "out-of-area coverage" but only in the case of medical emergencies.
    - HMOs emphasize treatment by primary care physicians to the greatest extent possible and subscribers must usually select a primary care physician to whom they will go initially for medical treatment of all types. These practitioners fulfill a *gatekeeper* function and historically have controlled access to specialists. The traditional HMO covers services provided by a specialist only if the primary care physician recommends the specialist, who may be a fellow employee in a group-practice plan or a physician who has a contract with the HMO. The patient has little or no say regarding the specialist selected. This has been one of the more controversial aspects of HMOs and one that has discouraged larger enrollment. In response to consumer concerns, many HMOs now make the process of seeing a specialist easier. Note that the 2010 Affordable Care Act requires most plans to allow female patients to directly schedule OB/GYN care with specialists without getting referrals from another physician.
- **cost control.** HMOs emphasize control of medical expenses. By providing and encouraging preventive care, HMOs attempt to detect and treat medical conditions at an early stage, thereby avoiding expensive medical treatment in the future.
    - The use of salaried employees by many HMOs may also result in lower costs since the physician or other care provider has no financial incentive to prescribe additional, and possibly unnecessary, treatment. In fact, the physicians and other medical professionals in

some HMOs may receive bonuses if the HMO operates efficiently and has a surplus.

PPOs. PPOs have evolved as a middle ground between the tight controls of HMOs over health care and the lack of controls by traditional major medical plans. Most PPOs are owned by insurance companies, but some are owned by HMOs to diversify their health plan portfolios.

A PPO is a benefit plan that contracts with preferred providers to obtain lower costs for plan members. PPOs typically differ from HMOs in several respects. First, the preferred providers are generally paid on a *fee-for-service* basis as their services are used. Second, employees and their dependents are not required to use the practitioners or facilities that contract with the PPO; rather, patients have a choice each time they need medical care, and benefits are also paid for care provided by nonnetwork providers. Employees are offered incentives to use network providers. These incentives include lower or reduced deductibles and copayments and increased benefits, such as preventive health care. Third, most PPOs do not use a primary care physician as a gatekeeper and employees do not need referrals to see specialists.

The basic benefit structure of a PPO is very similar to that of the traditional major medical contract. The most significant difference is that PPOs include a higher level of benefits for care received from network providers than for care received from non-network providers. Many PPOs have extensive networks of preferred providers, particularly in the geographic areas in which they operate; hence there is little reason normally to seek care outside the network.

A PPO may have annual deductibles that apply separately to network and non-network charges—for example, $100 within network and $250 outside the network, respectively. However, many PPOs have no deductible for network charges or waive this deductible for certain medical services, such as emergency or preventive care. Small copayments are usually required for physicians visits and prescription drugs.

POS Plans. A newer and fast-growing type of managed care arrangement is the point-of-service (POS) plan. A POS plan is a hybrid arrangement that combines aspects of a traditional HMO and a PPO. With a POS plan, participants in the plan elect, at the time medical treatment is needed, whether to receive treatment within the plan's tightly managed network, usually an HMO, or outside the network. Expenses received outside the network are reimbursed in the same manner as described earlier for non-network services under PPO plans.

A Comparison of Plan Types. While variations within each type of medical expense plan exist, some generalizations can be made. The degree of managed care increases as you move from left to right in the following table. However, the cost of the plans, on the average, decreases as the degree of managed care increases. In addition, a higher degree of managed care is generally associated with lower annual premium increases by a plan.

Table 3-1 Comparison of Health Insurance Plans				
	Traditional Major Medical Contracts	PPOs	POS Plans	HMOs
Provider Choice	Unlimited	Unlimited in network, but benefits are greater if network provider is used	Unlimited in network, but benefits are greater if network provider is used	Network of providers must be used; care from non-network providers covered only in emergencies
Use of Gatekeeper	None	None	Used for care of network specialists	Used for access to specialists
Out-of-pocket Costs	Deductibles and percentage participation	Deductibles and percentage participation, which are lower if network providers are used; may have small co-payment for network services	Small copayments for network services; deductibles and percentage participation for non-network services	Small copayments for some services
Utilization Review	Traditionally little, but a few techniques are likely to be used now	More than traditional plans, but less than HMOs; network provider may be subject to some controls	Like HMOs for network services; like PPOs for non-network services	Highest degree of review, including financial incentives and disincentives for providers

	Traditional Major Medical Contracts	**PPOs**	**POS Plans**	**HMOs**
Preventive Care	Little covered other than that required by law	Usually more coverage than traditional major medical plan but less coverage than HMOs and POS plans	Covered	Covered
Responsibility for Claims Filings	Covered person	Plan providers for network services; covered person for non-network services	Plan providers for network services; covered person for non-network services	Plan providers

Plan Provisions

Medical expense plans have numerous provisions that concern financial advisors. This section briefly looks at eligibility, covered expenses, coordination of benefits, and cost sharing.

Eligibility. Typically, the same medical expense benefits provided for an employee are also available for that employee's dependents. The term dependents traditionally referred to an employee's spouse who was not legally separated from the employee and any unmarried dependent children (including stepchildren, adopted children, and children born out of wedlock) under the age of 19. The Affordable Care Act of 2010 now requires virtually all medical plans to extend coverage to children until age 26. Plans that provide coverage for dependents were required to extend coverage of dependents (adult children) to age 26, regardless of their eligibility for other insurance coverage, effective September 23, 2010. Plans must provide coverage to all eligible dependents, including those who are not enrolled in school, not dependents on their parents' tax returns, and those who are married. In addition, coverage may also continue (and is required to be continued in some states) for children who are incapable of earning their own living because of a physical or mental infirmity.

Covered Expenses. Most medical expense plans today provide very comprehensive coverage. However, there are certain exclusions and limitations.

The following are common exclusions:

- care provided by family members or when no charge would be made for the care received in the absence of the insurance contract
- cosmetic surgery, except as required for breast reconstruction by the Women's Health and Cancer Rights Act or unless such surgery is to correct a condition resulting from either an accidental injury or a birth defect
- convalescent, custodial, or rest care
- dental care except for (1) treatment required because of injury to natural teeth and (2) hospital and surgical charges associated with hospital confinement for dental surgery
- eye refraction, or the purchase or fitting of eyeglasses or hearing aids.
- expenses either paid or eligible for payment under Medicare or other federal, state, or local medical expense programs
- experimental services

Most major medical plans also contain an exclusion for preexisting conditions. A *preexisting condition* is typically defined as any illness or injury for which a covered person received medical care during the 3-month period prior to the person's effective date of coverage. Usually, the condition is no longer considered preexisting after the earlier of (1) a period of 3 consecutive months during which no medical care is received for the condition or (2) 12 months of coverage under the contract by the individual. Again, the Affordable Care Act of 2010 mandated significant changes in regard to preexisting conditions. For example, the Act eliminated preexisting condition restrictions on children under age 19, effective for plans renewing on or after September 23, 2010. As currently written, health care reform legislation will require the elimination of preexisting conditions for all enrollees, effective January 1, 2014.

It is not unusual, particularly with large employers, for the preexisting-conditions clause to be waived for newly hired employees. In addition, the Health Insurance Portability and Accountability Act (HIPAA) limits the use of preexisting-conditions provisions with respect to newborn or adopted children. Preexisting-conditions provisions also cannot apply to pregnancy. HIPAA requires the preexisting conditions period to be reduced by the time a new employee had coverage under a prior employer-provided or individual medical expense plan as long as the gap in coverage was less than 63 days.

Limitations also exist for certain types of benefits. Some examples that may be found include

- hospital room charges limited to the cost of semi-private accommodations
- dollar limits on benefits (if available) for extended care facilities, home health care, and hospice care
- 50 percent percentage participation for infertility treatment
- limitations on the number of days of treatment or higher cost sharing for treatment of mental illness, alcoholism, and drug addition

coordination-of-benefits provision

Coordination of Benefits. In recent years, the percentage of individuals having duplicate group medical expense coverage has increased substantially and is estimated to be about 10 percent. One such situation occurs if a husband and wife both work and have coverage under their respective employers' plans.

In the absence of any provisions to the contrary, group medical expense plans are obligated to provide benefits in cases of duplicate coverage as if no other coverage exists. However, to prevent individuals from receiving benefits that exceed their actual expenses, most group medical expense plans contain a *coordination-of-benefits (COB) provision,* under which priorities are established for the payment of benefits by each plan covering an individual.

As a general rule, coverage under multiple policies will allow a person to receive benefits equal to 100 percent of his medical expenses. The coverage determined to be primary will pay as if no other coverage exists. If some expenses are not reimbursed (because, for example, of deductibles, copayments, or policy limitations), the secondary coverage will pick up the balance if it is less than what the coverage would have paid if it were the only coverage.

While the rules are complex, a few generalizations can be made:

- Coverage as an employee is usually primary to coverage as a dependent.
- Coverage as an active employee is primary to coverage as a retiree or a laid-off employee.
- If children live in a two-parent household, the plan of the parent whose birthday falls earlier in the calendar year is primary.
- If children do not live with both parents, a court order may spell out which parent's plan is primary. In the absence of such an order, the plan of the parent with custody is primary; the plan of a stepparent who lives with the custodial parent is secondary; and the plan of the parent without custody is tertiary.

Cost Sharing. Many employers pay all or the majority of an employee's medical expense coverage, although the trend in recent years has been toward employees paying more of the costs through premium sharing, higher deductibles and coinsurance, and higher stop-loss limits. In addition, a significant share of dependent coverage is also often paid by the employer.

The 21st century has seen considerable interest in the concept of the *defined-contribution medical expense plan.* A definition of a defined-contribution plan is difficult because the term has been used in many different ways. However, the common thread is that the employer makes a fixed contribution, which employees can use to "purchase" their own coverage. This practice enables an employer to control costs because the amount of the contribution can remain level from year to year or increase at any rate an employer chooses.

EXAMPLE

Defined Contribution Medical Expense Plan

The Weir Corporation makes three medical expense plans available to its employees—an HMO, POS plan, and a PPO. For self-only coverage, the corporation pays an amount equal to 90 percent of the cost of the least expensive plan, which is the HMO. For the three plans, the employee contribution is as follows:

HMO: Total Monthly Premium = $344.00; Employer Contribution = $309.60 (Note: this figure is 90% of $344.00); Employee Contribution = $103.74

POS Plan: Total Monthly Premium = $413.34; Employer Contribution = $309.60; Employee Contribution = $34.40

PPO: Total Monthly Premium = $523.86; Employer Contribution = $309.60; Employee Contribution = $214.26

The corporation uses a similar approach to determine the cost of dependent coverage for which it contributes an amount equal to 50 percent of the cost of HMO coverage.

Although some defined-contribution approaches for medical expense plans are still being developed, defined-contribution medical expense plans have actually been used for some time. For example, many employers make several medical expense plans available to their employees, such as an HMO, a PPO, and a traditional major medical plan. The employer's contribution to the cost of coverage for each plan may be a dollar amount pegged to a fixed percentage of the cost of the HMO plan, as in the example above. Therefore, an employee who elects a more expensive PPO or major medical plan must pay a greater out-of-pocket contribution for his coverage than if he had selected the HMO option.

Newer types of defined-contribution medical expense plans, often referred to as consumer-directed health care, have features other than just fixed employer contributions. At a minimum, these approaches force employees to make financial decisions involving their health care. For example, an employer might provide employees with a health plan that has a very high deductible, such as $5,000 per year. The employer might also contribute a lower amount, such as $2,500 per year, to an account, often called a *health reimbursement account (HRA),* from which the employee can make withdrawals to pay medical expenses not covered because of the deductible. The employee can carry forward any unused amount in the account and add it to the next year's employer contribution. Such a plan gives the employee an immediate incentive to purchase medical care wisely because, if the amount in the account is exceeded, employees will have to pay medical expenses out of their own pocket until the deductible is satisfied.

Additional Benefits for Executives

Some employers have plans that provide additional medical (and dental) benefits for executives. While this group of employees is most likely to be able to pay for the expenses covered by such plans, these supplemental benefits are frequently viewed as a way of attracting and retaining key employees.

From a purely administrative standpoint, it would be relatively easy to self-fund these benefits; however, the benefits, as explained later under the section on federal taxation, would most likely represent taxable income to employees. As a result, these additional executive benefits are usually insured as either a separate coverage or as a rider to the plan covering other employees.

Taxation

Employer contributions for an employee's or dependents' medical expense coverage do not currently create any income tax liability for an employee. Moreover, benefits are not taxable to an employee except in rare situations when the benefits exceed the medical expenses incurred.

One major difference between group medical expense coverage and other forms of group insurance is that a portion of an employee's contribution for coverage may be tax deductible as a medical expense if that individual itemizes his income tax deductions. Under the Internal Revenue Code, individuals can deduct certain medical care expenses (including dental expenses) for which no reimbursement was received. This deduction is limited to expenses (including amounts paid for insurance) that exceed 7.5 percent of the person's adjusted gross income. Note that the Affordable Care Act will raise the threshold for deducting eligible medical expenses to 10 percent, starting in the 2013 tax year. There is a delay of that increase for taxpayers over age 65 until the 2017 tax year.

Coverage after Termination of Employment

A concern of all employees is the effect of termination of employment on their medical expense coverage—whether it be by voluntarily quitting a job, being fired or laid off, or retiring. There are many provisions in medical expense plans that address these issues. They include COBRA, conversion, portability, and postretirement coverage.

COBRA

COBRA. The Consolidated Omnibus Budget Reconciliation Act of 1985 *(COBRA)* requires that group health plans allow employees and dependents covered under the plans to elect to have their current health insurance coverage extended at group rates for up to 36 months following a "qualifying event." The COBRA definition of group health plans is broad enough to include medical expense plans, dental plans, and vision care plans, regardless of whether benefits are self-funded or provided through other entities such as insurance companies or managed care organizations.

COBRA applies only to employers who had the equivalent of 20 or more full-time employees on a typical business day during the preceding calendar year; however, certain church-related plans and plans of the federal government are exempt from the act.

Under the act, each of the following is a qualifying event if it results in the loss of coverage by an employee or dependent:

- the death of the covered employee
- the termination of the employee for any reason except for the employee's gross misconduct. This includes quitting, retiring, or being fired for reasons other than gross misconduct.
- a reduction of the employee's hours so that the employee or dependent is ineligible for coverage

- the divorce or legal separation of the covered employee and spouse
- for spouses and children, the employee's eligibility for Medicare
- a child's ceasing to be an eligible dependent under the plan

COBRA specifies that a qualified beneficiary losing coverage is entitled to elect continued coverage without providing evidence of insurability. The plan must provide coverage identical to that available to employees and dependents for whom a qualifying event has not occurred. Coverage can continue until the earliest of the following:

- 18 months for employees and dependents when the employee's employment has terminated or coverage has been terminated because of a reduction in hours. This period is extended to 29 months if the Social Security Administration determines that the beneficiary was or became totally disabled at any time during the first 60 days of COBRA coverage.
- 36 months for other qualifying events (divorce, for example)
- the date the plan terminates for all employees
- the date the qualified beneficiary subsequently becomes entitled to Medicare or becomes covered (as either an employee or dependent) under another group health plan, provided the group health plan does not contain an exclusion or limitation with respect to any preexisting condition

The cost of the continued coverage may be passed on to the employee or dependent, but the cost cannot exceed 102 percent of the cost of the plan for a similarly situated active employee. The one exception to this rule occurs for months 19 through 29 if an employee is disabled, in which case the premium can be as high as 150 percent.

Conversion. Medical expense plans often contain a conversion provision, whereby covered persons whose group coverage terminates are allowed to purchase individual medical expense coverage without evidence of insurability and without any limitation of benefits for preexisting conditions. Covered persons commonly have 31 days from the date of termination of group coverage to exercise this conversion privilege, and coverage is then effective retroactively to the date of termination.

A person who is eligible for both the conversion privilege and the right to continue group insurance coverage under COBRA has two choices when eligibility for coverage terminates. She can either elect to convert under the provisions of the policy or elect to continue the group coverage under

COBRA. If the latter choice is made, COBRA rules specify that the person must again be eligible to convert to an individual policy after COBRA's maximum continuation-of-coverage period ceases.

> **EXAMPLE**
>
> Paul Wells, age 28 and single, recently lost his job in manufacturing when his company downsized. Paul had group medical coverage through his employer. Paul is eligible for coverage under COBRA for up to 18 months. He will pay a premium for COBRA that is 102 percent of the cost of individual coverage for current employees. In addition, when his COBRA coverage expires, Paul will be given 31 days to convert his group coverage to an individual medical insurance policy, and without having to show evidence of insurability. If he converts his coverage, Paul will pay all premiums for his individual policy.

The use of the word *conversion* is often a misnomer. Actually, a person whose coverage terminates is only given the right to purchase a contract on an individual basis at individual rates. Some plans offer a conversion policy that is written by another entity. For example, an HMO or self-funded plan might enter into a contractual arrangement with an insurance company to offer conversion policies.

Portability. The Health Insurance Portability and Accountability Act (HIPAA) makes it easier for individuals who lose employer-provided medical expense coverage to find alternative coverage in the individual marketplace. The purpose of the federal legislation is to encourage states to adopt their own mechanisms to achieve this goal and most states have complied. The federal rules apply in a state only if the state does not have its own plan. The state alternative must provide a choice of health insurance coverage to all eligible individuals and impose no preexisting-conditions restrictions.

Postretirement Coverage. Although not required to do so by the Age Discrimination in Employment Act, some employers continue coverage for "retired" employees, primarily those employers with 200 or more employees. Although coverage can also be continued for retirees' dependents, it is often limited only to spouses. Note also that retiree medical coverage may be made available to all employees or limited to certain classes of employees, such as executives. Retired employees under age 65 usually have the same coverage as active employees have. However, coverage for employees aged 65 or older (if included under the same plan) may be provided under a *Medicare carve-out* or a Medicare supplement.

With a Medicare carve-out plan, benefits are reduced to the extent that benefits are payable under Medicare for the same expenses. As an alternative, some employers use a Medicare supplement that provides benefits for certain specific expenses not covered under Medicare. These include (1) the portion of expenses that is not paid by Medicare because of deductibles, percentage participation, or copayments and (2) certain expenses excluded by Medicare, such as prescription drugs.

Changes in accounting rules for retiree medical expense coverage and increasing benefit costs have caused many employers to decrease or eliminate retiree benefits. However, there are legal uncertainties as to whether benefits that have been promised to retirees can be eliminated or reduced. Many employers also feel that there is a moral obligation to continue these benefits. As a result most employers are not altering plans for current retirees or active employees who are eligible to retire. Rather, the changes apply to future retirees only. These changes, which seem to be running the gamut, include:

- eliminating benefits for future retirees
- adding or increasing retiree sharing of premium costs after retirement
- shifting to a defined-contribution approach to funding retiree benefits. For example, an employer might agree to pay $5 per month toward the cost of coverage after retirement for each year of service by an employee.
- encouraging retires to elect benefits from managed care plans if they are not already doing so

Life Insurance

With the exception of paid holidays and vacations, life insurance is the most commonly provided employee benefit. Approximately 95 percent of the coverage in force is *group term life insurance*. This is yearly renewable term insurance that provides death benefits only and no build up of cash values. Because death benefits paid under a self-funded life insurance plan are taxable to beneficiaries, life insurance plans are almost always fully insured.

Benefit Schedule

The benefits under a life insurance plan may be based on a multiple of earnings or specified dollar amount. Benefits are also typically reduced for older employees.

Multiple-of-Earnings Schedules. The majority of group term life insurance plans use an earnings schedule under which the amount of life insurance is determined as a multiple (or percentage) of each employee's earnings. For example, the amount of life insurance for each employee may be twice (200 percent of) the employee's annual earnings. Most plans use a multiple between one and two, but higher and lower multiples are occasionally used.

Specified-Dollar-Amount Schedules. There are numerous types of benefit schedules that base benefits on specified dollar amounts. They include flat-benefit schedules and schedules that vary by earnings or position.

By far the most common type of specified-dollar-amount schedule is the flat-benefit schedule, under which the same amount of life insurance is provided for all employees regardless of salary or position. This type of benefit schedule is commonly used in plans covering hourly paid employees, particularly when benefits are negotiated with a union.

Some employers use schedules that have brackets based on income or position. Everyone within the bracket receives the same flat amount of coverage, but the amount varies by bracket, usually in a way that benefits higher-paid employees. For example, employees earning less than $30,000 might receive $20,000 of life insurance; employees earning between $30,000 and $69,999 might receive $75,000 of life insurance, and employees earning $70,000 or more might receive $200,000 of life insurance.

Reduction in Benefits. Group life insurance plans often provide for a reduction in benefits for active employees who reach a certain age, commonly 65 to 70. Such a reduction, due to the high cost of providing benefits for older employees, is specified in the benefit schedule of a plan. Any reduction in the amount of life insurance for active employees is subject to the provisions of the Age Discrimination in Employment Act.

Termination of Coverage

The termination of group life insurance coverage is usually accompanied by a conversion provision. In a few cases the coverage is also portable.

Conversion. All group term insurance contracts covering employees contain a conversion privilege that gives any employee whose coverage ceases the right to convert to an individual insurance policy without evidence of insurability. The conversion policy, however, must usually be a cash value policy rather than term insurance and the conversion is at attained-age rates. The employee retains ownership of the new policy and is responsible for paying all premiums.

Portability of Term Coverage. Some insurers issue contracts with a portability provision that allows employees whose coverage terminates to continue coverage at group rates, much like voluntary employee-pay-all plans. The rates are age-based and will continue to increase as an insured person ages.

Added Coverages

Group term insurance contracts often provide additional insurance benefits in the form of (1) supplemental life insurance, (2) accidental death and dismemberment insurance, and (3) dependent life insurance. These added benefits which are also forms of term insurance can be provided for all employees insured under the basic group term contract or may be limited to certain classes of employees.

Supplemental Life Insurance. The majority of group life insurance plans enable all or certain classes of employees to purchase additional amounts of life insurance. Generally, the employer provides a basic amount of life insurance to all eligible employees on a non-contributory basis. Although the employee may pay the entire cost of the supplemental coverage, either state laws that require employer contributions or insurance company underwriting practices often result in the employer paying a portion of the cost.

The amount of supplemental coverage available is specified in a benefit schedule. Under some plans, an employee must purchase the full amount of coverage; under other plans, an employee may purchase a portion of the coverage. The following table is an example of a benefit schedule for a basic-plus-supplemental life insurance plan.

Because giving employees the right to choose their benefit amounts leads to adverse selection, stringent underwriting requirements usually accompany supplemental coverage. These often include requiring individual evidence of insurability, except possibly when the additional coverage is modest. Higher rates may be charged for the supplemental insurance than for the basic coverage.

Table 3-2 Benefit Schedule for a Basic-Plus-Supplemental Life Plan	
Type of Coverage	**Amount of Life Insurance**
Basic insurance	1 times salary
Supplemental insurance	½, 1, 1½, or 2 times salary, subject to a maximum (including basic insurance) of $300,000

FOCUS ON ETHICS
Focusing on the Client's Need

One of the charges frequently made against financial advisors is that whole life policies are often proposed when additional insurance in the form of supplemental group term coupled with a basic amount of employer-provided group term would have provided better results for the client. The logic of this criticism is based on the fact that the advisor earns a commission on whole life and, therefore, emphasizes it in his or her planning.

The real issue is the importance of clearly focusing on the client's need. Consider a single earner family with young children and a limited budget. Their primary life insurance need is to replace the breadwinner's income in case of premature death. The amount of the insurance need is calculable and the funds available are limited. If a financial advisor encourages purchase of an insufficient amount of cash value whole life insurance instead of a sufficient amount of lower-cost supplemental group term insurance, that advisor has ignored the client's need. The advisor would then have traded compassion, integrity, and professionalism for commissions.

If a client died and was underinsured because the advisor had failed to focus on the client's need, the result would be more than an ethical lapse. It would be a financial catastrophe for the client's family.

Accidental Death and Dismemberment Insurance. Many group life insurance contracts contain an *accidental death and dismemberment (AD&D)* insurance provision that gives additional benefits if an employee dies accidentally or suffers certain types of injuries.

Under the usual form of AD&D insurance, an employee eligible for group life insurance coverage (and electing the life insurance coverage if it is contributory) automatically has the AD&D coverage if the employer adds it or if the insurer includes it as a standard part of its group term life insurance contract. Under the typical AD&D rider, the insurance company pays an additional amount of insurance equal to the amount of coverage under the basic group life insurance contract (referred to as the principal sum) if an employee dies as a result of accidental bodily injuries while she is covered under the policy. In addition to an accidental death benefit, the benefit schedule shown below is often used for certain specific types of injuries.

Death benefits are paid in accordance with the beneficiary provision of the group life insurance contract, and dismemberment benefits are paid to the employee.

Table 3-3 Benefit Schedule for Dismemberment Injuries	
Type of Injury	Benefit Amount
Loss of (including loss of use of):	
Both hands or both feet	The principal sum
The sight of both eyes	The principal sum
One hand and sight of one eye	The principal sum
One foot and sight of one eye	The principal sum
One foot and one hand	The principal sum
One hand	One-half the principal sum
One foot	One-half the principal sum
The sight of one eye	One-half the principal sum

Dependent Life Insurance. Some group life insurance contracts provide insurance coverage on the lives of employees' dependents. *Dependent life insurance* has been viewed as a method of giving the employee resources to meet the funeral and burial expenses associated with a dependent's death. Consequently, the employee is automatically the beneficiary. The employee also elects and pays for this coverage if it is contributory.

For purposes of dependent life insurance coverage, dependents are usually defined as an employee's spouse who is not legally separated from the employee and an employee's unmarried dependent children (including stepchildren and adopted children) who are over 14 days of age and younger than some specified age, commonly 19 or 21. To prevent adverse selection, an employee usually cannot select coverage on individual dependents. A few policies do allow an employee to elect coverage for the spouse only or for children only. If dependent coverage is selected, all dependents fitting the definition are insured. When dependent coverage is in effect for an employee, any new eligible dependents, such as newborn or adopted children, are automatically insured.

The amount of coverage for each dependent is usually quite modest. Employer contributions used to purchase more than $2,000 of coverage on each dependent result in income to the employee for purposes of federal taxation. However, amounts in excess of $2,000 may be purchased with employee contributions without adverse tax consequences. In some cases, the same amount of coverage is provided for all dependents; in other cases, a larger amount is provided for the spouse than for the children. the following table shows an example of a benefit schedule under dependent coverage.

Table 3-4 Benefit Schedule for Dependent Coverage	
Class	Amount of Insurance
Spouse	50% of the employee's insured amount, subject to a maximum of $5,000
Dependent children:	
at least 14 days old but less than 6 months	$ 500
6 months or older	$1,000

Taxation

Section 79 of the Internal Revenue Code (Sec. 79) gives favorable tax treatment to life insurance plans that qualify as group term insurance, and most employer plans are established to meet these requirements.

General Tax Rules. Under Sec. 79, the cost of the first $50,000 of employer-provided coverage is not taxed to the employee. The cost of coverage in excess of $50,000, minus any employee contributions for the entire amount of coverage, represents taxable income to the employee. For purposes of Sec. 79, the cost of this excess coverage is determined by a government table called the Uniform Premium Table I (typically referred to as Table I).

Table 3-5 Uniform Premium Table I	
Age	Cost per Month per $1,000 of Coverage
24 and under	$ .05
25–29	.06
30–34	.08
35–39	.09

Age	Cost per Month per $1,000 of Coverage
40–44	.10
45–49	.15
50–54	.23
55–59	.43
60–64	.66
65–69	1.27
70 and over	2.06

To calculate the cost of an employee's coverage for one month of protection under a group term insurance plan, the Uniform Premium Table I cost shown for the employee's age bracket (based on the employee's attained age at the end of the tax year) is multiplied by the number of thousands in excess of 50 of group term insurance on the employee. For example, if an employee aged 57 (whose Table I monthly cost is $.43 per $1,000 of coverage) is provided with $150,000 of group term insurance, the employee's monthly cost (assuming no employee contributions) is calculated as follows:

Coverage provided	$150,000
Minus Sec. 79 exclusion	− 50,000
Amount subject to taxation	$100,000

Monthly cost = $.43/$1,000 × $100,000 = $43

The monthly costs are then totaled to obtain an annual cost. Assuming no change in the amount of coverage during the year, the annual cost is $43 × 12, or $516. Any employee contributions for the entire amount of coverage are deducted from the annual cost to determine the taxable income that an employee must report. If an employee contributes $.25 per month ($3 per year) per $1,000 of coverage, the employee's total annual contribution for $150,000 of coverage is $450. This reduces the amount reportable as taxable income from $516 to $66. Note that if the employee contribution is $.30 rather than $.25 per month, the annual employee contribution in this example is $540. Since $540 exceeds the Table I cost, there is no imputed income to the employee.

Nondiscrimination Rules. Any plan that qualifies as group term insurance under Sec. 79 is subject to nondiscrimination rules, and the $50,000 exclusion is not available to key employees[11] if a plan is discriminatory. Such a plan favors key employees in either eligibility or benefits. In addition, the value of the full amount of coverage for key employees, minus their own contributions, is considered taxable income, based on the greater of actual or Table I costs.

Taxation of Proceeds. In most instances, the death proceeds under a group term insurance contract do not result in any taxable income to the beneficiary if they are paid in a lump sum. If the proceeds are payable in installments over more than one taxable year, only the interest earnings attributable to the proceeds are included in the beneficiary's income for tax purposes.

Treatment of Added Coverages. If an employer contributes to the cost of supplemental life insurance, the amount of coverage provided is added to all other group term insurance to calculate the Uniform Premium Table I cost. Any premiums the employee pays for the supplemental coverage are deducted to determine the final taxable income.

Premiums paid for AD&D insurance are considered to be health insurance premiums rather than group term life insurance premiums. Benefits paid to an employee under the dismemberment portion of the coverage are treated as benefits received under a health insurance contract and are income tax free. Death benefits received under the coverage are treated like death benefits received under group term life insurance.

Employer contributions for dependent life insurance do not result in taxable income to an employee as long as the value of the benefit is *de minimis*. This means that the value is so small that it is administratively impractical for the employer to account for the cost on a per-person basis. Dependent coverage of $2,000 or less on any person falls into this category. The IRS

---

11. A key employee of a firm is defined as any person (either active or retired) who at any time during the plan year containing the discrimination date is any of the following:

    - an officer of the firm who earns more than $165,000 (2012) in annual compensation from the firm
    - a 5 percent owner of the firm
    - a 1 percent owner of the firm who earns over $150,000 in annual compensation from the firm

considers amounts of coverage in excess of $2,000 on any dependent to be more than *de minimis*. If more than $2,000 of coverage is provided for any dependent from employer contributions, the cost of the entire amount of coverage for that dependent (as determined by Uniform Premium Table I rates) is taxable income to the employee.

Group Universal Life Insurance

A small amount of group life insurance is written under plans that provide cash value life insurance—usually group universal life insurance.

Coverage Available. Under group universal life insurance plans, employees pay the full cost of their coverage and can generally elect amounts of pure insurance equal to varying multiples of their salaries, which typically start at one-half or one and range as high as five times salary. Some plans require a minimum amount of coverage that must be purchased, such as $10,000. The maximum multiple an insurance company offers is influenced by such factors as the size of the group and the amount of insurance provided under the employer's basic employer-pay-all group term insurance plan.

Options at Retirement and Termination. Several options are available to the retiring employee. First, the employee can continue the group insurance coverage like an active employee. However, if premium payments are continued, the insurance company bills the employee, typically on a quarterly basis. With direct billing, the employee may also be subject to a higher monthly expense charge. Second, the employee can terminate the coverage and completely withdraw accumulated cash values. Third, the employee can elect one of the policy settlement options for the liquidation of the cash value in the form of annuity income. Finally, some insures allow the retiring employee to decrease the amount of pure insurance so that the cash value is adequate to keep the policy in force with reduced, or possibly no more, premium payments.

The same options are generally available to an employee who terminates employment prior to retirement.

Taxation. Group universal life insurance products are not designed to be policies of insurance under Sec. 79. Therefore, the tax treatment is the same to employees as if they had purchased a universal life insurance policy in the individual insurance marketplace.

Disability Income Insurance

The purpose of disability income (DI) insurance is to partially replace the income of employees who are unable to work because of a disability due to sickness or accident. Employers are less likely to provide employees with DI benefits than with either life insurance or medical expense benefits. It is difficult to estimate the exact extent of disability coverage because often benefits are not insured and workers are sometimes covered under overlapping plans. However, a reasonable estimate would be that at least 75 percent of all employees have some form of short-term employer-provided protection, and only about 40 percent have protection for long-term disabilities.

Disability income protection consists of two distinct types of benefits:

- short-term DI plans, which provide benefits for a limited period of time, usually 6 months or less. Benefits may be provided under uninsured sick-leave plans or under insured plans.
- long-term DI insurance, which provides extended benefits after an employee has been disabled for a period of time, frequently 6 months.

Short-Term Plans

The majority of short-term DI plans are uninsured and generally replace 100 percent of lost income for a limited period of time. These are commonly referred to as *sick-pay plans*.

Several approaches are used in determining the duration of benefits. The most traditional approach credits eligible employees with a certain amount of sick leave each year, such as 10 days. The majority of plans using this approach allow employees to accumulate unused sick leave up to some maximum amount, which rarely exceeds 6 months (sometimes specified as 180 days or 26 weeks). A variation of this approach is to credit employees with an amount of sick leave, such as one day, for each month of service.

Long-Term Plans

Long-term disability income plans are often limited to salaried employees, and have probationary periods of 3 months to one year. Most long-term disability contracts use a dual definition of disability. Under such a definition, benefits are paid for some period of time (usually 24 or 36 months) as long as an employee is unable to perform the duties of her regular occupation. After that time, benefits are paid only if the employee is unable to engage in any occupation for which she is qualified by reason of training, education, or experience.

Benefits. Long-term DI plans typically provide benefits that range from 50 to 70 percent of earnings, with 60 and 66 2/3 being the most prevalent percentages. Some plans also use a sliding scale, such as 66 2/3 percent of the first $4,000 of monthly earnings and 40 percent of earnings in excess of $4,000.

Long-term disability income benefits may be paid for as short a period as 2 years or as long as the lifetime of the disabled employee. In a few cases, the length of the benefit period may differ, depending on whether the disability was a result of an accident or a sickness. At one time, it was common for long-term disability income benefits to stop at age 65, but this is no longer permissible under the Age Discrimination in Employment Act. Several different approaches are now used for older employees. The most common approach is to use a schedule such as the one shown below.

Table 3-6 Disability Benefit Duration Schedule	
Age at Commencement of Disability	**Benefit Duration**
59 and younger	To age 65
60–64	5 years
65–69	To age 70
70–74	1 year
75 and older	6 months

To minimize the possibility that an employee will receive total benefits higher than her predisability earnings, disability income plans commonly stipulate that benefits be integrated with other sources of disability income. The effect of this integration is to reduce (either totally or partially) the benefits payable under the disability income plan to the extent that certain other benefits are available. In general, the insurance laws or regulations of most states allow such reductions (known as coordination of benefits) to be made as a result of benefits from social insurance programs (such as Social Security) and group insurance or retirement plans provided by the employer, but not as a result of benefits from individual disability income contracts unless they were purchased by the employer.

Supplemental Benefits. It is becoming increasingly common to find long-term disability income plans that provide employees with a base of employer-paid benefits and that allow each covered employee to purchase additional coverage at his own expense. For example, a plan may provide basic benefits of 50 percent of earnings and an option for an employee to increase this amount to 55, 66 2/3, or 70 percent of earnings.

Some plans are also designed to "carve out" benefits for certain employees, frequently key executives. For example, an employer might design one plan to cover most of its employees, but top executives are covered with another group plan that provides enhanced benefits in the form of a larger percentage of earnings and a more liberal definition of disability. Another variation of a carve-out plan would provide the executives with a lower benefit percentage than other employees receive, but it could provide supplemental benefits in the form of individual DI policies. In addition to more favorable policy provisions, an individual policy carve-out plan might offer better rate guarantees and an overall higher benefit than a group plan could offer. Furthermore, the portability of the individual policy might be especially attractive to executives.

Taxation

Employer contributions for disability income insurance result in no taxable income to an employee. However, the payment of benefits under an insured plan or sick-leave plan may or may not result in the receipt of taxable income. To make this determination, it is necessary to look at whether the plan is fully contributory, noncontributory, or partially contributory.

Under a fully *contributory plan*, the entire cost is paid by employee contributions and benefits are received free of income taxation. Under a *noncontributory plan*, the employer pays the entire cost and benefits are included in an employee's gross income.

Under a partially contributory plan, benefits attributable to employee contributions are received free of income taxation. Benefits attributable to employer contributions are includible in gross income, but employees are eligible for the tax credit described previously.

Dental Insurance

Since the early 1970s, *dental insurance* has been one of the fastest-growing employee benefits. It has been estimated that in the past 25 years the percentage of employees who have dental coverage has grown from about 5 percent to more than 60 percent. LIMRA statistics indicate that almost 75 percent of employers with 20–99 employees offer dental coverage.[12] More than 90 percent of firms with 500 or more employees make coverage available.

Many dental insurance plans have been patterned after medical expense plans, and they contain many similar, if not identical, provisions. Like medical expense plans, however, dental insurance has many variations. Dental plans may be limited to specific types of expenses, or they may be broad enough to cover virtually all dental expenses. In addition, coverage can be obtained from various types of providers, and benefits can be in the form of either services or cash payments.

Managed care has significantly affected the evolvement of group dental insurance plans. However, this evolvement has been somewhat different from that of medical expense plans. Group dental plans are more likely to provide benefits on a traditional fee-for-service basis. However, these traditional plans are also more likely to include some managed care approaches to providing benefits. The most common example of this is the emphasis on providing a higher level of benefits for preventive care. It is interesting to note that as group dental plans have become more prevalent, the percentage of persons receiving preventive care has continued to increase. As a result, the percentage of persons needing care for more serious dental problems has continued to decrease. Prevention works!

Benefits

Most dental insurance plans pay for nearly all types of dental expenses, but a particular plan may provide more limited coverage. One characteristic of dental insurance seldom found in medical expense plans is the inclusion of benefits for both routine diagnostic procedures (including oral examinations and X rays) and preventive dental treatment (including teeth cleaning and fluoride treatment). In fact, a few dental plans actually require periodic oral examinations as a condition for continuing eligibility.

In addition to benefits for diagnostic and preventive treatment, benefits for dental expenses may be provided for these categories of dental treatment:

- restoration (including fillings, crowns, and other procedures used to restore the functional use of natural teeth)

---

12. LIMRA International, *A Subtle Shift: Examining Benefits in the Midst of Economic Uncertainty*, 2009.

- oral surgery (including the extraction of teeth as well as other surgical treatment of diseases, injuries, and defects of the jaw)
- endodontics (treatment for diseases of the dental pulp within teeth, such as root canals)
- periodontics (treatment of diseases of the surrounding and supporting tissues of the teeth)
- prosthodontics (the replacement of missing teeth and structures by artificial devices, such as bridgework and dentures)
- orthodontics (the prevention and correction of dental and oral anomalies through the use of corrective devices, such as braces and retainers)

Most dental plans usually cover any expenses that arise from the first five categories listed above, and they may include more limited benefits for orthodontics. All benefits provided may be on a scheduled basis, on a nonscheduled basis, or on some combination of the two.

Scheduled Plans. A scheduled dental plan provides benefits up to the amount specified in a fee schedule. Most scheduled dental plans provide benefits on a first-dollar basis and contain no deductibles or percentage participation. However, benefit maximums are often lower than reasonable-and-customary charges, thereby forcing employees to bear a portion of the costs of their dental services.

Although once common, scheduled dental plans are now used less frequently than either nonscheduled plans or combination plans.

Nonscheduled Plans. Nonscheduled dental plans, often called *comprehensive dental plans,* are the most common type of dental coverage. They resemble major medical expense contracts because dental expenses are paid on a reasonable-and-customary basis, subject to any exclusions or limitations in the contract.

Nonscheduled dental plans usually have both deductibles and percentage participation provisions. Although a single deductible and a single percentage participation percentage may apply to all dental services, the more common practice is to treat different classes of dental services in different ways. The typical nonscheduled dental plan breaks dental services into three broad categories: diagnostic and preventive services, basic services (such as fillings, oral surgery, periodontics, and endodontics), and major services (such as inlays, crowns, dentures, and orthodontics).

Diagnostic and preventive services are typically covered in full and are not subject to a deductible or percentage participation. (They are, however, subject to any other contract limitations.) The other two categories, however, are generally subject to an annual deductible (usually between $25 and $100 per person). In addition to the deductible, the cost of basic services may be subject to a low percentage participation (most often 20 percent), while major services are subject to a higher percentage (most often 50 percent).

Combination Plans. Combination plans contain features of both scheduled and nonscheduled plans. The typical combination plan covers diagnostic and preventive services on a reasonable-and-customary basis but uses a fee schedule for other dental services.

Taxation

The federal taxation of dental insurance premiums and benefits is the same as the taxation described earlier for medical expense premiums and benefits.

Vision Insurance

More than half of the persons covered under employer-provided medical expense plans have some type of vision coverage provided by insurance companies, Blue Cross and Blue Shield plans, plans of state optometric associations, closed-panel HMO-type plans established by local providers of vision services, vision care PPOs, or third-party administrators. In most cases, however, the *vision benefit plan* is separate from the medical expense plan. Despite concerns with rising benefit costs in recent years, vision care is a benefit that employers continue to add. Routine eye exams can result in better overall health care because certain other types of health problems—such as high blood pressure, diabetes, and kidney problems—are first discovered during the course of such routine exams. Proper vision correction can also result in fewer accidents and greater productivity by minimizing eyestrain and headaches.

Benefits are occasionally provided on a reasonable-and-customary basis or are subject to a flat benefit per year that may be applied to any covered expenses. Normally, however, a benefit schedule will be used that specifies the type and amounts of certain benefits and the frequency with which they will be provided. The following table is an example of one such schedule.

Table 3-7 Vision Care Benefit Schedule

Type of Benefit	Maximum Amount
Any 12-month Period	
Eye examination	$ 45
Lenses, pair	
single vision	45
bifocal	75
trifocal	125
lenticular	200
contact (when medically necessary)	300
contact (when not medically necessary)	125
Any 24-month Period	
Frames	60

Vision care plans do not pay benefits for necessary eye surgery or treatment of eye diseases because these are covered under the regular coverage of a medical expense plan. However, many vision plans make benefits available for elective procedures to improve vision, such as LASIK surgery. The benefit is usually in the form of a discounted fee from a provider who has a relationship with the plan.

Voluntary Insurance Benefits

As previously mentioned, voluntary benefit plans make benefits available through the workplace. However, the employer does not share in the cost. Even though an employee must pay the full cost of his own coverage, these plans have several characteristics popular with employees. These include

- payment through payroll deduction
- more liberal underwriting than for similar coverage in the individual insurance marketplace
- lower cost than in the individual marketplace. It is estimated that voluntary benefits on the average are about 10 percent less expensive than coverage purchased outside the employment relationship. Each individual's situation is unique, and it should not be assumed that a voluntary benefit plan will always be the least

expensive way to purchase insurance. However, it is an alternative that should be evaluated.
- **portability of coverage.** Many voluntary benefit plans allow employees to continue coverage on a direct bill basis when they leave their employment.

Some types of insurance are most commonly offered as voluntary benefits. We will briefly discuss four of these benefits—legal expense insurance, long-term care insurance, supplemental medical expense insurance, and property and liability insurance.

Legal Expense Insurance

Legal expense insurance is designed to provide coverage for the legal services needed by employees. In many cases, this is a voluntary benefit provided through a contract purchased from an insurer, bar association, or group of attorneys. The cost of such coverage is often relatively small and frequently falls in the range of $80 to $100 per month per employee. A few larger employers, however, provide the legal services on a self-insured basis and provide the benefits at no cost to employees.

Some legal expense plans merely provide referrals to attorneys and discounts from their regular fees. However, most legal expense plans are referred to as comprehensive plans. In addition to telephone consultation, comprehensive plans cover in-office and trial work of attorneys. The term "comprehensive" may be a slight misnomer because most plans do not cover 100 percent of a plan member's potential legal services; 80 to 90 percent is probably a better figure.

Taxation. An employer has no tax implications from a legal expense plan if it is a voluntary benefit. Employees, however, have taxable income to the extent of any employer payments. If the plan is prefunded, the employee is taxed on her share of the premium paid and benefits are received tax free. If a plan is self-funded by the employer, the employee's taxable income is the value of any benefits paid by the plan.

Long-Term Care Insurance

Since the late 1980s, it has become increasingly common for employers to make long-term care insurance (LTCI) available as an employee benefit. For the most part, the coverage is voluntary and its tax treatment is identical to individual LTC policies. However, there are a few differences. Employees tend to have fewer choices with respect to benefit amounts, benefit duration, and the length of the elimination period. In addition to spouses being able to obtain coverage, eligibility is also often made available to other persons, such as children, parents, and parents-in-law.

Taxation

Employer-provided LTCI plans are designed to be tax-qualified for IRS purposes. This means that, as with individually purchased policies, a portion of the premium cost paid by an employee may be tax deductible, and benefits are generally received free of income taxation.

A few employers pay some or all of the cost of the LTCI premiums for employees. When this is the case, these premium payments typically are tax deductible to the employer and do not result in taxable income to employees.

Supplemental Medical Expense Insurance

There are three types of voluntary medical expense insurance designed to supplement an employee's primary medical expense plan by providing benefits that can be used for (1) out-of-pocket medical expenses not covered by even a comprehensive medical plan and/or (2) associated medical expenses such as travel, lodging, meals, child care, and lost income.

This type of insurance includes

- *hospital indemnity insurance*, which provides the insured with a fixed daily cash benefit (such as $250) during a covered hospitalization. There is also a maximum benefit duration, such as 90 days.
- *specified (dread) disease insurance,* which provides benefits to the insured upon the diagnosis of, or medical events related to the treatment of, a disease named in the policy. The list of diseases includes cancer and as many as 20 or 30 more diseases. Benefits may be based on expenses incurred, a fixed amount per day, or a lump sum.
- *critical illness insurance,* which provides a lump sum cash benefit upon the first diagnosis of a condition or specified surgical treatment. These policies usually cover such illnesses as Alzheimer's disease, heart attacks, organ transplants, paralysis, kidney failure, and strokes.

These supplemental policies are not a substitute for adequate medical expense insurance and disability income insurance. Moreover, if medical expense and disability income coverages are adequate, some financial advisors question whether these supplemental policies are necessary, particularly if a person has appropriate financial reserves for emergencies.

Property and Liability Insurance

A small number of employers make property and liability insurance coverage available to employees. Most plans offer automobile insurance, and a few also offer other coverages, such as homeowners insurance and umbrella liability insurance. Employees usually have the same choices regarding the amount and type of coverage they would have in the individual marketplace, and the contracts offered are usually identical. However, modifications that attempt to decrease the cost of the coverage are sometimes made. These include larger deductibles and provisions in the automobile insurance policy that eliminate coverage for medical expenses to the extent they are paid under the employer's medical expense plan.

Taxation

As with individual property and liability insurance, an employee cannot deduct property and liability premiums for income tax purposes, and benefits received are tax free. In the rare situation when an employer pays a portion of the premium, employees must report as taxable income any contributions made in their behalf.

Miscellaneous Fringe Benefits

The employee benefits previously discussed all fall into the broad category of insurance. However, employees often receive numerous other types of "fringe" benefits. Some of these *miscellaneous fringe benefits* important in the financial planning process are discussed here: education assistance, adoption assistance, dependent care assistance, and family leave.

Education Assistance

The Internal Revenue Code provides favorable tax treatment to employees for the first $5,250 of annual education assistance received from their employers. For benefits to be tax free, the employer's plan cannot discriminate with respect to eligibility in favor of officers, shareholders, highly compensated employees, or their dependents. In addition, no more than 5 percent of the benefits may be paid to shareholders or owners (or their dependents) who are more-than-5-percent owners of the firm.

Eligible benefits include tuition, fees, and books for undergraduate or graduate students. The costs of supplies and equipment are also included as long as they are not retained after completion of the course. Reimbursements for meals, lodging, and transportation associated with educational expenses cannot be received tax free. In addition, courses involving sports, games, or hobbies are ineligible for favorable tax treatment.

Adoption Assistance

While many types of benefits have long been available to natural parents because of the birth of a child, comparable benefits historically have not been available to adoptive parents. Over the last few years, this disparity has begun to change. Even before the passage of family-leave legislation, many employers had established comparable leave policies for natural parents and adoptive parents. For example, if an employer allowed maternity leave (either paid or unpaid) for a new mother, no distinction was made between natural mothers and adoptive mothers. Leave may also be available for time involved in qualifying for the adoption and taking possession of the child.

A smaller number of employers provide reimbursement for some or all of the expenses associated with adoption. Reimbursements are generally available only to employees who have satisfied some minimum service requirement, most commonly one year. Amounts typically range from $1,000 to $3,000 per adoption, but higher amounts may be paid for adoptions involving handicapped children or children from a foreign country. There may also be a lifetime cap, such as $6,000.

Employer payments of up to $12,650 (as indexed for 2012) per child for qualified adoption expenses are excludible from an employee's gross income if an employer has an adoption-assistance program that satisfies IRS requirements.

Dependent Care Assistance

Changes in society and the work force often create changing needs for both employers and employees. When the workforce was largely male and most families had two parents, caring for children and older parents frequently was the female spouse's responsibility. As the number of families headed by two wage earners or by single parents has increased, so has the need for dependent care. This change in demographics has also created problems for employers. Caring for family members can lead to increased absenteeism, tardiness, turnover, and time taken as family leave. Workplace morale can also suffer if the employer is viewed as insensitive to employee responsibilities.

The nature of employee benefit plans has changed as employers have increasingly responded to the need for dependent care. Child-care benefits are increasingly common, and a small but growing number of firms also make eldercare benefits available. Firms that have dependent-care assistance plans generally feel that such plans alleviate the problems cited in the previous paragraph. Furthermore, the availability of the benefit often makes it easier to hire new employees.

In addition to a formal dependent-care assistance plan, there are other ways in which employers can respond to employee needs to care for family members. These include flexible work schedules, part-time employment, job sharing, salary reduction options under cafeteria plans, and family-leave policies more liberal than those required by federal and state laws.

Child-Care Plans. Several alternative types of benefits can be provided under child-care plans. Some employers maintain on-site day-care centers, and the number is growing. Some employers provide benefits by supporting a limited number of off-site child-care centers. The employer may make arrangements to reserve spaces for employees' children at these centers and/or arrange for corporate discounts for employees. Probably the most common approach is to provide reimbursements to employees who make their own arrangements for child care, either at child-care centers or in their own home or with a caregiver. Reimbursement is sometimes tied to pay levels, with lower-paid workers receiving higher reimbursements.

Eldercare Benefits. Benefits to care for elderly dependents are much less prevalent than benefits for child care, but the need for them continues to grow as parents live longer. Although eldercare benefits take a variety of forms, frequently they are much like those provided under child-care plans. Within limits, the employer may pay for costs associated with home care for elderly dependents or care at adult day-care facilities for the elderly.

Taxation of Benefits. Under the Internal Revenue Code, dependent care is a tax-free benefit to employees up to statutory limits as long as certain requirements are met. The amount of benefits that can be received tax free is limited to $5,000 for single persons and married persons who file jointly and to $2,500 for married persons who file separately. The benefits must be for care to a qualifying individual—a child under age 13 for whom the employee is allowed a dependency deduction on her income tax return and a taxpayer's spouse or other dependent who is mentally or physically incapable of caring for himself or herself. Although benefits must generally be for dependent care only, educational expenses at the kindergarten or preschool level can also be paid.

Personal Time Off Without Pay (Family Leave)

Over the last two decades, an increasing number of employers have voluntarily begun to allow employees to take time off without pay, known generally as family leave. Reasons for such leave may include active military duty for reservists and national guard personnel, extended vacations, honeymoons, education, the birth or adoption of a child, and the illness of a family member. Usually, such time off has been subject to the approval of the employer. Family leave is becoming more and more common as many states and the federal government adopt family-leave legislation.

State Laws. In recent years, the legislatures of almost every state have considered family-leave legislation, and more than half the states have enacted such legislation. As a general rule, these laws allow an employee to take an unpaid leave of absence for such reasons as the birth or adoption of a child and the illness of a family member. The length of leave allowed varies considerably among states but usually ranges from 3 to 6 months. When the family leave is completed, the employer is required to allow the employee to return to the same or a comparable job.

At a minimum, most family-leave laws allow an employee to continue medical expense coverage at his or her own cost. Some laws require all employee benefits to be made available.

Federal Law. In 1993, the first federal family-leave legislation-the Family and Medical Leave Act—became effective. The legislation applies only to employers who have more than 50 employees within a 75-mile radius.

With some exceptions, a worker must be allowed to take up to 12 weeks of unpaid leave in any 12-month period for the birth or adoption of a child; to care for a child, spouse, or parent with a serious health condition; or for the worker's own serious health condition that makes it impossible to perform a job.

The act applies to both full-time and part-time employees. The latter must be allowed to take leave on a basis that is proportional to that given to full-time employees. However, leave can be denied to anyone who has not worked for the employer for at least one year and worked at least 1,250 hours during that period.

During the period of leave, an employer has no obligation to continue an employee's pay or most benefits, and the employee is not eligible for unemployment compensation. However, an employer must continue to provide medical and dental benefits during the leave as if the worker were still employed. The employee must continue to pay any required plan contributions and must be given a 30-day grace period for such payments.

Upon returning from leave, an employee must be given his former job or one that is equivalent. The employee must also be permitted to regain any benefits that he enjoyed prior to the leave without having to meet any requalification requirements.

Other Benefits

There are numerous other types of employee benefits that will not be discussed in detail in this chapter. However, they are of significance in evaluating an employee's overall benefit package. Some of them include

- vacations. Significant variations exist in the number of paid vacation days given to employees and how the number increases over time.
- holidays. Most employers provide somewhere between 6 and 12 paid holidays to employees per year.
- no additional-cost services and employee discounts. Employers in many service industries provide their employees with free or discounted services. Examples include telephone service to employees of phone companies, airline tickets to employees of airlines, and educational courses to employees (and their dependents) of educational institutions. Similarly, many manufacturers and retailers sell their merchandise to employees at a discount. As long as these services and discounts are provided in accordance with certain IRS rules, the benefits are tax free.
- wellness programs. Employers are increasingly aware that the well-being of employees increases productivity and lowers medical expense. Wellness programs may involve medical screening, such as tests for high blood pressure or high cholesterol, or lifestyle management programs to promote physical fitness or discourage smoking.

- work/life benefits. These include on-site ATMs, convenience stores, travel agencies, and dry cleaning pick-up. A few employers make dental clinics and pharmacies available.
- employee-assistance programs. These include treatment for alcohol or drug abuse, counseling for family and marital problems, legal advice, referrals for child care or eldercare, and crisis intervention.
- preretirement counseling and financial planning. The former is often made available to all employees, while the latter is frequently limited to executives.
- transportation and free parking. Under provisions of the Internal Revenue Code, an employer can provide significant tax-free benefits in the form of transit passes, van pools, and reimbursement for parking expenses.
- company vehicles. In addition to using a vehicle for business purposes, an employee is often allowed to use a company vehicle for personal purposes. However, an employee who drives a company vehicle for personal use must include the value of the use in his taxable income.
- subsidized eating facilities. In addition to convenience, this benefit can also be offered on a tax-free basis if there are inadequate facilities in the area for employees to obtain meals within a reasonable period of time.

CAFETERIA PLANS

cafeteria plan

Many organizations have benefit programs in which all (or almost all) of the employees can design their own benefit packages by purchasing benefits with a prespecified amount of employer dollars from a number of available options. Generally, these *cafeteria plans* (often referred to as flexible benefit plans or cafeteria compensation plans) also allow additional benefits to be purchased on a payroll-deduction basis. Today, it is estimated that more than 25 percent of employers with more than 500 employees have full-fledged cafeteria plans. Most of these employers and many smaller employers offer premium-conversion plans and/or flexible spending accounts.

Nature

In its purest sense, a cafeteria plan can be defined as any employee benefit plan that allows an employee to have some choice in designing her own benefit package by selecting different types or levels of benefits funded with employer dollars. At this extreme, a benefit plan that allows an employee to select an HMO as an option to a traditional major medical expense plan can be classified as a cafeteria plan. However, the more common use of the term cafeteria plan denotes something much broader-a plan that is designed to comply with Section 125 of the Internal Revenue Code (Sec. 125).

Prior to the addition of Sec. 125 to the Code, the use of cafeteria plans had potentially adverse tax consequences for an employee. If an employee had a choice among benefits that were normally nontaxable (such as medical expense insurance or disability income insurance) and benefits that were normally taxable (such as life insurance in excess of $50,000 or cash), then the doctrine of constructive receipt would result in an employee's being taxed as if she had elected the maximum taxable benefits possible under the plan.

Sec. 125 allows employees to choose between two or more benefits consisting of (1) qualified benefits and (2) cash. Qualified benefits essentially include any welfare benefits excluded from taxation under the Internal Revenue Code except medical savings accounts, long-term care insurance, scholarships and fellowships, transportation benefits, educational assistance, no-additional-cost services, employee discounts, and *de minimis* fringe benefits. Thus, medical expense benefits and long-term care insurance), disability benefits, accidental death and dismemberment benefits, vacations, and dependent-care assistance (such as day-care centers) can be included in a cafeteria plan. The Code also allows group term life insurance to be included, even in amounts exceeding $50,000. In general, a cafeteria plan cannot include benefits that defer compensation except for a qualified Section 401(k) or similar plan.

Sec. 125 requires that benefit elections under a cafeteria plan be made prior to the beginning of a plan year. These elections cannot be changed for that plan year except under limited and specified circumstances. Some of these circumstances, which are spelled out in IRS regulations, include such circumstances as a change in legal marital status, a change in the number of dependents, and increases or decreases in the cost of benefits under the plan.

Types

Under some cafeteria plans, employees are allowed to allocate only a predetermined employer contribution for benefits. Other cafeteria plans are designed so that employees can obtain additional benefits with optional payroll deductions or salary reductions.

Sec. 125 also allows employees to purchase certain benefits on a before-tax basis through the use of a *premium-conversion plan* and/or a *flexible spending account (FSA)*. Premium-conversion plans or FSAs, both of which are technically cafeteria plans, can be used by themselves or incorporated into a more comprehensive cafeteria plan. They are most commonly used alone by small employers who are unwilling to establish a broader plan, primarily for cost reasons. The cafeteria plans of most large employers contain one or both of these arrangements as an integral part of the plan.

An FSA allows an employee to fund certain benefits on a before-tax basis by electing to take a salary reduction, which can then be used to fund the cost of any qualified benefits included in the plan. However, FSAs are used almost exclusively for medical and dental expenses not covered by the employer's plan and for dependent-care expenses.

Cafeteria plans can take many forms, but the most common type of full-fledged cafeteria plan is one that offers a basic core of benefits to all employees, plus a second layer of optional benefits that permits an employee to choose which benefits he will add to the basic benefits. These optional benefits can be "purchased" with dollars, or credits, given to the employee as part of the benefit package. If these credits are inadequate to purchase the desired benefits, an employee can make additional purchases with after-tax contributions or with before-tax salary reductions under a premium-conversion plan and/or an FSA.

EXAMPLE
All employees receive a minimum level of employer-paid benefits, called basic benefits, as follows: • term life insurance equal to one-half of salary • travel accident insurance (when traveling on employer business) • disability income insurance • 2 to 4 weeks' vacation Employees are also given flexible credits, equal to between 3 and 6 percent of salary (depending on length of service, with the maximum reached after 10 years), which can be used to purchase additional or "optional" benefits. There is a new election of benefits each year, and no carryover of any unused credits is allowed. The optional benefits are the following:

- an array of medical expense options. Although there is no charge for HMO coverage, a charge is made for coverage under other options, and additional flexible credits are given if a person elects no medical expense coverage.
- additional life insurance, up to 4½ times salary
- accidental death insurance when the basic travel accident insurance does not apply
- dental insurance for the employee and dependents
- up to 2 weeks' additional vacation time
- cash

The Affordable Care Act made provisions for a new *simple cafeteria plan* for employers with fewer than 100 employees in either of the two preceding years. These new plans allow an employer to choose between two contribution methods; (1) a uniform percentage, not less than 2 percent of employees' compensation, for the plan year, or (2) an amount that equals or exceeds the lesser of (a) 6 percent of the employees' compensation for the year, or (b) twice the employee's salary reduction contribution.

The predominant advantages of the simple cafeteria plan are ease of implementation and, more importantly, a "safe harbor" granted to the plan from the nondiscrimination testing of the Internal Revenue Code. Simple cafeteria plans are sure to represent a significant opportunity for agents and brokers in the future.

CHAPTER REVIEW

Key Terms and Concepts are explained in the Glossary. Answers to the Review Questions are found in the back of the book in the Answers to Questions section.

Key Terms and Concepts

employee benefits
major medical plans
managed care plan
gatekeeper
HMO

PPO
POS plan
coordination-of-benefits provision
COBRA
cafeteria plan

Review Questions

1. Identify the five categories of employee benefits. [1]

2. Identify six reasons for the growth of employee benefits over the last 75 years. [2]

3. What are the steps in the benefit-planning process for employers? [2]

4. Explain why financial advisors should be aware of employee benefits. [2]

5. Describe six requirements that employee benefit plans may use to determine who is an eligible person for coverage purposes. [3]

6. What are the five basic characteristics of a true managed care plan? [4]

7. Describe three ways that PPOs differ from HMOs? [4]

8. Identify six qualifying events for which employees or their dependents can extend medical expense coverage under the provisions of COBRA. [4]

9. Explain how benefits under a group life insurance plan are determined. [4]

10. Describe two possible options that an employee may have for the continuation of life insurance coverage if he or she terminates employment. [4]

11. Bruce is age 25 and works for the ABC Company, which pays the total premium for his $100,000 of group term insurance coverage. If the Uniform Premium Table I rate for a person aged 25 is $.06 per month per $1,000 of coverage, what monthly amount will be reportable as taxable income to Bruce? [4]

12. Explain the tax treatment to employees under a noncontributory group long-term disability income insurance plan. [4]

13. Identify four characteristics of voluntary benefit plans that make them popular with employees. [1]

14. According to Sec. 125 of the Internal Revenue Code, what benefits are excluded from the definition of qualified benefits? [5]

INVESTMENT PLANNING 4

Learning Objectives

An understanding of the material in this chapter should enable the student to

1. Explain the meaning of investment, and contrast investing with speculating.
2. Explain both expected return and risk as they relate to investments.
3. Explain the relationship of financial risk tolerance to asset allocation models and asset selection.
4. Describe the categories of investment assets and the sources of investment risk.
5. Explain the importance of liquidity, marketability, taxation, and diversification to building a portfolio.
6. Describe three methods for comparing the investment returns from different investments, and identify the before-tax returns that can be expected from several different investment categories.
7. Describe several investment principles, strategies, and techniques used by successful investors.
8. Explain the major types of markets where investment trading occurs, and describe the major federal laws and regulations that affect investments.

THE MEANING OF INVESTMENT

investment assets   The assets that consumers buy are of two major types: *personal assets* and *investment assets*. Personal assets are bought primarily for the usage and creature comforts they provide. These include such items as homes, cars, and clothes. Investment assets are those acquired for investing, defined as the purchase of an asset with the expectation that the asset will provide a return associated with its risk. Returns (gains) come from price appreciation, income, or some combination of the two. Income is usually in the form of dividends (when the asset is stock), interest (when the asset is a bond), or rents (when the asset is a rental property).

The distinction between personal and investment assets is not always clear. For example, the purchase of an antique car may be for pleasure, in which case it is a personal asset. It might also be for investment purposes (price appreciation), and thus an investment asset. Or, it may be for both pleasure and investment purposes. Jewelry is another good example of where the asset may serve dual purposes. In such cases, the ultimate distinction depends on the intent of the buyer. The same asset may be a personal asset for one person, and an investment asset for another person. Fortunately, the categories of most assets held by consumers is clear and unambiguous.

Investment versus Speculation

speculative risk   Pure risks involve only the possibility of financial loss, whereas speculative risks involve both the possibility of financial loss and the possibility of financial gain. The distinction between pure risks and speculative risks is important because normally only pure risks are insurable. Speculative risks, on the other hand, are what people encounter when they purchase investment assets hoping to receive some form of return.

The term *speculative risk* is perhaps an unfortunate one because both investment and speculation involve speculative risk. This is true, despite the implication that speculative risk is only associated with speculating. However, even though both investment and speculation involve speculative risk, there is a very clear difference between them. *Investing* is based on a reasoned consideration of expected return and the risk associated with that return. *Speculating* occurs when a person buys an asset hoping to receive some form of return, without consideration or knowledge of the expected return or risk. It may also be the purchase of an asset in which the buyer expects to lose some or all of his purchase price, but which might have some huge payoff. One of the best examples of speculation is the purchase of a lottery ticket. A lottery may sell $10,000,000 worth of tickets, and have as a prize $1,000,000. Thus, while the average ticket buyer will receive back ten cents for each dollar paid for the lottery tickets, actually one person will receive $1,000,000 and everyone else will receive nothing! A rational analysis of expected return and risk would result in few or no people buying lottery tickets. However, most lotteries are successful because many people buy lottery tickets—hoping for the big payoff! Buying lottery tickets is speculating, not investing.

Another example of speculation is buying what are known as penny stocks. These are common stocks that trade for pennies a share. Often, these are stocks of companies that are about to become worthless. On a rare occasion, something favorable happens to one of these companies and it becomes quite valuable. Like lotteries, most buyers of penny stocks lose some, if not all, of their entire purchase price. While a few buyers get lucky and hit it big, again, this is speculating, not investing.

Expected Return and Risk

Expected return and risk are usually thought of in quantitative terms. Measurement of these two values can be quite complex for some securities. To obtain a feel for these concepts, consider the following example:

EXAMPLE

Imagine that a local bank offers a deal to its depositors. Because the city's football team is playing in the Super Bowl, the bank says that between now and the day of the game, customers can buy a one-year certificate of deposit (CD) that will pay 4 percent interest if the local team wins, but only 3 percent if the local team loses. The rate of interest a depositor expects to receive is dependent on the expected outcome of the football game. In national betting, the game is rated a toss-up, meaning it is equally likely that either team could win. Thus, there is a 50 percent probability that the depositor will receive 4 percent interest, and a 50 percent probability that he will receive 3 percent interest.

---

expected return

One way that an *expected return* is calculated is to multiply the probability of each outcome occurring by the value of that outcome, and add the products together. So in our example, the 50 percent probability of receiving 4 percent is multiplied by the value of 4 percent, and the 50 percent probability of receiving 3 percent is multiplied by the value of 3 percent. The first product is 2 percent (.50 × 4%), the second is 1.5 percent (.50 × 3%), and the sum is 3.5 percent. Thus, the expected return on this investment is 3.5 percent. Note that in this case, the actual return will be either 4 percent or 3 percent. It cannot be 3.5 percent for any single investor. We see it is not necessary that the expected return be one of the possible actual returns. The expected return serves as a proxy for the average return one would expect if she were to compare the one-year CD, or any specific investment for that matter, to other investments.

As previously mentioned, risk can be divided into (1) pure risks, which involve only the possibility of financial loss, and (2) speculative risks, which involve both the possibility of financial loss and the possibility of financial gain. Individuals typically handle their pure risks by purchasing insurance. Insurance is not, however, designed to protect individuals against losses arising out of speculative risks. With few exceptions, individuals assume speculative risks because they want the possibility of financial gain. To insure these risks against the possibility of financial loss would require a premium large enough to substantially reduce or eliminate the extent of gain that encouraged the assumption of the risk in the first place.

opportunity loss

If we apply the definition of speculative risk to the world of investments, it is important to recognize that there are two ways a financial loss can occur. The first and most obvious way is when there is a decrease in the value of something that an individual already possesses—for example, the loss of one's investment in the common stock of a firm that fails. The second and most common way is when there is a reduction in the value of something that an individual expects to receive in the future. This second type of financial loss, *opportunity loss*, is illustrated by the following example:

EXAMPLE

Brandon Jones has just inherited $10,000. He consults with his stockbroker about investment opportunities. His broker offers two choices. One is the purchase of a U.S. government bond that matures in one year and provides a 3 percent rate of return. As the chances of the United States government defaulting on this bond are virtually zero, this would be considered a risk-free investment. The broker offers an alternative investment in some common stock in a local company, described as having an expected return of 10 percent. However, the broker adds that the actual return could range anywhere from plus 30 percent to minus 10 percent over the coming year. If Brandon picks the stock and ends up with a rate of return of one percent for the year, he will have made money. However, Brandon ends up making less than he would have made had he bought the government bond, with a virtually certain 3 percent return. Brandon has suffered what is known as an *opportunity loss*. This loss is real to Tom, although he has not actually lost money— he has earned less than expected.

The definition of speculative risk works quite well in the investment world when it is used to describe the risk people face when making an investment. However, it presents mathematical problems for the advisor if he wants to quantify an estimate of an investment's risk. To do this, the advisor has to define investment risk differently. For this purpose, investment risk typically is measured by the variability in possible returns.

investment risk Since most people would agree that the probability of doing worse than expected is usually about equal to the probability of doing better than expected, the range of possible returns may well be described as symmetrical. *Investment risk* is measured by the likelihood that realized returns will differ from those that are expected. An asset with a wide range of possible returns (variability) is considered risky, while an asset with a narrow range of possible returns is considered more secure.

The range of returns is generally measured in terms of the distance or dispersion from the mean or expected (per-period) return. An asset's expected return is the average of its possible returns weighted by their respective likelihoods. Thus, the probabilities of below-expectation and above-expectation returns balance out. The actual yields of risky assets almost always differ from the market's expectations. The owner of a relatively risky asset whose return is expected to be between 2 percent and 18 percent bears the "risk" that the actual return could be anywhere within this range. The investor who owns a relatively secure asset with a 99+ percent probability of earning exactly 7.5 percent has little risk about which to be concerned. Simply stated, investment risk refers to the magnitude of the range of possible returns. In other words, the greater the range of possible returns, the riskier the investment.

Basic Investment Theorems

When engaged in investment planning, there are two theorems that you must always keep in mind. The first is that all investors are greedy! Everyone would like a risk-free investment with an incredibly high rate of return. The second is that there is no free lunch! This means that there is a well-established relationship in the world of investments between risk and expected return. Low risk investments have low expected returns, and high-risk investments have high expected returns. When an investment offers too low an expected return to justify its risk, the asset's price will fall, thus increasing its expected return. This adjustment process will continue until the market views the asset's expected return is in line with its risk. Rational investors will not willingly hold a high-risk investment unless they expect a rate of return that will, on average, compensate them for taking the risk.

This relationship between risk and expected return is known as the positive risk-expected return trade-off. In the end, some high-risk investments will have low or even negative rates of return. This is an illustration of risk. However, other high-risk investments will have rates of return greater than expected. On average, high-risk investments should provide returns greater than low-risk investments. However, it is critical to remember these two words: *on average*. A person who holds many different high-risk investments has a better chance of achieving this average than someone who holds only one high-risk investment. That fact introduces the importance of diversification, the spreading of one's investments among different assets.

SERVICE TO THE CLIENT

When engaged in investment planning for a client, the single most important service that you can perform is to determine the client's financial risk tolerance and make sure that the overall riskiness of the client's investment holdings is consistent with this tolerance level, along with her financial ability to handle the risk. Performing this service is never an easy task. It requires accurately determining the client's true tolerance for risk and her capacity to handle it. Investment planning is made much easier when these two items are consistent with each other. However, there are two cases when they are not consistent.

First, consider the case where a client has a high financial risk tolerance, but a low ability to deal with it. Consider the following example:

EXAMPLE

Winston is 84 years old. His portfolio is worth approximately $500,000. His only sources of retirement income are Social Security, a small pension, and investment income. Based on his current level of expenses at his assisted-living facility, his investment income is critical in meeting his annual expenses. Winston has been addicted to the stock market his entire life. He has made and lost large amounts of money in the stock market over the years. He always believes the market will do better in the future, and wants you to design an aggressive portfolio to increase his wealth for his old age and for a legacy.

In this scenario, Winston has a high tolerance for risk. In fact, he would almost seem to be addicted to gambling. The fact that his investment income is critical to his annual expenses would suggest, however, that he has a low capacity to handle financial risk. If he sustained any substantive losses, he might have to dramatically and unsatisfactorily change his standard of living. At his age and with his health, Winston has no capacity to resume working to rebuild any portfolio losses by additional savings. Therefore, despite Winston's desire to hold risky investments (that is, his financial risk tolerance is high), he should be advised to hold a low-risk portfolio that focuses on secure income.

Now, consider the case where the client has a low financial risk tolerance, but a high capacity to handle financial risk.

> **EXAMPLE**
>
> Edward is 55 and has been a successful business leader his entire adult life. He is worth $15 million. However, Edward's wife fixes him a brown-bag lunch every day, as he abhors the idea of spending a few dollars for lunch. Edward spends vacations at home because he finds the cost of vacations too expensive. He has a comfortable income, and as owner and president of his own company, he plans to continue working for many years.

Edward clearly has the ability to take on a substantial amount of financial risk. His assets are large enough to afford a well-diversified portfolio. He has a good income and can save prolifically. He also appears to be a miser who would find any loss (even a small one) extremely upsetting (that is, he has little tolerance for risk). Edward most likely should be advised to hold conservative (that is, not very risky) investments, not because he cannot afford to handle the risk, but because he psychologically is not equipped to deal with it.

Determining Risk Tolerance

Although determining the risk tolerance of a client is critically important to proper investment planning, there is no simple formula, tool, or technique that allows you to identify the client's financial risk tolerance and then relate it to an investment portfolio. Still, the fact that measurement of financial risk tolerance is not perfect does not mean it cannot or should not be done. For this reason, many companies have developed risk tolerance questionnaires.[13] These range from a few questions (5 to 10) to an extensive questionnaire requiring substantial time to complete.

---

13. *Survey of Financial Risk Tolerance,* American College, Bryn Mawr, PA, 1992.

Whether engaged in single-purpose, multiple-purpose, or comprehensive financial planning, you should make the use of a risk tolerance questionnaire a top priority in data gathering. This type of information is essential for you to develop a financial or investment plan for your clients. When the questionnaire has been completed and analyzed, it provides you with information that helps you assess the client's risk tolerance. Information about risk tolerance, however, is not a substitute for your professional judgment about the client's ability to sustain a financial loss. In fact, the answers on the risk tolerance questionnaire should provide the beginning point for broader discussions with the client about her experience, feelings, fears, and expectations for her investments.

> **EXAMPLE**
>
> Susan is a 60-year-old retired educator. After completing her financial risk tolerance questionnaire, she mentions that her uncle Fred had "been burned in the stock market 10 years ago" and that she wanted no risky investments. This is a great example of what many experienced advisors call "the sample of one." While Susan may have a capacity for equity investing, you would have a huge job of educating her on equity investing to get her acceptance of the risks and potential returns. Prudence would dictate that you avoid putting her money into the markets. One alternative would be to begin educating her about investing and then recommending a small portion of her portfolio to invest in equities. Later, if she is comfortable with the fluctuations in equity values, you could recommend a greater percentage, if appropriate.

The advisor is under a legal and an ethical obligation to help clients make investment choices suitable for the client's particular circumstances. Determining suitability requires consideration of the client's goals, in her capacity to sustain a financial loss, and her psychological attitudes toward risk taking. Developing a suitable financial or investment plan for the client should lead to a lasting and profitable relationship with the client. Not only will the client be happy, but you will have a deep sense of personal satisfaction and professional pride from having fulfilled the client's expectations. Conversely, extreme client dissatisfaction with an inappropriate plan can result in an unsuitability lawsuit. In such disputes, the charge is that the financial advisor knew—or should have known—that the plan was inappropriate for the client. Knowing and understanding your client is the starting point to determine whether a plan is appropriate or not. One more reminder here—always remember it is the client's plan! Do not superimpose your feelings, your values, or your own risk tolerance upon your client. You do so at your own peril!

Asset Allocation Models

After you gather information about the client's financial risk tolerance and have analyzed the situation, your next step in the investment planning process is to translate your knowledge about the client's risk tolerance into a portfolio recommendation. There is no simple formula, tool, or technique that allows you to define the optimal portfolio, even if you have obtained a perfect measure of the client's risk tolerance. At this step, many advisors develop their plans by constructing recommended investment portfolios for different levels of financial risk tolerance. These portfolios are based on categories of assets, rather than specific assets. For example, for the extremely conservative investor, a recommended portfolio might consist of the following: 25 percent in cash equivalents, 25 percent in U.S. government bonds, 30 percent in corporate bonds, 15 percent in preferred stocks, and 5 percent in common stocks. For investors with the highest degree of risk tolerance, the recommended portfolio might include up to 100 percent in common stocks.

asset allocation model

asset allocation

Portfolio recommendations such as these are known as *asset allocation models*. The emphasis is on the different categories of assets and the percentage to be placed in each category. You need to know the client's level of risk tolerance to properly determine both the categories and the appropriate percentages for your client. This leads to the next step in the investment planning process known as *asset selection,* whereby specific assets are recommended. Thus, in the case of a conservative client who has agreed to put 5 percent of his portfolio into common stocks, the final question deals with what specific stocks to buy.

Many new advisors think that the investment planning process works in the reverse order from what we just described. That is, they think that asset selection comes before asset allocation. They focus on the selection of specific assets by looking for "winners" that will have a high return with little or no risk, and then see if the client is comfortable with the selection. However, investment research has consistently shown that correct asset allocation is far more important to a client than asset selection. As a financial advisor you must make sure your client holds an asset allocation consistent with his risk tolerance and capacity to handle risk, rather than occasionally picking a few "winners."

CATEGORIES OF INVESTMENT ASSETS

Now that we have established the importance of asset allocation, let us examine the categories of assets. Basically, there are only two broad categories of investment assets: debt and equity. Debt is any investment in which the investor loans money to someone, receives interest during the life of the loan, and expects repayment of the money (that is, the principal) at the end of the loan. Equity is any investment in which the individual is the owner of the assets that generate the income.

There are three critical characteristics to any debt investment: the maturity of the loan (that is, when the principal will be returned), the risk of default on the loan, and the liquidity of the loan (that is, the ability to sell the investment or otherwise cash it out prior to maturity). The debt instruments with the shortest maturity, highest degree of safety with regard to default, and the most liquidity are known as cash equivalents. Common types of cash equivalents include savings accounts, negotiable and nonnegotiable certificates of deposit, U.S. Treasury bills, commercial paper, money market deposit accounts, and money market mutual funds. The next category of debt instruments is U.S. government bonds, which are assumed to have no default risk and good liquidity, but longer maturities. The last category of debt instruments is corporate debt, which may contain substantial default risk, have longer maturities, and may lack liquidity.

The primary equity investment is always common stock. Common stockholders are the owners of the corporation, in contrast to bond-holders who are creditors of the company or other entity. Another form of equity is preferred stock. There are many equity investments in which investors do not own common stock directly but own a claim on common stock. These include American Depositary Receipts and investment companies such as mutual funds or separate accounts in variable insurance and variable annuities. Other investment opportunities like gold bullion, artwork, and real estate are also classified as equity investments; we just do not typically refer to them as such. Let us consider these debt and equity investments in more detail.

Cash Equivalents

cash equivalent

Since nearly everyone needs to make transactions and have readily accessible money in case of an emergency, many individuals use instruments known as *cash equivalents*. Typically, cash equivalents either have no specified maturity date or have a date one year or less in the future. Investments in this category often provide a very modest current income and typically have little or no potential for capital appreciation. For example, in March 2012, the average U.S. one-year certificate of deposit was yielding less than one-half of one percent!

Bank Deposits

certificate of deposit (CD)

The most widely known cash-equivalent investments are savings accounts and nonnegotiable *certificates of deposit (CDs)* at banks, savings and loans, and credit unions. These investments are usually insured to a limit of $250,000 by the Federal Deposit Insurance Corporation (FDIC), and thus carry minimal risk. In addition, few restrictions are placed on withdrawals of deposits in savings accounts.

CDs, which are deposits for a specified period such as 3, 6, or 12 months (although maturities of up to 10 years are available), generally impose a loss of a portion of interest earnings as a penalty for a withdrawal before maturity. Since the depositor accepts the time commitment and the early-withdrawal penalty, the interest rates earned on CDs exceed that earned on most savings accounts.

Another characteristic of savings accounts and CDs is their ease of acquisition and disposal. Both can be opened or closed at any office of the issuer with little delay and at no cost. Savings accounts can be increased or decreased in virtually any desired sum. CDs can be acquired in sufficiently varied dollar amounts and with staggered maturities to allow the depositor to match maturity to future cash needs. At maturity, CDs can be automatically reinvested for an equivalent time period without the investor having to take any action.

Money Market Instruments

Money market deposit accounts (MMDAs) and *money market mutual funds (MMMFs)* are other popular cash equivalents. For both types of investments, minimum initial dollar amounts are typically required to open the account. In the case of MMDAs offered by banks, virtually any amount can be added to the account. MMDAs typically are FDIC insured like savings accounts and CDs. MMDAs allow withdrawals at the bank window or by check. However, a limit is imposed on the number of free checks per month, and additional checks can be quite costly. The earnings rate obtained from these instruments often increases depending on the size of the investor's account.

In contrast, MMMFs frequently require minimum dollar deposits, and they are not FDIC insured. MMMFs provide access by check, by wire transfer, and, in some cases, by phone. MMMFs are mutual funds, and investments are used to buy shares in the fund. Because MMMFs often belong to a commonly managed family of funds, these MMMF shares can be readily redeemed for shares in other funds within the family with little or no delay or transaction cost.

Both MMDAs and MMMFs hold portfolios of short-term obligations of the federal government and its agencies, of state and local governments, and of businesses. The securities usually have maturity dates averaging under 60 days.

Treasury Bills

U.S. Treasury bills (T-bills)

risk-free investment

Another popular cash-equivalent investment is *U.S. Treasury bills (T-bills)*. These short-term obligations of the U.S. government are issued with a term of one year or less, and they are backed by the full taxing authority of the U.S. government. With this backing, T-bills are the safest investment available and, thus, pay investors the lowest interest rate of the various money market instruments. When the term *risk-free investment* is used, it refers to T-bills. In this context, risk free means no possible risk of default on paying interest or principal when due. These instruments are sold at a discount from face value and do not pay interest before maturity. The interest is simply the difference between the purchase price of the bill and the amount paid either at maturity (the face amount) or when the T-bill is sold prior to maturity. T-bills require a minimum purchase of $100 (effective in 2008), making them readily available for clients of modest means. They can be acquired by bidding directly with the government in a program called Treasury Direct, or by bidding through brokers, dealers, or financial institutions. Also, T-bills can be readily sold and converted to cash at a modest cost to meet client needs.

Many other investments have the characteristics of cash equivalents, such as the short-term obligations of state and local governments (for example, tax anticipation notes or TANs) and of businesses (for example, commercial paper representing very short-term debt) and the long-term debt obligations of governments and businesses that mature within one year. Some of the characteristics of these long-term securities are described below.

Long-Term Debt Instruments

Long-term debt instruments are those whose term to maturity is one year or more. Some people refer to bonds with maturities of one to 10 years as being intermediate term. When bonds are issued with maturities of one to 10 years, they are frequently referred to as *notes*.

Bond issues of state and local governments (both of which are referred to as *municipals*) and of businesses typically are rated by agencies such as Standard and Poor's Corporation (S&P) and Moody's Investors Service on the likelihood that the issuer will default on the timely payment of interest or principal. Based on a financial analysis of the issuer, a letter grade is assigned to each bond issue. Bonds rated at the top of the B grade (BBB for S&P, Baa for Moody's) or higher are considered to be "investment quality." Lower ratings are assigned for bonds assessed as "speculative" (often referred to a "junk bonds"). These rating organizations evaluate the bond when it is issued and continue to monitor the issuer during the bond's life. The lower the quality rating, the greater is the risk of default and the higher will be the yield that the investor will expect to earn if the issuer does not default.

Governmental Debt Securities

agency bonds   Governmental debt includes securities of the federal, state, and local governments, and their agencies. Some federal bonds are backed by the full faith and credit of the U.S. government. For example, all U.S. Treasury obligations have such backing. Bonds issued by federal agencies or organizations, such as the Tennessee Valley Authority, are not direct obligations of the U.S. Treasury. These bonds, known collectively as *agency bonds*, provide investors with returns greater than U.S. Treasury bonds, although the difference in return is quite small. A few of these agency bonds have guarantees that effectively place the full faith and credit of the U.S. Treasury behind the bonds.

Some state and local government bonds, known as *general obligations (GOs)*, are backed by the taxing power of the state or local government. Others, usually issued by agencies of a state or local government, are known as *revenue bonds*. They are guaranteed by the revenues earned from such ventures as turnpikes, airports, and sewer and water systems. Without the taxing authority behind them, these revenue bonds are viewed as riskier and pay investors a slightly higher interest rate than do general obligation bonds.

GO's - general obligations - backed by state & local government taxing power

Revenue Bonds - guaranteed by revenues earned from turnpikes, sewer, airports, etc.

Typically, interest earned on debt issues of the federal government, although subject to federal income taxation, is exempt from income taxation by state and local governments. Exceptions to the exemption from state and local income taxation include mortgage-backed securities issued by federal agencies such as the Government National Mortgage Association (Ginnie Mae) or the Federal National Mortgage Association (Fannie Mae). Interest earned on most, but not all, municipal bonds is exempt from federal income taxation and income taxation by the state in which the bond originates. States generally tax the interest earned on municipal bonds issued in other states.

Corporate Debt Securities

indenture

junk bonds

Corporations are major issuers of debt instruments. These securities have various characteristics detailed in the *indenture*. The indenture is the legal contract associated with a bond issue, written by the issuer, that specifies the rights and protections afforded to the bond investor. Some of the more frequently encountered characteristics include the following:

- secured—a promise backed by specific assets as further protection to the bondholder should the corporation default on payment of interest or principal
- debenture—an unsecured promise, based only on the issuer's general credit status, to pay interest and principal
- callable—an option exercisable by the issuer to redeem the bond prior to its maturity date at a specified price
- convertible—an option exercisable by the bondholder to exchange the bond for a predetermined number of common or preferred shares of stock

For bonds of the same quality rating, these features affect the interest rate paid to the investor. If the feature provides a benefit to the bondholder, such as being secured or convertible, a lower interest rate is paid. If the feature provides a benefit to the issuer, such as the presence of a call feature, the interest rate is higher.

The market often assigns labels to securities. One label frequently heard in the news is *junk bonds,* now more commonly called high yield bonds. These bonds have weak quality ratings from Standard & Poor's (S & P) or Moody's and are risky because the firm either has excessive debt relative to its equity base or has suffered financial reverses and possibly is headed for serious trouble or bankruptcy. Since the risk on such junk bonds is high, their returns are also high—if the issuer does not default.

Note: The term "junk bonds" can also apply to certain municipal bonds if the government or agency tax or revenue base sharply deteriorates.

Equity Securities

Equity investments represent an ownership position in a business. As such, they represent a higher risk for the investor than do the debt investments. Although an equity interest can be as the sole owner of a proprietorship or as one of several partners in a partnership, this discussion will focus on equity as evidenced by shares of stock issued by a corporation.

Corporations acquire equity funds by selling ownership shares to either a few individuals or to the public. In the former case, the individuals often agree not to sell the shares to others, hence keeping the firm "closely held" and the shares are not marketable. When equity shares are sold to the public, a market for their resale emerges if enough shares are publicly held, and the ownership interest can be readily sold or purchased. Corporations can offer different types of ownership interests; the two most popular are common and preferred stock.

Common Stock

Investors in common stock have the ultimate ownership rights in the corporation. They elect the board of directors that oversees the management of the firm. Each common share receives an equal portion of the dividends distributed as well as any proceeds that remain after a liquidation. If the firm is unsuccessful, losses will occur that can lead to a cessation of any dividend payments and, if losses continue, to an eradication of the common equity ownership and eventual bankruptcy.

Payment of dividends to shareholders is at the sole discretion of the board of directors. The board is under no legal obligation to make dividend payments and may instead retain the profits within the business. The owners of common stock typically vote on issues such as mergers and stock splits. Common stockholders sometimes have a *preemptive right,* which is the right to maintain their relative voting power by purchasing shares of any new issues of common stock of the corporation.

Preferred Stock

Preferred stockholders usually have two privileges that provide them with a preferential position relative to common stockholders. The first privilege is the right to receive dividends before any dividends are paid to the common shareholders. This preference is usually limited to a specified amount per share each year. As previously stated, dividends are payable only if declared by the board of directors. If the preferred shares are noncumulative and no dividend is paid to the preferred shares in a year, the dividend is skipped and does not ever have to be paid. In the next year, the corporation can pay the specified annual preferred dividend and then pay a large dividend to the common shareholders. To prevent this from happening, many preferred stocks have a cumulative provision associated with the issue. This provision requires the corporation to pay all the skipped preferred dividends, as well as the current year's preferred dividend, before any dividends can be paid to the common shareholders.

The second privilege of preferred stockholders is the right to receive up to a specified amount for each share (plus current or cumulative dividends) at the time of liquidation. This liquidation value must be paid to the preferred stockholders in full before anything can be paid to common stockholders.

American Depositary Receipts (ADRs)

Many investors want to own shares in foreign corporations. These shares can be purchased abroad in the same way that domestic corporation shares are purchased in the United States. However, inconvenient trading hours due to time differences and large transaction fees make these transactions undesirable. To overcome these problems, some U.S. banks have acquired shares in foreign corporations and hold these shares in trust in one of their foreign branches. Then they sell negotiable instruments, called *American Depositary Receipts (ADRs)*, that represent a specified number of shares in a foreign company. ADRs are the equivalent of ownership of the stock, trade as such in domestic markets, and have rights and privileges as do the common shareholders in the country of issue.

Investment Companies

Investment companies can be distinguished in several ways. For example, there is a distinction between closed-end and open-end investment companies.

closed-end investment company

net asset value (NAV)

At formation, a *closed-end investment company* issues a given number of shares. Rarely, if ever, are additional shares issued. These shares are traded in the stock markets in the same manner as those of traditional corporations, such as Microsoft. That is, the forces of demand and supply for the stock determine the share price.

The closed-end investment company uses the proceeds from the initial sale of its stock to acquire a portfolio of securities. The market value of this portfolio influences, but does not directly determine, the market price of the closed-end company's shares. Theoretically, the value of a share in a closed-end investment company should equal the *net asset value (NAV)* of the portfolio. The net asset value is calculated as the fund's total assets − total liabilities divided by the number of shares outstanding, as in the following example:

[handwritten: net asset value NAV = fund's total assets − total liabilities ÷ # of shares]

EXAMPLE

The Top Dog Growth Fund reported total assets at the end of the trading day of $322,738,516, and total liabilities of $2,517,683. There were 4,698,245 shares outstanding. The NAV for this fund at this point in time is computed as: ($322,738,516 − $2,517,683)/4,698,245 or $68.64.

The shares of most closed-end investment companies sell at a discount to their net asset values. Occasionally, the shares of some closed-end funds trade at a premium, that is, a market price that is higher than the NAV.

open-end investment company

mutual fund

no-load fund

An *open-end investment company*, popularly called a *mutual fund*, continually sells and redeems its shares at net asset value. Hence, the shares are not traded in the stock market. Similar to closed-end companies, mutual funds acquire a portfolio of securities in which each of the fund's shares owns a proportionate interest. As sales and redemptions of the fund's shares take place, the size of the fund's total portfolio changes, increasing when additional shares are issued and decreasing when shares are redeemed.

The nature of the acquisition fees is another distinguishing characteristic among investment companies. Buyers of closed-end shares, because the shares are traded on securities markets, are subject to normal stock-brokerage commissions for both purchase and sale transactions. Some mutual funds charge a sales fee and are called load funds. The loading is regulated, and it can be as high as 8.5 percent of the value of the investment. If no sales fee is levied, the fund is called a *no-load fund*.

Technically, this load versus no-load distinction should refer to any initial sales fees and to other fees that carry different names but are used to compensate individuals for selling and marketing efforts. One of these fees is the 12-b(1) fee, which is an annual charge against the net assets of the fund that typically ranges from 0.1 to 1.0 percent. A fund may call itself a no-load fund as long as its 12-b(1) fee does not exceed one-quarter of one percent. In 2012, almost all "load" funds now charge 12-b(1) fees. A second type of marketing fee is called an exit fee, contingent deferred sales charge (CDSC), or back-end load. This is not a modest charge simply to cover the expenses of processing a redemption. Rather, the CDSC is sometimes as high as 4 or 5 percent of the dollar value of the shares being redeemed and is used to pay the marketing and selling costs. Some individuals believe that a true no-load fund (often called a 100 percent no-load fund) assesses investors neither a front-end, a 12-b(1), nor a CDSC, because these are all forms of marketing and selling costs. Whether the fund is load or no-load, shareholders must pay the administrative, transactions, and investment advising expenses incurred by the fund. These expenses (characterized by an "expense ratio" such as 1 percent) are deducted from the interest, dividend, and capital-gain fund income prior to distributing fund income to the shareholders.

prospectus Under federal laws that regulate security transactions, a *prospectus* (a document that gives a potential buyer the relevant information about a newly issued security) must be delivered to investors before purchase. The prospectus includes tables that show the amount of all loads and other expenses associated with the purchase, holding, and sale of the fund's shares. Therefore, the magnitude of these additional fees can be determined by the investor.

> **EXAMPLE**
>
> Craig's financial advisor has recommended that he purchase $50,000 of the GOODFUNDS Growth and Income Fund to build assets for Craig's retirement. The advisor provides a prospectus that describes the following expenses for the fund:
>
> 1. front-end load equal to 5.0 percent of initial purchase amounts up to $100,000. If total investments exceed $100,000, the front-end load is reduced to 4.0 percent up to $250,000, and so on.
> 2. 12-b(1) fees of 0.25 percent of NAV, assessed quarterly based on cumulative holdings in the fund
> 3. fund expense charges that have averaged 1.25 percent of NAV in the last 12 months
> 4. no deferred contingency sales charges (that is, surrender charges)

Investment companies also differ on the basis of their portfolio objectives. Although there are nearly 8,000 investment companies, they fall into several broad categories based on their portfolio objectives. For most of the portfolio categories, subcategories exist. The major categories are as follows:

- *money market mutual funds*—These funds own a portfolio of short-term interest-bearing securities. As mentioned earlier, they are used by investors as an alternative to cash. They operate only as open-end funds. Subcategories include funds that focus mainly on nontaxable securities or federal securities only, or on diversified portfolios.
- *index funds*—These funds own a portfolios of common stock that replicate a major market index, such as the S&P 500. They operate only as open-end funds. Index funds have substantially lower expenses and fees than actively managed funds. They are especially useful for passive investment strategies in which the investor simply seeks to match the performance of the index.
- *bond funds*—These companies own a portfolio of bonds. Subcategories include some that invest only in U.S. government issues, municipal issues, corporate issues, and low-quality (junk) bonds. Further subcategories can be short-term (up to 4 or 5 years), intermediate-term (5 to 10 years), or long-term (10 or more years duration) bond funds.
- *common stock funds*—These companies hold a portfolio of common stocks and perhaps a small number of preferred stocks. Subcategories include those that invest primarily in conservative

or *defensive stocks, growth stocks, value stocks, large cap stocks, small cap stocks*, and foreign stocks.

- *mixed (or blended) portfolio funds*—These companies own a portfolio of bonds, stocks, and other investment instruments. Subcategories include balanced funds and income funds.
- *specialty funds*—These companies have very specialized portfolios designed for investors who seek special investment opportunities. The most common is the *sector fund*, which specializes in stocks from a single industry or country.

In most cases, a fund is a part of a family of funds representing several categories or subcategories of portfolio objectives. This feature permits investors to switch their investments from stocks to bonds to money market instruments as conditions change, generally at no charge. However, every time a switch is made in a "nonqualified account," there is an income tax consequence because a sale, and then a purchase transaction has occurred.

Several reasons explain the current popularity of investment companies. The first is that each share in an investment company benefits from the pooled diversification of the portfolio. Second, the professional management that selects and continuously monitors the markets and the fund's securities should (it is hoped!) provide better overall portfolio performance than the typical individual investor. Third, many investors lack the time to properly select securities and can better delegate this responsibility to others. A fourth reason is that the wide diversity of investment companies allows an investor to select the diversified portfolio that best suits his investment objective. The tax and record keeping provided by the fund management is another reason for the popularity of investment companies. Last, as more companies institute 401(k) plans for their employees, shares of different mutual funds frequently are among the choices suitable for participants. The major disadvantage of mutual funds is that, on average, they underperform market averages by an amount equal to their annual fees.

Real Estate and Other Investments

Real Estate

real estate investment trust (REIT)

Many forms of real estate ownership are available to investors. One such form is the purchase of property directly, either as an individual or as a managing partner in a partnership. One way that requires less active management by the investor is owning shares in a *real estate investment trust (REIT)* (which is similar to an investment company in which the trust either owns property it manages or owns a portfolio of real estate mortgages). A second way is by owning a limited-partnership interest in a general partnership. This limited-partnership interest has no active role in the firm's management. Real estate investments usually involve more complexities than the previous investment categories because of

- the uniqueness of each property
- the differing rights associated with ownership of each property
- the absence of organized markets for the ready sale and purchase of the property or ownership interest (they are relatively illiquid)
- the complexity of the federal taxation of the income and appreciation from real estate (other than the investor's primary residence) since the passage of the Tax Reform Act of 1986

Before embarking into real estate for investment purposes, most investors should remember that they probably already have a major investment in real estate—their own home.

Other Investments

Virtually any asset can be used for investment purposes. Over the years, such activities as oil-and-gas drilling and exploration activities have been used as limited-partnership tax-advantaged investments. The growth of the options, futures, and commodities markets spawned investment instruments that offer many different objectives. The Cold War (through the 1980s) whetted investor preferences for ownership of precious metals that might rise sharply in value if relations between countries deteriorated. Although coins and stamps have long been collectibles, other types of collectibles have become popular because of the strong economic performance of stamps and coins. Art, ceramics, and china have captured the fancy of many individuals due to the appreciation of selected items.

Similar to real estate, each of these investments is a specialty field unto itself. Any technical treatment of the characteristics of these investments is well beyond the scope of this introductory discussion.

SOURCES OF INVESTMENT RISK

Earlier, we discussed the concept of speculative risk and the definition of investment risk as the magnitude of the range of possible returns. We will turn now to consider the sources of risk.

Purchasing Power Risk

inflation risk

real rate of return

One major source of risk is always *purchasing power risk,* sometimes called *inflation risk*. Inflation is the increase in the general level of prices. The Bureau of Labor Statistics estimates inflation based on what it would take to buy the basket of goods and services typically purchased by a family of four living in an urban community. Although inflation rates are published with great precision, they are at best an approximation because not everyone buys this same basket of goods and services, and changes in the quality of goods and services are impossible to incorporate into this calculation.

The impact of inflation is popularly misunderstood. Suppose someone had $100,000 to invest, and this person earned a 5 percent rate of return over the course of a year. If over that same year, the rate of inflation turned out to be 3 percent, then we would say that this person's *real rate of return* is approximately 2 percent. The rate actually earned, 5 percent, is referred to as the *nominal rate of return,* and the real rate can always be approximated as the nominal rate less the inflation rate. A more precise measure of the real rate of return is

$$\text{real rate of return} = \frac{(1 + \text{nominal rate of return})}{(1 + \text{current rate of inflation})} - 1$$

Both the nominal rate of return and the current rate of inflation must be expressed as decimals in this formula.

Thus, the real rate of return in the above example would be as follows:

$$\text{real rate of return} = \frac{(1 + .05)}{(1 + .03)} - 1$$
$$= 1.019 - 1$$
$$= .019 \text{ or } 1.9\%$$

The key point here is that even if this investor had taken the $100,000 and put it under a mattress, the inflation rate would still have been 3 percent, and he would have lost purchasing power. However, investing the money at the nominal rate of 5 percent overcame the impact of inflation.

Interest Rate Risk

interest rate risk

Another major source of risk for investors is *interest rate risk*. Due to the many economic forces in the economy, such as actions by the Federal Reserve System to control money supply, changes in demand for borrowed funds, and movements of foreign exchange rates, interest rates will change over time. With changes in general interest rates, the value of securities and the income earned on securities will also change over time. This effect, known as interest rate risk, has two segments: price risk and reinvestment rate risk.

Price risk exists because any change in market interest rates typically leads to an opposite change in the value of investments. When interest rates rise, the value of an investment declines, and *vice versa*. This inverse relationship is most pronounced for debt instruments, such as bonds, mortgages, and U.S. Treasury bills that specify a rate of interest and a specified time to maturity. The longer the time until maturity, the greater will be the resulting change in market price. For other instruments, such as common stock or real estate, the relationship is not as pronounced, but it still exists. In fact, changes in interest rates affect the valuation of securities and also affect the profitability of many companies, by making it more expensive for borrowers and more profitable for lenders. For example, when interest rates rise, some businesses, such as banks, tend to become more profitable.

The following example illustrates why the value of an investment changes when interest rates change. Suppose that an investor purchased a bond for $1,000 when the market interest rate for the bond's risk was 8 percent with a maturity date one year hence, so that the bond pays interest of $80 annually. Next, assume that on the following day the market interest rate for bonds of this same risk and maturity rises to 9 percent. Of course, our investor would now like to sell his bond for $1,000 to buy a new one yielding 9 percent. However, he could not do so because a potential buyer today can obtain $90 interest (instead of $80) by purchasing a newly issued, one-year maturity bond. However, a price can be determined that would make the total return, both interest income and appreciation in the market price of yesterday's 8 percent bond, such that today's buyer would be indifferent to either yesterday's 8 percent bond or today's newly-issued 9 percent bond. This price would have to be somewhat less than $1,000 so that the new buyer's total return would be exactly 9 percent. Alternatively, if the market interest rate had fallen to 7 percent, the value of the 8 percent bond (now more attractive than today's bonds) would rise above its $1,000 face amount so that the total return to a new buyer would be equal to 7 percent.

Reinvestment rate risk is the risk associated with reinvesting investment income at unknown future interest rates. Suppose an investor buys $100,000 worth of 10-year bonds that pay $5,000 in interest annually. At maturity, the investor would expect to receive back her $100,000 in principal, have accumulated $50,000 in interest payments (10 years × $5,000 per year), plus interest income from reinvesting the interest payments during that 10-year period. If interest rates rise during the 10 years, the investor can reinvest the interest payments for a higher rate of return than anticipated. If interest rates fall during the 10 years, the investor will have to reinvest the interest payments at a lower rate of return than anticipated. The level of interest rates over the 10-year period will have a substantial impact on the investor's final accumulation.

The important feature about price risk and reinvestment rate risk is that they work in opposite directions. For an investor holding a bond, there is always both good news and bad news when interest rates change, regardless of the direction of change. When interest rates rise, interest payments can be reinvested at higher rates, but the price of the bond falls. When interest rates fall, reinvested interest payments receive lower rates of return, but the price of the bond rises. The task for the investor when interest rates are changing is to have the opposing effects from price risk and reinvestment rate risk exactly offset each other. Then, the news from price risk, whether it be good or bad, exactly offsets the news from reinvestment rate risk.

Note that inflation risk and interest rate risk are related because the rate of inflation is the major determinant of the level of interest rates. When the rate of inflation increases, interest rates rise, and vice versa for decreases in the rate of inflation.

Business Risk

business (default) risk

Investors must consider the *business (default) risk* for their investments. For many reasons, such as changes in consumer preference away from a particular good or service, ineffective management, law changes, or foreign and domestic competition, some enterprises will experience financial difficulties and will be unable to repay bond principal or make interest payments on a timely basis. In such a default, investors in the bonds of these defaulting organizations may not receive interest payments, or worse yet, may even lose some or all of their principal. Defaults can affect investors in either profit-seeking businesses or nonprofit institutions such as municipalities.

Because the debts of bankrupt corporations being liquidated must be paid in full before any funds can flow to their stockholders, rarely is anything left for the owners (stockholders) of profit-seeking firms that have failed. (There is no equity ownership in nonprofit or governmental organizations.) In addition, it is still widely assumed that business (default) risk is not associated with debt instruments of the U.S. Treasury, which are backed by the full faith, credit, and taxing power of the federal government.

An investment strategy to minimize the business (default) risk is to purchase only bonds issued by organizations having a high credit rating. As mentioned earlier, both Moody's and Standard & Poor's provide assessments of the investment quality of various bond issues. Obtaining this type of information for other forms of investments, such as limited partnerships, requires a diligent investigation by the financial advisor or the investor.

SPECIAL PORTFOLIO CONSIDERATIONS

There are several concerns a financial advisor must consider when selecting securities for a portfolio. Two key aspects of investment planning, ascertaining the client's financial risk tolerance and making an appropriate asset allocation decision, were discussed earlier. Other important issues are liquidity, marketability, taxation, and diversification.

Liquidity

liquidity An asset is said to be liquid if it can be converted to cash (sold) quickly at any time with little or no loss of principal. Every portfolio should have some *liquidity* in it because it allows investors the flexibility to quickly obtain cash for emergency purposes. There are two different ways to obtain liquidity. One is to own liquid assets. Liquid assets were discussed earlier and include such investments as savings accounts, MMDAs, MMMF's, and U.S. T-bills.

There is, of course, a drawback to owning liquid assets, which is that they typically have the lowest expected rates of return. Although there is negligible risk in owning liquid assets, there is also negligible return. Put another way, there are often substantial *opportunity costs* to owning liquid assets.

An alternative way to have liquidity is to maintain ready opportunities for borrowing money. Consider the following example:

EXAMPLE

Ted Robbins has a portfolio worth about $500,000. The portfolio is mostly common stocks with a few bonds. It is held in a margin account, but there currently is no borrowing against this account. There are no money market securities in the account. Ted suddenly needs $30,000 to buy a new car. What are his choices?

Ted's first choice is to sell some securities, but this may trigger taxes and will certainly generate some transaction fees. A second choice for Ted is to borrow the cash from the brokerage firm. A margin account permits an investor to either borrow money from a brokerage firm to buy securities or pledge currently held securities as collateral for a loan. Current borrowing rules set by the Federal Reserve Board permit loans up to 50 percent of the value of an investor's portfolio. Therefore, Ted could borrow up to $250,000 against his portfolio, although he needs to borrow only $30,000 for a new car. The interest rate on a $30,000 margin account loan to Ted would be his cost for obtaining liquidity. In the meantime, Ted would have minimized his opportunity costs by not holding any low yielding money market securities in his portfolio

---

Interest expense accruing on margin account debt typically is tax deductible as investment interest if used to buy taxable securities. It would not be tax deductible for money borrowed to buy a new car. Thus, any interest expense on a $30,000 margin account loan to Ted to buy a new car would be considered nondeductible personal interest even though the debt would be secured by his investment portfolio.

Another method for Ted to have some liquidity is to establish a home equity line of credit (HELOC). Interest on up to $100,000 of home equity indebtedness typically is tax deductible even if the loan proceeds are used for personal expenditures, such as buying a new car.

The key point in this discussion is that everyone needs liquidity, and there are two basic ways to have liquidity. One is to own liquid assets, and the other is to own assets or employ techniques that allow for quick and convenient loans.

Marketability

Marketability is a little different than liquidity, but the two concepts are frequently confused. Marketability refers to the ability to sell an asset quickly. Thus, liquid assets are marketable, but not all marketable assets are liquid. Stock is a classic example of a marketable asset that is not liquid. If a stock is listed on a major exchange, it can be sold in a matter of seconds. However, there is no certainty as to the price at which the stock can be sold. It is important that portfolios have marketable assets, but this is not a substitute for liquidity. Also, this does not mean that investors should avoid holding any nonmarketable assets. For example, homes are nonmarketable assets. It often takes weeks, months, or even years to sell a home, and the transaction fees can be substantial.

Taxation

Financial advisors must pay close attention to their clients' tax situations when making investment recommendations. Different tax rates apply to different forms of income, and the timing of when the taxes are due can be quite different. The first critical feature to understand is that taxation of ordinary income varies depending on income level. The federal income tax is a progressive tax, and this means that higher tax rates apply to incremental income as the individual's total income increases.

EXAMPLE

Suppose you have two clients with different income levels. The first client, Robert, is single and is a bank teller with a taxable income of $30,000, placing him in the 15 percent income tax bracket for 2012. The second client, Sharon, is single, an executive vice president with a large firm, and she has a taxable income of $400,000. This places her in the top 35 percent income tax bracket. They each ask you to help them invest $100,000 in bonds, and you offer them two choices. They are Park District bonds, which pay an annual interest rate of 4 percent, and First National Bank bonds, which pay an annual interest rate of 5 percent. The Park District bonds have the lower interest rate because, as municipal bonds, they are exempt from federal income taxes. Both Robert and Sharon say they do not enjoy paying income taxes, and thus they want to buy Park District bonds. Is this a good choice for both of them?

A $100,000 investment in Park District bonds would produce interest income of $4,000 per year ($100,000 principal × 4 percent interest rate), while a $100,000 investment in First National bonds would produce interest income of $5,000 per year ($100,000 principal × 5 percent interest rate). For Robert, the purchase of First National bonds would provide an extra $5,000 of taxable income each year and would bring his total taxable income up to $35,000 per year. The entire $5,000 would still be taxed to Robert at the rate of 15 percent because his now larger taxable income of $35,000 would not be large enough to move him up to the next higher (25 percent) tax bracket. Thus, Robert's taxes on the $5,000 of interest income would be $750 ($5,000 × 15 percent). After the payment of taxes, he would still have $4,250 left. This is greater than the interest income from the tax-exempt bonds. Consequently, Robert should clearly invest in the First National bonds, even though he prefers not having to pay taxes.

In Sharon's case, the purchase of First National bonds would require her to pay $1,750 in taxes ($5,000 × 35 percent), leaving her with $3,250. Clearly, Sharon would be better off buying the Park District tax-exempt bonds even though the total interest income is only $4,000 (versus $5,000 for the First National bonds).

The following formula converts a tax-exempt yield to an equivalent taxable yield:

$$\text{equivalent fully taxable yield} = \frac{\text{tax-exempt yield}}{(1 - \text{MRT})}$$

$$\frac{.04}{1-.04}$$

where: MRT is the investor's marginal income tax rate

A second formula converts a fully taxable yield to an equivalent tax-exempt yield:

$$\text{equivalent tax-exempt yield MRT} = \text{fully taxable yield} \times (1 - \text{MRT})$$

To use these formulas, the tax-exempt yield or the fully taxable yield must be expressed as a percentage, while the marginal tax rate must be expressed as a decimal.

qualified dividends   Advisors must also understand the taxation rules for stock dividends and for capital gains and losses from the sale of equity investments such as stocks and mutual funds. Formerly, all dividend income was taxed as ordinary income. However, current tax treatment is that dividends are classified as ordinary (or nonqualified) and *qualified dividends*. "Qualified" dividends are taxed at a rate of 15 percent, except for taxpayers whose marginal tax bracket is

15 percent or less. For taxpayers in the two lowest marginal tax brackets (that is, 10 percent and 15 percent), the tax rate of qualified dividends is zero (that is, they are effectively tax exempt). Qualified dividends include dividends from most domestic corporations, whether or not publicly traded. Dividends from certain foreign corporations also qualify, including those paid by companies publicly traded on U.S. exchanges. Certain dividends are not qualified dividends, including those paid by credit unions or mutual insurance companies. Some other exceptions exist and advisors must stay current on applicable tax laws, since they are subject to frequent changes.

capital assets
Capital assets are defined under Sec. 1221 of the Internal Revenue Code as any property the taxpayer owns (whether or not connected with a business activity) with some exceptions. Financial assets such as stocks, bonds, and mutual funds clearly qualify as capital assets for tax purposes. When capital assets, such as stock, are sold at a price that exceeds their *cost basis*, then capital gains taxes can be imposed. Cost basis is normally the price paid for an asset, plus any expenses associated with the purchase. In the case of stock where a commission is normally paid, the cost basis would equal the price paid for the stock plus the commission.

EXAMPLE
Jennifer purchased 100 shares of Walmart (WMT) stock two years ago at $50 per share. In purchasing the stock, she paid a brokerage fee of $100. Her cost basis in the stock is computed as follows: (100 shares x $50) equals $5,000 plus $100 (brokerage fee) equals her cost basis of $5,100. If she sold her stock today for a net amount (after expenses) of $6,100, she would have a long-term capital gain of $1,000, reportable on her federal income taxes.

The key point of this section is that investors who are in high tax brackets can enhance the after-tax returns of their portfolios by investing in stocks of domestic (and qualified foreign) corporations, tax-exempt bonds, and/or assets with a large potential for capital appreciation. On the other hand, investors who are in low tax brackets can benefit by focusing their investment activity on assets that provide the largest amount of current taxable income. However, regardless of the investor's tax bracket, their investments must be commensurate with their financial risk tolerances.

Diversification

diversification

The importance of *diversification* in a client's portfolio can never be overemphasized. Asset allocation among a variety of investments is a first step in the diversification process. For example, a portfolio with a goal of asset allocation as shown below has a good degree of diversification.

5%	Cash equivalents
10%	Intermediate term government bonds
10%	Long-term government bonds
20%	Long-term corporate bonds
10%	Long-term foreign corporate bonds
15%	Large cap stocks
15%	Value stocks
10%	Sector mutual funds
5%	Foreign country mutual funds
100%	

However, within each of these categories, be sure there is not excessive concentration within an industry. For example, the large cap stocks category should not have large holdings of both General Motors and Ford. Similarly, there should not be concentration across categories. An investor should not hold both stock and bonds in the same company. Finally, the investor should be cautious about investing too heavily in investments closely aligned with his occupation. For example, if the investor is a software engineer for an internet firm, his portfolio should not be too heavily concentrated in internet stocks. When the internet industry collapsed in 2000, investors lost money on their internet ("dot.com") holdings, and many employees in the internet industry lost their jobs. It is tempting for people to want to invest in industries with which they are familiar, but it should be done with caution. The principle of diversification should always be practiced, no matter how strong the temptation to do otherwise. As a financial advisor, you should monitor your clients' portfolios to ensure they remain diversified.

INVESTMENT RETURNS

capital appreciation

The returns on an investment come in two forms: current income and *capital appreciation*. Not all investments produce both forms of return. Some investments, such as savings accounts, produce only current (interest) income. Others, such as undeveloped land, produce only capital appreciation (unless the land can be farmed or rented). Borrowing to purchase common stock, when the annual interest expense from borrowing is greater than the dividends being paid, produces negative current income. However, in the case of common stock, there is always the potential for capital appreciation or depreciation, regardless of whether current income is positive or negative.

Despite varying combinations of current income and capital appreciation, a method for comparing the investment returns from different investments is necessary. Over the years and before computers or calculators, three quick methods for measuring an investment's return acquired widespread acceptance within the investment community. Still widely used, these three methods of measuring return are the (1) current yield, (2) holding-period return (HPR), and (3) approximate yield.

Current Yield

current yield

The *current yield* is perhaps the most widely used of the three methods for measuring an investment's return. It is calculated by dividing an investment's current annual income by its current market price as follows:

$$\text{Before-tax current yield} = \frac{\text{current annual income}}{\text{current market price}}$$

For example, assume that an investor purchases a corporate bond for $1,050 that will pay her an annual interest income of $98. Under these circumstances, the investor's before-tax current yield from the bond would be as follows:

$$\text{Before-tax current yield} = \frac{\$98}{\$1,050}$$
$$= .0933 \text{ or } 9.33\%$$

One advantage of the current yield is that it provides a quick way to compare different investments being considered for purchase, retention, or sale. The current yield is particularly important when an investor needs a certain amount of annual income from his portfolio. For example, if an investor has a portfolio worth $500,000 and wants a before-tax income of $20,000 per year from the portfolio without spending the principal, the portfolio must produce a current yield of 4 percent ($20,000/$500,000) each year.

The major shortcoming of the current yield is that it fails to look beyond the present moment. The investments being compared may have different potentials for future increases or decreases in their income streams or market prices. This possibility is not considered when calculating the current yield. A second shortcoming is that the calculation is made on a before-tax basis. To calculate an after-tax current yield, the above formula must be modified so that the current annual income is adjusted (that is, reduced) by the investor's marginal rate of tax (MRT). The following formula makes this adjustment:

$$\text{After-tax current yield} = \frac{\text{current annual income} \times (1 - \text{MRT})}{\text{current market price}}$$

where MRT is the investor's marginal income tax rate

As previously mentioned, most dividends received by individuals today are taxed at the same rates that apply to capital gains. Consequently, an investor's MRT depends on the type of income being received (dividends versus interest) as well as the different tax rates imposed by the taxing authorities (state versus federal).

If a 28 percent marginal income tax rate applies to the investor in the previous example, his after-tax current yield would be

$$\text{After-tax current yield} = \frac{\$98 \times (1 - .28)}{\$1,050} = \frac{\$98 \times .72}{\$1,050} = \frac{\$70.56}{\$1,050}$$
$$= .067 \text{ or } 6.7\%$$

Alternatively, the investor's before-tax current yield of 9.33 percent shown above can be multiplied by one minus the investor's marginal tax rate to obtain the after-tax current yield of 6.7 percent [9.33% × x (1 − .28)].

Holding-Period Return (HPR)

holding-period return (HPR)

Although the name *holding-period return (HPR)* may imply that the method is used to measure an investment's return over any holding period, it is most appropriate for investment periods of one year. This is because no consideration is given to the timing of investment returns and, therefore, to the time value of money. The HPR is calculated by dividing the total amount of current income plus the total amount of capital appreciation by the beginning dollar value of the investment. The following formula shows this relationship for a before-tax HPR for a one-year period:

$$\text{Before-tax HPR} = \frac{\text{total current income} + \text{total capital appreciation}}{\text{total initial investment}}$$

For example, assume that an investor purchased common stock one year ago for $800 and that she wants to know what the HPR return is on the stock. During the one-year holding period, the investor received $50 of dividend income, and the stock's market price increased from $800 to $840. Based on this information, the before-tax HPR for the stock investment would be:

$$\text{before-tax HPR} = \frac{\$50 + (\$840 - \$800)}{\$800}$$

$$= \frac{\$90}{\$800}$$

$$= .1125 \text{ or } 11.25\%$$

If an after-tax HPR is desired, the formula becomes

$$\text{After-tax HPR} = \frac{[\text{TCI} \times (1 - \text{MRT})] + [\text{TCA} \times (1 - \text{TCG})]}{\text{total initial investment}}$$

where: TCI is the investor's total current income
MRT is the investor's marginal income tax rate
TCA is the investor's total capital appreciation
TCG is the investor's tax rate for capital gains

However, because the investor's MRT for dividends is 15 percent, the same as her TCG, her after-tax HPR return would be

$$\text{After-tax HPR} = \frac{\$50(1-.15) + [(\$840 - \$800)(1-.15)]}{\$800}$$

$$= \frac{\$50(.85) + \$40(.85)}{\$800}$$

$$= \frac{\$42.5 + \$34}{\$800} = \frac{\$76.5}{\$800}$$

$$= .0956 \text{ or } 9.56\%$$

Approximate Yield

approximate yield The true yield of an investment can be described as the rate of interest (called the internal rate of return) that makes the present value of the benefits derived from the investment exactly equal to the present value of the cost to purchase the investment. This calculation can be fairly complex, so investors often calculate a quick approximation. The most common approximation is known as the *approximate yield*, and it is found by using the following formula:

$$\text{Before-tax approximate yield} = \frac{\text{annual income} + \dfrac{\text{future price} - \text{current price}}{\text{number of years}}}{\dfrac{\text{future price} + \text{current price}}{2}}$$

For example, assume that an investor is interested in buying a particular stock that is currently selling for $50 a share but is expected to increase in value to $68 a share by the end of 3 years. The annual dividends from the stock are expected to average $3 for each of the next 3 years. Based on this information, the investor's approximate yield for the 3-year holding period would be

$$\text{Before-tax approximate yield} = \frac{\$3 + \frac{\$68 - \$50}{3}}{\frac{\$68 + \$50}{2}}$$

$$= \frac{\$3 + \$6}{\$59} = \frac{\$9}{\$59}$$

$$= .1525 \quad \text{or} \quad 15.25\%$$

The approximate-yield method can provide a meaningful estimate of an investment's yield over both short and long holding periods. Applications of this method include (1) estimating the yield over a planned holding period, as shown in the previous example, (2) determining the yield from the date of acquisition to the present on a currently owned investment, and (3) determining what the yield was for an investment that has been sold. Only the purpose of the calculation changes; the formula remains unchanged.

Whenever the rate of inflation exceeds the after-tax rate of return obtained over a holding period, an investor will realize a negative real after-tax rate of return. This was the situation for many investors during the late 1970s and early 1980s when inflation rates in the United States exceeded 10 percent and the before-tax return on some investments was 5 percent.

Historical Before-Tax Returns

At this point, the question might arise as to what size returns can be expected from different investments. This depends on the time frame used in the analysis and the particular events occurring during the time frame. One might, for example, examine the returns of different types of assets in the 1970s, 1980s, and the early 1990s and compare these returns to the consumer price index (CPI). The 1970s were a decade for tangibles, such as collectibles, commodities, and real estate. These assets had compound annual rates of growth ranging from 12 to 35 percent and outperformed both the CPI and financial assets such as stocks, bonds, and Treasury bills. However, the 1980s tell a different story, as shown in the table below. During that decade, stocks, bonds, and Treasury bills outperformed the CPI and tangibles. The first few years of the 1990s were turbulent. Foreign stocks (due to the sluggish domestic economy) and domestic bonds (due to falling interest rates) were the best performers. Nonetheless, most financial assets experienced returns in excess of the inflation rate. The late 1990s saw one of the greatest stock market booms in U.S. history, with the highest rates of return associated with companies involved with the internet. Early in 2000, stock prices started to fall, and they continued to fall throughout most of 2002. However, in 2003, stock prices recovered some lost ground.

In 2008, stock prices began to fall again as a result of the "Great Recession" from December 2007 through June 2009. The impact of what many observers consider the worst economic turmoil since the Great Depression caused many investors to move out of equities and into "safe havens" such as bonds and cash. However, while the S & P 500 Index lost 37 percent in 2008, it rebounded to a gain of over 26 percent in 2009, 15 percent in 2010, about 2 percent in 2011. As we revise this text in early 2012, the U.S. economy appears to be in a slow recovery, and many investors are still cautious about returning to the markets. As the table below shows, even with the tumultuous market gyrations over the last 30 years, stocks as a group have slightly out-performed bonds. While past performance is no guarantee of future performance, it appears that a judicious mix of stock and bond investments will remain a prudent way of overcoming the combined "threats" of taxes and inflation for most investors.

Table 4-1 Average Annual Pretax Return (Geometric Mean) Over 30 Years, 1981–2010	
U.S. Large-Cap Stocks *(S & P 500 Index)*	10.7%
U.S. Small-Cap stocks *(Russell 2000 Index)*	10.0%
International Stocks *(MSCI EAFE Index)*	9.7%
Municipal Bonds *(Barclays Muni Index)*	7.7%
Long-Term Government Bonds *(20-Year Treasuries)*	10.2%
Intermediate Government Bonds *(5-Year Treasuries)*	8.5%
U.S. Corporate Bonds *(Barclays U.S. Corporate Index)*	9.5%
Real Estate/Single Family *(Winans Int'l Real Estate Index)*	4.0%
T-Bills	5.1%
Inflation *(Consumer Price Index (CPI))*	3.2%
Used with permission. Ibbotson SBBI Classic Yearbook © 2011. All rights reserved.	

The table displays several asset categories and includes those assets most likely to be part of an investor's portfolio. The returns include both current income (dividends or interest) and capital appreciation when appropriate. For the various categories, the data shown represent before-tax returns. In general, the longer the time to maturity for debt instruments, the larger their returns will be. When risk rises, such as with corporate debt rather than U.S. Treasuries, before-tax returns also rise. However, common stock investments provide the highest returns over long holding periods.

INVESTMENT PRINCIPLES, STRATEGIES, AND TECHNIQUES

Now that the types of investments frequently used and various investment risks have been examined, this section will describe some of the investment principles, strategies, and techniques recommended by financial advisors and used by successful investors. Not all are appropriate in all situations, but collectively, they provide you with some guidelines that you can follow when advising clients.

Meeting Emergency and Protection Needs First

No investments should be undertaken unless the investor has first set aside some funds for emergency purposes. Obviously, a large portion of the investor's emergency funds could be placed in investments that provide a current return. However, the choices for these investments are limited to cash equivalents, such as bank savings accounts or MMDAs. These types of investments are highly liquid as required for emergency situations, but typically they do not provide much in the way of a return.

Besides preparing for possible emergency situations, an investor should also take steps prior to undertaking an investment program to protect himself from the various pure risks (categorized as personal risks, property risks, and liability risks). Insurance is the primary technique, and for many people the only appropriate technique, for dealing with the pure risks that people face in their everyday lives.

Matching Investment Instruments with Investment Goals

All investments must be appropriate for the personal financial goals being sought. For example, individual retirement accounts (IRAs) accumulate interest on a tax-free basis until the monies are withdrawn. Therefore, using tax-free municipal bonds as an IRA funding instrument is not prudent, since the IRA already provides tax deferral regardless of the type of funding instrument used. A better approach is to fund the IRA with investments that provide a higher rate of return commensurate with the client's financial risk tolerance and retirement goals.

When funds are being accumulated for purposes that are not deferrable, it is essential to have the precise amount available at the needed time. For example, investments whose market price fluctuates sharply or investments that are not readily marketable would not be appropriate for funding a child's expected education expenses. For this type of goal, the proper approach would match the investment's maturity with the date the funds are needed.

A young client who is funding for retirement should not use short-term investments, because these usually do not provide very high returns and offer little opportunity for appreciation over the planning horizon. Instead, investments that have long-term capital growth as their objective are more likely to offset the probable inflation over the next 10, 20, or 30 years.

Holding Periods for Equity Investments

Investments in common stocks that are owned individually or through investment companies should generally have a *planned holding period* of at least 5 years. Any period shorter than 5 years subjects the stocks to increased risk. The problem of market timing, or when to buy or sell the asset, and transactions costs for the purchase and sale combine to limit success with shorter-term holding periods.

In addition, the behavior of the stock market favors at least a 5-year holding period. Combined with the dividends earned on a portfolio of common stocks, the fluctuations of the market typically are such that only a relatively few 5-year holding periods fail to provide positive returns. However, many shorter holding periods, such as one year or less, have produced negative total returns.

Other equity investments, such as real estate, require even longer planned holding periods due to their relatively higher transactions costs and general lack of marketability. Indeed, for some limited partnerships that invest in real estate, financial advisors often advocate at least a 10-year planned holding period.

Tax-Saving Rationale

Investment analysis and decision making should focus on the underlying economic facts. Sometimes financial advisors who recommend investments focus too much on tax benefits for the client rather than on the economic soundness of the investment. Frequent tax legislation over the past three decades shows that government can drastically change the tax rules. Many investments made solely on the basis of tax considerations have generated problems and losses for their owners. Certainly, tax considerations influence investment decisions, and their effect must be analyzed. However, tax considerations are only one of many factors that determine the economic soundness of an investment.

Understanding the Investment

Selecting and managing some types of investments require little or no knowledge, facilities, or time commitment. For instance, an investor need not be an expert on short-term debt securities to understand the relevant characteristics (risk, expected return, liquidity, marketability, and tax treatment) of U.S. Treasury bills and similar securities. However, individuals who invest in real estate, collectibles, or commodities need special knowledge, talent, and tools. Similarly, some types of investments may be maintained with little or no effort (bonds), whereas others require constant management (an apartment complex). Accordingly, financial advisors and investors should carefully consider the expertise, talent, facilities, and time required to assemble and manage a particular type of investment portfolio. You should never recommend an investment unless both you and the client fully understand it. Following this simple rule would prevent many unpleasant situations for advisors and clients!

Using a Consistent Pattern of Investing

dollar-cost averaging

Attempts to outguess the market or to predict the start of the next downturn or upturn have proved fruitless over the decades. Trying to achieve superior returns through market timing for every investment is never worth the effort. To avoid trying to time the market, an investor can engage in *dollar-cost averaging*. This method requires the investment of a fixed amount of dollars at specified time intervals. Investing a fixed amount of dollars at set intervals means that the investor buys more shares when prices are low and fewer shares when prices are high. Unless the market goes into a persistent decline, dollar cost averaging will accomplish its objective, and it establishes a consistent pattern of investing. It works best when the stock has an early decline (shares are cheaper) and a later rise. Over normal market cycles, the overall cost of investing using dollar cost averaging is lower than it would be if a constant number of shares were bought at set intervals.

Many people have no other option but to engage in dollar-cost averaging; often, they are not aware they are doing so. For example, employees who contribute a certain dollar amount of their paycheck each month to their 401(k) plan are engaged in dollar-cost averaging. Employees may just think of it as a long-term savings program—and it is—but they are also using a dollar-cost averaging strategy.

The Power of Compounding

compound interest

Compound interest, or interest earned on interest, is a powerful force in accumulating funds for the future. The importance of this concept should be stressed in a client's investment program. Many investments provide easy reinvestment of current income that provides the benefit of compounding. Some of the more frequently encountered examples are:

- passbook savings accounts—The interest is automatically added to the account, and the investor must take specific action by withdrawing the interest to prevent compounding from occurring.
- certificates of deposit—Most CDs do not distribute interest during the life of the instrument. Rather, the interest is automatically reinvested, normally at the same rate being earned on the principal amount invested in the CD.
- mutual funds—Most mutual funds allow for the automatic purchase of additional shares with current income or capital gains credited to a shareholder's account.
- common stocks—Many large corporations permit the investor to reinvest dividends in additional shares of that corporation's common stock. Often, no brokerage charges are levied, and in a few cases the corporation subsidizes the purchase by providing up to a 5 percent discount from the average market price of its stock over the past 3 months.
- zero coupon bonds—Bonds that do not make an annual interest payment to the bondholder, such as U.S. government Series EE bonds and selected issues of corporate, government, and municipal bonds, have a built-in automatic compounding of interest over their life.

High-Pressure Sales Tactics

Many marketers possess persuasive sales skills, which sometimes leads to high-pressure selling. Unfortunately, marketers of investment products are no exception. Frequent tales of high-pressure, boiler-room, telephone solicitations receive widespread coverage in the news media. These are the most blatant examples. Although caution on your part as a financial advisor might lead to an occasional missed opportunity, that does not outweigh the benefits of careful investigation and sound recommendations. Your clients will appreciate you more and refer you to others frequently.

> **FOCUS ON ETHICS**
> **Understanding Investment Risk**
>
> In the 1980s, many headlines were written concerning junk bonds. Both the yields and the name of these securities implied high risk. Many families suffered financial loss directly or indirectly through investments in securities bearing a level of risk well above what their portfolios warranted.
>
> In the early 1990s, the same thing happened with derivatives, hybrid securities that few really understand. Although derivatives have valid uses in hedging and speculation, their high level of risk makes them a poor choice for all but the most sophisticated investors.
>
> In 2007–2009, the entire U.S. economy was damaged by risky investments in sub-prime mortgages. These mortgages had been "bundled" and sold with AAA ratings by several ratings agencies, and yet they failed when homeowners began to default on mortgages they could not afford. Once again, the old adage "if it looks too good to be true, it probably is not true" was demonstrated.
>
> It is the financial advisor's responsibility to comprehend and effectively communicate the risk associated with alternative investments. To do otherwise is an ethical, professional, and potentially legal error that can lead to disastrous results.

Avoiding Discretionary Power

Many clients prefer to have others perform the necessary work of managing their portfolios and grant broad managerial powers to accomplish this end. Although this indicates great trust in the judgment of the advisor receiving this power, conflict is likely to develop. Portfolio performance that does not meet a client's expectations, such as a sharp decline in market prices that generates portfolio losses, can precipitate this conflict. As we write this in early 2012, client complaints against advisors are up sharply from previous years leading to record numbers of arbitration cases under the Financial Industry Regulatory Authority (FINRA). To avoid this problem, you may want to obtain prior approval from the client before any action is taken. In fact, many broker/dealers will not allow their representatives to exercise discretionary authority for clients.

Applying Control through the Financial Planning Process

Investment planning typically is focused on selecting investments to help a client achieve the financial goals set forth in his financial plan. However, before selecting any investments, you should construct a recommended investment portfolio or asset allocation model tailored to the client's level of risk tolerance and capacity to handle risk. This asset allocation model outlines the client's investment strategy within the context of his overall financial plan. The asset allocation model should emphasize the different categories of assets and the percentages to be placed in each category. Once the client has an asset allocation model tailored to his unique circumstances, the next step is to actually select investments that match the parameters of the model.

The client's asset allocation model in conjunction with his financial goals determine the performance standards (typically "benchmarks" such as the total return of the S&P 500 stock index) by which selected investments are evaluated. Evaluating the performance of the individual investments in the client's portfolio provides the data to compare their performance with the standards. If an investment is not meeting the standards consistently over meaningful periods, then it should be replaced with one that will. Of course, this entire process of monitoring the performance of the client's portfolio is just another aspect of the financial planning process.

INVESTMENT MARKETS AND REGULATION

Many types of markets exist for investments. This section will first describe major types of markets where investments trading occurs on a regular basis. These markets are (1) true-auction markets, (2) negotiated markets, (3) dealer markets, and (4) organized-securities markets. Following this material, we will cover the purpose and thrust of the major federal laws and regulations affecting investments.

Investment Markets

True-Auction Markets

In true-auction markets, investment assets such as artwork, collectibles, or real estate are offered for sale to the highest bidder. The bidding continues until no one exceeds the last bid price. When this occurs, the sale is consummated. Since the advent of telecommunications, potential buyers need not physically attend these trading sessions. Normally, only a small number of potential buyers participate in true-auction markets for several reasons. First, buyers might not be aware that such an auction is being held. Second, buyers often prefer first-hand evaluation of the asset, and the cost of attending these auctions can be high. Third, for some of these assets (such as a particular artist's works), only a relatively few potential purchasers exist either regionally, nationally, or internationally. Finally, the high unit price of some of these investments dictates that only a handful of bidders will have the financial resources.

A variant of this form of auction market is used by the Treasury Department to sell T-bills. To buy T-bills at more than 150 auctions held throughout the year, investors must place bids. Bids may be entered on either a competitive or a noncompetitive basis. The Treasury accepts all noncompetitive bids, and buyers who enter these bids agree to pay the average price of the competitive bids that are accepted. Buyers entering competitive bids state a price they are willing to pay and the Treasury accepts these bids, taking the highest prices (which equate to the lowest yields) first until the issue is sold out. However, the price that all buyers who have accepted competitive bids actually pay is the same as the price that noncompetitive buyers pay. In other words, once the lowest price that the Treasury is willing to accept is determined, then all buyers (both competitive and noncompetitive) pay that same price.

Negotiated Markets

Negotiated markets predominate for the trading of real estate and similar investment assets. In these markets, sellers list their offerings with brokers who seek to attract buyers through advertising and other marketing methods. After a buyer has been located, negotiations determine the price.

Large institutional investors such as pension funds and mutual funds often employ brokers to locate buyers or sellers of large blocks of bonds or stocks. When these transactions involve listed securities (see subsequent treatment of organized-securities market), this negotiated market is called the *fourth market* because the transaction does not take place on the floor of an organized exchange. This market is similar to the true-auction market in the lack of general awareness that the asset is available for purchase and sale. Also, as in auction markets, there is often a need for physical examination of the asset, especially real estate. In addition, the high unit cost that restricts the number of participants in auction markets may have the same effect in negotiated markets.

Dealer Markets

over-the-counter (OTC) market

For many securities, one or more dealers make an active market by offering to buy (at a bid price) and sell (at an ask price) as much of a particular security as desired by investors. The difference between the bid and ask price is the dealer's *spread,* or compensation, for making the market and bearing the risk of holding an inventory of the security. The dealer makes the market. When demand for the security rises, the dealer raises the bid and ask prices; when demand falls, the dealer lowers these prices. Similar adjustments are made for changes in supply.

The *over-the-counter (OTC) market* is a network of securities dealers and includes over 30,000 different securities issues. Dealers profit from the bid-ask spread as described above. A numerical majority, but not the dollar-value majority, of all stocks are traded on this market. In addition to the stocks of operating corporations, this market also includes shares of some closed-end investment companies and most government and corporate bonds. In fact, the OTC market remains the primary market for bond trading. Commercial paper, large CDs (jumbos), municipal bonds, and other money market instruments trade in similar OTC markets.

Organized Securities Markets

Formal trading locations and markets exist for securities listed on one or more of the national or regional exchanges. The most dominant institution is the New York Stock Exchange, which lists the securities of approximately 2,800 firms and actively maintains trading in these corporations' common and preferred stocks and their bonds. Each security is assigned a trading post on the floor of the exchange where commission brokers, employed by the various stock-brokerage firms, meet to engage in auction trading for the buy and sell orders transmitted to them. Each listed security is assigned to a specialist who makes a continuous, fair, and orderly market for the issue.

All exchanges have membership requirements for individuals trading on the floor of the exchange. Also exchanges maintain listing requirements that must be met by a corporation before any trading of its securities can take place on the exchange. The New York Stock Exchange has the most stringent requirements, including a national rather than local interest in the security, a minimum number of shareholders and publicly traded shares, and a minimum dollar amount of profits, assets, and market value of the corporation's common stock.

Regulation of the Markets

Both state and federal regulations govern trading terms, conditions, and practices in all four markets. Federal laws dominate the organized securities and dealer markets, whereas state laws are of greater importance in the true-auction and negotiated markets. The focus of this discussion centers on the most important federal laws and briefly describes their main purpose.

Securities Act of 1933

The Securities Act of 1933 requires issuers of new securities to file a registration statement with the Securities and Exchange Commission (SEC). The issuing corporation may not sell the security until the SEC verifies that the information contained in the registration statement is complete and is not false or misleading. Once approval is obtained, a prospectus is prepared that contains a summary of information from the registration statement. Then the securities can be sold to the public and a copy of the prospectus must be given to all interested buyers.

No attempt to evaluate the investment merits of the proposal is made by the SEC. Rather, the SEC merely seeks to verify that the statements are accurate.

Securities Exchange Act of 1934

Securities Exchange Act of 1934

As the name implies, the emphasis of the *Securities Exchange Act of 1934* is to regulate the various securities markets. Its scope includes the organized securities exchanges, the over-the-counter markets, all stockbrokers and dealers, and the securities traded in these markets. In addition to requiring registration with the SEC, this act requires these institutions, individuals, and issuing corporations to file periodic updated data with the SEC.

Further, this regulation extends to many market practices that the SEC believes are detrimental or misleading. When this occurs, the SEC develops and promulgates, after public hearings and comments, rules and procedures that must be followed. Examples of such include methods of comparing different mutual funds' performance, advertising of returns earned on funds, and trading practices of dealers who purchase for their own account.

The Investment Advisors Act of 1940

Investment Advisors Act of 1940

The *Investment Advisors Act of 1940*, as amended by the Investment Supervision Coordination Act of 1996, requires that investment advisors register with either the SEC or state regulatory authorities, depending on the amount of assets under the advisor's management. Registration does not guarantee the competence or trustworthiness of any advisor; rather, it provides a modest protection from fraudulent or unethical practices by requiring the advisor provide full disclosure to clients. Critics point out that perhaps the most infamous investment fraud of this century surrounded Bernie Madoff, a registered investment advisor who defrauded clients of tens of billions of dollars over a long period. Madoff is now serving a life sentence in prison.

Investment Company Act of 1940

Investment Company Act of 1940

The *Investment Company Act of 1940* established rules and regulations that apply to all investment companies with respect to their dealings with their shareholders. This act requires investment companies (1) to provide adequate disclosure to shareholders and (2) to refrain from charging excessive advisory, management, or brokerage fees. Significant amendments to this act, which were passed in the 1970s, regulate fees associated with contractual purchase plans entered into by individual investors.

Securities Investor Protection Act of 1970

Securities Investor Protection Corporation (SIPC)

As part of the *Securities Investor Protection Act of 1970*, Congress set up the *Securities Investor Protection Corporation (SIPC)*. It is patterned after the Federal Deposit Insurance Corporation (FDIC), with the objective of protecting investors' property. SIPC protection is for when a clearing firm (which holds customers' cash and sends out statements) becomes insolvent. SIPC coverage also includes protection against unauthorized trading in a customer's account. Customers are insured by the SIPC for up to $500,000, not more than $100,000 of which may be in cash left on deposit incidental to transactions. Cash in a brokerage account simply to earn interest is not covered by the SIPC. The SIPC is a nonprofit, nongovernmental, membership corporation funded by member broker/dealers, although it can borrow from the SEC if its own funds are inadequate to meet its obligations.

A FINAL WORD

This chapter has provided a basic overview of the investment planning process. The process always starts with understanding the investment needs of the client and his financial risk tolerance and risk capacity. The overall riskiness of the portfolio should never exceed the client's risk tolerance or risk capacity. It is more important that the financial advisor identify the appropriate asset allocation for the client than that the advisor pick a few "hot tips." Making the appropriate asset allocation recommendations requires a detailed understanding of the various assets available.

The financial advisor then has to worry about such issues as purchasing power risk, interest rate risk, business risk, liquidity, marketability, taxation, and diversification. The advisor has a complicated job and one that requires continual learning to stay current, relevant, and helpful to one's clients.

CHAPTER REVIEW

Key Terms and Concepts are explained in the Glossary. Answers to the Review Questions are found in the back of the book in the Answers to Questions section.

Key Terms and Concepts

investment assets
speculative risk
expected return
opportunity loss
investment risk
asset allocation model
asset allocation
cash equivalent
certificate of deposit (CD)
U.S. Treasury bills (T-bills)
risk-free investment
agency bonds
indenture
junk bonds
closed-end investment company
net asset value (NAV)
open-end investment company
mutual fund
no-load fund
prospectus
real estate investment trust (REIT)

inflation risk
real rate of return
interest rate risk
business (default) risk
liquidity
qualified dividends
capital assets
diversification
capital appreciation
current yield
holding-period return (HPR)
approximate yield
dollar-cost averaging
compound interest
over-the-counter (OTC) market
Securities Exchange Act of 1934
Investment Advisors Act of 1940
Investment Company Act of 1940
Securities Investor Protection Corporation (SIPC)

Review Questions

1. Describe the two types of assets that consumers buy. [1]
2. Explain the difference between investing and speculating. [1]
3. Explain what is meant by investment risk. [2]
4. What are the two most basic theorems of investment? [2]
5. Explain what is meant by asset allocation models. [3]
6. What two privileges do preferred stockholders usually have that provide them with a preferential position relative to common stockholders? [4]
7. Explain what is meant by price risk. [4]
8. Explain the difference between liquidity and marketability. [5]

9. Jack owns some tax-exempt municipal bonds that provide him with a 3 percent current yield. If Jack is in the 33 percent marginal income tax bracket, what is his equivalent fully taxable yield? [6]

10. Joe purchased some stock one year ago for $50 per share. The stock just paid an annual dividend of $4 per share and is now selling for $60 per share. Joe is in the 28 percent marginal income tax bracket. On the basis of this information, calculate Joe's after-tax holding-period return. [6]

11. Sally is investing in commercial real estate that costs $100,000. She expects that it will generate $5,000 of annual rental income and that in 5 years it will be worth $200,000. Sally is in the 28 percent marginal income tax bracket. What would Sally's after-tax approximate yield be from this investment for the 5-year holding period? [6]

12. What two things should an investor do prior to beginning an investment program? [7]

13. Explain how dollar-cost averaging establishes a consistent pattern of investing. [7]

14. Describe the principal characteristics of each of the following types of securities markets: (a.) negotiated markets and (b.) dealer markets. [8]

15. What is the primary purpose of each of the following federal statutes? (a.) Securities Act of 1933 (b.) The Investment Advisors Act of 1940 [8]

INCOME TAX PLANNING — 5

Learning Objectives

An understanding of the material in this chapter should enable the student to

1. Explain the purpose of income tax planning, and describe the concept of gross income.
2. Explain the difference between exclusions and deductions, and distinguish above-the-line deductions from below-the-line deductions.
3. Distinguish the standard deduction from itemized deductions, and explain how the depreciation deduction differs from most other deductions.
4. Describe the structure of federal income tax rates.
5. Explain why a tax credit is more valuable than a tax deduction of an equal amount.
6. Describe the nature and purpose of the alternative minimum tax (AMT).
7. Explain the concept of the taxable year, and describe the two most popular tax accounting methods.
8. Describe the doctrines of economic benefit, fruit and tree, and constructive receipt.
9. Explain the use of some basic income tax planning techniques.
10. Identify several different types of taxable entities.

THE PURPOSE OF INCOME TAX PLANNING

It is said that the only things certain in life are death and taxes. Although death seems more certain than anything, it is likely that even Houdini would have had trouble defying Uncle Sam's tax collection. At the least, it would take a highly accomplished escape artist to evade both the federal income tax and a jail cell.

In any event, such extremes are not advisable for a variety of legal, ethical, and moral reasons. Yet, it is perfectly acceptable (and some would say commendable) to use every legal means to minimize and/or avoid the payment of federal income taxes.

This chapter outlines the most important basic concepts of our federal income tax law. It will not deal with advanced tax planning. It will provide, however, a firm grasp of fundamental concepts—always an excellent foundation to build upon. More advanced texts present planning techniques available to avoid paying taxes. Some tax-avoidance techniques (many call them loopholes) must be left to the experienced tax professional to recommend and implement.

Even though several planning techniques can help minimize and/or avoid paying taxes, tax relief may not be the only goal of income tax planning. The best tax plan is one that accurately reflects the client's overall financial goals. This requires that various tax strategies be explained to the client so that she can understand their limitations and benefits. With this knowledge and the recommendations of the financial advisor, the client can choose tax strategies that best fit her multiple-purpose or comprehensive financial plan. A tax plan that focuses on *tax minimization* and/or *tax avoidance* is a poor plan if it is inconsistent with the client's other financial goals. Nevertheless, almost all clients want to minimize and/or avoid paying taxes.

A working knowledge of tax law enables you to help clients, as well as to know when to seek assistance from a tax expert. Therefore, this chapter explains basic income tax concepts and introduces ways you can help a client plan for tax minimization and/or tax avoidance within the context of the client's overall financial plan.

THE PRINCIPLE OF GROSS INCOME

gross income

For you to learn about the federal income tax law, we begin with an understanding of the term *gross income*. Basically, gross income includes every item of value, including money or other property, that is either made available to, or comes into the possession of, the taxpayer. In other words, every item of value is included in gross income for income tax purposes unless—and this qualification is very important—the Internal

Revenue Code contains a specific provision that excludes the item from the taxpayer's gross income.

This explains why the provision in the Internal Revenue Code that provides the gross income rule is referred to as a "shotgun" clause. Although the provision lists 15 different items that are includible in a taxpayer's gross income, the provision states that gross income includes, but is not limited to, these items. Gross income means "all income from whatever source derived."

 However, certain items of money or other property are not includible in a taxpayer's gross income. These items include gifts, income from tax-exempt bonds, workers' compensation benefits, and many other items. Such items are called exclusions from gross income. The reason such items are excluded from a taxpayer's gross income is that a specific section in the Internal Revenue Code says so. In other words, no item of money or other property can be excluded from gross income unless there is a code provision stating that it is to be excluded. Therefore, in most cases it is fairly simple to determine whether an item is includible in the taxpayer's gross income.

exclusion

deduction

We must distinguish the concept of an *exclusion* from that of a *deduction* for tax purposes. An exclusion is an item of value that the taxpayer receives that is not includible in the taxpayer's gross income. A deduction, on the other hand, is an expense (not an item of receipt) that reduces the amount of income subject to tax.

EXAMPLE
Melissa has the following items of income and expense for the current year: a $35,000 salary from her job as a paralegal, a $5,000 gift from her aunt, and an alimony payment of $3,000 she made to her former husband. The $35,000 salary is includible in Melissa's gross income. The $5,000 gift is not includible in her gross income because there is a provision in the Internal Revenue Code stating that gifts are not includible in the recipient's gross income. The $3,000 alimony payment is deductible from Melissa's gross income in determining how much of Melissa's income will actually be taxed, because the Internal Revenue Code states that alimony payments are generally deductible by the payer.

EXCLUSIONS FROM GROSS INCOME

The Internal Revenue Code states that many items are excludible from a taxpayer's gross income. Among these items are:

- gifts and inheritances

- income from certain bonds issued by states and municipalities (so-called "muni" bonds)
- workers' compensation benefits
- life insurance proceeds
- benefits paid from medical expense insurance policies
- social security benefits (for taxpayers below certain income levels)
- amounts received under certain dependent-care-assistance programs and educational assistance programs
- certain qualified scholarships

The detailed rules that determine how and to what extent these items are excludible from gross income are beyond the scope of this text. Simply note that it is important for you to understand the concept of an exclusion, and know how exclusions are used in the overall process of computing an individual's tax liability. An item that is excludible generally does not have to be reported at all on the taxpayer's return.

DEDUCTIONS

As we stated earlier, a deduction is an item of expense that reduces the amount of the taxpayer's income subject to tax. Many different items are deductible for federal income tax purposes. However, before we discuss some of these items, you must understand the concepts of *adjusted gross income (AGI)* and *taxable income*.

Adjusted Gross Income = gross income − deductions

adjusted gross income

Adjusted gross income (AGI) is an intermediate calculation made in the process of determining an individual's income tax liability for a given year. Adjusted gross income is defined as your gross income from taxable sources minus allowable deductions, such as unreimbursed medical expenses, alimony, and deductible retirement plan contributions.

Although the calculation of AGI is an intermediate step, it is an important one. Two of the most significant reasons are as follows:

1. Above-the-line deductions allowable in determining AGI are available regardless of whether the taxpayer claims "itemized" deductions. As explained below, the taxpayer claims itemized or "below-the-line" deductions only if the total of such deductions

exceeds the available standard deduction. For this reason, above-the-line deductions are often more valuable to the taxpayer.

2. Many tax benefits are currently reduced if the taxpayer's AGI exceeds certain amounts. Certain other deductions are available only to the extent that the amount of such deductions exceeds a specified percentage of AGI (a deduction "floor"). For example, unreimbursed medical expenses that exceed 7.5 percent of AGI are deductible for taxpayers who itemize deductions. Also, the deduction for charitable contributions is allowed only to the extent that contributions do not exceed a specified percentage of AGI (a deduction "ceiling", generally 50 percent of AGI).

Taxable Income

taxable income

Taxable income is the amount of income actually subject to tax in a given year. How does taxable income differ from adjusted gross income? Taxable income is the taxpayer's AGI, reduced by certain deductions applied only after the individual's AGI has been computed. In other words, in the computation of an individual's tax liability, there are two basic types of deductions. The first type consists of those deductions subtracted from gross income to determine AGI. The second type consists of those deductions that are subtracted from AGI to determine taxable income. The first type are *above-the-line deductions,* while the second type are *below-the-line deductions.*

standard deduction

There are two basic reasons why the distinction is important. The first is that above-the-line deductions will change how certain other items on the taxpayer's return are treated. This is true since, as previously stated, AGI is used as a base for defining or limiting to what extent certain other items may be excluded or deducted on the individual's return. The second reason relates to the concept of the *standard deduction*.

> **FOCUS ON ETHICS**
>
> **The Ethics of "Playing the Odds"**
>
> Every year at tax time the media highlights the probability that certain categories of taxpayers will be audited. Usually the likelihood is quite low, and this can cause some clients to suggest "liberally interpreting" the tax law for their own financial gain. Among the myriad of possible approaches are deducting personal travel expenses by suggesting that they were business related, showing phony charitable donations, and failing to report cash income.
>
> Financial advisors have a responsibility to assist clients in legally minimizing their taxes, and tax counseling can be one of the most significant contributions a financial advisor can make. However, advisors must never participate in or condone fraudulent behavior. Regardless of the odds, an improper action could be disastrous to the client financially and legally, not to mention the impact on reputation. The same is true for the financial advisor.

The Standard Deduction or Itemized Deductions

itemized deductions

The standard deduction is a fixed amount that the individual may claim in lieu of claiming *itemized deductions* on Schedule A of Form 1040. Itemized deductions, or deductions listed on Schedule A, include medical and dental expenses, certain taxes, certain interest payments, charitable contributions, casualty and theft losses, and miscellaneous itemized deductions. The amount of the standard deduction depends on the tax status on which the individual is filing the return—that is, as a single taxpayer, an unmarried head of household, a married taxpayer filing jointly, or a married taxpayer filing separately.

If the individual has itemized deductions that total more than the amount of his standard deduction, then he will deduct his itemized deductions and not claim the standard deduction. The standard deduction amounts are indexed annually for inflation.

> **EXAMPLE**
>
> Arthur is a taxpayer who files a single tax return. For the 2011 tax year, Arthur's standard deduction was $5,800. For 2011, he had deductible expenses as follows: (1) charitable contributions equal to $1,000; (2) mortgage interest paid equal to $5,000; and (3) deductible taxes paid equal to $2,000. Since his total deductions equal $8,000 and exceed his standard deduction of $5,800, Arthur should itemize his deductions on his 2011 tax return.

All itemized deductions are below-the-line deductions (deductions taken in calculating taxable income). However, if these items were above-the-line deductions (deductions taken in determining adjusted gross income rather than taxable income), taxpayers could deduct these items regardless of whether they claim the standard deduction based on their taxpayer status. In such a case, the standard deduction can be taken in addition to other above-the-line deductions (such as contributions to some retirement plans). This is the second important difference between above-the-line and below-the-line deductions. The first type are deductible regardless of whether the individual claims the standard deduction. The second type may be claimed only in lieu of the standard deduction.

Categories of Deductions

Before we discuss the various types of deductions allowable under federal tax law, remember that a deduction may be claimed only if there is a specific provision in the Internal Revenue Code that allows it. If there is no provision in the Code regarding a given item, no deduction may be claimed for it.

Stated broadly, there are three basic categories of deductions allowable to individual taxpayers. The first category includes deductions for expenses incurred in the course of carrying on a trade or business. For example, the cost of employees' salaries or advertising would fall into this category. These are referred to as business deductions. The second basic category includes deductions for expenses incurred in the course of an activity that is not a trade or business, but is intended to produce income and make a profit. An example of a deduction in this category is an expense incurred for the maintenance of a taxpayer's investments, such as a fee for investment advice. The third basic category includes deductions for some expenses that are simply personal, family, or living expenses. While as a general rule these expenses are nondeductible, there are several important exceptions. Personal expenses deductible within limitations include charitable contributions, medical expenses, interest payments for home mortgages, and education loans. However, many of these personal deductions are subject to limitations on what and how much can be deducted.

When a client or advisor considers whether a given item of expense is deductible, certain questions should always be asked. Obviously, the first question is: Does the Code allows a deduction for the item? A second important question asks: What basic category does the expense falls under? In other words, is the item a *business expense,* an *expense for the production* of income, or a *personal expense?* A third question concerns whether the deduction is an above-the-line or below-the-line deduction. For tax planning purposes, you must know where an item will appear on the taxpayer's tax return.

If the deduction is allowed, you should determine next whether there is a particular restriction or limitation on the deductibility of the item. For example, certain deductions such as the medical expense deduction and the casualty loss deduction are subject to a floor. This floor is based on a percentage of the taxpayer's adjusted gross income (AGI). If the taxpayer's expenses in a given category are less than the applicable floor, no deduction will actually be allowed for the expenses.

EXAMPLE

Emily has medical expenses of $5,000 this year. Medical expenses are deductible, but only to the extent they exceed 7.5 percent of the taxpayer's adjusted gross income. Emily's adjusted gross income this year is $70,000. Although Emily has $5,000 of medical expenses, her deduction for these expenses is zero because the amount of the expenses ($5,000) is less than 7.5 percent of her adjusted gross income ($5,250).

Another type of restriction that may apply to a deduction is a dollar-amount restriction. Note that in the case of the deduction for home mortgage interest, the dollar amount limitation is based on the amount of the loan principal, not the amount of the interest expense itself. One example of a dollar-amount limitation is the limitation on deductible contributions to a traditional individual retirement account (IRA) for individuals who are covered by employer-provided retirement plans such as 401(k) or 403(b) plans.

Yet another type of restriction on the deductibility of certain expenses is a percentage limitation. For example, business entertainment expenses are generally deductible, but the deduction is limited to 50 percent of the actual expenses. There are many other ways in which the Internal Revenue Code limits the claiming of deductions.

Depreciation: A Special Type of Deduction

depreciation deductions

Not all tax deductions represent actual out-of-pocket expenses. Some deductions are allowable even though they represent no corresponding cash outlay. These are often referred to as *paper deductions*, because they are related to some entry on the books of a taxpayer's business or investment activity, but they are not a cash-flow item. They are also referred to as *cost recovery deductions,* which is a very descriptive term that aids in understanding them. The concept of cost recovery in the tax code allows taxpayers who invest capital in business and income-producing property to recoup their investment over time through deductions for the cost of the capital investment. This is important because it reflects the intent of Congress (through the tax laws) to encourage capital investment through favorable tax treatments.

What is the nature of these items? Why are they allowable as deductions against a taxpayer's income? These items represent a portion of a gradual decrease in the value or usefulness of property owned by the taxpayer. But they are only an arbitrary measure of such a decrease in value or usefulness. They are not a real-life measure of such a decrease.

The most important noncash deduction is the deduction for depreciation. The *depreciation deduction* allows a taxpayer to recover the cost of certain property by allowing the taxpayer to deduct a specified portion of the cost of the property each year against the taxpayer's income. We say that the taxpayer's cost of investment is "recovered" for tax purposes over a specified number of years that represent the "useful life" of the property. A simple example will illustrate the concept of depreciation.

EXAMPLE
Assume that Diane places property in service in January 2012 under the straight-line method of depreciation with a 25-year recovery period. Assume there is no special convention in determining the depreciation in the property for the first year the property is placed into service. The basis of the property is $100,000. Diane can claim $4,000 per year ($100,000 ÷ 25) in depreciation deductions for the property over the next 25 years.

Generally capital expenditures, such as the purchase of a building or piece of equipment, are not deductible in full for income tax purposes in the year the asset is acquired. The reason is that a capital expenditure is not considered to be an operating expense of a business, but a more long-term investment in the asset. As an investment, the capital expenditure would normally be recovered for tax purposes only when the asset is sold. In other words, the amount of the capital expenditure becomes the taxpayer's tax basis in the asset. This basis is subtracted from the amount realized when the asset is sold to determine how much of the sale proceeds should be taxed as a "capital gain."

But the depreciation deduction allows the taxpayer to deduct portions of the capital expenditure before the asset is sold, that is, on an annual basis as in the example above. The reasoning is that the asset experiences wear and tear while it is being used by the taxpayer, and thus a deduction is allowed for such wear and tear. However, in reality, the asset might actually be appreciating in real economic terms in spite of the wear and tear on the asset. This can happen with many types of assets, but is particularly common with real estate. In such a situation, the taxpayer is receiving a tax deduction, supposed to represent a decrease in the property's value, while the property is actually increasing in value. In such a situation, the owner enjoys a "win-win" but it is all legal!

income tax basis Note that any depreciation deductions claimed for an asset are subtracted from the taxpayer's *income tax basis* in the asset. This means that when the asset is sold later, the amount of depreciation deducted is recouped (or "recovered") by the government because the taxable portion of the sales proceeds will be increased. But, in the meantime, the taxpayer has enjoyed the economic benefit of the tax deductions for depreciation. The concept of income tax basis will be discussed in more detail later. Note also that there are several accounting methods for depreciation, but that study is beyond the scope of this text.

Depreciation is a deduction that often does not represent economic reality, such as when the property appreciates while it is in use. Thus, there is an element of social policy behind depreciation rules in the tax law. That social policy is to stimulate investment in business assets and properties held for the production of income.

What types of assets are eligible for this cost recovery by using the depreciation deduction? There are two basic requirements. First, the asset must be used either in the taxpayer's business or in some other activity intended to produce income for the taxpayer (such as a rental property). Assets held strictly for personal use, such as one's personal residence, are not eligible for the deduction. Second, the asset must have a limited useful life in order to qualify. This requirement explains why land, for example, does not qualify for a depreciation deduction. Land is considered to be an asset that does not wear out with time.

Income Tax Planning

There are some fairly complicated rules that determine how much of a qualifying asset's cost can be claimed each year as a depreciation deduction. These rules are based on two factors: the number of years over which the cost of the asset will be deducted, and the percentage of the cost of the asset that can be deducted each year. The details are beyond the scope of this chapter. In summary, it is fair to say that depreciation deductions are extremely beneficial to taxpayers and allow them to save tax dollars without a corresponding cash outlay over the years the property is in use.

PERSONAL AND DEPENDENCY EXEMPTIONS

personal exemption

dependency exemption

Each individual taxpayer is allowed to claim a *personal exemption* for himself or herself. A married couple filing jointly may claim an exemption for each spouse. The amount of the exemptions is subtracted from adjusted gross income (AGI) in computing taxable income. Personal exemptions are not itemized deductions claimed on Schedule A of Form 1040, however. Therefore, either the standard deduction or itemized deductions may be claimed in addition to the taxpayer's personal exemptions. Individual taxpayers are also permitted to claim a *dependency exemption* for each dependent individual supported by the taxpayer. There are strict rules regarding whom a taxpayer may claim as a dependent and under what circumstances. The exemption amounts change as they are indexed annually for inflation.

EXAMPLE

John and Alyson are a married couple filing a joint tax return in 2012 with an adjusted gross income (AGI) equal to $80,000. They are also the parents of two young children, David and Maggie. For 2012, John and Alyson have $20,000 of itemized deductions which exceeds their standard deduction of $11,900. Both John and Alyson can claim their personal exemption of $3,800. And finally, John and Alyson can claim a dependent exemption of $3,800 for each of their two children. In total, John and Alyson can reduce their AGI by $35,200 ($3,800 X 4 + $20,000) giving them a taxable income of $44,800 (assuming no other credits or deductions).

A final word on deductions and exemptions. The phaseout (elimination) of income limits that reduced the available deductions and exemptions has been extended through 2012 as part of Congressional tax legislation. As we revise this text in early 2012, it is unclear whether the phaseouts will be

Child support payments NOT tax deductible to payer.

TAX RATES AND BRACKETS

We now turn our discussion to the concepts of tax rates and tax brackets, keys to understanding a taxpayer's complete tax situation. Once the taxpayer's gross income has been determined, all "above-the-line" deductions allowed are subtracted from gross income to determine adjusted gross income (AGI). Next, all deductions and exemptions allowed are subtracted from AGI to determine the taxpayer's taxable income. The taxpayer's taxable income is the figure to which the income tax rates are applied to determine the amount of income tax due for the year. As we shall see, that tax liability may be further reduced by any *tax credits* for which the taxpayer is eligible.

marginal tax rate

filing status

tax bracket

For taxpayers other than corporations, there are six sets of tax rates that differ according to the taxpayer's filing status and which change slightly from year to year. For individuals, each filing status or set of rates includes different amounts of taxable income subject to each of the six basic federal income tax rates under current law. The Tax Relief, Unemployment Insurance Reauthorization and Job Creation Act of 2010 extended through 2012 the system of tax rates that had been effective in 2010. The lowest tax rates are 10 and 15 percent. Under current law, the four other rates are 25, 28, 33, and 35 percent. The tax rate applicable to each income bracket is called the *marginal tax rate*. The amount of taxable income subject to each marginal tax rate for each *filing status* is referred to as a *tax bracket*. The brackets are indexed annually for inflation. For 2012, the tax brackets (also referred to as "tax rate schedules") for each filing status are shown in the following example:

EXAMPLE

Gary and Karen Smith are married taxpayers filing jointly. Their taxable income for 2011 was $299,000. Their tax due was $76,124.50, computed as follows:

- Their taxable income not over $17,000 is taxed at a rate of 10 percent, which results in a tax of $1,700.
- Their taxable income over $17,000 but not over $69,000 (or $52,000) is taxed at a rate of 15 percent, which results in a tax of $7,800.
- Their taxable income over $69,000 but not over $139,350 (or $70,350) is taxed at a rate of 25 percent, which results in a tax of $17,587.50.
- Their taxable income over $139,350 but not over $212,300 (or $72,950) is taxed at a rate of 28 percent, which results in a tax of $20,426.
- Their taxable income over $212,300 but not over $379,150 (or $86,700) is taxed at a rate of 33 percent, which results in a tax of $28,611.
- The taxes computed under each of the brackets shown above are added together for a total of $76,124.50 ($1,700 + $7,800 + $17,587.50 + $20,426 + $28,611 = $76,124.50).

effective tax rate

This tax gives the Smiths an *effective tax rate* of about 25 percent (that is, the tax of $76,124.50 divided by their taxable income of $299,000). Note that as the taxpayer rises in the tax brackets, a greater percentage is applied to the dollars in that tax bracket. This points out what we call the progressive nature of the U.S. tax system. Except when a taxpayer is in the lowest tax bracket, a taxpayer's effective tax rate will always be lower than his marginal tax rate because of the progressive structure of the federal income tax system. A taxpayer in the lowest tax bracket has both an effective tax rate and a marginal tax rate equal to 10 percent.

As indicated above, the brackets of taxable income to which the various marginal tax rates apply depend on the individual's filing status. As previously described, an individual taxpayer files his or her tax return under one of four filing status categories: a single taxpayer, an unmarried head of household, a married taxpayer filing jointly, and a married taxpayer filing separately. The amount of taxable income in each tax bracket depends upon the individual's filing status.

Table 5-1 Tax Rate Schedules for Individuals in 2012 (Source: IRS.gov)		
	If Taxable Income is:	The Tax is:
Single (Unmarried Individuals) Filers	Not over $8,700	10% of taxable income
	Over $8,701 but not over $35,350	$870 plus 15% of the amount over $8,700
	Over $35,351 but not over $85,650	$4,868 plus 25% of the amount over $35,350
	Over $85,651 but not over $178,650	$17,443 plus 28% of the amount over $85,650
	Over $178,651 but not over $388,350	$43,843 plus 33% of the amount over $178,650
	Over $388,351	$112,863 plus 35% of the amount over $388,350
Heads of Household	Not over $12,400	10% of taxable income
	Over $12,401 but not over $47,350	$1,240 plus 15% of the amount over $12,400
	Over $47,351 but not over $122,300	$6,483 plus 25% of the amount over $47,350
	Over $122,301 but not over $198,050	$24,220 plus 28% of the amount over $122,300
	Over $198,051 but not over $388,350	$46,430 plus 33% of the amount over $198,050
	Over $388,351	$109,229 plus 35% of the amount over $388,350
Married Individuals Filing Joint Returns and Surviving Spouses	Not over $17,400	10% of taxable income
	Over $17,401 but not over $70,700	$1,740 plus 15% of the amount over $17,400
	Over $70,701 but not over $142,700	$9,735 plus 25% of the amount over $70,700
	Over $142,701 but not over $217,450	$27,735 plus 28% of the amount over $142,700
	Over $217,451 but not over $388,350	$48,665 plus 33% of the amount over $217,450
	Over $388,350	$105,062 plus 35% of the amount over $388,350
Married Individuals Filing Separate Returns	Not over $8,700	10% of taxable income
	Over $8,701 but not over $35,350	$870 plus 15% of the amount over $8,700
	Over $35,351 but not over $71,350	$4,868 plus 25% of the amount over $35,350
	Over $71,351 but not over $108,725	$13,868 plus 28% of the amount over $71,350
	Over $108,726 but not over $194,175	$24,333 plus 33% of the amount over $108,725
	Over $194,175	$52,531 plus 35% of the amount over $194,175

TAX CREDITS

tax credit After the tax has been computed on taxable income using the appropriate filing status, the actual tax liability can be reduced if the taxpayer qualifies for certain *tax credits*.

There is a very important difference between a tax credit and a tax deduction. A tax credit is a dollar-for-dollar reduction of the actual tax owed; deductions, on the other hand, only reduce the amount of income subject to tax. Both are good for the taxpayer, but credits are much better than deductions!

> **EXAMPLE**
>
> Philip is a single tax filer who has taxable income of $50,000 in 2012, which puts him squarely in the 25 percent marginal tax bracket. If he could find another deduction of $1,000, it would save him $250 in taxes (that is 25 percent of $1,000). However, if Philip qualified for a $1,000 tax credit, his actual tax owed would be reduced by $1,000...a dollar-for-dollar reduction!

There are several personal tax credits available for individual taxpayers. Numerous tax credits surface and become available annually, only to be eliminated or phased out in later years. Four of the most important tax credits available to individual taxpayers are: (1) the tax credit for children; (2) the adoption credit; (3) the dependent-care credit; and (4) credits for higher education. All personal tax credits reflect Congress's concern with providing tax incentives for individual taxpayers' socially beneficial or economically necessary activities. Each tax credit has its own set of rules for eligibility, availability based on the taxpayer's income level, and credit amounts. Knowledge of how tax credits operate is essential to a fundamental understanding of the income tax law.

THE ALTERNATIVE MINIMUM TAX (AMT)

alternative minimum tax (AMT)

The *alternative minimum tax (AMT)* is a separate method of calculating income tax liability. It is often referred to as a "parallel" system of income taxation. It applies in cases where the calculation of the AMT results in a higher tax liability than the calculation of the regular income tax. As you can expect, the computations for determining the AMT are different from those for determining the regular tax. The deduction rules are different. The credit rules are different. The tax rates are different.

The purpose of the AMT is to prevent the taxpayer from reducing his tax liability below reasonable levels (in the opinion of Congress!) through the use of certain tax benefits targeted by the AMT rules. Thus, in calculating the AMT, certain tax benefits available under the regular tax rules are limited or prohibited under the AMT calculation. For example, AMT rules require the individual to add back certain deductions for AMT purposes that are allowable to the taxpayer for regular tax purposes. Such benefits that are restricted under the AMT system are loosely referred to as *tax preference items*. These tax preference items generally produce no benefit to the taxpayer under the AMT system, as they would under the regular system.

While a detailed study of the AMT system is well beyond the scope of this course, you should know that some of the most common tax preference items include:

- the taxpayers standard deduction based on his/her/their filing status
- personal and dependency exemptions
- certain deductions such as for state and local taxes, real estate taxes, and miscellaneous itemized deductions
- a portion of certain deductions for depreciation

The tax rate under the AMT system is applied to income subject to the AMT. For individuals, there are two ordinary income brackets with rates of 26 percent and 28 percent, respectively. For corporations, it is a flat rate of 20 percent. Certain small corporations are not subject to AMT. Note that although the AMT tax rates for individuals are lower than the tax rates in the top brackets in the regular system, the tax payable may be greater because some exemptions and deductions are not allowed in calculating the AMT. If the AMT is higher than the regular income tax, the AMT must be paid instead of the regular tax.

For this course, you should simply be aware that the AMT tax system exists, and that certain taxpayers with certain types of deductions will be subject to it. The details for calculating the AMT and the various rules for determining what goes in and out of the AMT tax base are covered in more advanced texts such as The American College's HS 321 *Fundamentals of Income Taxation*. The advisor engaged in a tax practice or in comprehensive financial planning must acquire a basic understanding of these rules.

TAX PERIODS AND ACCOUNTING METHODS

Individuals file tax returns on an annual basis. For the vast majority of individuals, income tax is calculated based upon a calendar-year period. However, many partnerships and corporations (and a small number of individuals) report their tax liability based upon a 12-month period that does not coincide with the calendar year. Such a period is referred to as a *fiscal year*. In the past, using a fiscal year for tax purposes by a business entity provided an opportunity to defer taxable income. This was accomplished by paying or crediting income to a partner or shareholder in the beginning of a calendar year that was actually earned by the business during its fiscal year, which began several months before the onset of the calendar year. However, such techniques have been virtually eliminated by strict new rules governing the election of a fiscal year for tax purposes.

Taxable income must be computed on the basis of a fixed accounting period—that is, a *taxable year*—and complying with a method of tax accounting that clearly reflects income. Most financial advisors and their clients use the *cash-basis method*, which means they report income and pay taxes on the income only if it is received during the taxable year. Almost all individual taxpayers who do not own a business (and many who do) use this method of accounting.

However, there is an exception to the general rule that income is reported by a cash-basis taxpayer only in the taxable year when it is actually received. The exception is known as the constructive receipt doctrine, which is designed to prevent taxpayers from unilaterally determining the tax year when an item of income is "received by" them for federal income tax purposes. More about this doctrine later.

The other popular method of accounting is the *accrual method*, which typically is used by C corporations. Under this method, income is realized (and reported for taxes) when the right to receive it comes into being, that is, when all the events that determine the right have occurred. Under the accrual method, it is not the actual receipt but the right to receive the income that governs.

THREE IMPORTANT ISSUES

The preceding material has been an overview of the process by which an individual's tax liability is computed. To understand the income tax system more fully, it helps to consider three basic issues in addition to the computation process. These three issues are (1) what is taxed, (2) to whom is it taxed, and (3) when is it taxed. There are important tax law doctrines that clarify each of these issues.

The "What" Issue: The Economic Benefit Doctrine

We discussed the question of what is taxed in the section when we described the concept of gross income. In general, anything of value received by the taxpayer is taxed, unless it is specifically excluded such as a gift. An event or transaction that confers an economic benefit on the taxpayer will result in gross income to the taxpayer, as long as the economic benefit is certain and can be measured. For example, suppose the Carroll Corporation sets up an irrevocable trust in a nonqualified retirement account for a key employee Toby. The trust provides that beginning in 5 years Toby will receive $20,000 a year for a 10-year period. Toby's right to the money is nonforfeitable, and the trust assets are not otherwise available to the Carroll Corporation in any way. Even though Toby is not receiving any money currently, by U.S. tax theory the Carroll Corporation has conferred an economic benefit upon Toby that is certain and can be measured using time-value-of-money calculations. Therefore, Toby will be taxed currently on the present value of the payments to be made in the future.

Note the result would be different if the payments were contingent on Toby rendering future services to his employer, or if the assets of the trust were available to the Carroll Corporation or its creditors for uses other than to pay Toby. This is an example of the *economic benefit doctrine*, which holds that a taxpayer must pay tax when an economic benefit has been conferred on the taxpayer, regardless of whether the taxpayer has actually received any cash or property. Another application of this doctrine occurs when an employer pays life insurance premiums on a policy covering the life of an employee who has the right to name the policy's beneficiary. In such a case, the employer has conferred an economic benefit upon the employee (life insurance coverage) that is subject to income tax.

The "To Whom" Issue: The Fruit and Tree Doctrine

There are many types of assets that produce taxable income. The asset producing the income may be a corporate bond that pays interest, or it may be some real estate that generates rental income. The asset may be an individual, whose knowledge or expertise generates income from sales or services. In any event, an important tax principle that applies is this: income is taxable to the person who earns it, or to the person who owns the asset that produces the income. In other words, for income tax purposes, the "fruit" comes from the "tree" that produced it, and must be taxed accordingly. This is known as the *fruit and tree doctrine*.

> **EXAMPLE**
>
> Sandra owns a $1,000 bond issued by Ford Motor Company (Symbol: F). Sandra receives interest payments from the bond every 6 months and gives them to her son, Brett. Sandra retains ownership of the bond (that is, the "tree") itself. Despite the fact that Brett has received the actual income (that is, the "fruit"), Sandra is still taxed on it because she owns the asset that produced the income. Her gift of the interest income to Brett results in no taxation for him.

Similarly, income from personal services is taxed to the person who earns the income. The fruits of an individual's labor cannot be assigned to another individual for tax purposes. For example, suppose that Frank, an insurance advisor, irrevocably assigns in writing to his daughter the right to all future commissions from policies that he sold to clients in 2011. Will the daughter be taxed on the income? The answer is no. The advisor who earned the income must be taxed on it. This principle is often referred to as the *assignment of income doctrine*.

The "When" Issue: The Constructive Receipt Doctrine

constructive receipt doctrine

You have heard the expression "time is money" and that is very true! The current use of money is valuable. Therefore, if taxation can be deferred, the taxpayer gains a monetary benefit through the use of tax dollars until they are paid to the government at some future date. As a result, taxpayers often try to defer the receipt of income until a later tax year to defer the payment of tax due on the income. An important doctrine that limits the use of such delaying techniques is referred to as the *constructive receipt doctrine*. Without this doctrine, cash-basis taxpayers could shift, almost at will, the year in which they report income merely by not taking any steps to physically possess the income that is due to them.

Under the doctrine of constructive receipt, a cash-basis taxpayer is deemed to have received income for tax purposes when it is either credited to the taxpayer's account, set apart for the taxpayer, or otherwise made available so that it could be possessed by the taxpayer—even if the taxpayer fails to actually take possession.

> **EXAMPLE**
>
> Susan, a financial planner in Philadelphia, PA, submitted an application for life insurance on a client in November, 2011. The policy was issued in December, 2011, and a commission check dated December 22, 2011, was mailed to Susan's business address. Susan, however, was on an extended cruise and did not pick up and cash her check until January 4, 2012. Susan must report this income on her 2011 tax return under the doctrine of constructive receipt, even though she did not actually take possession of the money until 2012.

Notice, however, that if there are *bona fide* conditions or restrictions that limit the taxpayer's right to receive the income, the doctrine of constructive receipt will not apply.

> **EXAMPLE**
>
> Natalie is a realtor in Trenton, NJ. In November, 2011, her client signed an agreement to purchase a home that Natalie listed. The sale closed on January 4, 2012. Although Natalie was fairly certain in November 2011 that she would complete the sale and receive her commission, the client still had to go though the closing to make the sale final and allow Natalie to receive her money unconditionally. Therefore, the constructive receipt doctrine does not apply and Natalie will be taxed on her commission in 2012, not in 2011.

One more common example concerns investing in nonqualified mutual funds. These are mutual funds that are not held in a retirement account such as an IRA, Roth IRA, or 401(k). The mutual funds generally make distributions from both dividends and capital gains from stocks held by the fund. Most owners of the funds' shares reinvest these distributions to purchase more shares in the fund. However, since the investors have an unrestricted right to take the distributions in cash, under the constructive receipt doctrine they will receive a Form 1099 for the distributions and must report them for tax purposes in the year the distributions are made. Note, this can be particularly upsetting to the owner of a mutual fund whose share prices have declined and yet still makes taxable distributions for the year!

BASIC INCOME-TAX-PLANNING CONCEPTS

Despite repeated calls to simplify the tax laws (and politicians' promises to do so), much complexity remains in understanding and applying the U.S. Internal Revenue Code. Many highly intelligent people devote their entire professional lives trying to figure out how the Code can be employed (legally, of course) to save some tax money for their clients. This is proper, as long as the tax is saved through tax reductions or avoidance through a reasonable interpretation of tax laws and not through *tax evasion* (that is, ignoring or flouting the tax laws). Some wit has aptly said that the difference between tax avoidance and tax evasion is "about 20 years in prison!"

As previously stated, sophisticated tax planning is well beyond the scope of this text. However, it helps to outline some basic concepts used in tax planning to illustrate how accountants, tax attorneys, and other tax advisors help clients minimize and/or legally avoid taxes.

Income and Deduction Shifting

The principle behind income-shifting techniques is this: get taxable income into the hands of a taxpayer in a lower tax bracket than the taxpayer who would otherwise have to report the income. Proper income shifting techniques result in less tax paid on the income. For example, a taxpayer in the top 35 percent marginal tax bracket will pay $3,500 in tax on $10,000 of additional income. However, a taxpayer in the 15 percent bracket will pay only $1,500 of tax on the same $10,000 of income. Clearly, income shifting can provide substantial tax savings.

What are some income-shifting techniques that are available? Perhaps the simplest one is an outright gift of property. As previously discussed, under the fruit and tree doctrine, income is taxed to the person who owns the asset that produces the income. If the asset is transferred by gift, the donee (person receiving the asset) will be taxed on income generated by the asset. However, the gift tax consequences of giving away property to shift the income tax burden must always be considered.

EXAMPLE

Edward Brown owns a rental property worth $200,000, from which he receives a net (after expenses) of $10,000 in annual rental income. Edward is in the 35 percent marginal income tax bracket and thus pays $3,500 on the net income. For years, he has given the after-tax income (about $6,500) as a gift to his daughter Karen. In 2012, on advice of his tax attorney, Edward plans to gift the rental property to Karen who is in the 15 percent marginal tax bracket. If she earns the same net income from renting the property, she would pay $1,500 in taxes and would net $8,500 compared to the $6,500 given her by Edward. Note: there may be gift tax consequences for Edward in gifting the rental property to Karen...a topic for future discussion.

For planning purposes, a technique somewhat related to income shifting is deduction shifting. Deduction shifting is a simple, yet frequently overlooked, planning technique. Here, the idea is to shift deductions to a taxpayer in a higher tax bracket than the taxpayer who would otherwise claim the deduction. As a result, the deduction is taken against income that would be taxed in a higher bracket, thereby resulting in a greater tax savings.

> **EXAMPLE**
>
> Marie, age 25 and single, is ill and must enter a hospital for an extended stay. The cost of her care is only partially covered by insurance. Her out-of-pocket expenses are likely to be $10,000 or more. Although Marie has a few assets, she is not working and has no income. Her parents, Steven and Carol, are in the 28 percent tax bracket and have enough medical expenses of their own this year to claim a medical expense deduction. In 2012, Marie will be her parents' dependent for tax purposes, and therefore, Steven and Carol can deduct medical expense payments they make for Marie's care. By Steven and Carol paying for Marie's care, there will be a tax savings of 28 cents for every dollar of expense. If, on the other hand, Marie paid for her own expenses, there would be little or no tax savings.

Avoiding Limitations on Deductions

Although many types of expenses are deductible for income tax purposes, there may be limitations on how much of a given expense may actually be deducted. One common way the law limits deductions is through the use of a *deduction floor*. The taxpayer is allowed to deduct items subject to the floor, but only to the extent those items exceed a specified percentage of income (specifically, adjusted gross income (AGI) in most cases).

For example, an entire group of deductions claimed by individual taxpayers on Schedule A of Form 1040 is referred to as *miscellaneous itemized deductions*. This group of deductions includes unreimbursed employee business expenses (such as job travel, union dues, and job education), fees for investment advice, costs of tax preparation, and several other items. First, all of the taxpayer's deductions that fall within this miscellaneous group are added together. Then, the taxpayer's adjusted gross income is multiplied by 2 percent. The resulting figure is subtracted from the total of the items in the group to determine how much the taxpayer can actually deduct. The result is that the taxpayer can deduct miscellaneous itemized deductions only to the extent they exceed this 2 percent floor.

> **EXAMPLE**
>
> Jennifer reported an adjusted gross income (AGI) of $50,000 in 2011. She had unreimbursed business expenses of $1,000, and she paid $500 for tax preparation. Since her total of miscellaneous itemized deductions is $1,500, and 2% of her AGI is $1,000, Jennifer will be able to deduct only $500 in this category on her 2011 tax return ($1,500 − $1,000 = $500).

Other deductions subject to a floor include the medical expense deduction (7.5 percent of AGI) and the deduction for personal casualty losses (10 percent of AGI). Note: The Affordable Care Act passed in 2010 will change the floor for medical expense deductions to 10 percent of AGI beginning in the 2013 tax year. However, taxpayers over age 65 will continue to have the 7.5 percent floor through the 2016 tax year.

Deferral and Acceleration Techniques

Deferral of income and acceleration of deductions are basic and common tax planning techniques. These techniques are based on the time value of money. If income can be deferred to a later year, the tax payable on the income is also deferred, and the taxpayer has the use of that money for a longer time. Similarly, if deductible expenses are accelerated into an earlier tax year, the tax saving from those deductions is realized sooner, thereby giving the taxpayer the use of that money sooner. However, note that most tax deductions are attributable to actual out-of-pocket expenses. Therefore, the expense itself involves the loss of use of money, which over the same time period will be greater than the benefit realized by the tax savings. The point here is to not let the tax "tail" wag the overall financial "dog."

What is the potential benefit of accelerating deductions? If a taxpayer makes a deductible expense in December of 2011 rather than in January of 2012, he has lost the use of the money spent for only one additional month. However, the tax savings generated by the expense gives the taxpayer the use of the tax savings for an entire additional year. If the taxpayer makes the expense in January, he does in fact gain a net benefit from accelerating the expense.

> **EXAMPLE**
>
> Harry makes a $10,000 deductible business expense in December of 2011. Assume Harry's marginal tax bracket is 35 percent. By making the expenditure in December of 2011 rather than January 2012, Harry postpones the payment of $3,500 in taxes ($10,000 × .35) for one year. Assume Harry can invest money for one year at 6 percent annual interest, Harry will have $210 ($3,500 × .06) that he would not have if he had deferred the expense until next year. However, by paying the $10,000 in December instead of January, Harry loses one month's interest on the $10,000. This amount is $50 [($10,000 × .06) ÷ 12]. But note that Harry is still ahead $160 ($210 – $50) by accelerating the deductible expense and, in effect, deferring the payment of taxes on $10,000 of income for one year.

The Passive-Loss Rules

The IRS places special limitations on the deductibility of so-called *passive losses*. These tax losses are typically generated by activities in which the taxpayer has an ownership interest, but does not participate in the activity of the business. For example, suppose a taxpayer owns shares of a limited partnership that invests in rental real estate. Assume that the depreciation deductions and other deductions generated by the partnership properties exceed the income generated by the properties. Therefore, for tax purposes, the partnership generates losses.

Under tax laws in effect before the Tax Reform Act of 1986, there were few limitations on deductibility of such items by taxpayers owning interests in limited partnerships and other activities in which the taxpayer did not actively participate. Because these investments allowed taxpayers to write off tax losses from these ventures against salary and other income, the activities were referred to as *tax shelters*. Tax shelters were a very important weapon in the tax-avoidance arsenal; however, there were many abuses which eventually lead to legislation to dampen their benefits.

Under current law there are strict limitations on the deductibility of losses generated by tax-shelter investments. These rules are intended to prevent taxpayers from investing in activities merely for tax purposes, as distinguished from the actual economics of the investment. There are complicated rules and definitions as to what constitutes a passive activity subject to the strict deduction rules. The basic rule, however, is that tax losses generated by passive activities can be deducted *only* against income generated by the taxpayer's passive activities, and not against salary or other income of the taxpayer.

Income Tax Planning

There are qualifications, exceptions, and certain significant loopholes to these rules. This area of the tax law is a specialty in itself. For purposes of this discussion, you should simply be aware that if a taxpayer invests in an activity in which he does not participate, and the activity generates tax losses, the deductibility of those losses is limited by some very strict rules. Activities deemed to be passive include most rental activities in which the taxpayer owns an interest. However, investments in publicly traded stocks and bonds are not covered by these rules. Stocks, bonds, and mutual funds are deemed to be primarily for investment purposes—not primarily as a tax shelter.

Tax-Exempt Transactions

One of the best tax planning techniques is creating a transaction that produces a monetary benefit without the taxpayer being taxed on that transaction. Within this general category are two basic types of transactions. The first is where taxation is altogether eliminated, and the second is where taxation of the transaction is merely deferred. The first type can be described as a **tax-exempt transaction**. Such transactions are generally based on a specific exclusion from gross income.

[handwritten: muni's - income from bonds is tax free]

An example of a tax-exempt transaction is the receipt of income from a public-purpose municipal bond (often called a "muni"). The income from such bonds is excludible from the taxpayer's gross income for federal income tax purposes. As we noted earlier, all income is includible in gross income unless a provision in the Code specifically excludes it. There is such an exclusion for certain municipal bond income (IRC Sec. 103).

Note that unless the taxpayer is subject to a high marginal income tax rate, the interest rate on such bonds will generally not be greater than the after-tax rate on taxable obligations (say, from corporate bonds of equal ratings). Therefore such investments are generally of greater benefit to upper-bracket taxpayers.

Another valuable example of a tax-exempt monetary gain is the exclusion of the first $250,000 ($500,000 if married, filing jointly) of gain on the sale of a personal residence if certain requirements are met.

Nonrecognition Transactions

There are many types of transactions in which taxation is merely deferred rather than eliminated. These transactions may generally be referred to as *nonrecognition transactions*. Typically, such a transaction involves the sale or exchange of property at a gain realized by the taxpayer. However, because of a provision in the Internal Revenue Code, the realized gain is not currently recognized (that is, reportable on IRS Form 1040).

How do such transactions merely defer, rather than eliminate, taxable gain? To understand the mechanics of the nonrecognition transaction, we need to understand the basic tax treatment of a sale or exchange of property.

Computation of Gain or Loss

When property is sold, the taxpayer must determine what portion of the sale proceeds will be subject to taxation. In general, the gain realized from a sale of property is equal to the total amount realized from the sale, minus the taxpayer's cost basis in the property.

What does the term *cost basis* mean? Broadly stated, cost basis (or just "basis") is the amount that the taxpayer has invested in the property. Therefore, cost basis is generally the amount the taxpayer paid for the property, plus the cost of any permanent improvements to the property. Stated another way, the cost basis of property is generally equal to its cost. As a result, the gain realized from a sale of property is the sales price minus the taxpayer's cost.

EXAMPLE

Nancy bought 1,000 shares of stock in Cleanseco, Inc., a household cleanser manufacturer, 2 years ago. She paid $5,000 for the stock. In early 2012, she sold the Cleanseco stock for $10,000. The gross amount realized from the sale is $10,000. Nancy's cost basis is $5,000. Therefore, the realized gain from the sale is $5,000 ($10,000 – $5,000). She must report the sale and a long-term capital gain of $5,000 on her 2012 federal income tax return.

The rule that the portion of the sales price that represents a recovery of the taxpayer's cost basis is not taxable illustrates an important principle of tax law, namely, that money received as a return of one's capital is not treated as gross income. The Internal Revenue Code contains many provisions which reflect this basic principle. It is really a matter of common sense: Getting back money you have invested in property should not result in taxation, because there has been no profit (gain) returned to you, only your original investment.

How Nonrecognition Transactions Differ from Taxable Transactions

The Internal Revenue Code specifies that the gain on some sales and exchanges shall not be immediately recognized (that is, reported on Form 1040 and taxed). We stated earlier that the purpose of these transactions is not to eliminate taxation, but merely to defer it. How is this accomplished?

The answer to this question relates to the taxpayer's basis in property. Generally, a taxpayer's cost basis in property equals the cost of the property. In an exchange of property, the taxpayer's cost for the property received in the exchange is generally the fair market value of the property surrendered in the exchange. However, if the exchange is one in which gain is not recognized, the taxpayer's cost basis in the new property will generally be the same as the taxpayer's basis in the old property. We say that the exchange preserves the unrecognized gain and allows that gain to be taxed when the new property is later sold in a taxable transaction.

> **EXAMPLE**
>
> Robert owns a condominium (Red One) that he holds as a rental property. He paid $100,000 for the property and added $20,000 worth of permanent improvements. The fair market value of the property is now $180,000. Robert exchanges the property for another condominium (Blue Two) in a transaction that qualifies for nonrecognition treatment under the Internal Revenue Code. The property received in the exchange (Blue Two) is also worth $180,000. Robert's realized gain is $60,000 ($180,000 value of property received minus Robert's $120,000 basis in Red One). Robert's recognized gain is zero because the exchange qualifies for nonrecognition treatment. However, Robert's basis in the new property (Blue Two) will be the same as his basis in Red One ($120,000). As a result, if Robert sells Blue Two later, the gain that would have been recognized if the exchange was taxable earlier will be recognized when Blue Two is sold. On the other hand, if the exchange was taxable, Robert would have paid tax currently on the $60,000 of gain, but his cost basis in Blue Two would have increased to $180,000.

Clearly, the deferral of taxation in such a transaction has significant value. Moreover, the deferred gain may never be taxed if the taxpayer never sells the property received in the exchange. The intent of the nonrecognition provisions is merely to defer taxation. But there is no assurance that Uncle Sam will ever get his tax money, particularly if the taxpayer keeps the new property until death.

The example above is just one type of transaction that qualifies for nonrecognition. Other examples include exchanges of insurance policies (that is, Sec. 1035 exchanges) and involuntary conversions. These transactions, and the specific rules that govern their tax treatment, are important but are beyond the scope of this chapter.

Transactions That Result in a Taxable Loss

Some sales of property result in a loss rather than a gain to the selling taxpayer. This happens when the amount received for the property is less than the taxpayer's cost basis in the property. In such cases, the dollar amount of the loss is generally deductible for income tax purposes if the property sold is either business property or property held for the production of income. If the property is held for personal use, the loss resulting from a sale of the property is generally nondeductible.

EXAMPLE

Alexandra owns stock in the Hi-Five Corporation, a publicly traded corporation that sells sneakers. Alexandra paid $5,000 for the stock 2 years ago. In 2012, she sells the stock at a loss for $3,500. Alexandra has a realized loss of $1,500 ($5,000 basis minus $3,500 amount realized). Alexandra may deduct the $1,500 loss on her tax return this year.

Ordinary versus Capital Gain and Loss

Different rules apply to sales of a taxpayer's assets, depending on whether the gain or loss is treated as an ordinary gain (or loss) or a capital gain (or loss).

Capital Gain versus Ordinary Income

capital gain

ordinary income

One of the most important aspects of federal tax law is its broad scope of social policy considerations. Often, Congress attempts to mold parts of society by provisions of the tax laws. One policy issue that is a continuous source of controversy and change is whether a *capital gain* should be taxed at the same rates as *ordinary income*.

What is the difference between capital gain and ordinary income? Basically, capital gain is income realized through the sale or exchange of a capital asset. Capital assets are defined under Sec. 1221 of the Internal Revenue Code as any property the taxpayer owns (whether or not connected with a business activity) except for the following property types specifically excluded from the definition:

- "stock in trade" also known as inventory
- depreciable or real property used in the taxpayer's business
- intellectual or artistic property created by the taxpayer
- accounts or notes receivable acquired in the ordinary course of business
- publications of the U.S. government

The social policy issue surrounding the sale of capital assets is summarized as: Should the sale of such assets receive a tax break relative to other kinds of income? Those who favor the capital-gain tax relief argue that it encourages savings and investment. They also argue that full taxation of capital gain subjects the taxpayers to what is actually a tax on inflation, rather than one on real economic gains.

How does a capital-gain tax break favor savings and investment? Stocks, bonds, real estate, and other investment-type assets generally are treated as capital assets. When an investor sells such an asset, a greater portion of the amount realized from the sale will remain in the investor's pocket if favorable tax treatment applies to the realized gain. Therefore, the investor has a higher rate of return on the investment, which presumably provides an incentive to save and invest rather than spend.

It is argued also that a portion of the increase in value of an investment-type asset is attributable to inflation, rather than to real economic appreciation. Therefore, the argument goes, taxing the full amount of gain when the asset is sold is unfair and confiscatory, because the portion of the gain attributable to inflation has conferred no real economic benefit upon the taxpayer.

These theories have fueled varying legislative measures over the years that provide relief for the taxation of capital gain. For example, through an exclusion from gross income for some percentage of an individual's capital gain, or by applying a lower tax rate on capital gains, a lower tax bill on the overall gain results.

Under the 2003 Jobs and Growth Tax Relief Reconciliation Act, the maximum rate applicable to capital gains on assets held by individual taxpayers for more than 12 months is generally 15 percent, as opposed to the much higher maximum marginal tax rate of 35 percent that applies to ordinary income. Follow-on legislation passed in 2006 and 2010 have extended the favorable capital gains rates through the 2012 tax year. Gains from collectibles and real estate gains attributable to "unrecaptured" depreciation are taxed at the higher rates of 28 percent and 26 percent, respectively.

What are the arguments against favorable tax treatment for capital gain? The principal argument is that a preferential treatment for capital gain favors wealthy taxpayers at the expense of the average citizen. The theory goes that most stocks, bonds, and other investment assets are owned by the rich, and that by taxing gains from the sale of these investments at a lower effective rate, the government is playing Robin Hood in reverse: stealing from the poor to feed the rich.

These arguments for and against the lower capital gains tax rates are heard almost daily as the 2012 presidential election draws closer. Arguments on both sides can be persuasive; draw your own conclusions!

Tax Treatment of Dividends as Capital Gains

Dividends represent income that has already been taxed at the corporate level before it is distributed to individual stockholders. Under the 2003 Jobs and Growth Tax Relief Reconciliation Act and extended through 2012, dividends paid to individual stockholders typically are taxed at the same rates that apply to capital gains. Taxpayers in the 10 percent or 15 percent tax bracket pay a 0 percent rate of tax on qualified dividends, while taxpayers in the 25 percent tax bracket or above pay a 15 percent rate of tax on qualified dividends.

Tax Treatment of Capital Losses

When a capital asset is sold at a loss rather than at a gain, special rules apply. Basically, capital losses can be deducted only against the taxpayer's capital gains. In other words, a taxpayer cannot deduct capital losses against ordinary income (such as her wages for the year). Capital losses cannot be deducted against dividends either. Nonetheless, in the special case of individual taxpayers, capital losses can be deducted against ordinary income (including dividends) in an amount up to $3,000 per year. Capital losses in excess of $3,000 can be carried over to future tax years.

EXAMPLE 1
Justin sold 200 shares of Walmart (WMT) in 2011, for which he incurred a long-term capital loss of $5,000. He also sold 100 shares of ExxonMobile (XOM) and realized $8,000 of long-term capital gains. On his 2011 federal income tax return, Justin can offset $5,000 of his long-term capital gain with $5,000 of the long-term capital loss. He would then report a $3,000 net long-term capital gain for the tax year.
EXAMPLE 2
Elizabeth sold shares of Home Depot (HD) at a long-term capital loss of $5,000 in 2011. She had $50,000 of ordinary income, but she had no other capital gains for the year. Elizabeth can deduct $3,000 of the long-term capital loss against $3,000 of ordinary income in 2011. She can "carry over" the remaining $2,000 of long-term capital loss into the 2012 tax year.

Sec. 1231 Assets: Depreciable Property and Real Property Used in a Trade or Business

Sec. 1231 assets receive different tax treatment, depending on whether the assets are sold at a gain or at a loss. If the asset is sold at a gain, the gain is treated as a capital gain. If the asset is sold at a loss, the loss is treated as an ordinary loss, not as a capital loss.

What is the significance of this hybrid form of tax treatment? The sale of an asset falling into this category is not subject to the limitations that apply to the deductibility of capital losses. Therefore, if such an asset is sold at a loss, the loss can be deducted against the taxpayer's salary or other income. This is a very favorable provision for the taxpayers with Sec. 1231 assets.

If the asset is sold at a gain, the gain will be treated as capital gain and enjoy the lower rates that (at least currently) apply. Even though there is currently no partial exclusion or other preferential treatment available for capital gains, capital-gains treatment can still provide a benefit for taxpayers who have capital losses for the year. This is because the capital losses from Sec. 1231 assets can be deducted against capital gains, but not against ordinary income.

EXAMPLE
Pat sells a piece of machinery this year used in his business (that qualifies as a Sec. 1231 asset). The machinery is sold at a gain of $40,000. Pat also has a long-term capital loss of $40,000 this year from stock sales from his investment portfolio. Since the gain from the sale of the machinery is treated as a capital gain and not ordinary income, Pat can offset his stock losses in full against the gain from the sale of the machinery.

The assets that receive this hybrid form of tax treatment include all depreciable property plus land that is used in the taxpayer's business (land is not depreciable for tax purposes). Sec. 1231 assets provide the best of both worlds for taxpayers, and the rules that govern them are designed to stimulate investment in assets used in the conduct of a business.

TAXABLE ENTITIES

Subchapter S corporation

C corporation *taxable*

This chapter has focused mostly on the individual taxpayer who receives income from salary, investment, or a sole proprietorship. However, in addition to individuals, trusts, estates, and corporations also are subject to the federal income tax. Certain corporations can elect to have their shareholders taxed on the corporation's taxable income. This is called a Subchapter S election. The effect of such an election is to have the corporation treated for tax purposes very much like a partnership. Like a partnership, a corporation that makes a Subchapter S election is not subject to income tax at the entity level. Rather, the owners of the business pay the taxes. Partnerships and *Subchapter S corporations* are often referred to as "pass-through" entities because the responsibility for paying their taxes is passed through the entity to the owners of the entity.

pass thru = responsiblity of paying taxes passes thru to owners.

However, trusts, estates, and C corporations (that is, corporations other than S corporations) do pay taxes at the corporate level. Special rules apply to each of these entities that do not apply to individual taxpayers. In addition, each of these entities has a different tax rate structure than the rate structure for individual taxpayers.

C corp = taxable + not pass-through entity

CONCLUSION

We have outlined basic income tax concepts and planning techniques that should be familiar to financial advisors. However, there is far more to be learned about each of these topics. If you plan to be a tax specialist or offer comprehensive financial planning for your clients, then you need to study more advanced tax sources. Tax planning involves the analysis, evaluation, and client acceptance of the tax consequences of every capital and financial transaction—before the transaction is made! Tax and economic advantages and disadvantages must be balanced against the risk tolerance profiles and objectives of each client. As both your client's tax bracket and complexity of her financial affairs increases, it becomes more urgent that you provide sound tax planning as a central element in comprehensive financial planning.

CHAPTER REVIEW

Key Terms and Concepts are explained in the Glossary. Answers to the Review Questions are found in the back of the book in the Answers to Questions section.

Key Terms and Concepts

gross income	marginal tax rate
exclusion	filing status
deduction	tax bracket
adjusted gross income	effective tax rate
taxable income	tax credit
standard deduction	alternative minimum tax (AMT)
itemized deductions	constructive receipt doctrine
depreciation deductions	capital gain
income tax basis	ordinary income
personal exemption	Subchapter S corporation
dependency exemption	C corporation

Review Questions

1. Explain what is considered to be gross income for income tax purposes. [1]

2. Explain the difference between an exclusion from gross income and a deduction from gross income. [2]

3. Explain the difference between an above-the-line deduction and a below-the-line deduction. [2]

4. Explain what is meant by the standard deduction. [3]

5. Describe the three basic categories of deductions allowable to individual taxpayers. [3]

6. This year George has medical expenses totaling $9,500. If George has an adjusted gross income of $80,000 and he itemizes deductions, how much of these medical expenses will he be allowed to deduct for income tax purposes? [3]

7. Explain the difference between a taxpayer's marginal tax rate and effective tax rate. [4]

8. Compare the effect on the amount of federal income tax payable of a $10,000 tax deduction versus a $10,000 tax credit for a taxpayer in the 25 percent marginal tax bracket. [5]

9. Explain the nature and purpose of the alternative minimum tax (AMT). [6]

10. Explain the meaning of each of the following federal income tax doctrines: (a.) the economic benefit doctrine, (b.) the doctrine of the fruit and tree, and (c.) the doctrine of constructive receipt. [8]

11. Distinguish between federal income tax avoidance and federal income tax evasion. [9]

12. Contrast the basic purpose of income-shifting techniques with that of deduction-shifting techniques. [9]

13. (a.) Explain the meaning of the term passive losses. (b.) What is the general effect of the current federal income tax treatment of passive losses? [9]

14. Explain how a nonrecognition transaction may result in more than simply a deferral of federal income taxes on the transaction. [9]

15. Briefly describe the social policy issue surrounding taxation of the sales of capital assets. [9]

RETIREMENT PLANNING   6

Learning Objectives

An understanding of the material in this chapter should enable the student to

1. Explain why clients need to start retirement planning when they are young.
2. Explain the role of the retirement advisor, and describe the holistic approach to retirement planning.
3. Describe the responsibilities of the retirement advisor, and explain how retirement planning parallels the financial planning process.
4. Explain why clients are never too old to plan for retirement, and describe several roadblocks to saving for retirement.
5. Explain the difficulties in estimating client financial needs during retirement, and describe two methods for determining how much retirement income may be needed.
6. Describe the potential sources of retirement income available to clients to meet their financial goals during retirement.
7. Describe several strategies that clients can use to overcome their having inadequate retirement resources.
8. Describe the most common types of qualified and tax-advantaged retirement plans.
9. Understand the unique planning problems associated with nonqualified plans.
10. Understand the basic rules for traditional and Roth IRAs, and know who can contribute to each.

STARTING RETIREMENT PLANNING WHEN YOUNG

Not so long ago retirement meant getting the gold watch after 30 years with the company and then quietly living out one's few remaining years with family. But changing lifestyles, increased longevity, and improved expectations have drastically altered the nature of retirement. Today, people anticipate active, vibrant retirements in which they enjoy life and economic self-sufficiency. They see retirement not as the short final phase of life but as the reward phase of life—the icing on the cake. Moreover, a significant percentage of the population has become increasingly interested in achieving the financial independence currently associated with retirement. Put another way, the so-called graying of America resulted in a maturing retirement planning movement.

However, instead of waiting until one is middle-aged or older to start planning for retirement, it is best for people to start planning when they are relatively young. Getting younger people to take retirement planning seriously, however, often requires some convincing. With this in mind, you may be able to motivate younger clients to act by sharing the following information with them:

- Starting early can mean the difference between success and failure. Assuming a 7 percent rate of return, saving $200 a month beginning at age 30 will result in an accumulation of $300,000 by age 65. With a start at age 40, only $162,000 is accumulated. This example dramatically illustrates the power of compounding.
- A majority of Americans are saving far less than needed to fund even the basic lifestyle in retirement.
- As companies switch to defined-contribution type plans, more responsibility for retirement planning falls on employees. In many cases, participants must decide how much to save, when to start doing so, and how their retirement money is invested.
- Careful planning requires preparing for contingencies. Realistic possibilities include Social Security cutbacks, reduction in company pension benefits, periods of high inflation, higher tax rates, and forced early retirement.
- In the future, retiring at age 65 or earlier may not be realistic. Those individuals born in 1938 or later will not be entitled to full Social Security benefits until age 66 or 67, depending on their year of birth.

- Retirement may last longer than planned, because life expectancies continue to rise. People retiring now at age 65 can reasonably expect to live 20 or more years in retirement.
- To be sure funds are not depleted too early, clients need to plan on beating the odds and living beyond the average life expectancy.
- For most people today, maintaining the preretirement standard of living requires 60 to 80 percent of preretirement earnings.
- Working with a financial advisor helps an individual focus on the right issues, prepare a retirement plan, and follow through with it. The advisor provides expertise, a dispassionate viewpoint, and motivation.

Retirement planning is no easy process, however. Financial advisors who engage in retirement planning must be prepared to answer some tough questions. Several of these questions concern their role as retirement advisors, the amount of income their clients will need for retirement, the sources of retirement income available to their clients, and strategies for maximizing their client's retirement incomes. This chapter examines these questions and provides financial advisors with the knowledge and tools to properly serve their clients' retirement needs.

THE ROLE OF THE RETIREMENT ADVISOR

Retirement planning is a multi-dimensional field. As such, it requires that the advisor be schooled in the nuances of many financial planning specialties and related areas. Unfortunately, many so-called advisors approach retirement planning from only one point of view (investments, for example). This perspective offered by specializing in just one field is too limited to deal with the diversified needs of the would-be retiree. A client is better served by a team of advisors who have specialized but complementary backgrounds or by a single advisor who is educated and experienced in a variety of important retirement topics.

Holistic Retirement Planning

holistic retirement planning

Whether the retirement team or the multi-talented individual is the vehicle, the holistic approach to retirement planning is the only means by which a client's needs can be fully and adequately met. Under *holistic retirement planning,* the advisor must communicate with clients concerning such topics as

- employer-provided retirement plans
- Social Security considerations
- personal savings and investments
- income tax issues
- insurance coverage
- IRAs and Roth IRAs
- Medicare choices
- tax planning for distributions and other distribution issues
- health insurance planning including medigap insurance and long-term care insurance
- wealth accumulation for retirement
- selecting a retirement community or another living arrangement
- relocation possibilities and reverse mortgages
- asset allocation and risk
- wellness, nutrition, lifestyle choices, and other aging-related issues
- assessment of current assets and future savings needed to achieve retirement goals

Because the advisor must be conversant in so many disciplines, he must be somewhat of a renaissance person. Nevertheless, retirement planning practice is complicated because of the broad-based knowledge needed for the job. The advisor must integrate retirement planning strategies with other financial planning needs such as tax, estate planning, and investment goals—not an easy task!

A word of caution is in order here. Understanding how to plan for a client's retirement is more art than science. There is no one-size-fits-all approach to retirement planning. For example, an attempt to describe the average retiree is like trying to describe the average book—even if it could be done, the information would not be very useful. Retirees are wealthy and poor, male and female, old and not-so-old. They are single, married, and widowed; some have children and some do not. Retirees are healthy and unhealthy, happy and miserable, active and sedentary, and sophisticated and naïve.

A further complication is that retirement planning does not always begin early enough in the financial life cycle. While the old axiom "it's never too early or too late to plan for retirement" is true, it is a huge challenge to plan for a client's retirement when it is too late to influence the client's ability to retire with financial security. Conversely, planning at a relatively young age for clients opens up a multitude of opportunities and presents its own planning challenges.

Because client situations are like snowflakes—there are no two alike—you must be able to meet a variety of situations creatively and cannot rely on a "formula approach" to solve your clients' problems. Some examples will help demonstrate the varied topics discussed during retirement planning.

EXAMPLE 1

Adam, aged 65, is retired and he and his wife Evelyn receive $30,000 in pension income and $10,000 in Social Security income. Adam would like to know how he will be taxed for federal tax purposes. Adam and Evelyn file jointly.

The general rule that applies to all retirees is that pension income is fully taxable as ordinary income. However, taxpayers filing a joint return can exclude all Social Security benefits from income for tax purposes if their provisional income is $32,000 or less. (Provisional income is defined as adjusted gross income plus tax-exempt interest plus half of Social Security benefits.) For provisional income between $32,000 and $44,000, as much as 50 percent of Social Security benefits are taxable. If provisional income exceeds $44,000, as much as 85 percent of Social Security benefits are taxable.

In this case, the couple's provisional income is calculated by adding his $30,000 pension to one-half of their $10,000 Social Security benefit ($5,000). Since a provisional income of $35,000 ($30,000 + $5,000) exceeds the base amount of $32,000 by $3,000, Adam and Evelyn will have to pay tax on a portion of their Social Security benefit, in addition to the $30,000 pension. (The exact amount of the taxable Social Security benefit is determined by complex formulas beyond the scope of this discussion.) However, Adam and Evelyn can take heart in the fact that married taxpayers age 65 and over are each entitled to an additional standard deduction of $1,150 (as indexed for 2012) over their regular standard deduction of $11,900.

EXAMPLE 2

Barbara, aged 58, has questions about investing for retirement. Barbara's investments are heavily concentrated in aggressive growth equities. Barbara's advisors told her she should become less growth oriented and begin to be more concerned with a portfolio that provides enough income for retirement needs. Also, it is appropriate to make the portfolio less volatile because now there is less time to recover losses should the higher-risk growth stocks suffer reverses.

Barbara's advisor should not, however, offer her one-time advice to change portfolio strategies, but should help her to implement the recommendations while continuing to offer Barbara investment advice. Moving toward more current income and less volatility usually means taking less risk, which normally reduces the long-term total return each year from the portfolio. This factor must be considered in any long term retirement planning.

Today, advisors have a number of strategies to accomplish the above goals. Traditional approaches include changing the asset allocation mix to include fewer stocks and more bonds, and/or to change the stock portfolio to include more income producing stocks. Another approach is to maintain a large position in more aggressive equity investments, but to also retain a significant amount of cash as an emergency fund.

EXAMPLE 3

Charlie and his wife, Ann, have heard about long-term care insurance from a friend and wonder if it would be right for them. Charlie, aged 65, has recently retired and his personal disability income policy has expired. Ann, also retired with no personal disability income policy, is slightly older than Charlie and is currently enjoying good health. Charlie and Ann have a retirement income of $95,000 per year and are not in a position to spend down (that is, shed assets to qualify for Medicaid to pay for nursing home care). Charlie and Ann are covered by Medicare but their advisor informed Charlie that long-term nursing home stays are not covered by Medicare to any significant degree.

Charlie and Ann are good candidates for long-term care insurance. The majority of newer long-term care policies pay benefits on a reimbursement basis. These contracts reimburse the insured for actual expenses up to the specified policy limit every day that the insured utilizes long-term care supports and services. Without a long-term care insurance policy, the costs of a nursing home or even significant home care would quickly deplete Charlie's and Ann's assets.

Charlie and Ann are uncertain about what level of benefits to purchase. The average cost for a nursing home stay is $75,000 annually in their area, but the facilities that Charlie and Ann would be comfortable with cost over $80,000 per year. Charlie's financial advisor informed him that premiums for, say, a $200 a day policy ($73,000 annually) would be approximately $2,500 per year each ($5,000 total). The additional cost of a nursing home (beyond $73,000) would have to be paid out-of-pocket by the couple, unless they purchase more expensive long-term care policies that cover more than $200 per day.

Responsibilities of the Retirement Advisor

Financial advisors engaged in retirement planning must accept several responsibilities that may not have been a part of their traditional financial practice. These aspects of a retirement planning practice include doing the following:

- incorporating retirement planning as a segment of comprehensive financial planning. This means using financial planning techniques such as fact finding, budgeting, income flow regulating, and the rendering of investment advice.
- dealing with other professionals who advise the client. These professionals typically include the client's lawyer, accountant, banker, investment advisor, and insurance advisor. By working closely with this group, the retirement planner enjoys many

- advantages, including a better understanding of the client's needs, offering a team approach for clients, and excellent referral sources for future business.
- dealing with relatively young clients. A common mistake is to start retirement planning only after a client has satisfied his other long-term responsibilities, such as buying a home or educating a child. Retirement planning is enhanced, however, if clients start saving for retirement at a relatively young age. In particular, young clients must be encouraged to take full advantage of defined contribution plans (a 401(k), for example) in which the employer matches some percentage of employees' salary.
- monitoring and/or updating the client's plan. Whether you provided a comprehensive, multiple-purpose, or a single purpose financial plan, you need to continually monitor and update your client's retirement plan because of changes in family circumstances (such as job changes, births, deaths, divorces, and receipt of inheritances) and changes in the tax and economic environment.
- being familiar with available resources. The advisor should be familiar with the various resources available in the retirement planning field. These resources include the National Council on Aging, the American Society on Aging, the Financial Planning Association, and the New York Life Center for Retirement Income at The American College, all of which provide newsletters, conferences, and a chance for interaction with other advisors. In addition, advisors should make their clients aware of AARP that provides information on services for the elderly and is a valuable resource for retirement information.

Retirement Planning and the Financial Planning Process

As one of the major planning areas that should be part of any comprehensive financial plan, retirement planning follows the same process used in financial planning.

Step 1: Establishing and Defining the Client-Planner Relationship

Retirement planning begins with advisors meeting with the client, establishing rapport, and clearly defining what the client-planner relationship will be. The advisor must structure the conversation, describe his planning philosophy, his compensation model, the scope of the engagement, and responsibilities of both the client and planner. This initial meeting is of vital importance and sets the tone for the entire planning experience. Advisors must carefully set the agenda; the goal must be for the client to have a clear understanding of the process. It is especially important that the client understand, and accept the time commitment necessary for data-gathering, plan presentation, plan implementation, and monitoring.

Step 2: Gathering Information Necessary to Fulfill the Engagement

After the client understands and indicates acceptance of pursuing the retirement planning engagement, the next step is also vitally important. It is here that the advisor leads a discussion to help the client define goals and expectations for retirement. Most clients will have only the vaguest of ideas about their own retirement. A huge percentage of clients have never attempted to determine how much they will need to retire comfortably. A good financial plan must be built on a foundation of specific, reasonable, achievable goals. The skilled advisor performs a great service in helping the client define and refine retirement goals. Next, advisors must gather a considerable amount of information about their clients. This can be time-consuming, especially when the client's situation is complex with lots of assets, trusts, or multiple sources of income. Again, a comprehensive fact-finder is extremely valuable to ensure that critical items are not missed. Remember: G-I-G-O or "garbage in, garbage out." If the data you collect is inaccurate or incomplete, the entire plan can be grossly misleading or even dangerous for your clients. While data-gathering can be tedious and complicated, resolve as a retirement planner to give it the close attention it deserves. Your clients will be the benefactors of your patience and professionalism!

Step 3: Analyzing and Evaluating the Client's Current Financial Status

In this step, you look at the client's current situation and her retirement goals to evaluate appropriate strategies for the client. This includes a retirement needs analysis, consideration of the client's financial risk tolerance, risk management strategies, and risk exposures. For example, does the client have adequate disability insurance and long-term care insurance? Are the client's current asset allocations likely to achieve her financial and/or retirement goals? Is the client saving enough for retirement? What tax planning and distribution strategies are available to the client, and do they make sense for her? You need to evaluate and analyze the client's current retirement plan exposures (for example, the penalty tax for premature distributions), current retirement plans, projected Social Security benefits, and retirement income strategies.

> **EXAMPLE**
>
> Kirk, our financial planner in Philadelphia, is working with Craig, a 35 year-old sales vice president with a small but successful internet marketing corporation, I-Tell, Inc. In analyzing Craig's current situation, Kirk notes that Craig has no retirement plans available to him through his employer. Craig has been granted a number of stock options in I-Tell, Inc., which could pay handsomely if I-Tell goes public in the future. Kirk realizes that Craig is exposed to a serious risk because his assets are not diversified. If I-Tell, Inc. has a reversal of fortune, Craig could lose his job and his stock options could become worthless (remember Enron?). Kirk will recommend that Craig start a Roth IRA and fund it to the maximum each year and invest in either mutual funds or a well-diversified stock portfolio to build other funds for eventual retirement.

Step 4: Developing the Recommendation(s)

You should develop and prepare a client-specific retirement plan tailored to meet your client's goals and expectations, considering the client's values, attitudes, temperament, and financial risk tolerance. In addition to the client's current financial position, include the client's projected retirement status under the status quo as well as projected status if the client follows your recommendations. You should also provide a current asset allocation model along with strategy recommendations. Investments should be summarized, and you should recommend an investment policy. The retirement plan should also include an assessment of distribution options and tax strategies. Finally, the plan should include a list of prioritized action items and address issues such as housing, health care, and long-term care.

Step 5: Communicating the Recommendation(s)

Normally, your retirement plan will be presented in writing, although single-purpose plans such as a retirement plan rollover into an IRA may not be in a formal written report. Many advisors use laptop computer presentations to inform the client and demonstrate "what if" scenarios for different inflation rates, rates of return, or longevity assumptions. A word to the wise here. Many younger retirement planners feel they can impress their clients with long, complicated, 80 page financial plans. Such reports are rarely read and infrequently understood by most clients. In general, the simpler the report, the easier for clients to understand the recommendations and commit to them. Many experienced advisors gravitate toward plans of 15–20 pages with good visual aids such as charts, graphs, and summaries to inform the client. This step in the retirement planning process requires you to get the client's acceptance of your recommendations and agreement to move toward implementation. This is an important step which you should carefully document in your clients' records.

Step 6: Implementing the Recommendation(s)

A plan that is never implemented is an exercise in futility. After all your work in meeting with your client, gathering data, developing recommendations, and obtaining your client's approval, do not drop the ball at this point! Part of your next responsibility is to motivate and assist your client in implementing each step of the retirement plan. The plan must include an "action list" in which the action, the responsibility, and a timeline for completion are clearly displayed. For example, if a rollover of a 401(k) is part of the plan, the client must obtain and complete rollover forms (perhaps with the advisor's help). If new investment accounts must be established, or if a reallocation of assets is to be done, the plan must clearly define responsibilities for implementing these steps. In some cases, the retirement planner must coordinate with the client's other advisors such as an attorney, CPA, or life insurance agent. Again, the goal here is to get it done—without delay. Often, the advisor must drive the process—not just wait for things to happen!

Advisors must also have a system to monitor the recommendations and retirement plan for their clients. You should plan to meet with most clients at least once per year and more frequently with some. Changes in the client's situation such as death of a family member, divorce, remarriage, birth or adoption of children, loss of a job and other major changes would warrant a review and update of the client's plan. The frequency of reviews should be agreed upon by the client in Steps 1 and 6 along with any compensation for the advisor associated with the monitoring requirements.

THE ART OF FINANCIAL PLANNING FOR RETIREMENT

To be a successful financial advisor, you must have a working knowledge of a variety of financial planning and retirement-related topics and know how to apply that knowledge to a client's particular situation. You must help determine and fully understand the client's goals, attitudes, and personal preferences. For example, you should be prepared to help a client meet important goals such as maintaining her preretirement standard of living during retirement, becoming economically self-sufficient, minimizing taxes on retirement distributions, adapting to the retirement lifestyle, and taking care of a dependent parent or dealing with special health needs. In addition, you should be able to deal with issues such as how long the client wants to work, the client's prospects for health and longevity, whether the client can be disciplined enough to save for retirement, and the client's acceptance of investment risk. Retirement planning is large in scope and demands a great deal of preparation, continual study to maintain currency, and the advisor's devotion to helping people succeed in retirement. It involves both facts and feelings and perception by the retirement planner. This application of a broad range of knowledge to a diverse group of clients makes financial planning for retirement more art than science.

As a financial advisor, your primary responsibility in the "art of financial planning for retirement" is to make clients aware they are making choices about their retirement every day. For example, should your client take an expensive vacation or take a moderately priced vacation and save the difference for retirement? Should the client purchase the latest model of a new automobile or buy a three-year-old vehicle with low mileage but at 70 percent of the cost of the new one? The advisor cannot force the client to make lifestyle choices today that will provide an adequate source of retirement funds in the future. The advisor can, however, make the client aware of the huge amount of funds needed for a long retirement and point out that a spendthrift lifestyle during the client's active working years hurts him upon retirement in two ways.

First, a spendthrift lifestyle reduce's the client's ability to accumulate enough savings to complement his employer pension and/or defined contribution plans and Social Security. These three elements—private savings, employer-sponsored retirement plans, and Social Security—are considered essential for a secure retirement. If any leg on this "three-legged stool" is missing, the client risks falling short of an economically secure retirement. Second, over years of lavish spending the client becomes accustomed to an unnaturally high standard of living. By living at or below his means before retirement, the client establishes a lifestyle more easily maintained through the retirement years.

Influencing clients to think about financial planning for retirement and lifestyle choices is a primary responsibility of the financial advisor. However, two other important facets to financial planning for retirement exist. First, the advisor must devise different retirement strategies for clients who are prepared for retirement than for those who are not prepared. Second, the advisor must help clients overcome roadblocks to retirement saving.

Older Clients Still Need to Plan for Retirement

Advisors new to the retirement planning field soon discover that clients are never too old or too young to plan for retirement. Retirement planning, however, takes on different characteristics for different age groups, and you must deal with clients of all ages. Starting young, however, can mean all the difference in the world.

Unfortunately, many workers do not start saving for retirement until the time to retire is upon them. As a result, they forgo the opportunity to set aside savings on a systematic basis and to let compound interest work for them over more years. Nevertheless, retirement planning can still be conducted for these clients. Clients must make important decisions about distributions from qualified plans, liquidation of personal assets, and investment of private savings. Developing retirement plans for clients who have procrastinated involves determining what funds are available for retirement and creating strategies, even if the funds are inadequate. In some cases, you can recommend the best of several "bad" alternatives such as working longer or reducing living expenses in retirement.

Let us consider in more detail the strategy of delaying retirement for the client with insufficient funds to retire at his desired age. The combined effect of both lengthening the accumulation period and shortening the retirement period provides a significant financial benefit. If delaying retirement from his current job is not feasible, the client can achieve similar results by working for another employer after a forced retirement. By doing so, the client can give more time for retirement assets to grow, possibly contribute more to retirement accounts, and obviously delay having to draw down retirement assets. A second strategy is to recommend that the client move to an area with a lower cost of living. This strategy will help the client stretch his retirement dollars. Moreover, by freeing up some of the equity in his home, the client can make assets available for investment purposes.

After recommending these strategies, you should help the client change his expectations about retirement. By forcing the client to look realistically at the lifestyle he can afford, you can save the client from overspending during the early retirement years and avoid becoming financially destitute in the later retirement years. Remember the high stakes involved in retirement planning. You may have only one chance to get it right! The client who runs out of money at age 75 or 80 is in dire straits. It is difficult to start a new career at that age, and bankruptcy, moving in with relatives, or worse may be the alternatives.

Table 6-1 IRA Funding Plans: The Advantages of Starting Young*

Plan One			Plan Two		
Age start		18	Age start		27
Age end		26	Age end		65
Amount per year		$3,000	Amount per year		$3,000
Rate of return		8%	Rate of return		8%
Value at age 65		$753,572	Value at age 65		$713,823
Total amount contributed		$27,000	Total amount contributed		$114,000
Age	Amount	Value	Age	Amount	Value
18	$3,000	$ 3,240	18	0	0
19	3,000	6,739	19	0	0
20	3,000	10,518	20	0	0
21	3,000	14,600	21	0	0
22	3,000	19,008	22	0	0
23	3,000	23,768	23	0	0
24	3,000	28,910	24	0	0
25	3,000	34,463	25	0	0
26	3,000	40,459	26	0	0
27	0	43,696	27	$3,000	$ 3,240
28	0	47,192	28	3,000	6,739
29	0	50,967	29	3,000	10,518
30	0	55,044	30	3,000	14,600
.	.	.	.	.	.
.	.	.	.	.	.
.	.	.	.	.	.
60	0	512,869	60	3,000	472,880
61	0	553,898	61	3,000	513,950
62	0	598,210	62	3,000	558,306
63	0	646,067	63	3,000	606,211
64	0	697,752	64	3,000	657,947
65	0	753,572	65	3,000	713,823

* This comparison is hypothetical; no guarantees are implied for specific investments. The interest rate is assumed to remain unchanged for the entire period.

Overcoming Roadblocks to Retirement Saving

Perhaps the biggest roadblock to retirement planning is the tendency of many working people to use their full after-tax income to support their current standard of living. These people will have little if any private savings to supplement Social Security and pension funds. Many of them also may have experienced adversities like unemployment that pushed them into debt. In many cases, however, a lifestyle that incurs debt stems from a spendthrift attitude or from the desire to match (or exceed) their parents' standard of living. Regardless of the reasons for their lack of retirement savings, clients must live within their means and provide for retirement. Multiple studies show that a huge percentage of American workers are ill-prepared for retirement in which the bare basics of living can be obtained.

An old rule of thumb which has merit is for clients to save a minimum of 10 percent of their gross earnings for long-term financial goals such as retirement. As with all rules of thumb, the client's personal situation may modify the rule. For example, if the client has a physically-demanding job that may require him to retire at age 55 or 60, he may need to save even more than 10 percent of earnings. Furthermore, you should routinely recommend that as a client's income rises, the percentage spent on current living expenses should decline.

A second obstacle to retirement saving is unexpected expenses, including uninsured medical bills; repairs to a home, auto, or major appliance; and unforeseen periods of unemployment. Every client should set up emergency funds to handle these inevitable problems. Advisors typically recommend 3 to 6 months' income to set aside for this purpose. If a client's salary is stable and other income, such as dividends, is part of the individual's income flow, then a 3 to 4 months' income level in the emergency fund can be sufficient. However, if the main source of income is commissions that fluctuate between pay periods, 6 months' income held for emergencies is more appropriate. In the economic recession or 2008–10 and subsequent slight recovery, many workers were out of a job for a year or more. For some clients, an emergency fund of 12 months may be prudent in today's uncertain economy.

Inadequate insurance coverage is a third roadblock to retirement saving. Many Americans remain uninsured or underinsured for life, disability, health, home or auto risks. Because clients cannot always recover economically from such losses, an important element of retirement planning is protection against catastrophic financial loss that would drain existing savings and make future saving impossible. You should always conduct a thorough review of your clients' insurance needs to see if they are adequately covered. Two frequently overlooked areas are disability insurance and umbrella liability insurance. Make sure your client is adequately protected with both coverages.

qualified domestic relations order (QDRO)

A fourth roadblock to saving for retirement is incurred by a divorced client. Divorce often leaves one or both parties with little or no accumulation of pension benefits or other private sources of retirement income. These clients may have only a short time to accumulate any retirement assets and may not accrue significant pension or Social Security benefits. If the marriage lasted 10 years or longer, however, divorced persons are eligible for Social Security as early as age 62 based on their former spouse's earnings record. In addition, a spouse may be entitled to a portion of the former spouse's retirement benefits if the divorce decree includes a *qualified domestic relations order (QDRO)*. QDROs are judgments, decrees, or orders issued by state courts that allow a participant's plan assets to be used for marital property rights, child support, or alimony payments to a former spouse or dependent.

Another common retirement planning problem is the lack of a retirement plan at the place of employment. Some workers have no opportunity to participate in a retirement plan because their employer(s) do not provide such benefits. In fact, according to the most recent data from a survey of 501 small businesses sponsored by Nationwide Insurance in 2011, only about one in five (19 percent) offer their employees any sort of retirement plan.[14] Many companies cited the excessive costs of implementing plans along with their administrative burdens. Furthermore, only 11 percent of the small employers in the survey said they are likely to add an employer-sponsored plan in the next two years.

Workers who have frequently changed employers also may arrive at retirement with little or no pension. Statistics show that employees today are unlikely to remain with one employer for their entire working life and will, typically, hold seven full-time jobs during their career. Generally, these people will not accumulate vested defined-benefit pension benefits because they do not remain with an employer long enough to become vested. Even if they did become vested, they may have received a distribution of their accumulated pension fund upon leaving the job and many have spent this money

---

14. Summary accessed at http://www.marketwatch.com/story/study-small-business-owners-say-number-of-workers-financially-unprepared-for-retirement-at-crisis-level-2011-11-28.

rather than investing it or rolling it over for retirement. You should strongly recommend to clients who change jobs that they roll over vested benefits into an IRA or into their new qualified plan to preserve the tax-deferred growth of their retirement funds. You should also advise clients who have recently changed jobs that if they are not eligible for their new employer's plan, they may be eligible to make tax-deductible contributions to an IRA until they do meet the requirements.

Roadblocks to Retirement Saving

1. Tendency to spend all income
2. Unexpected expenses
3. Inadequate insurance coverage
4. Divorce
5. No employer plan available
6. Frequent employment changes
7. Lack of financial literacy
8. Other accumulation needs

Another huge problem that inhibits people from saving for retirement is a lack of financial literacy. Many employees have never been properly schooled about investments and finance. Few high schools have any courses on financial planning topics, and many people do not get financial educations even with a college degree. For this reason, investment education ranks with health care as a top concern for employee benefit professionals and employees. In many cases, in your role as a retirement planner you must educate your clients on fundamental principles of investing, expected rates of return, impact of inflation, advantages of tax-deferred growth, and many other topics. The good retirement planner is also a good teacher!

A final impediment to the acquisition of adequate retirement savings involves other long-term goals that clients desire to fund. The down payment on a primary residence or vacation home and the education of their children can consume long-term savings people have managed to accumulate. Because these goals are closer, they tend to have a greater urgency for completion than retirement, and they often supplant retirement as a saving priority. Although these other accumulation goals are worthy, it is important to remind clients that savings must be carved out for retirement purposes in addition to other long-term goals. A good technique is to inform clients that education and retirement are "two sides of the same coin." Every dollar spent for education, plus the future investment gains on that dollar, will not be available for the parents' retirement years. While education is extremely important for one's children, it must be balanced with the need to secure the parents' retirement so (it is hoped) they will not have to depend on their children for assistance.

DEVELOPING A RETIREMENT PLAN

Another important task in financial planning for retirement is determining how much the client should save to achieve her retirement goals. Estimating a client's financial needs during retirement is not an exact science because it entails trying to predict the future. Such estimates are filled with complicating factors and clouded by unknown variables. For example, you and your client must define what standard of living is desired during retirement, when retirement will begin, inflation assumptions before and after retirement, and interest (or total return) expected on invested funds. In addition, for the client who must liquidate her retirement nest egg during retirement, you and the client must estimate the life expectancy over which liquidation will occur. Many of these variables can dramatically change overnight and without warning. The following are examples of how variables could change:

- The client may plan to retire at age 65 but health considerations, or perhaps a plant shutdown, forces retirement at age 62.
- A younger client may plan on a relatively moderate retirement lifestyle but business success may lead to a higher retirement income expectation.
- Forecasters may predict that long-term inflation will result in an annual 4 percent increase in the cost of living when in reality 6 percent increases occur. (Even a one percentage point difference can make a significant difference!)
- Clients may hope for an after-tax rate of return of 7 percent when in fact investment returns are adversely affected by a bear market, or the real after-tax rate of return is reduced by rising tax rates.
- Clients may plan on a short life expectancy and have the "misfortune" of living longer.

> **EXAMPLE**
>
> Kirk, our Philadelphia financial planner is preparing a retirement plan for Karl and Barbara Burke, both age 62. Kirk obtains agreement from the clients to use the following assumptions in the plan:
>
> - Karl and Barbara will both retire at age 66.
> - Karl's life span will be set to age 88 and Barbara's to age 92.
> - Inflation will average 3.5 percent throughout the retirement years.
> - Social Security benefits will start at age 66 for Barbara and age 70 for Karl.
> - Social Security benefits will increase at an average rate of 2.5 percent annually throughout retirement.
> - Their investments will average a 5 percent after-tax rate of return.
> - They will require an after-tax income of $4,000 per month, adjusted for inflation to maintain purchasing power.
>
> Note the number and types of assumptions in even a simple retirement plan. The retirement plan is like a travel plan. It lays out the path one would like to take, but it is sure to require detours and changes as one progresses. For example, if inflation spikes to 6 percent for a year or two, that could have a major impact on the Burkes' retirement plan. Similarly, if they have two or three years of poor investment returns, their plans may have to be significantly revised. Periodic monitoring and updating of your client's retirement plans are crucial.

While retirement planning is, at best, an educated guess, it still beats the alternative of no planning at all. A failure to plan is certainly tantamount to planning to fail for most clients. Moreover, changing variables can be overcome if the retirement plan is monitored and evaluated periodically. Once you have explained to your client the tentative nature of the plan and the need for hands-on monitoring, then the task of setting out a plan for the client begins.

The second step of the retirement planning process (gathering information necessary to fulfill the engagement) involves determining the standard of living the client expects during retirement. You must also determine where the client stands financially for retirement purposes. This involves gathering the data and adding up the client's existing resources. These may include expected Social Security benefits; anticipated pension benefits; any private savings the client has accumulated to date, including IRAs and personally owned life insurance; and any other sources of retirement income, such as the proceeds from the sale of a home or business interests.

Once you have taken a financial inventory of possible sources of retirement income, you must determine how much annual income will be needed in the first year of retirement to achieve the client's goals. There are two common ways of determining this, the *replacement ratio method* and the *expense method*.

Replacement Ratio Method

replacement ratio method

The replacement ratio method of determining retirement income assumes that the standard of living enjoyed during the years just prior to retirement will be the determining factor for the standard of living during retirement. For clients at or near retirement, it is much easier to define the target. For example, if a 64-year-old near-retiree is earning $100,000, then her retirement income should maintain most of her current purchasing power. However, if a younger client is involved, growth estimates should be made to approximate what his salary will be at retirement.

Note that the entire final salary may not be needed to maintain a client's purchasing power and lifestyle in retirement. A 60 to 80 percent replacement ratio of a client's final average salary is typically used for individual retirement planning purposes. This "rule of thumb" rests upon the elimination of some employment-related taxes and some expected changes in spending patterns that reduce the retiree's need for income.

Table 6-2 Justification of a 60 to 80 Percent Replacement Ratio

In 2012, Joe Jones, who is aged 64 and single, has a fixed salary of $100,000 and is in the 28 percent marginal tax bracket. He would like to maintain his current purchasing power when he retires next year. If Joe has no increased retirement-related expenses, he can do this by having a retirement income of 67.3 percent of his final salary as illustrated below. If Joe has increased retirement-related expenses, a somewhat higher figure should be used. (Note that post-retirement inflation will be accounted for later.)

Working salary			$100,000
less annual retirement savings		$18,000.00	
less Social Security and Medicare taxes		7,650.00	
less reduction in federal taxes	(extra standard deduction of $1,150 for being 65)	287.50	
	(no tax on portion of Social Security received)	1,650.00	
less annual commuting expenses to work		622.00	
less mortgage expenses	(mortgage expires on retirement date)	4,492.20	
Reductions subtotal			32,702
Total purchasing power needed at 65			$ 67,298
Percentage of final salary needed			67.3%

Reduced Taxes

Retirees can assume that a lower percentage of their income will go toward paying taxes in the retirement years because, in many cases, there is an elimination or a reduction of certain taxes they had to pay in their working years. Tax advantages for the retiree include the elimination of the Social Security wage base tax, the health insurance tax (that is, for Medicare Part A), an increased standard deduction depending on the retiree's age and filing status, the exclusion of all or part of Social Security retirement benefits from gross income, reductions in state and local income taxes, and an increased ability to use deductible medical expenses.

Reduced Living Expenses

Retirees incur a variety of changes in spending patterns after retirement, and some of these changes will reduce their living expenses. These reductions often include the elimination of work-related expenses such as purchases of uniforms or equipment; no home mortgage expenses; no dependent care, that is, child-rearing expenses; the elimination of long-term savings obligations; and a reduction in automotive expenditures.

Additional Factors

It is not all good news for retirees, however. Retirees also face several factors that may increase the amount of income they will need during the retirement period. These may include increases in long-term inflation, medical expenses, travel expenses, and in other retirement-related expenses. On the other hand, many retirees typically spend less later in their retirement when travel and other activities become more difficult to manage. Some surveys have found that spending (in real terms) may drop by an average of 20 percent for retirees age 75 or greater, as compared to retirees age 65 to 74. Findings in multiple surveys show that spending decreases are natural, voluntary, and acceptable to most retirees—a fact that should be reflected in the most realistic computer models used in retirement planning.

Expense Method

expense method   The expense method of determining retirement income focuses on the projected expenses the retiree will have. As with the replacement ratio method, it is much easier to define the potential expenses for clients at or near retirement. For example, if the 64-year-old near-retiree expects to have $5,666.67 in monthly bills ($68,000 annually), then the retirement income for that retiree should maintain approximately $68,000 worth of purchasing power in today's dollars. If, however, a younger client is involved, more speculative estimates of retirement expenses must be made (and periodically revised).

Expenses to consider include expenses unique to a specific client as well as other more general expenses.

Some expenses that tend to increase for retirees include the following:

- utilities and telephone
- medical/dental/drugs/health insurance
- house upkeep/repairs/maintenance/property insurance

- recreation/entertainment/travel/dining
- contributions/gifts

On the other hand, some expenses tend to decrease for retirees:
- mortgage payments
- food
- clothing
- income taxes
- property taxes
- transportation costs (car maintenance/insurance/other)
- debt repayment (charge accounts/personal loans)
- child support/alimony
- household furnishings

The Effects of Inflation

Both the replacement ratio method and the expense method can be used to determine the income level a retiree will need in the first year of retirement. They do not, however, calculate the amount of savings the client must accumulate to achieve a consistent level of financial security throughout retirement. The amount the client needs to accumulate to achieve retirement goals is a function of two opposing factors, both of which are influenced by inflation. The first factor is the savings that the client currently has, while the second is the income the client will need. To better understand the effects of inflation over time, consider the loss of purchasing power that occurs in the following example.

EXAMPLE

Glenn Edwards, aged 65, is retiring this year and needs $50,000 of retirement income to maintain his current standard of living. If the inflation rate is 4 percent per year over Glenn's retirement period, he will need an increasing amount of retirement income each year of retirement just to maintain his lifestyle. The following table illustrates the amount of annual income Glenn will need at specified intervals to maintain a consistent amount of purchasing power.

Retirement Income Glenn Edwards Needs to Maintain a Consistent Amount of Purchasing Power (Assuming a 4 Percent Rate of Inflation)	
Glenn's Age	Income Needed
65	$ 50,000
70	60,833
75	74,012
80	90,047
90	133,292
100	197,304

To calculate the true retirement income needed, the financial advisor must provide inflation protection both before and after retirement for all the client's resources. To accomplish this, identify which of the client's resources are subject to a decline in purchasing power due to effects of inflation.

Any Social Security retirement benefits the client might receive may not be subject to a decline in purchasing power, because Social Security is indexed each year to reflect inflation (at least currently). Therefore, you will not have to provide inflation protection for a client's Social Security benefit. You cannot, however, generally assume any inflation protection built into defined benefit pension income. Thus, the client should fund for an amount that can be used to bolster a noninflation-protected pension benefit during retirement. Said another way, the client should accumulate funds specifically to cover the decline in purchasing power created by a level income from a defined benefit pension plan.

The next step in mapping a client's retirement needs is to calculate the target amount of savings needed. To do this, most financial organizations provide computer programs that "crunch the numbers" you need for accurate retirement planning. Advisors must fully understand the assumptions their retirement planning software uses in creating a retirement plan. Some simply use arithmetic averages to estimate growth of investments, while others employ a "Monte Carlo" or probability-based approach. Advisors should use their planning software as a helpful tool—not as a substitute for sound planning practices. The results using planning software will only be as good as the assumptions and data that you supply—garbage in, garbage out!

POTENTIAL SOURCES OF RETIREMENT INCOME

Understanding how much a client will need for retirement is a tremendously important factor; however, it is only one part of sound financial planning. Advisors must also know the potential sources of retirement income available to a client, and how the sources can be optimized during the retirement years. For purposes of this discussion, various types of tax-advantaged retirement plans can be divided into *qualified plans* and those that are not. Qualified plans are those subject to Code Sec. 401(a) and include defined-benefit pension plans, cash-balance pension plans, money-purchase pension plans, target-benefit pension plans, profit-sharing plans, 401(k) plans, stock bonus plans, and employee stock ownership plans (ESOPs). All qualified plans can be sponsored by for-profit and nonprofit employers.

Three other very common types of tax-advantaged plans are not qualified, although they are excellent programs in their own right. These are SEPs, SIMPLEs, and 403(b) plans. Like qualified plans, SEPs and SIMPLEs can be sponsored by both for-profit and nonprofit employers. 403(b) plans, on the other hand, can only be sponsored by public school systems and nonprofit organizations that have tax-exempt status under Code Sec. 501(c)(3). Whether qualified or not qualified, all employer-sponsored tax-advantaged plans share some characteristics.

Another very different type of employer-sponsored retirement planning vehicle is the *nonqualified plan*.

nonqualified plan   Here we must be careful with the terminology, which can be confusing at times. Most advisors use the term "nonqualified plan" to refer to deferred compensation plans instead of the tax-advantaged plans identified above (the SEP, SIMPLE, or 403(b) plan). Unlike tax-advantaged plans, nonqualified plans are generally for only a few key people and have few design restrictions regarding the benefit structure, vesting requirements, and coverage. However, in exchange for the added flexibility in plan design, the tax rules are not as kind to nonqualified plans as they are to qualified plans and other tax-advantaged plans.

Another type of retirement plan is the individual retirement account (IRA). As its name implies, this type of plan is established by or for individuals, not by employers. At times, a business owner or employee will be faced with the choice of participating in a company-sponsored plan or establishing an IRA. In some cases as we shall see, the individual can choose to participate in both.

Retirement Planning

Another very important source of retirement income is Social Security. Retirement benefits under Social Security are based more on social adequacy than on individual equity. Under the principle of social adequacy, benefits are designed to provide a minimum floor of income to all recipients regardless of their economic status. Above this floor, clients are expected to provide additional sources of retirement income from their own individually established plans and from employer-sponsored plans. Because Social Security benefits are so thoroughly interrelated to individually-established and employer-sponsored retirement plans, it is important that you have a good understanding of this government program.

Tax-Advantaged Qualified Plans

qualified plan

Perhaps the most valuable way to save for retirement is through a tax-advantaged *qualified plan*. The advantages of a qualified plan stem from its tax benefits. While an employer is able to take a tax deduction when it contributes to a qualified plan on behalf of employees, the employee does not have to pay income tax on those contributions when they are made. Instead, the employee pays income tax when plan funds are distributed to him years later. In addition, investment earnings on plan assets are also tax-deferred while they remain in the plan. This combination of tax-deferred contributions and tax-deferred earnings is like receiving an interest-free loan from the government, and qualified plans permit the employee to invest funds for retirement that otherwise would be lost to taxation.

EXAMPLE
Roy Cassidy is employed by HorseMasters, Inc., which offers a qualified 401(k) plan to all eligible employees. Roy contributes $200 per month to his 401(k) on a pre-tax basis. This means that his $200 per month contribution reduces his taxable income dollar-for-dollar. In addition, HorseMasters, Inc., matches the first 5 percent of a participating employee's contributions. In Roy's case, his gross income is $48,000, so he receives a match for his entire $200 per month contribution. The employer's contributions are also deductible to the corporation in the year they are made. Finally, the assets in Roy's 401(k) grow tax-deferred until he requests a distribution. The distributions will be fully taxable as ordinary income in the year they are distributed. Other tax penalties may apply in some circumstances, such as for taxable withdrawals before age 59½.

A final tax advantage afforded by qualified plans is that distributions from these plans can be rolled into an IRA or other tax-advantaged plan with taxation continuing to be deferred until the funds are finally withdrawn as retirement income.

Tax-advantaged qualified plans can be categorized in several ways, and one method for categorizing is based on what the employer provides. Under this method of categorizing, one type of plan includes the employer's promise to pay an annual retirement benefit (a defined-benefit plan). A second type of plan is based on the employer's annual contribution to an employee's individual account (a defined-contribution plan).

A second method for categorizing qualified plans distinguishes plans primarily geared to sharing employer profits (profit-sharing plans) from those geared to providing retirement benefits (pension plans).

Yet another method to categorize qualified plans focuses on the business entity adopting a plan. If a corporate entity sponsors a qualified retirement plan, the plan is simply known as a qualified plan. If a partnership or self-employed person sponsors a qualified plan, the plan is known as a *Keogh plan*. Over the years the rules for Keogh and corporate plans have evolved so that only a few minor distinctions exist between the two types of plans. Therefore, only the differences between defined-benefit/defined-contribution plans and pension/profit-sharing plans are examined in the following paragraphs.

Defined-Benefit versus Defined-Contribution Plans

defined-benefit plan

defined-contribution plan

All qualified plans are either defined-benefit or defined-contribution plans. One way to look at these dissimilar approaches is to say that a *defined-benefit plan* provides a fixed predetermined benefit for the employee but has an uncertain cost to the employer, whereas a *defined-contribution plan* has a predetermined cost to the employer but provides an uncertain benefit for the employee. Let us examine each of these two types of plans more closely.

Under a defined-benefit plan, the required employer contributions vary depending on what is needed to pay the promised benefits. The maximum annual benefit that can be provided to a retired employee from a defined-benefit plan must not exceed the lesser of $200,000 (as indexed for 2012) or 100 percent of the employee's average compensation for his 3 consecutive years of highest pay while an active participant in the plan. A defined-benefit plan typically uses a benefit formula to stipulate a promised retirement benefit. This promised benefit is typically a percentage of the employee's salary (for example, 50 percent of the employee's final salary or 50 percent of the employee's final-average salary, such as the average of the final 3 to 5 years' salary).

EXAMPLE

Susan Dean has been an employee for PaperWorks, Inc. for over 25 years. Her company has a defined-benefit plan that will pay Susan a lifetime annuity payment based on the following formula: the annual payment, starting at age 65, will be 2 percent times the average of the employee's last three years of salary, times the number of years of service credited to the employee. In Susan's case, she can retire at age 65 with 30 years of service. She anticipates her average salary over her last 3 years to be $60,000. As a result, she estimates her retirement benefit will be $36,000 (0.02 X $60,000 X 30 years = $36,000). While Susan may take her benefit as a single (or straight life) annuity payment, the company will offer other options that are actuarially equivalent.

Defined-contribution plans do not promise to pay a specified retirement benefit; instead, they specify (or define) the contribution the employer will make annually to an employee's individual account. The maximum annual contribution made to a defined-contribution plan on behalf of an employee must not exceed the lesser of $50,000 (as indexed for 2012) or 100 percent of the employee's compensation. Annual contributions include both employer and employee contributions, as well as any forfeitures allocated to the employee's account. By their nature, defined-contribution plans base an employee's benefit on the employee's entire career earnings and not the employee's final or final-average salary. Because defined-contribution plans allocate contributions to the accounts of individual employees, they are sometimes called individual account plans.

EXAMPLE

Juan Ramirez is a 45-year-old participant in his employer-sponsored 401(k), a defined-contribution plan. Juan's annual salary is $70,000. By rule, he can contribute up to $17,000 (for 2012, as indexed) to his 401(k). His employer will match up to 5 percent of salary for employees who contribute to their plan. The total additions to Juan's 401(k) from all sources (his contributions, employer's matching contributions, or a share of forfeitures) cannot exceed $50,000 (for 2012).

Most defined-contribution plans allow the employee to select from among a group of available investments. Some plans offer dozens of options such as stock funds, bond funds, money market funds, balanced, real estate, and so on. The risk in defined-contribution falls squarely on the employee/investor. As studies continue to show, many workers have inadequate knowledge or experience in selecting their funds and managing them effectively. Clients covered by defined-contribution plans may find themselves short of retirement income if investment results are unfavorable. With a defined-contribution plan, unlike a defined-benefit plan, the employer's obligation begins and ends with making the annual contribution. If plan investments are poor in a defined-contribution plan, the employee suffers the loss and may have inadequate retirement resources. In a defined-benefit plan, the benefits are promised and by law the employer must make additional contributions to compensate for poor investment performance.

A second problem with defined-contribution plans is that contributions are based on participants' salaries for each year of their careers, rather than on their salaries at retirement as in most defined-benefit plans. Consequently, if inflation increases sharply in the years just prior to retirement, the chances of a participant achieving an adequate income-replacement ratio are diminished because most of the annual contributions would have been based on lower salaries paid prior to the inflationary spiral. In contrast, if the participant had been covered by a final-average defined-benefit plan, the employer would have had to compensate for the higher final-average salary due to the increased inflation.

An instance where either a defined-benefit plan or a defined-contribution plan may provide inadequate retirement income occurs when a client joins a plan late in his working life. In this situation, since the years until retirement are few, a defined-contribution plan may not provide enough time to accumulate adequate assets. A defined-benefit plan, where the benefit is based in part on length of service, would also provide a relatively small benefit. The following table provides a summary of differences between these two types of plans.

Retirement Planning

Table 6-3 Differences Between Defined-Benefit and Defined-Contribution Plans	
Defined-Benefit Plans	**Defined-Contribution Plans**
Defines the benefit; the law specifies the maximum allowable benefit payable from the plan—the lesser of 100 percent of salary or $200,000 per year (2012, indexed)	Defines the employer's contribution; the law specifies the maximum allowable annual contribution—the lesser of 100 percent of salary or $50,000 (2012, indexed)
Contributions not attributed to specified employees but are managed by the employer, trust, or other account.	All contributions allocated to individual employee accounts
Employer assumes risk of preretirement inflation, investment performance, and the promised amount of retirement income	Employee assumes risk of preretirement inflation, investment performance, and the adequacy of retirement income
Unpredictable costs for the employer. Contributions are established by adequate funding requirements and may vary year to year.	Predictable costs to the employer, based on contribution formula

Pension versus Profit-Sharing Plans

pension plan

profit-sharing plan

Under a *pension plan*, the employer commits to making annual contributions to the plan, since the main purpose of the plan is to provide a retirement benefit. Under a *profit-sharing plan*, however, the employer retains the flexibility and can avoid funding the plan annually, at least for some number of years. Moreover, a profit-sharing plan is not necessarily intended to provide a retirement benefit as much as to provide tax deferral of present compensation. To this end, under certain profit-sharing plans employees are permitted to withdraw funds after they have been in the plan for at least 2 years.

Two important factors apply to a profit-sharing plan: First, the financial advisor should help a client closely monitor the funding of the plan. A common mistake is to assume that the employer is making scheduled payments to the plan when the employer actually is not contributing because employer contributions are discretionary. Another common mistake is assuming that the employee is allowing the funds to accumulate for retirement when the employee is actually depleting the account by taking withdrawals.

The second factor concerning profit-sharing plans is that since funds can be withdrawn prior to retirement under some profit-sharing plans, this opens up some interesting planning possibilities for the client and advisor. For example, the client may want to gradually take money out while employed (starting after age 59½ to avoid the 10 percent penalty tax) to reposition assets or take advantage of some excellent investment opportunity. In addition, the client may want to prepay any debt that would carry over into retirement, such as prepaying a mortgage or reducing interest expenses on a major capital purchase. The following table provides a summary of differences between pension and profit-sharing plans.

Table 6-4 Differences between Pension and Profit-Sharing Plans

Characteristic	Pension Plan	Profit-Sharing Plan
Employer commitment to annual funding	Yes	No
Withdrawal flexibility for employees	None	Yes, after 2 years

Types of Tax-Advantaged Qualified Plans

After you understand the basic characteristics of each category of qualified plans, you are well on the way to understanding the specific type of plan your client has. For example, if your client has a plan that is a defined-contribution, profit-sharing plan, you will know that employer contributions are optional and that the employee assumes the risks associated with investment performance and preretirement inflation.

The final component you need to understand is the plan's benefit or contribution formula. These formulas are unique to the specific type of plan involved.

defined-benefit pension plan

unit-benefit formula

Defined-Benefit Pension Plans. As its name implies, a *defined-benefit pension plan* is both a defined-benefit plan and a pension plan. The employer's contributions under this type of plan are determined actuarially based on the benefits promised by the plan. These benefits must be determined using a benefit formula, and there are several different types of defined-benefit formulas. The most common type, the *unit-benefit formula*, directly accounts for both the participant's service with the employer and the participant's salary in determining the pension benefit. An example of how a unit-benefit formula might read is as follows:

> **EXAMPLE**
>
> Each plan participant will receive a monthly pension commencing at the normal retirement age and paid in the form of a life annuity equal to 2 percent of final-average monthly salary (annual salary considered in the benefit formula is limited to a maximum amount of $250,000 as indexed for 2012) multiplied by the participant's years of service. Normal retirement age in this plan is defined as the later of age 65 or 5 years of plan participation. Service is limited to a maximum of 30 years.

Under this unit-benefit formula, an employee with 20 years of service and a $300,000 final-average annual salary will receive $8,333.33 per month in the form of life annuity payments [.02 × $20,833 (not $25,000 because of the compensation limit) x 20].

There are a number of less common formulas that are also used. One of these is a *flat-percentage-of-earnings formula* under which the benefit is tied to salary. Length of service, however, is also a factor, albeit indirect. To prevent discrimination in favor of participants hired later in their careers, the IRS passed regulations that required this type of formula to have a 25-year minimum period of service for participants to receive the full benefits promised. For those with less service, the benefits are proportionately reduced.

Understanding the benefit formula is not all that is required to understand how much a client will receive from a defined-benefit plan. Every element of a benefit formula affects the ultimate benefit. In the unit-benefit formula previously discussed, the benefit is tied to four factors: final-average salary, years of service, the timing of when benefits begin, and the form of the benefit. In a defined-benefit plan, compensation can be defined inclusively to cover all wages paid, or it can be limited to only base salary, excluding bonuses, overtime, or other extraordinary pay. Final-average salary is usually defined to include the highest 3-to-5 years of salary, although this also can vary. In any event, compensation used in the formula cannot exceed $250,000 (as indexed for 2012), meaning that an employee earning more than the $250,000 compensation cap will not receive retirement benefits on the amount of salary that exceeds the cap.

Even the definition of years of service can vary from plan to plan. Some plans exclude years prior to plan participation, and some exclude part-time service or give only partial credit for part-time service. For an early retiree, the timing of when benefits begin is a key element. For example, a plan may provide for full retirement benefits to begin at age 65, but allow early retirement at age 62 with actuarially reduced benefits to reflect the longer payout period. This can be a bit tricky for the advisor helping a client determine what benefits she will receive, especially if the client is going to retire early, late, or has an unusual employment history with the company. A safe practice is for the client to request an estimate of benefits, in writing, from the plan's administrator prior to retirement.

cash-balance pension plan

Cash-Balance Pension Plans. A *cash-balance pension plan is a defined-benefit plan* designed to look like a defined-contribution plan. As a defined-benefit plan, employers are committed to funding it each year, but its defined-contribution "look" means that its benefit formula is more easily explained to employees.

The heart of the cash-balance pension plan is the benefit formula. As in a defined-contribution plan, the benefit is stated as an account balance that increases with contributions and investment experience. However, in the cash-balance plan the account is fictitious. Contributions are a bookkeeping credit only—no actual contributions are allocated to individual participants' accounts. Investment credits are also hypothetical. Nonetheless, to the participants, this plan looks like a traditional defined-contribution individual account plan. An example of how a cash-balance formula might read follows:

EXAMPLE

The participant is entitled to a single-sum benefit based on a credit of 5 percent of compensation each year. The credited amounts will accumulate with interest. Interest will be credited annually using the U.S. 30-year treasury rate on the crediting date of December 31 each year. Actual investment experience will not affect the value of the benefit.

From the employer's perspective, a cash-balance pension plan is still a defined-benefit plan, and as in any qualified pension plan, the employer is ultimately responsible for making the contributions necessary to pay promised benefits—meaning that the sponsor bears the risk for the plan's investment experience. If a cash-balance pension plan's assets earn a higher rate of return than expected, then the employer's future contributions can be reduced, and vice versa.

money-purchase plan

Money-Purchase Pension Plans. A *money-purchase pension plan* is a type of defined-contribution plan. It is also, as its name states, a pension plan. Under a money-purchase pension plan, the employer's annual contributions are mandatory and are specified in the plan. For example, a money-purchase contribution formula may require annual contributions equal to 10 percent of each participant's compensation. The definition of compensation will vary from plan to plan.

target-benefit pension plan

Target-Benefit Pension Plans. A *target-benefit pension plan,* like a money-purchase pension plan, is both a defined-contribution plan and a pension plan. Thus, target-benefit plans have many of the same characteristics as money-purchase plans. Despite the similarities, however, target benefit plans are a unique form of defined-contribution plan because they have some features associated with traditional defined-benefit plans. One feature is that a defined-benefit formula is used to determine the annual contribution.

Table 6-5 Hybrid Plans: Mirrors of Each Other	
Target-Benefit Pension Plan	**Cash-Balance Pension Plan**
Defined-contribution plan	Defined-benefit plan
Participant entitled to vested account balance	Participant entitled to promised benefit, regardless of actual plan assets
Looks and feels like a defined-benefit plan because contributions target a monthly benefit at retirement *employee assumes risk*	Feels like a defined-contribution plan because promised benefit is based on an accumulated hypothetical account balance
Contribution is fixed based on the contribution formula determined by an actuary	Employer's contribution is determined annually by an actuary *employer assumes risk*

At the inception of a target-benefit plan, an actuary takes into account final-average salary assumptions, age, mortality, interest earnings, and other assumptions to project the annual level contribution for each participant. While the employer hopes to provide a specific benefit (the target) at retirement, the employer does not guarantee that the targeted benefit will be paid. The investment risk falls on the participants, and an amount less than or greater than the target may be available, depending on the investment performance of the participants' accounts.

profit-sharing plan

allocation formula

Profit-Sharing Plans. A profit-sharing plan is also a type of defined-contribution plan. Under a profit-sharing plan, there are two parts to the contribution formula. One part relates to how much the employer contributes to the plan, and the other relates to how the contribution is allocated—or spread—among the participants.

In most profit-sharing plans, employer contributions are made on a discretionary basis. This means the employer decides whether a contribution will be made and how much that contribution will be. Typically, contributions are geared to profits, although the employer can make contributions even if there are no profits. However, a profit-sharing plan can also be written to require a specified contribution. The plan may state the required contribution as a specified percentage of profits or some other objective formula stated in the plan. This approach is appropriate when the employer wants employees to feel that they have a clear and determinable stake in the performance of the company.

The heart of a profit-sharing plan is the method of allocating the employer contribution among the participants—the *allocation formula*. This formula must be definite and predetermined. The most common type of allocation formula allocates the total contribution so that each participant receives a contribution equal to a percentage of compensation, for example, 3 percent or 5 percent. This allocation formula is popular, because it satisfies the ERISA requirement that contributions or benefits cannot discriminate in favor of highly compensated employees. Qualified plan rules do allow profit-sharing plans to allocate contributions by a formula that integrates the contributions with Social Security. While somewhat complicated and beyond the scope of this text, an integrated profit-sharing plan allows employees who earn more than the Social Security taxable wage base ($110,100 in 2012, as indexed) to receive a higher portion of the employer's profit-sharing contributions. Other approaches allocate even a larger portion of the contribution to older, more highly compensated employees. However, even a brief explanation of these other approaches is beyond the scope of this introductory chapter on retirement planning. You are encouraged to strengthen your knowledge of those approaches, such as age-weighted and cross-tested allocation methods covered in other American College courses.

401(k) plan

401(k) Plans. One of the most popular types of qualified plans is the 401(k) defined-contribution profit-sharing plan. A *401(k) plan* allows employees to defer current salary, which is then contributed to the plan on a pretax basis. In addition to the salary deferral feature, a 401(k) plan can contain a traditional profit-sharing feature, an employer matching contribution feature, or both. Some 401(k) plans even allow for employee after-tax contributions. This means a 401(k) plan can be as simple as a stand-alone plan (salary deferrals only) or one that allows both pretax and after-tax employee contributions, employer matching contributions, and employer profit-sharing contributions. In today's market, many employers, even those that already have defined-benefit or money-purchase pension plans, opt to sponsor 401(k) plans. From a retirement planning perspective, 401(k) plans are an excellent way for employees to save for retirement, and in most cases clients should be encouraged to take full advantage of them. Frequent mistakes by younger employees include (1) not participating at all in their 401(k) plan; (2) not contributing enough to get the entire matching funds from the employer; and (3) investing far too conservatively when they have a long time horizon until retirement.

The heart of a 401(k) plan is the salary deferral feature that employees may elect. The amount of elective deferrals cannot exceed a specified annual limit. For 2012, the limit is $17,000. In addition, the maximum salary deferral is increased for those individuals who have attained age 50. For 2012, the additional allowable contribution (a "catch-up") is $5,500.

In addition to encouraging clients to participate in 401(k) plans and deferring part of their salaries, you should know about the following factors that apply to 401(k) salary deferrals:

- 401(k) salary reductions are immediately 100 percent vested and cannot be forfeited, but matching contributions can be subject to a vesting schedule.
- Participants may have limited access to salary deferral contributions while still employed. The law only allows in-service withdrawals upon a severe financial hardship or the attainment of age 59½. However, many plans allow employees to borrow against their assets in the 401(k).

> **EXAMPLE**
>
> Julie Reagan, age 45, is a participant in her employer-sponsored 401(k) plan. Julie's vested balance in the plan is $100,000. Her plan allows her to borrow up to $50,000 for any reason. She must pay the money back to the plan on a 5-year schedule, including a 5 percent interest rate on the remaining balance. She must also make repayments of principal and interest at least quarterly. If Julie defaults on her loan, the entire amount of the loan will be "deemed" by the IRS to be an early withdrawal; Julie would then owe ordinary income taxes on the full amount, plus a 10 percent penalty tax since she is under age 59½.

In addition to pretax salary deferrals by participating employees, most employers make additional contributions to the plan. The employer can choose how to make the contributions for employees—as matching or as profit-sharing contributions or both. A common practice today is to choose a matching contribution feature in which the employer matches employee contributions to a certain extent. For example, the employer might agree to contribute 50 cents to the plan for each dollar the employee contributes up to the first 6 percent of the employee's salary. In this example, the maximum employer match is 3 percent of the employee's salary. Other contribution designs can be more complex to meet specific employer objectives.

Both the matching percentage and the maximum match must be carefully chosen to meet the employer's objectives and budget. The primary reason for the match is to stimulate plan participation through the offer of an instant return on the participant's contributions. Another goal is to create a retirement planning partnership between the employer and the participants. Under this philosophy, an employer commits to contribute toward an employee's funds for retirement, but only if the employee also commits to save.

A profit-sharing feature in a 401(k) plan works the same way as in a traditional profit-sharing plan. Contributions are made for all eligible participants, regardless of whether they make salary deferral contributions. The profit-sharing contributions must be allocated according to some formula designated in the plan documents. When a 401(k) plan is the only plan offered by an employer, it is not uncommon—in a good year—for the employer to make both matching contributions and profit-sharing-type contributions.

stock bonus plan

employee stock ownership plan (ESOP)

Stock Bonus Plans and ESOPs. Both a *stock bonus plan* and an *employee stock ownership plan (ESOP)* are variations of profit-sharing plans and are, therefore, similar in many ways:

- Stock bonus plans, ESOPs, and profit-sharing plans are all defined-contribution plans and fall into the profit-sharing (not pension) category.
- Contributions need not be fixed and need not be made every year.
- Similar allocation formulas used under a profit-sharing plan may be used under either a stock bonus plan or an ESOP.
- Contributions for all three types of plans are usually based on profits, although they are not required to be.

Stock bonus plans and ESOPs differ from profit-sharing plans, however, in three important ways:

- Both stock bonus plans and ESOPs typically invest plan assets primarily in the employer's stock (in fact, an ESOP is required to invest primarily in employer stock). Profit-sharing plans, on the other hand, are usually structured to diversify investments and do not concentrate investments in employer stock (even though they are legally permitted to do so).
- Both stock bonus plans and ESOPs provide a market for employer stock, especially for small corporations or closely-held companies. This, in turn, generates capital for the corporation and can help finance a company's growth. Profit-sharing plans, however, are not viewed as a way to finance company operations but are more concerned with providing tax-favored deferred compensation for retirement purposes.
- Stock bonus plans and ESOPs allow distributions to participants in the form of employer stock. Profit-sharing plans generally do not. This creates a distinct advantage for participants in a stock bonus plan or an ESOP. Participants receive a tax break since any unrealized appreciation (gain in value) in their stock is not taxed until the stock is sold.

Despite the many similarities between stock bonus plans and ESOPs, there is one major difference. An ESOP allows the plan to borrow to purchase employer stock. Under this technique, the employer guarantees repayment of the loan, and the plan repays the loan with employer contributions to the ESOP.

Other Tax-Advantaged Plans

In this section, we discuss three types of tax-advantaged retirement plans, that are not technically qualified plans. These are the simplified employee pension (SEP), the savings incentive match plan for employees (SIMPLE), and the 403(b) plan. We shall see that each of these plans has its own unique set of rules.

Simplified Employee Pension (SEP)

simplified employee pension (SEP)

A *simplified employee pension (SEP)* uses an individual retirement account (IRA) or an individual retirement annuity (IRA annuity) as the vehicle for contributions. As its name implies, this plan is simpler than a qualified retirement plan, which makes it attractive to many small business owners.

A SEP is quite similar in design to a profit-sharing plan—that is, employer contributions are made on a discretionary basis, although the plan can require specified employer contributions. No employee contributions can be made to a SEP. What makes the SEP different from a qualified profit-sharing plan is that contributions must be allocated to participants as a level percentage of compensation. (For example, all employees may receive an allocation of 10 percent of compensation.) The only exception to the level-percentage-of-compensation rule is that the allocation formula may be integrated with Social Security in the same manner as other defined-contribution plans. This provides highly compensated employees with contributions that are slightly larger (as a percentage of pay) than those for the rank-and-file employees. All employer contributions to a SEP must be immediately and 100 percent vested.

SIMPLEs

savings incentive match plan for employees (SIMPLE)

Beginning in 1997, employers had a new plan option available, referred to as the *savings incentive match plan for employees (SIMPLE)*. Like SEPs, a SIMPLE plan is funded with individual retirement accounts, which means the following requirements apply to the SIMPLE:

- Participants must be fully vested in all benefits at all times.
- Assets cannot be invested in life insurance or collectibles.
- No participant loans are allowed.

Any type of business entity can establish a SIMPLE; however, the business cannot have more than 100 employees (only counting those employees who earned $5,000 or more of compensation). If the employer grows beyond the 100-employee limit, the law does allow the employer to sponsor the plan for an additional 2-year grace period. Also note that to be eligible, the sponsoring employer cannot maintain any other qualified plan, 403(b) plan, or SEP at the same time it maintains the SIMPLE.

Note that the employee's maximum salary deferral contributions are less under a SIMPLE than with qualified plans such as a 401(k). For 2012, an employee under age 50 can defer up to $11,500. Employees age 50 or older can defer an additional $2,500 in 2012.

Unlike with the 401(k) plan, there is no discrimination testing with the SIMPLE, meaning that highly-compensated employees can make contributions without regard to the salary deferral elections of nonhighly-compensated employees. However, the SIMPLE has a mandatory employer contribution requirement that can be made in either of two ways:

1. The employer can make a dollar-for-dollar matching contribution on the first 3 percent of compensation that employees defer, or
2. The employer can make a 2 percent nonelective contribution for all eligible employees, regardless of whether they defer.

Note that with the SIMPLE, the employer must choose only one of the contribution methods. In other words, if the employer elects the matching contributions, nonelective contributions are not allowed. If the employer elects the nonelective contribution, then the 2 percent contribution is required, and matching contributions are not allowed.

Salary Deferral Contributions. The maximum salary reduction contribution that can be made by an individual is subject to the same dollar limitations that apply to 401(k) plans. For 2012, the dollar limit is $17,000. Also, as with the 401(k) plan, additional contributions can be made by individuals who have attained age 50 by the end of the current year.

Also, it is important to note that the dollar limit applies to all contributions made by the individual to any 403(b) plan, 401(k) plan, simplified employee pension (SEP), or savings incentive match plan for employees (SIMPLE). This is true even if the individual is covered by plans of unrelated employers. For example, a 40-year-old participant deferring $10,000 in a 403(b) plan for 2012 would only be able to defer a maximum of $7,000 under a 401(k) arrangement for 2012.

403(b) Plans

403(b) plan

tax-sheltered annuity (TSA)

The plans we have studied up to this point are not limited to any particular type of industry. For the most part, they are available to any organization. In contrast to other retirement plans, a 403(b) plan can be established only by tax-exempt organizations and public schools. Despite these limitations, 403(b) plans represent a separate and lucrative opportunity for financial advisors, particularly those who sell annuity products. A 403(b) plan, which is also referred to as a *tax-sheltered annuity (TSA)* or a tax-deferred annuity (TDA), is similar to a 401(k) plan. Like the 401(k) plan, the 403(b) plan

- allows deferrals as a salary reduction chosen by the employee
- allows before-tax employer contributions to the employee's individual account
- can be used in conjunction with, or in lieu of, most other retirement plans

However, 403(b) plans differ from 401(k) plans both in the market they serve and in their makeup.

The maximum salary reduction contributions that can be made by an employee to a 403(b) plan are subject to the same dollar limitations that apply to 401(k) plans. For 2012, the dollar limit is $17,000. As with the 401(k) plans, individuals who are at least age 50 by the end of the current year can make additional "catch-up" contributions ($5,500 in 2012).

Note here that the dollar limits apply to contributions made by an individual to all plans collectively, such as to a 403(b) plan, 401(k), or SIMPLE. For example, a 40-year-old participant deferring $10,000 in his 403(b) plan for 2012 could defer a maximum of $7,000 under a 401(k) plan with a different employer in 2012.

Nonqualified Plans

nonqualified plans

Another very different type of employer-sponsored retirement planning vehicle is a *nonqualified plan*. These plans are primarily established for highly compensated executives, managers, and officers of a company. The plans help business owners and selected employees save for retirement without being subject to the many regulations and restrictions that come with qualified plans. In some plans, the employer provides an additional benefit or "supplemental" plan. In other cases, the participants are allowed to defer their right to compensation, along with deferring the taxation on it.

As a trade-off for allowing the employer nearly complete discretion in plan design and choosing employees covered by the plan, the employer loses the central advantage of a qualified plan—that is, the ability to make a before-tax contribution on the employee's behalf that is simultaneously deductible to the business. With nonqualified plans, the tax savings stem from the fact that, in most cases, the employer defers the business deduction so that specifically chosen employees can defer compensation promised to them. In some plans, the employer provides an additional ("supplemental") benefit, while other plans are similar to 401(k) plans, allowing participants the right to defer salary.

Financial advisors must be alert for some potential problems for clients covered by nonqualified plans. One trap is that clients will typically have somewhat inflexible withdrawal provisions. In qualified plans, distributions can generally be rolled over into an IRA, which will delay taxation until the client withdraws funds as required from the IRA. Nonqualified benefits cannot be rolled over to an IRA. In addition, the participant generally is not given a choice of distribution options at retirement time. The distribution options are generally defined when the nonqualified plan is established and are quite limited. The following illustration gives you the flavor of a typical nonqualified plan.

EXAMPLE

Under Woodworth Company's nonqualified plan for employee Tara Ross, 10 percent of her annual compensation is credited on her behalf on December 31 of each year. In addition, a reasonable rate of interest is credited quarterly on the balance. All amounts credited under the plan are 100 percent vested after Tara completes 5 years of service. Tara was hired on March 1, 2006, and began participation in the plan on January 1, 2007. When Tara became vested in 2012, her account had a balance of $88,450 as of December 31, 2011. The company must treat the $88,450 account balance as wages for employment tax purposes for 2012. Tara will have "constructive receipt" of the balance, which will be taxable income to her in 2012.

A second trap for clients covered by nonqualified plans is that promised benefits are typically subject to loss for a variety of reasons. For example, a nonqualified plan may contain a forfeiture provision stipulating that benefits will be forfeited if certain conditions are not met. In some circumstances, the client may be either unwilling or unable to meet her part of the commitment, such as working for the employer a certain period. A second way nonqualified benefits can be lost is when an employer sponsoring the plan goes bankrupt. Nonqualified plan funds are typically held as corporate assets subject to the claims of corporate creditors in bankruptcy. This is in sharp contrast to funds in a qualified plan that are held in a trust or insurance contract completely separate from business assets. Qualified plan assets no longer belong to the employer and are not subject to forfeiture in case of bankruptcy. Nonqualified plan assets, on the other hand, must be subject to forfeiture to prevent constructive receipt by the employee that would trigger taxable income.

A final issue associated with nonqualified plans is the threat of immediate taxation to the employee that would result in a lower overall retirement accumulation. For example, despite the employer's best intentions to the contrary, some nonqualified plans are construed by the IRS as providing an immediate economic benefit to the employee, or the employee may be deemed to be in constructive receipt of the income. In either case, the prefunded benefit will be taxable while the client is still employed, and the advantages of tax deferral will be lost.

Despite all these problems, nonqualified plans have an important role in retirement planning for executive clients. The major reason is that qualified and tax-advantaged plan rules limit plan benefits, and a nonqualified plan may ensure that the executive will have an adequate income replacement ratio. Nonqualified plans represent a very lucrative market for financial services professionals servicing the retirement needs of businesses and business owners.

IRAs

One of the most important sources of retirement income that financial advisors can help their clients with is an individual retirement account (IRA). There are two types of IRAs designed to accumulate retirement funds: traditional IRAs and Roth IRAs. Traditional IRAs are similar to qualified plans in many respects. Both encourage retirement savings by allowing contributions to be made with pretax dollars (if the taxpayer is eligible). Both allow earnings to be tax deferred until retirement, at which time all withdrawals are taxable. In contrast, Roth IRA contributions are not deductible, but qualifying withdrawals are not subject to income tax.

Traditional IRAs and Roth IRAs are subject to certain limitations. The most important are the maximum contribution limits. Total contributions to both traditional and Roth IRAs may not exceed $5,000 a year (for 2012) or 100 percent of compensation, whichever is smaller. These contribution limits are indexed and subject to change each year. In addition, an IRA owner who has attained age 50 before the end of the taxable year can contribute an additional "catch up" amount of $1,000. The catch-up amount is also scheduled to increase in future years. Other important IRA rules include the following:

- Traditional IRA contributions may not be made during or after the year in which the client reaches age 70½; however, Roth IRA contributions may continue during and after that year if the owner has earned income.
- IRA funds may not be commingled with the client's other assets; the funds may contain only IRA contributions and rollover contributions.
- IRA funds may not be used to buy a life insurance policy.
- Funds contributed to an IRA may not be invested in collectibles.
- No loans may be taken from IRA accounts.

Traditional IRAs

traditional IRA Any person under age 70½ who receives $5,000 in compensation (either salary or self-employment earned income) may make a $5,000 contribution (for 2012) to a *traditional IRA*. In addition, if a person is married, even if he does not work, that person can contribute $5,000 as long as his spouse's salary is at least $10,000 (then each spouse can make a $5,000 contribution).

A contribution to a traditional IRA, however, is only deductible if certain eligibility requirements are satisfied. The contribution will be fully deductible if neither the taxpayer nor his spouse is an active participant (as discussed below) in an employer-maintained retirement plan. If the taxpayer is an active participant, then the contribution is deductible only if his modified adjusted gross income falls below prescribed limits (designed to approximate a middle-class income). If an individual is not an active participant, but his spouse is, then the contribution is deductible for the spouse who is not an active participant if the couple's income is less than a different and higher income threshold. Note, while these rules appear somewhat complicated at first reading, it is important that financial advisors master these rules to adequately advise their clients.

active participant

Active Participant. The first eligibility issue concerns whether the client is an active participant in an employer-maintained plan. Employer-maintained plans include every type of qualified plan, as well as all federal, state, and local government plans. Nonqualified plans, however, are not considered. Thus, an employee who is covered only by a nonqualified plan is not considered an active participant under IRA rules, and can make fully deductible IRA contributions.

The term *active participant* has a special meaning that depends on the type of plan involved. Generally, a person is an active participant in a defined-benefit plan unless she is excluded under the eligibility provision of the plan for the entire year. This is true even if she elects not to participate in the plan. In the case of a defined-contribution plan, a person is an active participant if the plan specifies that employer contributions must be allocated to the individual's account (such as a money-purchase pension plan). This category also includes SEPs, 403(b) plans, and SIMPLEs. In a profit-sharing or stock plan where employer contributions are discretionary, the participant must actually receive some contribution to be considered an active participant for the plan year. Furthermore, mandatory contributions, voluntary contributions, and salary deferral contributions made within a 403(b) plan, SIMPLE, or 401(k) arrangement will also trigger active-participant status.

EXAMPLE
Sharon Davis, age 45, first became eligible for the XYZ Corporation's profit-sharing plan for the plan year ending December 31, 2011. The company is on a calendar fiscal year and decided to make no profit-sharing contributions for the 2011 plan year. Sharon is not considered an active participant in the 2011 plan year. Therefore, she could make a fully deductible IRA contribution of $5,000 for 2011. If XYZ Corp. makes a profit-sharing contribution for 2012, Sharon will be considered an active participant for 2012. In that case, the deductibility of any IRA contributions will be subject to limits on her modified adjusted gross income for 2012.

Monetary Limits. The second issue of IRA deductibility is the taxpayer's income. If a taxpayer is an active participant, fully deductible contributions are still allowed only if the taxpayer has a modified adjusted gross income (MAGI) that falls below a specified level. The level for unreduced contributions depends on the taxpayer's filing status. For 2012, married couples filing a joint return will get a full IRA deduction if their modified AGI is $92,000 or less. Married persons filing separately cannot get a full IRA deduction. Single taxpayers and taxpayers filing as heads of households will get a full

IRA deduction if their modified AGI is $58,000 or less. For taxpayers whose modified AGI falls between the no-deduction level and the full-deduction level, their reduced deduction is determined on a pro rata basis. For example, in 2012, a single taxpayer, under age 50, who is an active participant and has a modified AGI of $63,000 (exactly in the middle of the phaseout amounts) can make a $2,500 deductible contribution to his IRA.

Table 6-6 2012 Modified AGI*Limits for Deductible IRA Contributions			
Filing Status	Full IRA Deduction	Reduced IRA Deduction	No IRA Deduction
Individual or head of household	$58,000 or less	$58,001–$67,999	$68,000 or more
Married filing jointly	$92,000 or less	$92,001–$111,999	$112,000 or more
Married filing separately	Not available	$1.00 –$9,999	$10,000 or more
*The explanation of how AGI is modified is beyond the scope of this introductory chapter.			

Special Spousal Rule. If a married taxpayer and her spouse are both active participants, then the deduction rules just described apply to both IRAs. However, the rules are different when only one spouse is an active participant. In this case, a $5,000 deductible IRA contribution is allowed for the nonactive participant spouse as long as the couple's modified AGI does not exceed $173,000. The deduction is phased out if the couple's joint modified AGI exceeds $173,000 and will be gone entirely if their modified AGI is $183,000 or more. A deductible contribution is not available for the non-active participant spouse if the couple files separate tax returns.

EXAMPLE

In 2012, Joe and Jane Morgan, each age 45, ask you whether they are allowed to make deductible IRA contributions for 2012. They file a joint tax return. Only Joe works outside the home, and their expected modified AGI for 2012 is $150,000. Joe is an active participant in a retirement plan and Jane, of course, is not. As an active participant, Joe cannot make a deductible IRA contribution on his own behalf for 2012 because the couple's modified AGI exceeds the limit of $112,000. However, Joe can make a $5,000 deductible IRA contribution for Jane because their joint modified AGI is less than the higher spousal IRA limit of $173,000. Note, if Joe and Jane filed separate returns, Jane would not be able to deduct any IRA contributions.

Distributions. Taxpayers can withdraw all or part of their IRAs any time they wish. Unless the participant has made nondeductible contributions, which can be withdrawn tax free on a pro rata basis, all distributions are treated as ordinary income for federal income tax purposes. If distributions are taken prior to age 59½, however, they are also subject to the 10 percent penalty on the taxable portion of the early withdrawals unless an exception applies. Exceptions are made for

- payments on account of the participant's death
- payments on account of the participant's disability
- the payment of certain medical expenses
- substantially equal periodic payments over the remaining life of the participant and a chosen beneficiary
- payments for qualified higher education expenses for the participant, spouse, or any child or grandchild of the participant or spouse
- payments to cover qualified first-time home buyer expenses for the participant, spouse, or any child, grandchild, or ancestor of the participant or spouse. Note, this exception has a $10,000 lifetime limit per IRA participant.

Traditional IRAs are also subject to the rules that control the maximum length of the tax-deferral period. These are the required minimum-distribution (RMD) rules that generally require distributions to begin for the tax year in which the participant attains age 70½. The RMD rules also require specified payments following the death of the participant.

Roth IRAs

Roth IRA Individuals have a choice between contributing to a traditional IRA or to a *Roth IRA* each year. The Roth IRA is subject to maximum contribution rules in that total contributions for the year (to either type of IRA) cannot exceed $5,000 (2012, as indexed) (and spousal IRAs are allowed). Contributions to a Roth IRA are not deductible, but distributions are tax free as long as certain eligibility requirements are satisfied. The maximum contribution to a Roth IRA in 2012 is phased out for single taxpayers with a modified AGI between $110,000 and $125,000 (a pro rata reduction over a $15,000 income spread). For married joint filers the maximum contribution to a Roth IRA is phased out for a modified AGI between $173,000 and $183,000 (a pro rata reduction over a $10,000 income spread). Note, for Roth IRA contributions, there is no consideration of being an active participant in an employer-provided retirement plan, as with deductibility for traditional IRA contributions. Thus, even if a taxpayer is an active participant in, for example, a 401(k) plan, he can still contribute to a Roth IRA if his modified AGI is under (or within) the phaseout limits.

> **EXAMPLE**
>
> Todd Deal, age 55, is a participant in his employer-sponsored 401(k) plan for 2012 and contributed the maximum amount of $17,000 for his regular contribution plus a $5,500 catch-up contribution. Todd files as a single taxpayer, and in 2012 his modified adjusted gross income is $100,000, which is below the lower phaseout limit of $110,000. Todd can make a full contribution of $6,000 to a Roth IRA for 2012 ($5,000 regular plus a $1,000 catch-up contribution).

Unlike traditional IRAs, the owner of a Roth IRA can make contributions even after she attains age 70½. Moreover, the required minimum distribution rules that apply to traditional IRAs do not apply to a Roth IRA while the owner is alive. The owner of a Roth IRA is not required to take distributions at any age. However, after the death of a Roth IRA owner, certain required minimum distribution rules that apply to traditional IRAs also apply to Roth IRAs.

For distributions to be "qualified distributions" that are entirely tax free, they have to meet two requirements. First, the distribution must be made at least 5 years after the Roth IRA was established. Second, the distribution must be made after one of the four following events has occurred:

- The owner has attained age 59½ by the end of the year in which distributions are made.
- The distribution is paid to a beneficiary because of the owner's death.
- The owner has become disabled.
- The withdrawal is made to pay qualified first-time home buyer expenses.

Qualified first-time home buyer expenses include acquisition costs of a first home (paid within 120 days of the distribution) for the owner, his spouse, or any child, grandchild, or ancestor of the owner or spouse. This exception, however, has a $10,000 lifetime limit per IRA (or Roth IRA) owner. Any distribution that does not meet these requirements is a nonqualifying distribution. With the Roth IRA, even nonqualifying distributions receive somewhat favorable tax treatment. Contributions can be withdrawn first, without having to pay any taxes. Any amounts withdrawn above total contributions would then be subject to income tax and the 10 percent penalty on early withdrawals.

> **EXAMPLE**
>
> Maria Salidore, now age 48, has a Roth IRA that she established in 2009. She has contributed $15,000 to the Roth IRA and her account balance is now $20,000. Maria needs $10,000 to make some extensive home repairs. She can withdraw the entire $10,000 tax-free as a return of her (already taxed) contributions. Since the withdrawal is not taxable, she will not have to pay any penalty for being under age 59½. Note, if Maria had withdrawn the entire $20,000, she would have to pay ordinary income tax on $5,000 plus a penalty tax of $500 (that is, 10 percent of the taxable portion of $5,000).

OVERCOMING INADEQUATE RETIREMENT RESOURCES

In addition to determining how much income clients will need to retire, you should understand how to help clients produce as much retirement income as possible from their existing resources. The final part of this chapter addresses four strategies that you can recommend to accomplish this objective:

- trading down to a less expensive home
- obtaining a reverse mortgage
- postretirement employment
- pension maximization

Trading Down to a Less Expensive Home

If a client sells her home and relocates to a smaller, less expensive residence, the money from the transaction can be a valuable source of retirement income. For example, if a retiree sells her home for $300,000 and buys a new residence for $200,000, the $100,000 cash difference can produce extra income from an immediate annuity or other investment. This is very desirable from a financial perspective, because it enables retirees to capitalize on what for many of them is their single most important financial asset—their home. In addition, the Internal Revenue Code allows single taxpayers to exclude up to $250,000 of gain ($500,000 on a joint return in most situations) from the sale or exchange of their homes if the following restrictions are met:

- During the prior 5 years, the house was owned and used by the taxpayers as their principal residence for periods aggregating 2 years or more.
- The taxpayers may not have excluded a gain from the sale of their principal residence in the prior 2 years.

EXAMPLE

Fred and Wilma Stone purchased their home in a Philadelphia suburb in 1980 for $50,000. In early 2012, they sold their home for $350,000 and realized a gain of $300,000. As a married couple filing a joint return, the entire $300,000 in gain is excluded from federal income taxation. If they purchase another primary residence and live in it for at least two years within the next five years, they could then sell that home and qualify for another exclusion of up to $500,000 in gains.

Obtaining a Reverse Mortgage

reverse mortgage

Often, a client would like to take some equity out of her home but is reluctant to sell it and move to a less expensive one. One alternative that is becoming increasingly common is a *reverse mortgage.* A reverse mortgage is a nonrecourse loan against an individual's home that requires no repayment as long as the individual lives in and maintains the home. In other words, a reverse mortgage allows a client to live in her home while withdrawing substantial amounts of money from the home's equity. This money from the reverse mortgage can be used for any purpose, and there is no need to repay it. A reverse mortgage is available only when all of the home's owners are aged 62 or older and when the home is the principal residence. Also, the home must either have no debt or only a relatively small debt that can be paid off with part of the reverse mortgage loan.

The federally-sponsored Home Equity Conversion Mortgage (HECM) program is the most popular type of reverse mortgage. The Federal Housing Administration (FHA) insures HECM loans to protect lenders against loss if amounts withdrawn exceed equity when the property is sold. Any lender authorized to make Housing and Urban Development insured loans, such as banks, mortgage companies, and savings and loan associations, can participate in the HECM program. There are also a number of other privately sponsored programs.

The amount of loan payments made to the client depends on the client's age (or clients' joint ages), the amount of equity the home currently has, the interest rate and fees being charged, and the specific reverse mortgage program used. Payment options vary depending on the specific program, but generally they include an immediate lump sum payment, a credit line account, or a specified monthly amount for a specific number of years.

The amount of the debt to the lender grows based on the amount paid to the homeowner(s) and accumulated interest. Typically, the loan only has to be repaid when the last surviving borrower either dies, sells the home, or permanently moves away. Most loans are non-recourse, meaning the maximum amount that has to be repaid is the value of the home. If property values erode, the borrower receives a windfall and the lender suffers a loss. Because reverse mortgages are truly loans, if the retiree wants or needs to sell the home, any home equity that exceeds the loan balance belongs to the retiree. If the property is sold after the borrower dies, her heirs receive any remaining equity after the loan is repaid. In addition, because reverse mortgages are loans, payments received by the home owner are not considered taxable income.

As a financial advisor, you are likely to get many questions about reverse mortgages, so you will need to go beyond this brief introduction. Suffice to say, reverse mortgages are not for everyone. There are some downsides that you should know. First, homeowners who get a reverse mortgage must continue to live in and maintain the property adequately to preserve the lender's interest in the home. Second, the homeowner must continue paying for homeowner's insurance, which can be very expensive in some areas such as Florida and California. Third, many seniors may want to leave their residence to their children via their will; however, for the children to retain the property, they would have to repay the lender for the amount of the outstanding loan to take full possession of the home. For more information on reverse mortgages, visit the National Reverse Mortgage Lenders Association at *reversemortgage.org*.

Postretirement Employment

A third strategy to provide the retiree with extra cash is a part-time job during the retirement years. Many retirees find that working on a scaled-back basis not only meets their financial needs but also helps them adapt psychologically to the changes that retirement brings. This is especially true for retirees whose self-esteem and sense of self-worth were tied to their careers.

Working after retirement poses a potential problem for retirees who have begun receiving Social Security retirement benefits but have not yet attained the full retirement age (age 66 for those retiring in 2012 and gradually rising to 67 for workers born after 1954) if they have earned income that exceeds a specified level. Social Security beneficiaries under the full retirement age are allowed earnings of $14,640 in 2012. If a beneficiary earns more than that, his Social Security benefit is reduced $1 for every $2 of excess earnings. A different formula applies for the calendar year the individual attains the full retirement age. For that year, the reduction is only $1 for every $3 of excess earnings and counts only earnings before the month the individual reaches full retirement age. Also, for that year the threshold is higher, $38,880 in 2012.

Once an individual reaches the full retirement age, the earnings limitation no longer applies. At that point the individual can earn any amount without a reduction of Social Security retirement benefits.

EXAMPLE

Raul Chavez retires from his long-time employment in December 2011 at age 63. Raul's full Social Security retirement age is 66. Raul begins taking a reduced Social Security retirement benefit of $1,000 per month. In addition, he begins a part-time job as a consultant and earns $24,640 in 2012. In July 2013, Raul is notified by the Social Security Administration that he exceeded the earnings limit of $14,640 in 2012 and his Social Security benefits will be reduced by $5,000 (that is, by $1.00 for each $2.00 he earned above the limit). Thus, starting in August 2013 and continuing for 5 months, Raul will receive no Social Security payments until the full $5,000 is repaid. Assuming that Raul does not earn more than the earnings limit for 2013, he will begin receiving his Social Security payments again in January, 2014.

As a point of understanding, when one's Social Security benefits are reduced because the retiree earned more than the earnings limit, Social Security will recalculate the benefit at the retiree's full retirement age, resulting in a higher benefit than originally paid at the retiree's earlier age. The following is taken from the Social Security website (ssa.gov) to illustrate this point:

> **EXAMPLE**
>
> Suppose you claim retirement benefits upon turning 62 in 2012 and your payment is $750 per month. Then, you return to work and have 12 months of benefits withheld. We would recalculate your benefit at your full retirement age of 66 and pay you $800 a month (in today's dollars). Or, maybe you earn so much between the ages of 62 and 66 that all benefits in those years are withheld. In that case, we would pay you $1,000 a month starting at age 66.

> **FOCUS ON ETHICS: Who Is the Client?**
>
> One of retirement planning's unique challenges is focusing on the question: Who is your client? This needs further explanation.
>
> Current law requires married retirees to accept a joint-and-survivor annuity rather than a single-life annuity (in the absence of a spousal waiver). Obviously, the monthly check is lower for the joint-and-survivor payout.
>
> What should the financial advisor do if the client wants the higher single-life benefit and tries to talk the spouse into signing a waiver? Should the retiree die first, this could leave the spouse with little or no income. While the advisor cannot force the married retiree to take the joint-and-survivor option, the ethical course is to defend the welfare of the vulnerable spouse. This is more easily done when the client is viewed as the couple as opposed to only the pension-receiving spouse.

Pension Maximization

pension maximization

The final strategy we will discuss here is so-called *pension maximization*. Qualified plans typically stipulate the type of distribution your client will receive. The normal form of benefit for a married client is a joint-and-survivor benefit that pays between 50 and 100 percent of the joint benefit amount to the survivor. One strategy for the married client is to elect a different payment option than the normal benefit form with the spouse's written consent. If a married client elects a benefit paid in the form of a life annuity, he can increase his retirement income significantly. If, prior to retirement, life insurance is purchased (or kept in force) on the retiree/life annuitant, the spouse's financial well-being can also be secured.

> **EXAMPLE**
>
> Karl Klass, aged 65, and his wife Hilda, aged 62, are eligible to receive a $2,300 joint-and-survivor benefit monthly from the $500,000 they have in Karl's retirement plan. (This is a qualified joint-and-survivor benefit that pays 100 percent of the joint benefit amount to the survivor.) If they elect to receive a life annuity based on Karl's life, they will receive $500 more each month ($2,800). The extra $6,000 a year represents a 22 percent increase in annual income for them. If they can purchase (or keep in force) enough life insurance on Karl to provide for Hilda at a premium that is less than the $6,000 a year, they can stretch their retirement savings and improve their financial situation. For example, if Hilda died before Karl, he could change the beneficiaries on the life insurance policy(ies). He could also possibly sell the policies in a life settlement, or he could surrender them for their cash values. Note, because of the uncertainty of the timing of Karl's and Hilda's deaths, only permanent life insurance is suitable in a pension maximization plan. In addition, if Karl is in poor health, is a tobacco-user, or is otherwise uninsurable at standard rates, he is not likely to be a good candidate for a pension maximization. In such cases, he should be advised to elect the qualified joint-and-survivor benefit to protect Hilda.

CHAPTER REVIEW

Key Terms and Concepts are explained in the Glossary. Answers to the Review Questions are found in the back of the book in the Answers to Questions section.

Key Terms and Concepts

- holistic retirement planning
- qualified domestic relations order (QDRO)
- replacement ratio method
- expense method
- nonqualified plan
- qualified plan
- defined-benefit plan
- defined-contribution plan
- pension plan
- profit-sharing plan
- defined-benefit pension plan
- unit-benefit formula
- cash-balance pension plan
- money-purchase plan
- target-benefit pension plan
- profit-sharing plan
- allocation formula
- 401(k) plan
- stock bonus plan
- employee stock ownership plan (ESOP)
- simplified employee pension (SEP)
- savings incentive match plan for employees (SIMPLE)
- 403(b) plan
- tax-sheltered annuity (TSA)
- nonqualified plans
- traditional IRA
- active participant
- Roth IRA
- reverse mortgage
- pension maximization

Review Questions

1. Describe two ways in which a spendthrift lifestyle during a client's active working years makes retirement planning more difficult. [4]

2. Explain how each of the following may constitute important roadblocks preventing the client from accumulating adequate retirement saving: (a.) inadequate insurance coverage, (b.) divorce, and (c.) frequent changes of employer. [4]

3. Explain how the variables affecting the amount a client will need to save to achieve his retirement goals can change due to forces largely beyond the client's control. [5]

4. Distinguish between the replacement ratio method and the expense method of determining how much income a client will need in the first year of retirement to achieve his goals. [5]

5. Identify several factors that make it likely that clients will have a lower annual federal tax burden after retirement than before retirement. [6]

6. Identify several categories of general living expenses that, for most retirees, will be (a.) lower after retirement than before retirement (b.) higher after retirement than before retirement. [6]

7. Distinguish between (a.) a defined-benefit plan and a defined contribution plan and (b.) a pension plan and a profit-sharing plan. [8]

8. Describe several factors associated with a defined-contribution plan that may result in inadequate retirement income for a client. [8]

9. Describe two important factors that the retirement advisor should keep in mind if a client is a participant in a profit-sharing plan. [8]

10. Present a typical benefit formula of each of the following types that might be found in a qualified defined-benefit pension plan: (a.) unit-benefit formula, (b.) flat-percentage-of-earnings formula. [8]

11. Describe the principal characteristics of 401(k) plans. [8]

12. Identify several potential retirement planning problems that participation in a nonqualified plan may pose for a client. [9]

13. Describe the principal characteristics of traditional IRAs with respect to (a.) limitations on contributions and (b.) eligibility for deductible contributions. [10]

14. Describe the principal characteristics of Roth IRAs with respect to (a.) deductibility of contributions and (b.) taxability of distributions. [10]

15. Explain how each of the following strategies can be used to maximize a client's retirement income: (a.) trading down to a less expensive home, (b.) obtaining a reverse mortgage, (c.) postretirement employment. [7]

ESTATE PLANNING 7

> **Learning Objectives**
>
> *An understanding of the material in this chapter should enable the student to*
>
> 1. Describe both the narrow view and the broader view of estate planning, and explain why the client needs to answer the who, how, and when questions.
> 2. Describe several different types of property interests.
> 3. Explain the significance of wills, trusts, durable powers of attorney, and advance medical directives in developing a cohesive estate plan.
> 4. Explain why knowledge of how property is transferred at death is necessary to plan an estate.
> 5. Describe the various federal and state taxes imposed on transfers of wealth.
> 6. Describe several planning techniques for preserving a client's wealth.

THE GOALS OF ESTATE PLANNING

Planning the client's estate is an essential step in life-cycle financial planning. A narrow view of estate planning is that the process involves merely the conservation and distribution of a client's estate. The broader view, however, is that estate planning is an integral part of financial planning, and the role of a financial advisor is to maximize the client's distributable wealth and transfer that wealth appropriately to the client's beneficiaries. Following this broader view, the estate plan should employ life-cycle financial planning strategies that increase the client's distributable wealth, along with planning for the disposition of such wealth. Estate planning, then, is included in a comprehensive financial plan and must also consider other major planning areas (that is, insurance planning, employee benefits planning, investment planning, income tax planning, and retirement planning) within a comprehensive plan.

> **Three Primary Questions in Estate Planning**
>
> - Who should receive the client's property?
> - How should beneficiaries receive the property?
> - When should beneficiaries receive the property?

Because the other major planning areas in a comprehensive financial plan are covered elsewhere, this discussion will follow the narrow view and focus on the conservation and distribution of a client's estate. However, bear in mind that a client's estate plan typically is broader as an integral part of a comprehensive financial plan.

Selecting appropriate alternatives in estate planning involves answering the "who," "how," and "when" questions. The client must determine who will be the recipients of his property. The "who" question is generally the easiest for the client to answer and can often be determined without significant professional advice.

The client must also determine how his beneficiaries will receive the property. For example, property can be distributed outright to beneficiaries. Alternatively, the property can be left to beneficiaries in trust with various restrictions on their use and enjoyment rights. Beneficiaries could also receive a partial interest in property. One example of a partial interest is a life estate.

The client will generally need significant professional advice to answer the "how" question. Competent financial advisors should be able to determine a client's goals and design a transfer mechanism that meets the goals and complies with state property laws.

Transfer taxes imposed on a specific transfer of property often depend on the form of the transfer. Planning for the "how" question will often focus on minimizing transfer taxes within the framework of the client's goals.

Finally, it must be determined "when" a client's estate will be distributed. Typically, distributions are not made from the client's property until his death. However, it is sometimes appropriate to transfer specific items of a client's wealth during his lifetime. The reasons behind lifetime gifts are numerous, but the primary estate planning purpose of lifetime giving is the reduction of the client's estate tax base. Systematic, planned lifetime giving is often recommended for wealthy clients to reduce the amount of death taxes payable on *testamentary* (that is, occurring at death) dispositions.

STARTING THE PROCESS

The estate planning process begins early in the client's financial life cycle with the financial advisor helping the client define her goals and gathering relevant data from the client. Data gathering usually involves interviewing the client and completing a fact finder. Although the estate plan should be an integral part of any client's comprehensive financial plan, the fact remains that estate planning concerns generally gain prominence later in the client's financial life cycle. Other than having a simple will to direct the disposition of assets, most clients typically are well on the way toward reaching their wealth accumulation and retirement planning goals before estate planning becomes paramount. Nonetheless, as part of the financial planning process, you need to gather data early in the client's financial life cycle to help her answer the "who," "how," and "when" questions. You must also ensure that both you and your client fully understand the client's asset inventory as revealed on the completed fact finder form. An accurate asset inventory indicates the composition and magnitude of the client's assets available for distribution. This data will help you and the client determine whether the assets are in an appropriate form for distribution and whether their total value can provide the desired distributions to the client's beneficiaries. Planning to convert the assets into the appropriate form and/or to accumulate additional wealth could logically follow.

After you have helped the client define her goals and gathered the necessary data, you must analyze the data and develop a clear and efficient plan to distribute the client's assets. In other words, once the client answers the "who" questions, the advisor then assists the client by developing an estate plan that answers the "how" and "when" questions. In many cases, answering the "who" question is fairly easy for the client. For example, a married individual may want to leave all of his wealth to a surviving spouse. In other cases, however, the "who" decision is more difficult and will require some soul-searching by the client. You should be aware that the client may not be able to answer the "who" question immediately. For example, the client may want to disinherit some children or provide for children from a prior marriage.

> **EXAMPLE**
>
> Kirk, our financial planner in Philadelphia, has met with Mike and Brenda Giles, now both age 70, who have agreed to have Kirk build an estate plan for them. They have a distributable estate approaching $5 million. Mike was in a previous marriage to Elizabeth and they had two children, Christopher and Karen. Brenda was a widow from a previous marriage in which she had a child Dorothy. Mike and Brenda have one child David from their marriage. Mike and Brenda are having a very difficult time answering the "who" question for their estate plans. Mike is estranged from his two children, Christopher and Karen, and has not had any contact with either of them for more than 10 years. Brenda and Dorothy are extremely close, and Brenda wants to leave a substantial portion of their estate to Dorothy. Mike and Brenda want to provide substantial assets to their son David. However, David who is now age 30, is a spendthrift and a very poor manager of money. Mike's and Brenda's questions include:
>
> - Should they treat Mike's estranged children (Christopher and Karen) equally as their own child David and Brenda's daughter Dorothy?
> - Should they leave a significant inheritance to David, whom they feel will squander his assets?

Once the client has determined who should receive the property, the client, with the advisor's assistance, must determine both how and when the property will be distributed. Frequently, as in the previous example, some beneficiaries may lack the ability to handle outright distributions of property. Moreover, the client may wish to restrict the ultimate right of some beneficiaries to dispose of any property they receive from the client. You will need to inform the client about alternative forms of property transfers and the benefits and risks of each method. This will help the client determine how and when her property should be distributed and permit the advisor to draft a more complete estate plan and recommendations for the client.

Interviewing to gather data for estate planning is often an uncomfortable event for the client. Many clients feel uneasy talking about their own death and personal family matters. Moreover, it is not unusual for a client to modify his initial goals during the estate planning process. The alternative distribution choices discussed with the advisor will often raise issues the client had initially overlooked. You may need to interview spouses separately if an estate plan is being drawn up for a married couple. This is particularly true if the goals of the spouses are widely divergent. Nonetheless, a thorough interview with appropriate follow-up gives the greatest probability that you will receive an accurate picture of the client's goals and enable you to design a plan that will satisfy the client.

TYPES OF PROPERTY INTEREST

A client's asset inventory may not always provide a complete financial picture for the advisor. The manner in which the client owns the property is also an important factor. It is essential that you determine the form of property ownership and determine any additional property rights held by the client that are not indicated on the asset inventory form. Some forms of property ownership provide for less than full use and enjoyment and may have been ignored by the client in completing the fact finder. Your knowledge of the various forms of property ownership is necessary to determine all possible property rights a client can hold, and the possible types of dispositions that a client can make to beneficiaries.

Types of Property Interest
• Individual ownership of property
Fee simple estate
Life estate
Term interest
Future Interest
• Joint concurrent ownership of property
Tenancy in common
Joint tenancy with right of survivorship
Tenancy by the entirety
Community property

Individual Ownership of Property

Fee Simple Estate

fee simple estate   The most complete interest in property is a *fee simple estate* (outright ownership of property). It is an interest that belongs absolutely to an individual. The individual who holds such an unlimited interest in property owns all the rights associated with the property. The rights include the current rights of possession and use and the ability to transfer the property at any point during his lifetime or at death. Most property ownership falls into the category of the fee simple estate. In planning a client's estate, property that is held outright is an obvious asset to be considered in the distribution scheme (also called the "dispositive" plan). If the estate being planned is for a married couple, either spouse might own substantial property individually.

Life Estate

life estate

A more limited, but still common, form of property ownership is a *life estate* in the property. The life estate provides the life tenant with the right to possess and enjoy the property for a time period measured by the life of an individual (typically the life tenant, although it may be another person). The life estate gives the life tenant the absolute right to possess, enjoy, and derive current income (rental income, for example) from the property until the life estate terminates.

> **EXAMPLE**
>
> Under his father's will, Brock Storm has been given the exclusive use and possession of his father's residence for Brock's lifetime. When Brock dies, the residence will be transferred to a beneficiary also named in his father's will. Brock can live in the house until he dies, allow others to live in it, or rent it. He can also sell his life interest; however, his interest (or a buyer's interest) will cease upon Brock's death. In other words, the duration of this possessory interest is limited by the life of the life tenant (Brock).

Estate for Term of Years

estate for a term of years

term interest

Another type of estate that may or may not outlast a life estate is one created for a definite, limited period of time. An interest in property for a specific duration is called an *estate for a term of years.* It is also known as a *term interest*. This form of estate may be as short as a month, or it may last for many years. It may extend beyond the lifetime of the tenant. Remember that it provides the right to possess, enjoy, and receive income from the property during a specified term. The interest of the current tenant ceases at the end of the specified term.

> **EXAMPLE**
>
> Suppose that Brock (in the previous example) was given an estate for 10 years in his father's residence instead of the life estate. Thus, Brock would possess the estate for 10 years, after which it would pass to a beneficiary named in his father's will. This transfer is known as an estate for a term or years, or a term interest estate.

Estate Planning

Future Interest

future interest

remainder interest

reversionary interest

A *future interest* in property is the current right to future enjoyment of the property. A future interest in property could either be fixed and determined or contingent on the occurrence of some future event. The future interest holder has no immediate right to use and enjoy the property.

One type of future interest is a *remainder interest*, which is an interest that takes effect immediately on the expiration of someone else's interest in the same property. For example, a remainder interest might take effect on the termination of a life estate or a term interest. A remainder interest is often held by one individual, the "remainderperson," on property contained in a trust that currently benefits another individual—for example, a life estate beneficiary.

EXAMPLE
Don is given a life estate in his deceased father's property. Upon Don's death, the property will pass to his younger sister Rachel absolutely. Don possesses a life estate and Rachel is the remainderperson, who will receive the property contingent upon Don's death. Rachel's right to the possession, use, and enjoyment of the property begins when Don's expires. In this situation, Rachel has a current, absolute future interest, that is to take possession upon Don's death.

Another type of future interest is a *reversionary interest*. The reversionary interest occurs when the current property owner transfers possessory rights to another. The reversionary interest gives the transferor (also called the "grantor") the right to receive the property back at the end of the possessory term of the transferee. For example, a parent could create a trust for a child for a specified term of years and retain a reversionary interest in the trust property upon the end of the child's interest.

EXAMPLE
James owns Richland Hills in fee simple absolute. He conveys Richland Hills to his sister Ellen for her life. Ellen now has a life estate in the property. However, because James conveyed less than his total interest, he retained a reversionary interest in Richland Hills. With the reversionary interest, at Ellen's death Richland Hills reverts to James absolutely if he is living, or to his estate if he is deceased when Ellen dies.

Joint Concurrent Ownership of Property

A property can be owned entirely by one individual. A person may also own a portion of the property with others owning the remainder of the property. Such a partial current interest in property is often generically referred to as joint ownership of property. Joint ownership, in its various forms, is an important concept in estate planning.

Tenancy in Common

tenancy in common

Property owned concurrently by two or more persons who may be but are not necessarily related is generally called a *tenancy in common*. There may be any number of owners who hold property as tenants in common. We say each tenant's share is an undivided part of the entire property. However, each tenant need not own equal shares with the other cotenants; ownership interests may or may not be equally divided. Unless restricted by contract or agreement with the other co-owners, each tenant may dispose of his interest during his lifetime or at death.

> **EXAMPLE**
>
> Adam, Brent, and Charlie are tenants in common of an office building in West Chester, PA. Adam owns 50 percent of the property, Brent owns 30 percent, and Charlie owns 20 percent. Charlie choked on a fish bone in early 2012 and expired. His 20 percent interest in this property will pass to his heirs either by his will (if he has one) or by the intestate laws of Pennsylvania if Charlie had no will.

Joint Tenancy with Right of Survivorship

joint tenancy with right of survivorship

Joint tenancy with right of survivorship is similar to tenancies in common in that there may be two or more joint tenants. As with tenants in common, joint tenants may or may not be related to each other. During lifetime, each joint tenant may sell his interest in the property to someone who is not a joint owner without consent of the other joint tenants; however, such a transaction will sever the joint tenancy with right of survivorship. This is a major distinction between the tenancy in common and the joint tenancy with right of survivorship. Another primary difference is that jointly-held property passes to the surviving tenants upon death of one of the joint owners. When there are more than two joint tenants, the property ultimately passes to the last surviving joint tenant, who, as sole surviving owner, has all rights in the property. This represents a major advantage of joint tenancy with right of survivorship, namely that the property passes free of probate in many states.

> **EXAMPLE**
>
> Alice, Barbara, and Charlene Colter are three unmarried sisters who are joint tenants with right of survivorship in their residence in Norristown, PA. If Alice were to pass away, her interest would pass by title to Barbara and Charlene. If Barbara then passed away, Charlene would take absolute and sole ownership of the residence. Upon her death, the property would pass by Charlene's will or according to Pennsylvania's intestate laws if Charlene had no will.

Tenancy by the Entirety

tenancy by the entirety

A *tenancy by the entirety* is similar to a joint tenancy with right of survivorship although it is more restrictive. It is limited to co-ownership of property held jointly by a husband and wife. By definition, a tenancy by the entirety exists only during marriage and will be terminated upon divorce of the spouses. Local law determines some features of a tenancy by the entirety. For example, in most states each tenant is entitled to half of any income from the property.

A primary difference between a tenancy by the entirety and jointly held property with right of survivorship is that neither spouse/owner may unilaterally terminate the tenancy by conveying his or her interest to a third party while living. Thus, a tenancy by the entirety cannot be severed without the consent of both tenants. Husband and wife must join in a sale or other conveyance to a third party.

Tenancy by the entirety represents joint ownership by the spouses with rights of survivorship. Property is transferred automatically to the surviving spouse upon death of a husband or wife. Thus, the property bypasses probate and is not subject to disposition by the will of the deceased spouse.

Financial advisors must know the laws within their state jurisdiction with respect to joint property since property held jointly by spouses may or may not be presumed to be held with such rights of survivorship. Generally, it is presumed that the ownership is a tenancy in common if the co-owners are not married; however, if the co-owners are married, a tenancy by the entirety may be presumed. Some jurisdictions insist that the words "right of survivorship" are necessary in the property title to clear up any misunderstanding.

Community Property

community property

Community property is another form of co-ownership limited to interests held between husband and wife that has particular significance today because of our mobile society. Only nine states—Arizona, California, Idaho, Louisiana, Nevada, New Mexico, Texas, Washington, and Wisconsin— are community property states. The laws of the particular community-property state in which a married couple resides must be examined to determine accurately the specific effect on the spouses' property ownership. Property in such states is treated as either separate or community property. Generally speaking, property acquired during the marriage is treated as community property and is equally owned by the spouses. Although community property is not technically jointly held, the community property laws limit the ability of each spouse to transfer community property to individuals other than his or her spouse.

The chart below compares the ownership forms of tenancy in common, joint tenancy with right of survivorship, and tenancy by the entirety.

Property Ownership	Tenancy in Common	Joint Tenancy with Right of Survivorship	Tenancy by the Entirety
Permitted number of owners?	Ownership by two or more individuals.	Ownership by two or more individuals.	Ownership only by two individuals.
Must owners be related?	No.	No.	Yes, they must be married.
Can ownership be unequal?	Yes, ownership may be equal or unequal.	No. Contribution can be unequal, but each has equal ownership rights.	No. Each has equal ownership rights.
Kind of property—real or personal?	Either real or personal.	Either real or personal.	Either real or personal. (Some states require real property only.)
Can owner sell or make a gift of the property without other owners' consent?	Yes, owner can dispose of his/her share without the consent of the other joint owners.	Yes, owner can dispose of his/her share without the consent of the other joint owners, but the joint tenancy is severed.	No. Both owners must consent.
Can owner transfer his/her share by will?	Yes.	No. Share automatically passes to the survivor(s) by operation of law.	No. Survivor automatically becomes sole owner by operation of law.
Is property reachable by an individual's creditors?	Yes, to the extent of his/her contribution to the property.	Yes, to the extent of his/her contribution to the property.	Only creditors of both owners can reach the property.

Estate Planning

Other Property Rights

Other property interests may be held by a client and used as a vehicle to transfer the client's wealth. These other rights generally provide varying restrictions on the ability of the holder to enjoy or transfer the property. These forms of property ownership should be used when the restrictions are appropriate for the goals and objectives of the client.

Beneficial Interests

beneficial interest Certain property interests may provide one individual with a *beneficial interest* in property. Beneficial interests (also known as *equitable interests*) refer to such rights to use, possess, or enjoy the property, as well as the right to derive income from the property. An example of a beneficial interest is the interest owned by the beneficiary of a trust. The trust is created by a grantor who transfers title to the trust property to a trustee. The trustee's function is to hold legal title to the property, guard it and administer the trust property for the benefit of the beneficiary. The trustee's ability to make distributions to the beneficiary is determined by the terms of the trust. The trustee may be required to make specific distributions or may have broad discretion as to the size and/or timing of distributions and even the identity of the beneficiaries. Thus, the trustee may have substantial dispositive decisions. Upon termination of the trust and final distribution of the trust property to the ultimate beneficiaries, the beneficiaries become absolute owners.

Other Property Rights
• Beneficial interests
• Powers
Power of appointment
General power of appointment
Special power of appointment
Power of attorney

Powers

Certain powers to make property decisions may be held by (or transferred by) the client.

power of appointment

Power of Appointment. A *power of appointment* provides the holder of the power with the ability to transfer property subject to the power. The holder, known also as the donee, may have a broad power to transfer the property to virtually any recipient. This is known as a *general power of appointment*. Or the holder may have a *special power of appointment*, which typically restricts the holder to designate the property to a limited class of potential recipients. The time period during which a power of appointment may be exercised can also be restricted by the donor of the power.

power of attorney

Power of Attorney. Another power that can be held or granted by a client is a *power of attorney*. A power of attorney gives the holder of the power (the attorney-in-fact) the ability to stand in the place of or represent the grantor of the power (the principal) in various transactions. Among the possible transactions is the power of the attorney-in-fact to transfer property for the principal. The advantages of using a power of attorney will be discussed later in this chapter.

ESTATE PLANNING DOCUMENTS

An estate plan (a subset of a comprehensive financial plan) is a roadmap that directs how a client's wealth will be assembled and disposed of during the client's life and/or at her death. An estate plan is useless unless the documents to execute the plan have been drafted appropriately. The documents, such as a will, trusts, and others must be drafted carefully to avoid hidden traps and provide direction to the appropriate personal representatives, *fiduciaries,* and beneficiaries of the client. These directions must be drafted according to principles of state law and should clearly state the intent of the client. Because these documents involve compliance with state law, they should be prepared by an attorney who specializes in estate planning in the local jurisdiction.

Estate Planning Documents
• Wills
• Trusts
• Durable powers of attorney
• Advance medical directives

Wills

intestacy

Despite the importance of a will in a client's estate plan, an estimated seven out of ten Americans die without a valid will. Unfortunately, these individuals leave the disposition of their estates to the provisions of state *intestacy* law. In addition, the estates of these intestate individuals will be handled by a court-appointed administrator. In many cases, the estate will be subject to unnecessary taxes and administration expenses. In any event, a valid will is necessary to implement a cohesive estate plan, whether that plan results from single purpose, multiple purpose, or comprehensive financial planning.

Requirements for a Valid Will

testator

Although the requirements for wills are established in the laws of the various states and differences do exist, several items are universal. With some minor exceptions for very rare circumstances, the following are generally required for a valid will:

- The will must be in writing.
- The will must be dated.
- the *testator* (maker) of the will must have the legal capacity (that is, in terms of age and mental capacity) to make a will.
- The testator, or creator of the will, must sign the will at the end of the document, usually in the presence of witnesses.
- A number of witnesses (generally two or three) must sign the will after the testator's signature. The witnesses are simply attesting that the signature of the testator is his or her true signature.

What Can a Valid Will Accomplish?

probate assets

The client's will is the centerpiece of the estate plan. Although the will's primary function is to direct the disposition of the client's wealth, it serves other purposes as well. A properly drafted will can accomplish the following objectives:

- Direct the disposition of the client's *probate assets,* that is, assets disposed through the probate process in the probate court in the county where the deceased person resided.
- Nominate the personal representative of the testator, known as the executor (or executrix), who will handle the administration of the client's estate.
- Nominate the guardians of any minor children of the testator.

- Create testamentary trusts that will take effect at the testator's death to hold the property of the testator for the benefit of named beneficiaries.
- Name the trustee(s) of any trust(s) created under the will.
- Provide directions to the executor–executrix and/or trustees named in the will to define how these fiduciaries will manage assets contained in the estate or testamentary trust.
- Provide directions for payment of the estate's taxes and expenses.
- Establish the compensation of executors and/or trustees named in the will.

Trusts

trust
fiduciary capacity
grantor
trustee

A *trust* is a legal relationship in which one acts in a *fiduciary capacity* (position of trust) with respect to the property of another. Fiduciary capacity requires that a person (the fiduciary) receive and hold title to the property that is held for the benefit of another person (a beneficiary), to whom the fiduciary owes the highest duty of good faith. In the case of a legal trust, the fiduciary is typically known as a *trustee*. The beneficial (or equitable interest) in the trust property is owned by the beneficiaries of the trust. The trustee has the duty to manage the trust property provided by the *grantor* for the benefit of the beneficiaries. A trust is often used to provide for beneficiaries when, for some reason, they are unable to administer the trust assets for themselves. For example, a trust may be created to provide for minor beneficiaries. Minor beneficiaries are incapable under state law of holding property in their own name and perhaps lack the necessary experience and financial skills to manage the trust property. The trust is an excellent tool for handling and/or consolidating accumulations of wealth.

The trustee manages the trust property under specific terms of the trust. The trust terms are the directions and intentions of the grantor with respect to management of the trust. For example, there may be directions concerning the investment objectives of trust assets. More importantly, there are directions to provide for the beneficiaries of the trust. The trust terms may be quite specific and restrictive and provide the trustee with very little discretion. For example, the terms may provide for specified distributions of income and/or principal to designated beneficiaries at various points in time. In some cases, however, the trustee may be provided with "sprinkle" powers, permitting the trustee to determine when distributions of either income or principal are appropriate for beneficiaries. The trustee has a legal obligation to manage the trust prudently and, to the extent the trustee has discretionary powers, to act impartially with respect to the beneficiaries.

The five elements common to all trusts are:

1. the creator (generally known as the grantor)
2. the trustee
3. the property in trust
4. the beneficiaries
5. the terms of the trust (generally in a written document)

> **FOCUS ON ETHICS: Trusts, "Don't Trusts," and Loss of Trust**
>
> Financial planning often includes the use of trusts to save taxes. An equally important goal is to control wealth distribution. Sometimes clients want to retain control, even from the grave; their trusts might more appropriately be called "don't trusts."
>
> Estate planning can involve many moral and ethical pitfalls. For example, a divorced and remarried person may elect to leave her entire estate to her second spouse with no provision for children of her first marriage. Another example is a client who, anticipating an irrevocable life insurance trust, applies for coverage before establishing the trust. Informed that this premature application invalidates gift tax advantages of the trust, the client may want to re-date legal documents or simply claim the tax benefit anyway, hoping never to be audited. Financial advisors must never be a party to such actions.
>
> For an advisor to decline business because of moral, ethical, or legal objections may be financially painful in the short run. However, in the long run, the financial advisor with an unquestioned reputation will inevitably attract more and higher quality business. That same advisor also has a clear conscience and the knowledge that the likelihood of legal, ethical, and malpractice charges is dramatically reduced.

Because the trust terms describe the intentions of the grantor, a trust should be drafted carefully under the direction of an attorney who specializes in such matters. In addition, the grantor should select the trustee, whether a private individual or a corporate trustee, with great care.

Living (Inter Vivos) Trust

inter vivos trust
revocable trust
irrevocable trust

A trust created during the lifetime of a grantor is called a *living trust* or, using the Latin, an *inter vivos* trust. It could be created for several reasons. The trust could hold property and operate prior to the death of the grantor. Or, it could be created during the lifetime of the grantor simply to receive assets at the grantor's death, perhaps from another trust. Such a trust is known as a *pour-over trust*.

A trust can be either revocable or irrevocable. A *revocable trust* is created when a grantor transfers property to a trust but reserves the power to alter or even revoke the agreement, and thereby reclaim the trust property while he is still alive. Because a revocable trust is an incomplete transfer, a revocable trust has no effect on a client's income, gift, or estate tax situation.

The revocable trust does not enjoy many of the tax advantages of irrevocable trusts. Another very important point here is that putting assets into a revocable trust will not protect the grantor from a Medicaid "spend down" if he requires nursing home care. A revocable trust gives a grantor the ability to observe the management of the trust assets without relinquishing ultimate control of the assets. Thus, the grantor can reclaim the trust assets at any time. A revocable trust becomes irrevocable only when the grantor modifies the trust to become irrevocable or dies and, therefore, is no longer able to modify the trust.

The revocable trust has gained popularity in recent times as an estate plan in itself. This occurs when it is drafted to provide the dispositive directions normally contained in a client's will. The client then transfers all appropriate assets to the trustee to be retitled in the trustee's name. At the grantor's death, the trust becomes irrevocable and all property contained in the trust is managed or disposed of under the terms of the trust. The revocable trust has become popular as an estate plan because property disposed of by a revocable trust avoids the publicity, delay, and some expenses associated with the probate process. Note again, however, the revocable trust does not protect a grantor from estate taxation on property in the trust. The revocable trust can reduce estate settlement costs by removing property from the probate estate. If probate costs are 5 percent of the estate value, placing $1.0 million of assets in the revocable trust can save $50,000 in estate settlement costs.

A living trust can also be designated as irrevocable by the grantor. Because a transfer to an *irrevocable trust* is a completed gift, it will affect the grantor's income, gift, and/or estate tax situation. A properly designed irrevocable trust can receive property from the grantor that avoids inclusion in the grantor's estate at her death. In addition, funds placed in an irrevocable trust become the property of its trustee and are exempt from the claims of the grantor's creditors. The irrevocable trust is a common and effective estate planning tool for older grantors who face substantial estate tax burdens.

Some advantages of the irrevocable trust are:

- It can reduce the estate and thus reduce the estate tax.
- The trustee can provide investment and asset management skills that the grantor does not have.
- The trust property avoids probate at the grantor's death, which can reduce estate settlement costs.
- Beneficiaries must deal with the trustee, freeing the grantor from pressures to alter provisions of the trust.
- The trust can protect assets from spousal claims to ensure benefits for the grantor's children from a previous marriage.

Testamentary Trust

testamentary trust

A *testamentary trust* is created under the will of a *testator*. Because the will can be revoked or amended as long as the testator retains legal capacity, the testamentary trust is never irrevocable until the client's death. A testamentary trust does not receive property until the testator dies and the proceeds are transferred into the trust by the executor. Since the trust is contained in the client's will, it is subject to probate and is thus open to the public. In a fairly simple estate plan, testamentary trusts are often drafted to provide for the testator's children should the spouses die in a common disaster. In a more complex estate plan, testamentary trusts are often the vehicles for the A or marital trust and B or family trust described later in this chapter.

Durable Powers of Attorney

durable power of attorney

springing durable power of attorney

A power of attorney is a written document that enables the client, known as the principal, to designate an agent, known as the *attorney-in-fact,* to act on the client's behalf. The agent has the power to act on behalf of the client only with respect to powers specifically detailed in the document.

Under a general or *conventional power of attorney,* the client authorizes the agent to act on his behalf. The client may choose anyone to act as the agent but most often selects a trusted relative or friend. The power may be quite limited, perhaps permitting the agent only to make deposits to the client's bank account. Alternatively, the power can be broad and authorize the agent to engage in nearly any transaction the client could perform. However, regardless of how limited or broad the power, a conventional power becomes inoperative if the client is incapacitated. In short, the conventional power of attorney becomes useless at the time it is needed most!

Enter the *durable power of attorney*. Unlike a conventional power, a durable power of attorney remains valid and operative despite any subsequent incapacity of the client. A durable power is definitely an integral part of a client's estate or comprehensive financial plan.

> **EXAMPLE**
>
> Mildred Spencer is an 85-year-old woman with a net worth of over $1 million. In early 2012, while she was still in good health, she created a durable power of attorney upon the recommendation of her financial advisor. Mildred authorized her adult daughter Louise as the agent to act on her behalf. In June 2012, Mildred suffered a severe stroke and was mentally and physically incapacitated for 6 weeks. During that time, Louise was able to manage all of her mother's financial affairs, which included writing checks for utilities, insurance, and other purposes; cancelling the TV cable service in her mother's home; and paying Medicare deductibles and co-payments incurred during her mother's hospitalization and subsequent treatments. If Mildred recovers sufficiently, she could revoke the durable power of attorney. In any event, if Mildred passes away, the durable power of attorney is no longer in effect, and Mildred's executor named in her will would then dispose of Mildred's estate in accordance with her will.

A durable power of attorney takes effect immediately upon execution—though it may not be needed until much later, if ever. Some clients, however, are reluctant to grant another person wide powers to act when they themselves are still mentally and physically capable. Such clients might prefer a *springing durable power of attorney*.

Recognized in several jurisdictions, a springing power lies dormant and ineffective until it is needed, typically upon the physical or mental incapacitation of the principal. For example, a determination that the client has become incapacitated would trigger the springing power.

Since family members may dispute whether a disability has properly triggered the springing power, clear language is necessary in the instrument that defines incapacity and gives the mechanism to determine whether incapacity has occurred.

Clearly, a power of attorney provides the attorney-in-fact (or agent) with the potential to abuse the privileges granted by the document. Therefore, these documents are construed very narrowly in transactions with third parties. The agent must look to the legal document for scope of authority and may not deviate from the power of attorney. The document should be drafted so that the powers granted the agent are very specific. Third parties, such as banks, brokers, and other businesses, typically are not eager to assume risks by relying on powers not specifically expressed in the document. Therefore, the more specific the language, the more likely that third parties will honor the power.

Many potential uses for a durable power of attorney arise during estate or financial planning. However, while the durable power is useful during a person's lifetime, it is only one part of an estate plan and cannot serve as the primary planning vehicle. In addition, a durable power may be difficult to use if it is dated long before it is operative. Banks, brokers, and health care personnel may be reluctant to accept a document executed years ago that grants broad powers to an agent. Good practice is to renew the durable power on an annual basis while the client has capacity.

As indicated above, a power of attorney should be drafted prudently for the specific circumstances of the client. The client should choose the agent very carefully along with the powers granted.

The advantages of a durable power of attorney include the following:

- An older client can execute a durable power of attorney and avoid the trouble and expense of having a guardian or a conservator appointed if the client loses legal capacity.
- The agent can be given the power to manage the client's assets should the client suffer a permanent or temporary loss of legal capacity. This is particularly important for owners of a closely held business.
- The durable power can replace or complement a revocable trust. The agent can manage a client's assets upon the client's legal disability and, if empowered, continue the client's dispositive scheme. For example, the agent could continue making annual gifts or charitable contributions after the client's legal incapacity but prior to the client's death.
- Most states allow a durable power of attorney for health care in which the agent can make medical care decisions on behalf of the client.

Advance Medical Directives

advance medical directives

durable power of attorney for health care

living will

A *durable power of attorney for health care* along with a *living will* are referred to as *advance medical directives*. These documents are receiving more attention because advances in medical technology that prolong life have increased fears of lengthy artificial life support and family financial disaster. Modern medicine can keep a person alive by artificial mechanisms even though the individual is unconscious and essentially nonfunctional. Life-sustaining procedures are used in cases of accident or terminal illness where death is imminent and recovery highly improbable. Individuals by law have the right to make their own medical choices based on their own values, beliefs, and wishes. However, what happens if a person has an accident or stroke and can no longer make decisions? Advance medical directives have evolved in response to these situations. Preparing advance directives lets the physician and other health care providers know the kind of medical care a client wants, or does not want, if she becomes incapacitated. Advance medical directives will go into effect only when the client cannot make and communicate her own health care decisions.

EXAMPLE

Mildred Spencer, cited in an earlier example, had created a durable power of attorney to grant power to her daughter to conduct Mildred's financial affairs if Mildred became incapacitated. Mildred had also prepared a durable power of attorney for health care, again as recommended by her financial advisor. In this document, Mildred granted contingent powers to her daughter to make health care decisions for Mildred if she became incapacitated either temporarily or permanently. After Mildred's stroke in June 2012, Mildred was unable to respond to her doctor's communications. The doctors wanted to surgically implant a "port" through which Mildred could receive nourishment. Mildred's daughter was consulted and was able to authorize the surgery on Mildred's behalf as authorized in the durable power of attorney for health care.

By executing a durable power of attorney for health care (known as a health care proxy in some circles), clients are giving authority to some other person to carry out their health care instructions. A durable power of attorney for health care is a signed and witnessed legal document that names the person (agent) the client authorizes to make medical decisions about his care. The document then relieves family and friends of the responsibility for making decisions regarding life-prolonging actions.

The other type of advance medical directive is a living will. It describes the types of medical treatment a client wishes to receive and also the types of medical treatment the client does not want to receive. The living will communicates the client's medical wishes, should he or she become terminally ill and lie in a persistent vegetative state, unable to communicate. You should be aware that while a living will makes the client's medical wishes known, it does not guarantee those wishes will be followed. Someone still has to make medical decisions regarding whether or not to continue treatment. That person typically is the agent named in a durable power of attorney for health care to carry out the client's medical wishes as expressed in a living will. Together, these two types of advance medical directives are an important part of any estate or comprehensive financial plan.

A final word on this subject. There is no national standard on living wills. States have their own authorized versions that may have substantially different terminology and provisions. Encourage your clients to have a living will that is current and compliant with the state's laws in which they reside. In addition, your clients must make sure family members and medical personnel know that a living will exists for the client.

TRANSFERS AT DEATH

Knowledge of how property is transferred at death under the laws of the jurisdictional state is necessary to plan an estate. A common misconception is that the client's will determines the distribution of the entire estate at his death. Under most circumstances, the will actually affects the distribution of only a small portion of the client's property. A carefully drafted will is still very important, but the will must be coordinated with all of the client's testamentary transfers for effective estate and financial planning.

Transfers at Death
Probate estate:
• Fee simple ownership
• Nonterminating ownership interests (certain life estates, term interests, future interests, beneficial interests, and powers that do not terminate at the client's death)
• Tenancy in common
Nonprobate estate
• Transfers by operation of law

Transfers at Death
Joint tenancy with right of survivorship
Tenancy by the entirety
Community property (in community property states)
Living trusts
Totten trusts
• Transfers by operation of contract
Life insurance proceeds payable to a named beneficiary (rather than to the client's estate or executor)
Annuity benefits payable to a named beneficiary
Retirement plan death benefits payable to a named beneficiary
Payable at death investment accounts

The Probate Estate

Transfers through Will Provisions

There are many misconceptions about the various goals associated with the estate and financial planning process. One popular opinion is that a primary goal of estate planning is to reduce the size of the probate estate. The probate estate includes all assets passing by will or intestacy. Probate property is owned outright by the deceased and is not transferred by operation of law or contract, such as by title or by naming a beneficiary. For married individuals, probate property is generally limited to the individually-owned property of the deceased spouse. Thus, the probate estate is often minimized by the usual form of property ownership between spouses—tenancy by the entirety. Note here that if otherwise nonprobate, assets such as life insurance on the decedent are made payable to the estate, the assets become probate property and are then subject to estate administration. For that reason, except in rare cases it is not advisable to name one's estate as beneficiary on life and annuity contracts.

Probate (which technically means the process of proving the validity of the will) begins when the original will is deposited in the court with jurisdiction over the deceased's estate, normally the county in which the decedent resided. The probate court oversees matters involving the settlement of the estate, distribution of probate property, appointment and supervision of fiduciaries, and disputes concerning the deceased's will. If a valid will exists, the probate court will ensure the probate property is distributed according to terms of the will after all estate settlement costs are paid. The executor (or a court-appointed administrator) has the right and obligation to distribute the probate property, with approval and supervision of the probate court. Although the court has jurisdiction solely over probate property, the state and federal taxing authorities may have the statutory authority to collect any unpaid taxes from nonprobate property if probate assets are insufficient.

Transfers by Intestacy

intestacy laws

If a client dies without a valid will, all probate property passes under the laws of *intestate succession* of the state that has jurisdiction. Intestate means "without making a will." A person who dies without a will, or with a will that has been revoked, annulled or in some other way declared invalid is said to die intestate. If there is no will, there is no way to determine how the deceased wanted her property distributed. In such cases, the *intestacy laws* legally replace the intent of the deceased in the distribution of her probate property. In other words, if you die without a will, the state will distribute your property according to its laws of intestacy, which may be very different than how you would have desired.

States vary significantly with respect to intestate laws. Distribution under intestacy laws depends on which relatives survive a deceased client. A deceased client's spouse usually receives primary consideration and will receive the entire probate estate if the deceased is not also survived by children or parents. Generally, a surviving spouse receives from one-third to one-half of the decedent's estate if there are living children or parents of the decedent. As an advisor, you must know the specific intestacy laws of the state (or states) of clients for whom you conduct estate planning.

Note again that state intestacy laws also apply to transfers under a will that is deemed invalid.

> **EXAMPLE**
>
> Henry dies in 2012, leaving $900,000 worth of property with Henry as the sole owner. He never got around to making a will, and so he died intestate. In his state, the intestacy laws dictate that $300,000 passes to Henry's wife, and the remaining $600,000 is divided equally among his three adult children. Henry was very close to his younger sister, and he had often spoken about leaving her a significant amount of assets upon his death. However, by dying intestate, Henry's wishes to bequeath his sister are not realized. In addition, Henry's wife is only 70, is in good health, and cannot live comfortably on $300,000 over what could be 20–30 more years of life. She had expected to receive the entire $900,000 as Henry's wife of almost 50 years. Henry's wife is not happy!

The Nonprobate Estate

Transfers by Operation of Law

Totten trust

We have already seen that certain ownership interests in property causes the property to pass automatically at the death of an owner. Such property is not subject to probate and it does not pass under the will or intestacy rules. A significant example of property transferred by operation of law is property held jointly with rights of survivorship. The survivorship provisions cause such property to automatically pass to the surviving joint tenant(s). As discussed earlier, property held as tenants by the entirety is also an example of a transfer by operation of law. Many married clients own property acquired during their marriage in this fashion. For example, the family home, automobile, and significant investments are often held jointly by spouses. At the death of one spouse, the property automatically passes to the surviving spouse outside the jurisdiction of the probate court.

> **EXAMPLE**
>
> Martin and Mona were married for 30 years and lived in Pittsburgh, PA. Their residence and primary bank account were titled as joint with rights of survivorship. Martin's automobile (a Lexus convertible), however, was titled in Martin's name only. Upon Martin's death in early 2012, the residence and bank account passed by operation of law to Mona. She merely had to provide evidence of Martin's death and complete some forms to retitle the residence and bank account into her name as sole owner. Martin's automobile was part of his probate property, and according to his will, the automobile went to Marie, his daughter from a previous marriage.

As we noted earlier, living trusts can be effective tools in estate and financial planning. Recall that only irrevocable living trusts have an effect on the grantor's income, gift and/or estate tax situation. However, both revocable and irrevocable living trusts are efficient methods of transferring property by operation of law, thus avoiding some of the expense, publicity, and delay of probate.

In addition, it is quite common for elderly parents to reduce their probate estates by creating operation-of-law transfers to their descendants. One such transfer is the establishment of joint bank and securities accounts with their children and giving the children survivorship rights. A similar vehicle for transfer by operation of law is the *Totten trust*. A Totten trust, also known as a *pay-on-death (POD)* account, is established when an individual client (generally a parent or grandparent) opens up a bank account in trust for a named beneficiary (generally a child or grandchild). At the client's death, the account will pass automatically by operation of law to the named beneficiary. Note that since the donor retains rights of withdrawal while living, these kinds of transactions are incomplete gifts and, while effective in reducing probate, have no impact on the taxable estate.

Transfers by Operation of Contract

Another form of nonprobate transfer is transfer by contract. The most common forms of transfer by contract involve life insurance or employee benefits to a named beneficiary. For example, life insurance policy death benefits are distributed to the policy's designated beneficiary. The same result occurs if an employee has named beneficiaries to receive various employment benefits, such as death benefits from a retirement plan. These benefits pass by operation of contract and will not become part of a deceased client's probate estate unless they are made payable to the estate's executor (or the estate) in lieu of named beneficiaries.

> **EXAMPLE**
>
> David and Dawn have been married for 10 years. David's will specifies that all of his probate assets are to transfer to Dawn upon David's death. In addition, all other property such as bank accounts, residence, and securities are titled as joint with right of survivorship. David was previously married to Jennifer for three years, during which time he purchased a $1 million term life insurance policy with Jennifer as the beneficiary. David never got around to changing the beneficiary. When David died in an auto accident in June 2012, the $1 million in life insurance proceeds went to Jennifer, not to Dawn. Dawn was not happy! Note that, as in this case, transfers by operation of contract supersede any provisions in one's will.

TAXES IMPOSED ON TRANSFERS OF WEALTH

The most significant costs of transferring wealth are various transfer taxes imposed at the federal and state levels. The tax rates applicable to affected transfers can be quite high. The relatively large impact of these transfer taxes makes tax reduction a primary focus in the estate and financial plan to conserve a client's wealth. By optimizing the solutions to the "who," "how," and "when" questions, the client can implement a plan to achieve his stated goals and holds the transfer-tax reduction of his estate to a minimum. The primary focus of our discussion will be the federal gift and estate transfer taxes, but we will briefly discuss the federal generation-skipping transfer (GST) tax and state death taxes.

We should also mention here that the estate, gift, and GST tax provisions have been in a state of flux for several years. In December, 2011, President Obama signed into law the Tax Relief, Unemployment Insurance Reauthorization, and Job Creation Act ("TRA 2010" for short). The new law made sweeping changes to rules governing federal estate taxes, gift taxes, and generation-skipping transfer taxes, but the changes only apply to the 2010, 2011, and 2012 tax years. As we revise this text in early 2012, TRA 2010 is scheduled to sunset on December 31, 2012. If that occurs, most of the provisions would revert back to their status in 2002. For example, the current estate tax exemption of $5,120,000 in 2012 would revert back to $1,000,000 if the law is allowed to expire.

We emphasize the fluid nature of estate laws and the need for financial advisors to stay current as things develop. Other complications arise from various state-imposed estate taxes which conflict significantly with federal law. For example, in 2012, some states still exempt as little as $1 million (or less) from their estate taxes, while federal laws exempt $5,120,000.

Federal Transfer Taxes

The federal transfer tax system consists of three components—gift taxation, estate taxation, and generation-skipping transfer (GST) taxation. The federal estate and gift taxes are separate tax systems imposed on different types of transfers, but the systems are unified with respect to tax brackets and tax base. The interplay between the gift tax rules and the estate tax rules must be understood, and there are several differences between the two systems that make lifetime gifts very attractive. The GST taxes are separate taxes applied under different rules and *in addition* to any applicable estate or gift taxes.

Federal Transfer Taxes
• Federal gift tax
• Federal estate tax
• Generation-skipping transfer (GST) tax

Gift taxes are imposed only if transfers exceed various exemptions, exclusions, deductions, and credits. The initial gifts made by a client will be exempt from taxation due to the exclusions and credits. Once gift taxes become payable, they are imposed by a progressive tax rate structure, with a tax rate of 35 percent levied on taxable gifts for 2012. As we will discuss later, qualifying gifts of up to $13,000 (2012, indexed amount) may be made annually by a donor to any number of donees without paying any gift tax.

Although the gift tax and the estate tax are again unified with respect to their taxation, the estate tax is quite different from the gift tax in several regards. First, there is no exclusion for the estate tax return analogous to the gift tax annual exclusion. Second, all appreciation on property included in the gross estate is subject to estate tax. That fact gives rise to strategies that remove appreciating property from the estate through the use of certain trusts and gifting programs while the client is alive. Third, estate taxes are paid at the highest marginal rate imposed on the deceased client's transfers due to the nature of the estate tax calculation. Fourth, the estate tax is a tax-inclusive system—that is, estate taxes are imposed on all property included in the gross estate, including the estate assets used to pay the estate taxes, subject to any estate tax exemptions.

Table 7-1 Federal Gift and Estate Tax Rate Schedule: 2012	
If the amount subject to the tentative tax is: . . .	The tentative tax is. . .
Not over $10,000	18% of such amount
Over $10,000 but not over $20,000	$1,800, plus 20% of excess of such amount over $10,000
Over $20,000 but not over $40,000	$3,800, plus 22% of excess of such amount over $20,000
Over $40,000 but not over $60,000	$8,200, plus 24% of excess of such amount over $40,000
Over $60,000 but not over $80,000	$13,000, plus 26% of excess of such amount over $60,000
Over $80,000 but not over $100,000	$18,200, plus 28% of excess of such amount over $80,000
Over $100,000 but not over $150,000	$23,800, plus 30% of excess of such amount over $100,000
Over $150,000 but not over $250,000	$38,800, plus 32% of excess of such amount over $150,000
Over $250,000 but not over $500,000	$70,800, plus 34% of excess of such amount over $250,000
Over $500,000 but not over $750,000	$155,800, plus 35% of excess of such amount over $500,000
Over $750,000	$248,300, plus 35% of excess of such amount over $750,000

Table 7-2 Illustrative Chart Showing the Steps for Computing Federal Estate Tax (Actual Computations are Beyond the Scope of This Book)

	STEP 1	(1) Gross estate		$_____
minus				
		(2) Funeral and administration expenses (estimated as _____ % of _____)	$_____	
		(3) Debts and taxes	_____	
		(4) Losses	_____	(–)_____
equals				
	STEP 2	(5) Adjusted gross estate		$_____
minus				
		(6) Marital deduction	$_____	
		(7) Charitable deduction	_____	
		(8) State death tax deduction	_____	(–)_____
equals				
	STEP 3	(9) Taxable estate		$_____
plus				
		(10) Adjusted taxable gifts (taxable portion of post-1976 lifetime taxable transfers not included in gross estate)		+_____
equals				
		(11) Tentative tax base (total of taxable estate and adjusted taxable gifts)		$_____
compute				
		(12) Tentative tax		$_____
minus				
		(13) Gift taxes payable on post-1976 gifts		(–)_____
equals				
	STEP 4	(14) Estate tax payable before credits		$_____
minus				
		(15) Tax credits		
		(a) Applicable credit amount	$_____	
		(b) Credit for foreign death taxes	_____	
		(c) Credit for gift tax for pre-1977 gifts	_____	
		(d) Credit for tax on prior transfers	_____	(–)_____
equals				
	STEP 5	(16) Net federal estate tax payable		$_____

Table 7-3 Federal Gift and Estate Tax Credit and Exclusion Amounts Schedule

The applicable credit amount applies to both gratuitous lifetime (gift) transfers and testamentary (after-death) transfers. The credit amount can be elected during a donor's lifetime to offset gift taxes with any remaining credit applied against federal estate taxes. The following table shows the applicable credit amount and the applicable exclusion amount (that is, the value of the gross estate sheltered from taxation) for each year from 1982 through 2012.

Year	Applicable Credit Amount	Applicable Exclusion Amount (Size of Estate Sheltered)
1982	$ 62,800	$ 225,000
1983	79,300	275,000
1984	96,300	325,000
1985	121,800	400,000
1986	155,800	500,000
1987 to 1998	192,800	600,000
1998	202,050	625,000
1999	211,300	650,000
2000 and 2001	220,550	675,000
2002 and 2003	345,800	1,000,000
2004 and 2005	555,800	1,500,000
2006, 2007, and 2008	780,800	2,000,000
2009	1,455,800	3,500,000
2010	1,473,800	3,500,000
2011	1,730,800	5,000,000
2012	1,772,800	5,120,000

The requirement to file an estate tax return has been adjusted upward to reflect increases in the applicable credit amount. Executors of estates (including lifetime adjusted taxable gifts) having a gross value that is less than the applicable exclusion amount shown in the right column above are not required to file federal estate tax returns. Only estates having values exceeding the applicable exclusion amount are potentially subject to the federal estate tax.

Certain transfers, whether made by lifetime gift or at the client's death, are subject to the generation-skipping transfer tax (GST). Generally, the GST applies to outright transfers that skip a generation in the client's family and are taxable under either the gift tax or the estate tax. Transfers subject to the GST are taxed at a flat rate equal to the highest current estate or gift tax bracket on every taxable generation-skipping transfer. Thus, taxable transfers are taxable at the 35 percent rate in 2012. When the GST applies, it is in addition to any estate or gift tax otherwise applicable to the transfer.

Federal Gift Tax

federal gift tax

The federal gift tax applies only if the following two elements are present:

- There is a completed transfer and acceptance of the property.
- The transfer of the property is for less than full and adequate consideration.

These essential elements of a taxable gift are premised on several facts. First, only property transfers are subject to gift taxation. A transfer of services by a client is not a taxable gift. Second, all completed transfers including direct and indirect gifts of property are taxable. Finally, for transfer tax purposes, the less than full and adequate consideration requirement generally does not contain an element of intent. Therefore, it is not necessary that the grantor intends to make a gift. It is merely required that the transfer be for less than full and adequate consideration. However, such transfers between unrelated individuals in a business setting typically are treated as "bad bargains" and are not treated as taxable gift transfers.

EXAMPLE

Rich Mann is a wealthy businessperson in Harrisburg, PA, and has a net worth of over $3 million. In May 2012, he "sold" his 2006 BMW 330i to his son Richie for $1.00. The market value of the BMW was $43,000 at the time of the transfer. The IRS considers the sale as a completed gift of $42,999, which is approximately $30,000 above the 2012 annual gift exclusion of $13,000. Rich should be advised to file a gift tax return and either pay the applicable gift taxes, or elect to apply the gift against his $5.12 million total gift tax exclusion.

---

exempt transfers

Exempt Transfers. A few types of gratuitous transfers (that is, gifts) are statutorily exempted from gift tax. A qualified disclaimer, in which an intended donee "disclaims" or refuses the gift, results in the gift not being treated as a taxable gift. Tuition paid directly by a donor to an educational institution on behalf of a student is exempt from gift tax, regardless of the amount or the relationship of the parties. It is not required that the donor and donee be related for the gift to be exempt. Still another exempt transfer concerns payments for medical care. A donor can pay for the medical care of a donee without making a potentially-taxable gift.

Again, the transfer (gift) must be made directly to the provider of medical services on behalf of the individual to make it an exempt transfer. Finally, transfers of money or property to a political organization (defined in IRC Sec. 527(3)(1)) are exempt from the gift tax if the transfer is for use of the political organization. The exemption does not apply to contributions made to an individual politician.

EXAMPLE
In March 2012, Eddie Baker made a payment of $50,000 to a Philadelphia hospital for emergency medical services on behalf of his nephew Butch, who was seriously injured in a neighborhood flag football game. Butch had no medical insurance. Ed made the payment directly to the hospital on Butch's behalf; as such, the transfer was an exempt transfer, and no gift taxes were applied.

gift tax annual exclusion

Gift Tax Annual Exclusion. Much of the design and complexity involved in gift tax planning involves the gift tax annual exclusion. In 2012, qualifying gifts of up to $13,000 (indexed for inflation in increments of $1,000 and equal to $14,000 in 2013) may be made by a donor to any number of donees without gift tax. The exempt amount can be increased to $26,000 (also indexed) if the donor is married and the donor's spouse elects to join in making the gifts on a timely filed gift tax return.

To qualify for the annual exclusion, a gift must provide the donee recipient with a present interest. Outright interests or current income interests in a trust will provide the beneficiary with a present interest. Trust provisions that give beneficiaries current withdrawal powers can be used to qualify gifts to a trust for the annual exclusion, even if the trust provides for deferred benefits. Use of the gift tax annual exclusion in the estate planning process is discussed later.

EXAMPLE
Barry May has a net worth of approximately $10 million and has no spouse or other close relatives. He plans to leave his entire estate at death to his longtime housekeeper Martha. While Barry is alive, he can make present interest gifts of $13,000 (2012, indexed) to any number of individual donees. In 2011, Barry wrote checks for $13,000 to 25 close friends who are members of his local Kiwanis Club. Barry did not have to pay any gift taxes on these gifts, and the recipients paid no income tax for them either.

Estate Planning

marital deduction

charitable deduction

Deductions from the Gift Tax Base. Two types of gifts are fully deductible from the transfer tax base. First, the *marital deduction* provides that unlimited qualifying transfers made by a donor to his or her spouse are fully deductible from the gift tax base. The marital deduction is quite useful if it is necessary to rearrange ownership of marital assets to implement an estate plan. This deduction is similar to the marital deduction used in computing the federal estate tax.

The *charitable deduction* provides that qualifying transfers to a legitimate charity are also deductible against the gift tax base. Thus, all qualifying transfers made to a qualified charity will avoid transfer tax.

applicable credit amount

Applicable Credit Amount. A cumulative credit is currently available against federal gift and/or estate taxes due on taxable transfers. For 2012, the *applicable credit amount* for gift tax purposes is $1,772,800, and this tax credit exempts cumulative taxable gifts up to $5,120,000 from gift taxes. Since the estate and gift tax systems are now unified, the applicable credit applies to both taxable gratuitous lifetime transfers (gifts) and testamentary (after-death) transfers. While the client is alive, this credit amount is first used to offset gift taxes, with any remaining credit being applied against estate taxes.

Under the current structure of the federal gift and estate tax system, the applicable credit amount provides a dollar-for-dollar reduction in transfer taxes otherwise payable for lifetime and/or testamentary transfers. The credit amount can be used against each dollar of transfer tax until it is exhausted. The 2012 gift tax credit amount of $1,772,800 shelters $5,120,000 of taxable transfers from federal gift and/or estate taxation. Since no taxes are due in 2012 until aggregate lifetime and/or testamentary transfers exceed $5,120,000 million, the first tax bracket applicable to a taxable transfer is 35 percent.

> **EXAMPLE**
>
> Mona Lister is a wealthy retired widow in Lancaster, PA with a net worth over $8.0 million. In January 2012, Mona made a $200,000 charitable contribution to her alma mater, Penn State University. No gift taxes applied to this charitable gift. Mona also transferred $1,013,000 into an irrevocable trust for the benefit of her granddaughter Missy. The transfer (gift) exceeded the annual gift exclusion by exactly $1.0 million. Mona will file a gift tax form with her 2012 income taxes. She will declare the $1.0 million taxable gift as part of her (current) lifetime exclusion amount of $5,120,000 (for 2012). Assuming no changes in tax laws and no other taxable gifts, if Mona died in 2013, she would be able to exclude only another $4,120,000 from estate taxes. ($5,120,000 — $1,000,000 = $4,120,000)

Federal Estate Tax

federal estate tax

The *federal estate tax* is a tax imposed on the privilege of transferring wealth at the time of death. Hence, it applies to assets held by the decedent, benefitting the decedent, or in some control of the decedent at death. Often the most difficult task in calculating the federal estate tax is determining the assets that are included in a deceased client's estate tax base. Some of the included assets are obvious, such as individually owned property. However, the estate tax rules often cause the inclusion of property in surprising circumstances. For example, property previously transferred by a decedent can be brought back into the estate tax base by provisions of the statute.

gross estate

The Gross Estate. The starting point in the estate tax calculation is determining the property included in the *gross estate*. The gross estate not only includes the property included in the client's probate estate, but it also includes property transferable at the client's death by other means. The client's gross estate includes

- property individually owned by the client at the time of death
- (some portion of) property held jointly by the client at the time of death
- the proceeds of any insurance on the client's life if either (1) incidents of ownership are held by the client within 3 years of death or (2) the proceeds are deemed payable to the estate
- pension or IRA payments left to survivors
- property subject to general powers of appointment held by the client at the time of death

- property transferred by the client during his or her lifetime if he or she retained (1) a life interest in the property, (2) a reversionary interest valued greater than 5 percent of the property at the time of death, or (3) rights to revoke the transfer at the time of death

As the list above indicates, the gross estate of the client is defined much more broadly than the probate estate, and consequently, a reduction in the size of the probate estate will often have little effect on the amount of the federal estate tax paid.

Items Deductible from the Gross Estate. Analogous to the federal gift tax rules, certain items are deductible from the gross estate to determine the adjusted gross estate for estate tax calculation purposes. First, legitimate debts of the deceased client are deductible from the gross estate if they are obligations of the gross estate. Second, reasonable funeral expenses and other death costs of the deceased client are deductible from the gross estate. Third, the costs of estate settlement, such as the executor's commission and attorney fees, are deductible to the extent such fees are reasonable.

marital deduction

Marital Deduction. As with the gift tax, qualifying transfers to a surviving spouse are deductible under the marital-deduction rules. Since the marital deduction is unlimited, the usual dispositive scheme (100 percent to the surviving spouse) will result in no estate taxes for a married couple until the death of the surviving spouse. As a client's wealth increases, sophisticated planning may be needed to make optimal use of the marital deduction. Planning for the marital deduction is discussed later in this chapter.

Charitable Deduction. The federal estate tax charitable deduction provides that transfers at death to qualifying charities will be fully deductible from the estate tax base. The charitable deduction is an excellent device to reduce the gross estate of a wealthy client. As discussed later in this chapter, the transfer of a remainder of current term interest to charity can substantially reduce the estate tax burden of a wealthy client without significantly disrupting her dispositive goals.

applicable exclusion amount

Applicable Exclusion Amount. The applicable exclusion amount shows the size of the gift or estate that can be sheltered by the corresponding applicable credit amount. The 2012 estate tax credit amount of $1,772,800 corresponds to a $5,120,000 applicable exclusion amount. As we mentioned earlier, if the applicable

$1,772,800 credit is not exhausted by employing it against lifetime gifts, any remaining amount is available against transfers made at the client's death.

State Death Tax Credit. Before it was phased out and then eliminated in 2005, the state death tax credit provided a dollar-for-dollar reduction against the federal estate tax due for any state death taxes paid by the estate. Since repeal of the state death tax credit, states have opted for various estate and inheritance tax provisions as discussed below.

Generation-Skipping Transfer Tax (GST Tax)

The GST tax was created (by the Tax Reform Act of 1986) to prevent the federal government from losing transfer tax revenue if a transferor attempts to skip one generation's level of transfer tax by transferring property to a generation more than one generation below the level of the transferor. An example would be when a grandparent make gifts of property to a grandchild. Although the GST tax was designed to prevent a transferor from finding a transfer tax loophole in the federal estate/gift tax system, it is different from the estate and gift tax system in many ways. The GST tax is applied at a flat rate equal to the highest current gift or estate tax rate on every taxable generation-skipping transfer. Thus, in 2012, any taxable transfer is subject to a 35 percent rate if the GST applies. Moreover, if the GST applies, it is in addition to any gift or estate tax that otherwise applies to the transfer. Thus, if the GST applies, a transfer could be subject to a tax rate in excess of 100 percent of the value of the asset transfer. Obviously, planning to avoid the GST tax is of paramount importance for wealthy clients.

Types of Transfers. The GST tax applies to three different types of transfers. First, the GST applies to a *direct skip*. A direct skip is an outright transfer during life or at death to a skip person, an individual who is more than one generation below the level of the transferor. In most instances, a skip person is a grandchild of the transferor, and nonskip person is a child of the transferor. In application, a direct skip can be a transfer in trust for the benefit of a skip person. A transfer in trust will be treated as a direct skip if (1) the trust benefits only one skip person, (2) no portion of the trust property may be distributed to anyone else during the skip person's lifetime, and (3) the trust property will be included in the skip person's (that is, the beneficiary's) estate if he dies before the termination of the trust.

To be a direct skip, the transfer to the skip person must also be subject to gift or estate tax. Transfers that are not subject to gift tax because of the gift tax annual exclusion or the exemption for direct payment of medical and/or tuition expenses are not subject to the GST rules. Moreover, for all types of transfers, if the parent of the skip person is deceased at the time of the transfer, the transfer is not subject to the GST. In this instance, the GST does not apply because the grandchild is the natural recipient of the grandparent's wealth if the grandchild's parent is deceased.

> **EXAMPLE**
>
> James Dollar, Sr., a widower with a taxable estate of approximately $10.0 million, left a fully furnished condominium that he had owned for 15 years to his only grandchild, James Dollar, III (Jimmy) under terms of his will. If Jimmy's father, James Dollar, Jr., was still alive upon James Dollar, Sr.'s death, the transfer of the condo will be considered as a direct skip under the GST rules, and the generation-skipping (GST) tax would apply. Note, if James Dollar Jr. was deceased when his father, James Dollar, Sr., passed away, the transfer of the condo would NOT be subject to the generation-skipping tax. However, in either event, the regular federal estate tax applies to the transfer.

The GST rules also apply to a *taxable termination*. A taxable termination occurs when there is a termination of a property interest held in trust as a result of death, lapse of time, or otherwise, and a skip beneficiary receives the remainder interest outright in the trust.

> **EXAMPLE**
>
> Alice Summer's will directed that the income from her investment portfolio was to pass to her daughter Barbara for life, with the remainder interest to pass at Barbara's death to Alice's grandson, Charles. When Barbara died in March 2012, her life interest in the property (that is, to receive income) terminated and Charles received all the assets in the investment portfolio. Charles is a skip beneficiary. A taxable termination occurred at Barbara's death.

The third type of transfer subject to the GST tax is a *taxable distribution*. A taxable distribution is a distribution of either income or principal from a trust to a person more than one generation below the level of the trust grantor. The recipient of the taxable distribution is a skip beneficiary of the trust. Thus, a taxable distribution can occur when a trustee makes a distribution to a skip beneficiary even if a nonskip beneficiary still holds a current beneficial interest in the trust.

> **EXAMPLE**
>
> Arthur Webb created an irrevocable trust 10 years ago for the benefit of his son, Bradley, and his grandson Chris. In January 2012, the trustee made a distribution of $20,000 of trust income to Bradley and $10,000 of trust income to Chris. The distribution to Chris is characterized as a taxable distribution that triggers GST. Note that the original transfer to the trust could have been subject to gift taxes under any applicable gift tax rules at that time.

Lifetime Exemption and Annual Exclusion. The GST has a $5.12 million exemption in 2012 available to each taxpayer to be applied against all potential generation-skipping transfers. The exemption will return to $1.0 million for 2012 absent any further legislation. The exemption is applied against transfers during life or at death of a transferor. The exemption must be affirmatively allocated to specific transfers in the tranferor's appropriate tax return. If this GST exemption is not allocated on a gift tax return during the life of a transferor or in the transferor's will, the taxing authorities will allocate the exemption by default. A client would make a substantial mistake by failing to appropriately allocate the GST exemption.

Note that a lifetime allocation is particularly appropriate because the exemption is leveraged. That simply means the exemption will be applied to the value of the property at the time of the transfer, and any posttransfer appreciation will not be subject to the GST or need to be sheltered by part of the exemption. Consequently, wealthy clients can make lifetime transfers of appreciating property that will eventually expand into substantial wealth at a huge total transfer tax savings. Any exemption not used at the time of the taxpayer client's death and not made by his or her executor will be allocated according to the default rules.

Similar to the gift tax annual exclusion discussed earlier in this section but with specific rules of its own, an exclusion of $13,000 (as indexed for 2012) from the GST is available for direct skips. As previously indicated, a direct skip is either an outright gift to a skip person or certain gifts in trust providing a present interest to a skip person.

State Death Taxes

Frequently, the subject of state death taxes is overshadowed by the attention given to the federal estate tax. Although the emphasis on federal estate taxation is warranted for estates that have a value of more than the applicable exclusion amount, statistically the federal tax affects a relatively small percentage of all estates settled. On the other hand, many more estates are within reach of the death taxes levied by states. Therefore, state death tax planning should not be ignored since taxable transfers for state purposes can often be avoided by simple planning that might otherwise be ineffective (and thus disregarded) for federal estate tax planning purposes. For example, many states exempt life insurance benefits paid to a named beneficiary.

State Inheritance Tax

state inheritance tax

A *state inheritance tax* is a tax imposed on a beneficiary's right to inherit property from a deceased person's estate. The tax rate is based on the amount of property received by each beneficiary and may be based on the relationship of the beneficiary to the deceased. An inheritance received by a close relative, such as a son or daughter, is generally subject to a lower tax rate than an inheritance received by a more distant relation, such as a niece or nephew. In many cases, the inheritance tax on property received by relatives outside the deceased's immediate family (surviving spouse and children) is subject to a tax that can be significant. In fact, in many instances, the state inheritance tax could be more significant than any federal estate tax due.

State Estate Tax

state estate tax

A *state estate tax* is similar to the federal estate tax. It differs from a state inheritance tax in that an inheritance tax is imposed on a beneficiary's right to inherit, while an estate tax is imposed on a deceased person's right to transfer or pass property to beneficiaries.

Credit Estate Tax

credit estate tax

States previously used a *credit estate tax* (also known as a "sponge tax") to capture the maximum amount of taxes up to the amount of state death taxes allowed to be credited against the federal estate tax. In other words, if the computed state inheritance or estate tax was less than the federal estate tax credit allowed for state death taxes, the state assessed the difference. This allowed the states to collect at least as much as the federal estate tax credit amount. Prior to 2005, all states imposed a credit estate tax. A dollar-for-dollar credit amount was applied against any federal estate taxes payable. The revenue that states derived from the credit estate tax represented sizable additions for many states' coffers.

However, beginning in 2005, the state death tax credit was fully repealed by EGTRRA and replaced with simply a deduction for any amount of state death taxes paid. Hence, the new federal rules have encouraged some states, especially those states having only a federal state death tax credit, to either create or reenact different state death tax rules of their own. Suffice to say, the situations in the states vary considerably. It is well beyond the scope of this introductory course to examine the states' rules in detail. For advisors working with estate planning clients, be aware that you must learn the particular state rules for the jurisdictions in which your clients reside, or even own property subject to state taxations.

Planning for State Death Taxes

While a detailed analysis of each state's inheritance or estate tax is well beyond our scope of discussion, there are some peculiarities in the state death tax base that you should understand. First, jointly-held property is included in the federal estate tax base. However, there are some states that do not tax property held jointly by an individual at the time of his death. Therefore, without affecting federal estate taxes, an individual in one of these states can avoid state death taxes by transferring property to joint ownership prior to his death.

In addition, some states provide for no marital deduction for individually owned property transferred to a surviving spouse. Therefore, severing a joint ownership of property with a surviving spouse may create state death taxes even if that property is transferred to the surviving spouse in a transfer deductible for federal estate tax purposes.

After EGTRRA 2001 rules repealed the state death tax credit completely starting in 2005, many states have since acted to prevent future death tax revenue losses by "decoupling" or removing themselves from their interrelationship with the federal estate tax system. At present, 17 states are decoupled from the federal estate tax system and currently impose some form of estate tax. A person who resides in one of those states could pay state death tax even though no federal estate tax was due. For example, in 2012 the federal estate tax exemption is $5,120,000, but the state of New Jersey's estate tax exemption is only $675,000. While a client might plan to take full advantage of the federal estate tax exemption that may result in no federal estate taxes due, a resident of New Jersey may incur state estate taxes on an estate above the $675,000 threshold.

Some states impose a stand-alone inheritance tax (payable by the recipient of the property) and not based on federal rules. In either event, the states that impose an estate or inheritance tax are in the minority. For states with an estate or inheritance tax, the taxes are imposed at a significantly lower rate than the federal estate tax. However, the taxes apply to estates with values well before the federal exemption amount (that is, $5.12 million in 2012). For this reason, it is important to know the tax picture for any state that may impose a tax on your client's property at death.

Finally, life insurance owned individually by an insured at the time of his death is often not taxable at the state level if payable to a named beneficiary.

PRESERVING THE CLIENT'S WEALTH

There are many techniques to reduce the transfer tax burden associated with transferring a client's wealth to his or her heirs. The appropriate answer to the "who" question may be used to reduce estate taxes. For example, qualifying transfers to a surviving spouse are fully deductible from the client's gross estate under the unlimited marital deduction. The optimal resolution of the "how" question could also reduce estate taxes. For example, transferring assets to a family trust takes advantage of the applicable credit against federal estate taxes. Finally, if the "when" question is answered appropriately, the gross estate of a client can be substantially reduced through a systematic lifetime gifting program, and substantial wealth can be transferred free of all transfer taxes.

The Advantages of Lifetime Gifts

Nontax Advantages of Lifetime Gifts

Clients give away property during their lifetime for many reasons. The nontax advantages of making lifetime gifts are as follows:

- The donor can provide for the support, education, and welfare of the donee.
- The donor gets the pleasure of seeing the donee beneficiary enjoy the gift.
- The donor avoids the publicity and administrative costs associated with a probate transfer at death.
- The donated property is protected from the claims of the donor's creditors.

Tax Advantages of Lifetime Gifts

Although the federal gift tax and estate tax share the same set of progressive tax rates, there are some distinctions that make lifetime gifts more favorable from a tax standpoint. These tax advantages of lifetime gifts are as follows:

- The gift tax annual exclusion for gifts up to $13,000 (2012, indexed for inflation) provides a complete loophole from federal transfer gift and estate taxes. In 2012, any number of $13,000 gifts can be made by clients ($26,000 if their spouses join with them) to reduce their transfer tax bases.
- The gift tax is imposed on the value of the gift at the time a completed transfer is made. Thus, any posttransfer appreciation in the property avoids all transfer tax.
- The gift tax payable on gifts made more than 3 years prior to the donor client's death is excluded from the donor's estate tax base.
- The income produced by gifted property is shifted from the donor client to the donee beneficiary for income tax purposes. In other words, lifetime gifting may be used to move taxable income-producing property from a high-bracket donor client to a lower-bracket donee beneficiary.
- Unlimited qualifying transfers can be made between spouses without incurring gift taxes. Spouses can advantageously shift assets between themselves to meet the needs of the estate and financial plan of each spouse.

Opportunities Created by the Gift Tax Annual Exclusion

As discussed earlier, the annual exclusion allows a donor to give up to $13,000 tax free to any number of donees in 2012. If the donor client's spouse elects to split gifts with the donor client for the tax year, the annual exclusion is increased to $26,000 per donee. If the donor has a substantial estate and several individuals to benefit, the systematic use of annual exclusion gifts can facilitate the transfer of substantial wealth free of transfer tax.

EXAMPLE

Tom Taxplanner, a 65-year-old widower, has two children and four grandchildren. Tom can give up to $78,000 of qualifying transfers annually to his heirs without ever subjecting the transfers to federal gift taxes. If Tom lives an additional 16 years (his actual life expectancy), he can give away $1,248,000 and save up to $436,800 of estate tax (assuming a maximum 35 percent bracket in 2012). The actual tax savings are even greater because any appreciation on the property transferred also escapes transfer taxes.

Estate Planning

The annual exclusion is available only for gifts that provide the donee beneficiary with a present interest. For example, an outright transfer of property provides a present interest. Because an outright transfer is often unfavorable (for example, the donee beneficiary is a minor), significant planning is often necessary to design gifts that restrict the donee beneficiary's current access to the funds while still qualifying for the annual exclusion.

Gifts to Minors

Quite often, annual exclusion gifts will be made to minor children or grandchildren as part of the estate plan of a wealthy client. This creates problems for the donor and the donee. First, there are restrictions on the ability of minors to hold or otherwise deal with property under state law. In addition, the donor will naturally be concerned about the safety of the funds if the minor has significant access rights. Fortunately, there are several methods for making annual exclusion gifts with restrictions on the minor's access to the property.

Transferring Assets to Minors: Techniques That Restrict Access

- Uniform Gifts to Minors Act (UGMA)
- Uniform Transfers to Minors Act (UTMA)
- Sec. 2503(b) trust
- Sec. 2503(c) trust
- Irrevocable trust with current withdrawal powers

Uniform Gifts to Minors Act (UGMA)

Uniform Transfers to Minors Act (UTMA)

Uniform Gifts to Minors Act (UGMA) or Uniform Transfers to Minors Act (UTMA). The *Uniform Gifts to Minors Act (UGMA)* and the *Uniform Transfers to Minors Act (UTMA)* statutes are model laws that have been adopted in various forms in individual states. They permit the transfer of funds to a custodial account for the benefit of a minor. The custodian of a UGMA or UTMA account manages the property under the rules provided by state law. There are restrictions on the type of property permissible as an investment for these purposes. The original model act, UGMA, has been expanded in many states to increase the types of permissible investments. In a majority of states, the newer model act, UTMA, has been adopted, and relatively few restrictions exist in these states on the permissible investments. A UGMA or UTMA transfer is particularly favorable for smaller gifts because it provides for the protection of the assets without the expense of administering a trust. The provisions for distribution from a UGMA or UTMA are provided under the various state laws. Generally speaking, UGMA or UTMA funds can be accumulated during the minority of the donee beneficiary, but the custodial assets must be distributed to the beneficiary upon reaching majority in the state jurisdiction—generally 18 to 21 years of age. Some states allow a donor to select ages up to age 25.

> **EXAMPLE**
>
> Marie McKay created a Uniform Transfer to Minors Act (UTMA) mutual fund account under Pennsylvania law for her granddaughter Maggie. Under the PA state law, Marie selects the age of 25 at which Maggie can take possession of the assets in the account. Marie can gift up to the annual exclusion amount ($13,000 in 2012) each year into the account with no gift tax consequences, and as custodian she can make investment decisions for the account. Any taxable transactions, such as distributions of dividends and capital gains, are taxable to Maggie. A so-called "kiddie tax" may apply.

Sec. 2503(b) Trust. A *Sec. 2503(b) trust* is an irrevocable trust created by a donor during his lifetime to receive annual exclusion gifts for a minor beneficiary. The trust requires that income be distributed at least annually to (or for the benefit of) the minor donee. The minor would receive distribution of the trust principal whenever the trust agreement specifies. A distribution of principal does not have to be made at the majority of the donee. The annual gift tax exclusion is limited to the value of the income interest provided by the trust. The Sec. 2503(b) trust should be invested in income-producing property and is less favorable in some respects than the UGMA/UTMA gift because the income cannot be accumulated.

Sec. 2503(c) Trust. A *Sec. 2503(c) trust* is another type of irrevocable trust designed to receive annual exclusion gifts for a minor donee. This type of trust requires that both income and principal be distributed to the minor at age 21. However, the trust is allowed to accumulate current income prior to the termination of the trust, unlike the Sec. 2503(b) trust.

Crummey powers

Irrevocable Trust with Current Withdrawal Powers. A client often wishes to make gifts to a minor in trust with the purpose of accumulation. If the trust provides for accumulation and does not currently benefit the donee, the gift tax annual exclusion would normally be forfeited. Provisions of the tax law, however, permit the annual gift tax exclusion if current beneficial rights are given to the donee. These rights, known as *Crummey powers*, provide the beneficiary with temporary donee rights to the funds contributed to the trust. Under these rules, a gift to a trust will qualify for the annual exclusion if the donee has the noncumulative, temporary (for example, 30 days) right to demand up to the annual exclusion amount from his share of the funds contributed to the trust by the donor.

The Crummey powers are named after the taxpayer who litigated the landmark decision in 1968 authorizing an annual gift tax exclusion for gifts and trusts subject to these powers. Irrevocable trusts with Crummey withdrawal powers are often used to hold a life insurance policy on the life of the grantor. Since the life insurance premiums are paid with annual premium additions to the trust, it is intended that these premiums will accumulate in the policy and that no distributions will be made until the death of the grantor. If each beneficiary is provided with the ability to withdraw a pro rata share of the annual premium contributions to the trust, the premium contributions will qualify for the annual exclusion gift to the donees. Thus, an irrevocable life insurance trust can be created without gift tax costs. The estate tax advantage of a life insurance trust will be discussed below.

Federal Estate Tax Planning

Despite the advantages of systematic annual gifting, most individuals will desire to retain a significant portion of their wealth until death. To the extent this wealth is included in the gross estate of the decedent, it will be included in the estate tax calculations. Due to the deductions and credits provided by the estate tax laws, a properly designed estate and financial plan can distribute significant wealth to a decedent's heirs while minimizing or deferring federal estate taxes.

Planning for the Marital Deduction. The marital deduction provides that certain transfers at death from a deceased spouse to a surviving spouse are fully deductible from the gross estate for federal estate tax purposes. This deduction is unlimited as long as the property is included in the gross estate of the deceased spouse and is transferred to the surviving spouse in a qualifying manner.

Through *maximum* use of the marital deduction, a married couple can, at their option, eliminate all federal estate taxes due at the first death of the two spouses. The estate plan of the marital unit making full use of the marital deduction merely defers the estate taxes until the second spouse dies. The marital deduction will be available at the death of the surviving spouse only if he or she remarries and transfers the property to the new spouse. Thus, a married couple can avoid all federal estate taxes on the first death of the two spouses by making a qualifying transfer of all property included in the deceased spouse's gross estate (both probate and nonprobate property) to the surviving spouse. As we shall explain shortly, a new provision under the Tax Relief Act of 2010, allows for "portability" of the unused portion of the estate tax exemption by the first spouse to die, so that the surviving spouse can use the exemption, along with her own, upon her death.

Simply answering the "who" question in favor of the surviving spouse will not necessarily qualify such transfers for the marital deduction. The tax laws provide that only qualifying transfers will be eligible for the marital deduction. Thus, the "how" question must also be answered appropriately.

Portability Under the New Estate Tax Law. The Tax Relief Act of 2010 (TRA 2010) introduced a new concept into the estate tax system—portability in regard to use of a deceased spouse's unclaimed estate tax exemption. An understanding of this concept is vitally important to anyone involved in estate planning for a married couple, as it will radically affect planning if it remains in effect after 2012. Portability allows a surviving spouse to use a predeceased spouse's unused applicable exclusion amount ($5.12 million in 2012), effectively doubling the amount that a married couple can pass to beneficiaries free of tax.

TRA 2010 defined a new concept in estate planning lexicon, the "deceased spousal unused exclusion amount." This simply describes the applicable exclusion amount that remains unused at the death of the first spouse to die. The concept can be illustrated with a simple example:

EXAMPLE

George and Betty Ward were married for 50 years before George died in early 2012. His tentative taxable estate was $10,000,000 which he left in total to his surviving spouse Betty. The executor of the estate, in accordance with prior estate planning, used the unlimited marital deduction to avoid paying any federal estate taxes on George's estate. In effect, George's estate passed up the opportunity to exempt $5.12 million of his taxable estate available in 2012. Under the TRA 2010 portability provision, Betty can claim the unused applicable exclusion amount upon her eventual death. Assuming her taxable estate was also $10,000,000 and that the applicable exclusion amount remained at least $5,120,000 at her death, then Betty could pass her entire estate free of federal estate taxes by claiming both her $5.12 million exclusion and George's unused exclusion of $5.12 million.

For decades, married couples have used estate planning techniques to accomplish the same results that portability, at least in part, now provides. A married couple's estate plan often used a "credit shelter" disposition of assets to fully use the applicable exclusion amount of the first spouse to die. Such estate planning techniques as "A/B Trust" arrangements were designed to use the marital deduction for the "A trust" (with no subsequent federal estate taxes) and put enough assets into the "B trust" to fully use the applicable exclusion amount that applied when the first spouse died. Although, credit shelters will continue to play an important role in estate planning, portability definitely provides some relief for couples who fail to plan properly.

Outright Transfers. The simplest and most common method of transferring property to a surviving spouse—the unrestricted transfer—is eligible for an unlimited marital deduction. This includes all property included in the deceased spouse's gross estate that passes directly to the surviving spouse. Therefore, outright transfers of probate assets by will or intestacy qualify for the marital deduction. In addition, transfers by operation of contract or law that pass outright to the surviving spouse at death similarly qualify. Thus, life insurance proceeds payable to a surviving spouse or jointly-held property received by the surviving spouse qualify for the marital deduction.

Property transfers that place restrictions on the surviving spouse's use or enjoyment of the property may or may not qualify for the marital deduction. The marital deduction was designed to prevent a substantial first-death tax to a married couple if the usual dispositive scheme (100 percent to the spouse) is followed. However, Congress intended that federal estate taxes would be payable at the second death of the two spouses, now subject to the new portability rules of TRA 2010. Thus, a general rule of thumb is that the marital deduction is available only for transfers to a surviving spouse that would cause the ultimate inclusion of the property in the surviving spouse's gross estate. Property transferred to a surviving spouse typically will not qualify for the marital deduction if the interest is terminable at the death of the surviving spouse.

An interest in property left to a surviving spouse will be nondeductible if

- it terminates on the occurrence of an event or a contingency, such as death, and
- a third party gains possession of the property after the surviving spouse's interest terminates.

A common example of a nondeductible terminable interest is the transfer of a life estate to a surviving spouse with the remainder interest being paid to the couple's children under the terms of the deceased spouse's will. Such a transfer would not create a second-death tax because the surviving spouse's interest terminates and, therefore, would not be included in her estate. However, a first-death tax would be payable because the life estate transferred to the surviving spouse would not qualify for the marital deduction.

Congress recognized that many married individuals prefer leaving property in trust for the surviving spouse. The transferor may be concerned that the surviving spouse may be unable to properly manage the trust property. Or, the transferor-spouse may want to limit the invasion rights of the surviving spouse. In addition, it is generally the intent of individuals to leave their property ultimately to their children. The transferor-spouse may want to control the ultimate disposition of the property to preserve the rights of his children. This is particularly true if the transferor spouse has children from a prior marriage. Fortunately, the marital-deduction rules have created several opportunities that meet many of these objectives.

estate trust

Estate Trust. A transfer to a surviving spouse through an *estate trust* qualifies for the marital deduction. Under this arrangement, a deceased spouse leaves a life estate in trust to the surviving spouse. The surviving spouse's estate is the remainderperson of the trust. Income from the estate trust can either accumulate or be paid to the surviving spouse at the discretion of the trustee. Because the remainder interest is transferred to the surviving spouse's estate, the property will be included in the surviving spouse's gross estate, and a second-death federal estate tax may be payable at that time.

power of appointment trust

Power-of-Appointment Trust. Another common marital-deduction trust is the *power-of-appointment trust*. This trust is designed to distribute income to the surviving spouse during life and to provide the surviving spouse with a general power of appointment over the trust property. The general power of appointment may be exercisable by the surviving spouse in all events, or it may be exercisable only at the death of the surviving spouse. Because the surviving spouse has a general power of appointment over the trust principal, the principal is included in the gross estate for federal estate tax purposes.

Transfers Qualifying for the Marital Deduction

- Outright transfers
  - By will or intestacy
  - By operation of law
  - By operation of contract
- Estate trust
- Power-of-appointment trust
- QTIP trust

QTIP marital-deduction trust

QTIP Marital-Deduction Trust. A special provision of the tax law provides for a marital deduction if qualifying terminable interest property (QTIP) is left to a surviving spouse. Under these rules, a terminable property interest can be transferred to a surviving spouse with the interest qualifying for the marital deduction. The QTIP deduction is available if the executor of the deceased spouse's estate elects QTIP treatment on the estate tax return. The QTIP trust can be funded by probate assets or other types of testamentary dispositions. The surviving spouse must have the right to all income annually from the QTIP trust for life. At the death of the surviving spouse, the QTIP election provides that the trust property *will be included* in the surviving spouse's gross estate.

The primary advantage of a QTIP trust for the transferor-spouse is the ability to control the ultimate disposition of his or her assets. The ultimate disposition of the QTIP property would be predetermined by the terms of the QTIP trust as specified by the transferor-spouse. Thus, a QTIP trust permits a transferor-spouse to provide income for the surviving spouse, but still protect the interests of his or her children.

To summarize the QTIP elective provision, it allows even terminal interests passing to a surviving spouse to qualify for the marital deduction. Property passing to the spouse for life with the remainder going to some other person (often children of the transferor-spouse) is eligible for the marital deduction, on the condition that the property will be subject to tax upon the surviving spouse's death.

Planning for the Gift and Estate Tax Applicable Credit Amount. The applicable credit against gift and/or estate taxes is designed to prevent the imposition of transfer taxes on moderate-sized estates. In 2012, as previously noted, a credit amount of $1,772,800 is available to shelter up to $5,120,000 of property transfers from gift taxes during a transferor's lifetime. However, if this credit is not exhausted sheltering gifts, any remaining portion of the credit is available to shelter transfers made at death.

Keep in mind that the exclusion amount of a decedent is increased by a "deceased spousal unused exclusion amount" (DSUEA) after 2010, under terms of TRA 2010. Hence. if the first spouse to die does not leave a taxable estate, by employing the unlimited marital deduction against his entire gross estate, the surviving spouse would have up to $10.24 million (2012, as indexed) of exclusion available at the second death. Be aware, however, the exclusion will return to $1.0 million for 2013, and the portability of the exclusion to a surviving spouse will be repealed unless Congress extends these provisions.

However, before any of the available credit can be used to offset gift or estate taxes, there must first be a property transfer that creates gift or estate taxes. Thus, the applicable credit amount cannot be used when a property transfer is already exempt or deductible from the tax base as a result of other federal transfer tax rules. For example, if a transfer is already exempt from tax because of the gift tax annual exclusion or because of the marital deduction, the transferor's credit cannot be used.

deceased spousal unused exclusion amount (DSUEA)

Coordination of the Marital Deduction and the Applicable Credit Amount. In the past, the maximum use of a marital deduction has been the typical dispositive scheme for most married individuals. All property is generally left either outright to the surviving spouse, or in some other manner the transfer qualified for the marital deduction at the first spouse's death. Since no estate tax was payable under these circumstances, the lifetime exclusion for the first spouse was wasted.

A married couple can now make maximum use of the applicable exclusion amount, and the marital unit as a whole can shelter up to $10.24 million (with the current 2012 individual exclusion of $5.12 million) in marital wealth from federal estate taxes. The new rules of the Tax Relief Act of 2010 provide that the exclusion amount left unused at the first death can be "inherited" by the surviving spouse. The surviving spouse's applicable exclusion amount is $5.12 million plus the *deceased spousal unused exclusion amount (DSUEA)*.

Estate Planning

The portability of the exclusion amount between spouses would appear to eliminate the need to create the marital and exemption (exclusion) trust transfers at the first death. Under the rules existing prior to the portability provision, it was necessary to use the exclusion amount at the death of the first spouse to die. This arrangement is commonly referred to as an A/B trust arrangement. The A/B trust arrangement is designed to operate as follows:

- The A trust is some form of marital-deduction trust. This trust receives assets in a manner qualifying for the marital deduction and provides for maximum use of these assets by the surviving spouse. The remainder of the assets transferred by the decedent are placed into the B trust.

- The B trust is designed *not* to qualify for the marital deduction. Instead, the B trust, funded with approximately $5.12 million, will be part of the taxable estate since the transfer will not be deductible under the marital deduction. However, the $5.12 million transferred to the B trust is sheltered from tax at the first death by the applicable credit available to the estate of the first spouse to die.

Much of today's estate planning strategy revolves around how to best use the portability provisions in TRA 2010 with various trusts available to married clients. This planning can get somewhat complicated and is beyond the scope of this introductory course.

Table 7-4 Characteristics of the AB Trust Arrangement (under which both spouses create two testamentary trusts)	
A Trust	**B Trust**
• Surviving spouse is beneficiary • Receives all assets not placed in B trust • Qualifies for marital deduction • Subject to estate taxation at death of surviving spouse	• Surviving spouse receives no more than life income interest and limited invasion powers; children may receive current and/or remainder interest. • Receives $5.12 million of assets (for 2012) • Does not qualify for marital deduction; makes use of the applicable credit amount • Escapes estate taxation at death of surviving spouse

Planning Charitable Contributions. Qualifying gifts of property to charities may generate deductions against federal income, gift, and estate taxes. Although some limitations exist for the charitable deduction for income tax purposes, qualifying gifts of property are deductible in full against either the federal gift or estate tax base.

Charitable contributions are deductible for federal income, gift, and estate tax purposes only if made to qualified organizations. Generally speaking, an organization is qualified if it is operated exclusively for religious, charitable, scientific, literary, or educational purposes. In addition, the charity must hold such qualified status under the rules of the Internal Revenue Service (IRS). A list of qualified charities is published by the IRS and may be used by individuals interested in making a charitable contribution.

Advantages of Gifts to Charity. The value of property gifted to a qualified charity is fully deductible from the federal gift or estate tax base. In addition, the value of property gifted to charity will be deductible from the federal income tax base of the donor client. (Some limitations exist on the size of the income tax deduction, but they are not discussed here.) Thus, a donor can reduce current income taxes and the eventual size of her taxable estate. Quite simply, any property gifted to charity will remove the property (including any postcontribution appreciation) from the transfer-tax base of the donor. Because the gift tax charitable deduction is unlimited, charitable contributions can be even more effective than gifts to non-charitable donees in reducing the size of the gross estate of a wealthy client. The estate tax charitable deduction is similarly unlimited for testamentary bequests to charities. Through the techniques discussed below, charitable contributions can significantly reduce a deceased client's estate tax liability without completely divesting other heirs of the donated property.

charitable remainder trust

Gifts of Remainder Interests to Charity. One disadvantage of an outright lifetime contribution of property to charity is that the donor loses the current enjoyment of the property. Fortunately, there are methods to take advantage of the tax benefits provided by charitable contributions while retaining the donor's use or enjoyment of the property. A certain type of trust arrangement, known as a *charitable remainder trust,* can be employed to retain the current enjoyment of the property for the life of the donor (or lives of the donor's family members) while providing income, gift, and estate tax advantages. The charitable remainder trust can be established during the donor's lifetime or at her death. The charitable remainder trust permits the donor to retain the current income for the client or her family. The income from the trust's assets will be retained for a time period (usually measured by the life of the donor or lives of selected family members) with the charitable institution holding the remainder interest. The current charitable deduction is measured by the present value of the remainder interest held by the charity. Thus, the donor (or possibly members of the donor's family) receives not only the current enjoyment of the trust property but also a current tax deduction, while the charity receives outright ownership of the property sometime in the future when the remainder interest is distributed by the trust. To prevent abuses of the transfer tax system, tax rules carefully specify the types of charitable remainder trusts eligible for such tax benefits.

charitable lead trust

Donating Income Interests to Charity. Under some circumstances, a donor may give a current income interest to charity instead of a remainder interest. To accomplish this, a type of trust known as a *charitable lead trust* is established to provide the charity with a current term income interest. At the end of the term period, the property either reverts to the donor or passes to a member of his family. The donor gets an up-front income and gift or estate tax deduction for the present value of the lead income interest donated to the charity. However, careful planning is required with this type of trust because even though the donor receives a charitable tax deduction, all trust income is still taxable to the donor.

Charitable lead trusts generally are used for testamentary dispositions. If the current income interest bequested to the charity is substantial, the estate will receive a tax deduction in an amount equal to a large portion of the value of the property placed in trust. Thus, the taxable estate will be significantly reduced while the family retains ultimate control of the trust property through its remainder interest. The charitable lead trust is an excellent planning tool for extremely wealthy clients who have a substantial amount of other assets to leave to their heirs currently, since the assets placed in the charitable lead trust may not be available for several years.

Life Insurance in the Estate and/or Financial Plan

Life insurance can serve either as an estate liquidity or estate enhancement tool. The most appropriate use of life insurance in an estate plan depends on the age, family circumstances, and financial status of the particular client.

Life Insurance for Estate Enhancement. Life insurance is generally used for estate enhancement by (1) younger clients, (2) clients with dependent family members, and (3) clients with small to moderate-sized estates. Clients in these categories generally cite protection as their primary need for life insurance. They want to protect their families from the loss of future earnings needed for support. These clients are either in or are headed toward their peak earning years, and their families are relying on these future earnings to maintain their standard of living, educate the children, and accumulate retirement assets. In a family with a special needs child or grandchild, the support needs might well continue long beyond the death of the child's parents. In this instance, the estate enhancement will continue beyond the parents' working years.

The death taxes facing younger clients with small to moderate-sized estates are relatively minor. The applicable credit amount, marital deduction, and portability provisions will generally remove the danger of federal estate taxes for these individuals. Thus, estate liquidity is not their primary concern. Nonetheless, it is highly improbable that these clients have accumulated enough wealth to replace their future incomes and support of a breadwinner who dies prematurely. Life insurance is the perfect estate enhancement tool to replace some or all of the financial loss created by a premature death.

Life Insurance for Estate Liquidity. For older clients with larger estates, estate liquidity becomes their primary focus in the use of life insurance. Older clients with families generally have completed or nearly completed the heaviest support and educational expense years for dependent children. These clients are usually well along in their funding for retirement and have fewer years of employment ahead of them.

Because older clients may have accumulated substantial wealth, the protection offered by the applicable exclusion amount, the marital deduction and the TRA 2010 portability of unused exclusion amounts may be inadequate to shelter their estates from taxation. Although the marital deduction will generally shelter all of the estate from tax at the death of the first spouse, the second death can create a substantial tax problem. As noted earlier, with optimal planning the marital unit can shelter up to $10.24 million of total family wealth from taxes in 2012. Consequently, marital wealth in excess of these amounts will be subject to taxation and may well create liquidity problems for these large estates as they struggle with how best to pay the taxes. Besides, the client's accumulated wealth may not be liquid and available for paying taxes. For example, an interest in a closely held family business is often assigned a high value for federal estate tax purposes. However, the reality is that the business interest may be unmarketable to purchasers outside the family group. If the heirs are to remain in the business, they must discover a method to pay any estate taxes due.

Under the circumstances described above, life insurance can provide death proceeds equal to the size of the wealth lost in the form of substantial state death taxes, federal estate taxes, and other end-of-life final expenses. In addition, the life insurance proceeds provide cash, which, unlike illiquid estate assets such as real estate, is more readily available to provide the liquidity needs to settle the estate. Without the liquidity provided by life insurance, illiquid and often unmarketable estate assets may have to be sold at a fraction of their value just to cover the settlement costs.

The estate tax treatment of the life insurance selected by these clients is critical. Since affluent clients hope to solve liquidity problems rather than add to a tax burden, the life insurance should be purchased and owned in a manner that keeps the death proceeds out of the gross estate, if possible. Thus, wealthy clients often make arrangements for using life insurance that provide the insured with no incidents of ownership. This can be accomplished by having either their spouses or children apply for and own the policies. Or, as discussed below, a trust can be created specifically to own the insurance. In either case, neither the estate nor the executor should ever be the beneficiary of the policy because that designation would place the proceeds in the gross estate for tax purposes.

revocable life insurance trust

Revocable Life Insurance Trusts. A *revocable life insurance trust* is designed to own and/or be the beneficiary of life insurance on the grantor's life. This type of trust, however, serves no estate tax planning purposes. Since the trust is revocable, the insured is treated as the owner of the policy, and the death proceeds will be included in the insured's gross estate. The revocable life insurance trust is ordinarily used when a specific, perhaps temporary, protection need exists.

The revocable life insurance trust is an excellent method of providing life insurance benefits to protect young children. If the insured dies, the trust becomes irrevocable and the children can be provided for by the beneficial terms of the trust. The revocable life insurance trust is also an excellent method of providing protection for children following a divorce.

irrevocable life insurance trust (ILIT)

Irrevocable Life Insurance Trusts. An *irrevocable life insurance trust (ILIT)* is generally used by older clients who have a more stable family and financial situation. The ILIT can be designed to provide life insurance benefits for a client's heirs that will be excluded from the client's gross estate. In addition, contributions to the trust can be designed to avoid gift and generation-skipping taxes. Thus, an irrevocable life insurance trust is a perfect tool for the estate liquidity needs of older, wealthy clients without adding to their tax burden. Since the trust is irrevocable, the client needs to be certain of his or her beneficial intent and estate planning objectives when the trust is drafted.

CONCLUSION

Although the drafting of estate planning documents suggests a certain finality, the process should be ongoing. The financial advisor should never be satisfied just because a client has an approved plan because change is the one constant that is guaranteed. The advisor and the client should take the necessary steps to coordinate the estate plan with the other components of the client's comprehensive financial plan.

In addition, all appointed individuals, such as executors, trustees, and attorneys-in-fact, should be informed of their roles and the intentions of the client. In many cases, members of the client's family will be relied upon to make responsible decisions with respect to the estate plan. These family members must be informed, to the extent necessary, of the client's dispositive intentions.

Finally, periodic follow-up is necessary for all the components of a comprehensive financial plan. Many aspects of the estate plan component will be revocable, although such flexibility may provide additional opportunities for both the advisor and the client. Changes in tax or Medicaid laws should be monitored and may necessitate new planning steps as a result. The failure to follow up would probably result in client dissatisfaction and perhaps malpractice claims against the estate planner.

A final word of admonition: As you see from just this one introductory chapter, estate planning is a very complex subject. Advisors who plan to practice as estate planners will need far more knowledge than this limited treatment can provide. In addition, many of the estate planning tools, such as wills, trusts, powers-of-attorney, require professional legal assistance to your clients. Financial advisors who engage in estate planning must avoid giving unauthorized legal advice. Savvy estate planners who are not attorneys will create professional relationships with competent, trustworthy attorneys who specialize in the field to provide the maximum in estate planning services to their clients.

CHAPTER REVIEW

Key Terms and Concepts are explained in the Glossary. Answers to the Review Questions are found in the back of the book in the Answers to Questions section.

Key Terms and Concepts

fee simple estate
life estate
estate for a term of years
term interest
future interest
remainder interest
reversionary interest
tenancy in common
joint tenancy with right of survivorship
tenancy by the entirety
community property
beneficial interest
power of appointment
power of attorney
intestacy
testator
probate assets
trust
fiduciary capacity
grantor
trustee
inter vivos trust
revocable trust
irrevocable trust
testamentary trust
durable power of attorney
springing durable power of attorney
advance medical directives
durable power of attorney for health care

living will
intestacy laws
Totten trust
federal gift tax
exempt transfers
gift tax annual exclusion
marital deduction
charitable deduction
applicable credit amount
federal estate tax
gross estate
marital deduction
applicable exclusion amount
state inheritance tax
state estate tax
credit estate tax
Uniform Gifts to Minors Act (UGMA)
Uniform Transfers to Minors Act (UTMA)
Crummey powers
estate trust
power of appointment trust
QTIP marital-deduction trust
deceased spousal unused exclusion amount (DSUEA)
charitable remainder trust
charitable lead trust
revocable life insurance trust
irrevocable life insurance trust (ILIT)

Review Questions

1. Of what value to a financial advisor doing estate planning is the inventory of assets section of a fact finder form? [1]

2. Why might an interview by a financial advisor gathering information for a client's estate plan be an uncomfortable event for the client? [1]

3. Explain each of the following ways in which an individual might have an ownership interest in property: (a.) life estate, (b.) estate for a term of years (or term interest), and (c.) future interest. [2]

4. Explain each of the following ways in which two individuals might have a joint concurrent ownership interest in property: (a.) tenancy in common, (b.) joint tenancy with right of survivorship, and (c.) tenancy by the entirety. [2]

5. Explain the difference between a general power of appointment and a special power of appointment. [3]

6. (a.) Describe the requirements for a valid will. (b.) What objectives can be accomplished by a properly drafted will? [3]

7. Explain the difference between a conventional power of attorney and a durable power of attorney. [3]

8. Briefly describe the process of probating an estate. [4]

9. Briefly describe the typical distribution system provided by state intestacy laws. [4]

10. Describe the types of gratuitous transfers that are exempt from the gift tax base by statute. [4]

11. Identify the types of property that are includible in the gross estate of a deceased for federal estate tax purposes. [5]

12. (a.) Describe the purpose of the federal generation-skipping transfer tax (GST) tax system. (b.) Identify the three types of transfers that are subject to the GST tax. [5]

13. Explain the difference between a state inheritance tax and a state estate tax. [5]

14. (a.) Describe several nontax advantages from making lifetime gifts. (b.) Describe several tax advantages from making lifetime gifts. [5]

15. Describe each of the following techniques for making gifts to minors that will not be subject to federal gift taxes: (a.) UGMA or UTMA gifts, (b.) irrevocable trusts [6]

16. Explain how each of the following trusts may be used to qualify property left by a deceased to his or her spouse for the federal estate tax marital deduction: (a.) an estate trust, (b.) a power of appointment trust, (c.) a QTIP marital-deduction trust. [6]

17. Explain how an AB trust arrangement can make maximum use of each spouse's applicable credit amount while also making optimal use of the marital deduction. [6]

18. Explain how a charitable remainder trust can be used advantageously in planning a client's estate. [6]

19. Describe the type of client for whom life insurance may be particularly appropriate for purposes of estate enhancement. [6]

20. Explain why a revocable life insurance trust is not a very useful device for estate tax planning purposes. [6]

SOCIAL SECURITY, MEDICARE, AND MEDICARE SUPPLEMENTS   8

> **Learning Objectives**
>
> *An understanding of the material in this chapter should enable the student to*
>
> 1. Explain the importance and extent of coverage under the Social Security and Medicare programs, and describe how the programs are financed.
> 2. Explain the requirements for eligibility under Social Security, and describe the types and amounts of benefits available.
> 3. Explain the requirements for eligibility under Medicare, and describe the benefits available under Parts A and B.
> 4. Explain the options available to beneficiaries under Part C of Medicare.
> 5. Explain how Medicare Part D provides prescription drug coverage, and describe a typical Medicare prescription drug plan.
> 6. Explain how Medicare supplement coverages fill some gaps in Medicare benefits, and describe the eligibility requirements for buying a Medigap policy.

SOCIAL SECURITY AND MEDICARE

old-age, survivors, disability, and health insurance (OASDHI)

In a broad sense, the term Social Security refers to several programs resulting from the Social Security Act of 1935 and its subsequent amendments. Taken together, these programs constitute the old-age, survivors, disability, and health insurance *(OASDHI)* program of the federal government. This program is often separated into two broad parts. The first part is the old age, survivors, and disability insurance (OASDI) program. Over the years, OASDI has become synonymous with Social Security, which is the term used in this chapter. The remainder of the OASDHI program is called Medicare, with its Part A (hospital insurance) and Part B (supplemental medical insurance).

Social Security and Medicare programs are of major importance to financial advisors as a foundation upon which they can develop comprehensive financial plans for clients. The following discussion about Social Security and Medicare begins with a brief explanation of why the programs are important, how many people they cover, and how they are financed. We will then discuss the eligibility requirements and benefits of each separate program.

The Importance, Coverage, and Financing of Social Security and Medicare

Importance of Programs

The Social Security and Medicare programs are important to financial advisors and clients for at least two reasons. First, the largest insurance expense for most individuals is their contributions to Social Security and Medicare. For many workers, this contribution will exceed the combined cost of all other insurance purchased directly by the individual. Second, these programs form the foundation on which employee benefit programs and individual insurance plans are built. In fact, nearly one-quarter of the money employers spend on benefits for their employees goes toward legally required payments to these programs. Moreover, it is impossible to do a proper job of personal insurance planning or financial planning without considering Social Security and Medicare benefits.

Extent of Coverage

Over 95 percent of the workers in the United States are in covered employment under the Social Security program and over 98 percent under the Medicare program. These workers have wages (if they are employees) or self-employment income (if they are self-employed) on which Social Security and Medicare taxes must be paid.

Tax Rates and Wage Bases

All the benefits of the Social Security program and Part A of Medicare are financed through a system of payroll and self-employment taxes paid by all persons covered under the programs. In addition, employers of covered persons are also taxed. (These taxes are often referred to as FICA taxes because they are imposed under the Federal Insurance Contributions Act.) Part B of Medicare is financed by a combination of monthly premiums paid by persons eligible for benefits and contributions from the federal government.

Social Security, Medicare, and Medicare Supplements

In 2012, an employee and his employer pay a tax of 7.65 percent each on the first $110,100 of the employee's wages. This figure, $110,100 (for 2012, indexed) is known as the Social Security *taxable wage base (TWB)* and is adjusted annually for changes in the national level of wages. Of this tax rate, 6.2 percent is for Social Security, and 1.45 percent is for Part A of Medicare. The Part A tax rate of 1.45 percent is also levied on all wages in excess of the taxable wage base. The tax rate for self-employed persons is 15.3 percent on the first $110,100 of self-employment income and 2.9 percent on the balance of any self-employment income. This is equal to the combined employee and employer rates.

Note, as we revise this text in early 2012, the Social Security tax rate for 2012 was temporarily reduced to 4.2 percent, effective through December 2012. Without additional legislation, the percentage will revert back to 6.2 percent for workers in January 2013.

Paying for Social Security and Medicare

- Social Security—Employees pay 6.20 percent of the first $110,100 (2012) of earnings. Employers pay the same. Self-employed persons pay 12.40 percent of first $110,100 (2012) of self-employment income. Note, legislation passed in February 2012 extends a reduction of the Social Security tax rate for employees to 4.2 percent through December 2012. Without Congressional action, the tax rate will revert to 6.2 percent in January 2013.

- Medicare Part A—Employees pay 1.45 percent of all earnings. Employers pay the same. Self-employed persons pay 2.9 percent of all self-employment income.

- Medicare Part B—Most covered persons pay a $99.90 (2012) monthly premium. Taxpayers in the highest income tax brackets pay $319.70 for Part B premiums. General revenues of the federal government cover the remainder (about 75 percent) of the program's cost.

Over the years, both the tax rates and wage bases have risen dramatically to finance increased benefit levels under Social Security and Medicare, as well as new benefits that have been added to the program. In 1950, a tax rate of 1.5 percent was levied on the first $3,000 of wages. These figures increased to 4.8 percent and $7,800 in 1970, and 7.65 percent and $51,300 in 1990. Starting in 1991, a two-tier program was introduced with a tax of 7.65 percent on the first $53,400 of wages and a Medicare tax of 1.45 percent on the next $71,500. By 1994, all wages and self-employed income were subject to the Medicare tax.

The adequacy of the current funding structure to pay for Social Security and Medicare benefits continues to be a source of public concern and political debate.

Eligibility for Social Security

quarters of coverage

To be eligible for benefits under Social Security, an individual must have credit for a minimum amount of work under the program. This credit is based on credits or *quarters of coverage*. For 2012, a worker receives credit for one quarter of coverage for each $1,120 in annual earnings on which Social Security taxes were paid. However, credit for no more than four quarters of coverage may be earned in any one calendar year. Consequently, a worker who pays Social Security taxes on as little as $4,480 ($1,120 X 4) at any time during the year will receive the maximum four credits for that calendar year. As in the case of the wage base, the amount of earnings necessary for a credit under Social Security is adjusted annually for changes in the national level of wages.

Quarters of coverage are the basis for establishing an insured status under Social Security. The three types of insured status are fully insured, currently insured, and disability insured.

Fully Insured

fully insured

A person is *fully insured* under Social Security if either of two tests is met. The first test requires credit for 40 quarters of coverage. Once a person acquires such credit, he is fully insured for life even if covered employment under Social Security ceases.

Under the second test, a person who has credit for a minimum of six quarters of coverage is fully insured if she has credit for at least as many quarters of coverage as there are years elapsing after 1950 (or after the year in which age 21 is reached, if later) and before the year in which she dies, becomes disabled, or reaches age 62, whichever occurs first. Therefore, a worker who reached age 21 in 2000 and who died in 2012 would need credit for only 11 quarters of coverage for her family to be eligible for survivors benefits.

Currently Insured

currently insured

If a worker is not fully insured, certain survivors benefits are still available if a *currently insured* status exists. To be currently insured, it is only necessary that a worker have credit for at least six quarters of coverage out of the 13-quarter period ending with the quarter in which his death occurs.

Disability Insured

disability insured   To receive disability benefits under Social Security, it is necessary to be *disability insured*. At a minimum, a disability-insured status requires that a worker (1) be fully insured and (2) have a minimum amount of work under Social Security within a recent time period. In connection with the latter requirement, workers aged 31 or older must have credit for at least 20 of the last 40 quarters ending with the quarter in which disability occurs; workers between the ages of 24 and 30, inclusively, must have credit for at least half the quarters of coverage from the time they turned 21 and the quarter in which disability begins; and workers under age 24 must have credit for 6 out of the last 12 quarters, ending with the quarter in which disability begins. A special rule for the blind considers them disability insured as long as they are fully insured.

Social Security Benefits

As its name implies, the Social Security program provides three principal types of benefits: retirement (old-age) benefits, survivors benefits, and disability benefits.

Retirement Benefits

full retirement age   A worker who is fully insured under Social Security is eligible to receive monthly retirement benefits as early as age 62. However, the election to receive benefits prior to the full Social Security retirement age results in a permanently reduced benefit. Full retirement benefits are payable when a participant attains *full retirement age*.

Full retirement age (sometimes referred to as normal retirement age), or the age at which non-reduced retirement benefits are paid, is 65 for workers born in 1937 or before. This age, however, is still transitioning from age 65 to age 67. Individuals born in 1960 and later will have a full retirement age of 67. As shown in the following table, a gradually increasing full retirement age applies to workers born in 1938 and later.

Table 8-1 Retirement Age for Non-reduced Benefits

Year of Birth	Full Retirement Age
1937 and before	65 years
1938	65 years, 2 months
1939	65 years, 4 months
1940	65 years, 6 months
1941	65 years, 8 months
1942	65 years, 10 months
1943–54	66 years
1955	66 years, 2 months
1956	66 years, 4 months
1957	66 years, 6 months
1958	66 years, 8 months
1959	66 years, 10 months
1960 and later	67 years

In addition to the retired worker, the following dependents of persons receiving retirement benefits are also eligible for monthly benefits:

- a spouse aged 62 or older. However, benefits are permanently reduced if this benefit is elected prior to the spouse's reaching full retirement age. This benefit is also available to a divorced spouse under certain circumstances if the marriage lasted at least 10 years.

- a spouse of any age if the spouse is caring for at least one child of the retired worker who is (1) under age 16 or (2) disabled and entitled to a child's benefit as described below. This benefit is commonly referred to as a *mother's/father's benefit.*

- dependent, unmarried children under 18. This child's benefit will continue until age 19 as long as a child is a full-time student in elementary or secondary school. In addition, disabled children of any age are eligible for benefits as long as they were disabled before reaching age 22.

Note that Social Security retirement benefits, and other benefits under Social Security and Medicare, are not automatically paid upon eligibility; the beneficiary must apply for them.

Survivors Benefits

All categories of survivors benefits are payable if a worker is fully insured at the time of death. However, three types of benefits are also payable if a worker is only currently insured. The first is a lump-sum death benefit of $255, payable if there is a surviving spouse or dependent child who meets certain requirements.

Two categories of persons are eligible for income benefits as survivors if a deceased worker was either fully or currently insured at the time of death:

- dependent, unmarried children under the same conditions as previously described for retirement benefits
- a spouse (including a divorced spouse) caring for a child or children under the same conditions as described for retirement benefits

EXAMPLE
Bill Ross was a 63-year-old retiree drawing Social Security retirement benefits when he died in March 2012. Bill's wife Karen is only 50 years old and is caring for the couples' 14-year-old daughter Jennifer. After Bill's death, Karen can draw a Social Security survivor income until Jennifer reaches age 16. Jennifer can also draw a survivor income until her 18th birthday, or until she is 19 if she is still attending high school. Karen can draw a Social Security widow's benefit as early as age 60 based on her marriage to Bill.

Social Security *Blackout Period*

No benefits are payable for the surviving spouse of a deceased covered worker from the time the youngest child reaches age 16 (or is no longer disabled in certain cases) until the surviving spouse is age 60.

The following categories of persons are also eligible for benefits, but only if the deceased worker was fully insured:

- a widow or widower aged 60 or older. However, benefits are reduced if taken prior to full retirement age. This benefit is also payable to a divorced spouse if the marriage lasted at least 10 years.
- a parent aged 62 or over who was a dependent of the deceased worker at the time of death

Disability Benefits

A disabled worker under full retirement age is eligible to receive benefits under Social Security as long as he is disability insured and meets the Social Security definition of disability. The definition of disability is very rigid and requires a mental or physical impairment that prevents the worker from engaging in *any substantial gainful employment*. The disability must also have lasted (or be expected to last) at least 12 months or be expected to result in death. A more liberal definition of disability applies to blind workers who are aged 55 or older. They are considered disabled if they are unable to perform work that requires skills or abilities comparable to those required by the work they regularly performed before reaching age 55 or becoming blind, if later. Note that since Social Security's definition of disability is so restricted, approximately 65 percent of applicants for disability are denied when they first apply. Many applicants obtain legal assistance on subsequent attempts to obtain the benefits.

> **EXAMPLE**
>
> Dan Dillon is a 40-year-old X-ray technician who was covered for disability benefits under Social Security. On New Year's Eve of 2011, he and a friend were setting off fireworks in celebration of the New Year. A large package of fireworks caught on fire and blew up, blinding Dan in both eyes. Dan will be permanently unable to perform the duties of his former X-ray technician job. He applied for Social Security disability benefits in late January 2012 and was approved. However, his monthly payments will not start until July 2012 because of the waiting period for disability benefits.

Disability benefits are subject to a waiting period and are payable beginning with the sixth full calendar month of disability. In addition to the benefit paid to a disabled worker, the other categories of benefits available are the same as those described under retirement benefits.

As previously mentioned, certain family members not otherwise eligible for Social Security benefits may be eligible if they are disabled. Disabled children are subject to the same definition of disability as workers. However, disabled widows or widowers must be unable to engage in any gainful (rather than substantial gainful) employment.

Eligibility for Dual Benefits

In many cases, a person is eligible for more than one type of Social Security benefit. The most common situation occurs when a person is eligible for both a spouse's benefit and a worker's retirement or disability benefit based on her own Social Security record. In this and any other case when a person is eligible for dual benefits, only an amount equal to the higher benefit is paid.

EXAMPLE
Ramon and Barbara Ramirez are a married couple, both aged 66 and both are at their Social Security full retirement age. Barbara is eligible for a retirement benefit of $700 per month, based on her own work history. She is also eligible for a benefit based on 50 percent of Ramon's benefit, which would calculate to $600 per month. Social Security will only pay the higher amount, in this case the $700 per month, not both of the benefits.

Termination of Benefits

Monthly benefits to any Social Security recipient cease upon death. When a retired or disabled worker dies, the family members' benefits that are based on the worker's retirement or disability benefits also cease, but the family members are then eligible for survivors benefits.

Disability benefits for a worker technically terminate at full retirement age but are then replaced by comparable retirement benefits. In addition, any benefits payable because of disability cease if medical or other evidence shows that the definition of disability is no longer satisfied. However, the disability benefits continue during a readjustment period that consists of the month of recovery and 2 additional months. As an encouragement for them to return to work, disabled beneficiaries for whom there is no evidence their disability has otherwise terminated are allowed a 9-month trial work period during which benefits are not affected regardless of how much the beneficiary earns. At the end of that period, a beneficiary's earnings are evaluated to determine if the earnings are substantial ($1,000 per month in 2012). If earnings then exceed this amount for 3 months, benefits are suspended but can be reinstated during the next 36 months without starting a new application process should the earnings fall below this level.

As long as children are not disabled, benefits will usually terminate at age 18 but may continue until age 19 if the child is a full-time student in elementary or secondary school.

The benefit of a surviving spouse terminates upon remarriage unless remarriage takes place at age 60 or later.

Social Security Benefit Amounts

Calculating Benefits

primary insurance amount (PIA)

With the exception of the $255 lump-sum death benefit, the amount of all Social Security benefits is based on a worker's *primary insurance amount (PIA)*. When a beneficiary is eligible for benefits, his actual PIA is calculated by the Social Security Administration using a complex formula that is heavily weighted in favor of lower-income workers.

The PIA is the amount a worker receives if he retires at full retirement age or becomes disabled, and it is the amount on which benefits for family members are based. In 2011, the average PIA for a retired worker was approximately $1,177. A worker who has continually earned the maximum income subject to Social Security taxes can expect to have a PIA for retirement purposes of $2,366 if he retired at age 66 in 2011. The average monthly benefit for a retired couple with both receiving benefits was $1,907 in 2011. The maximum PIA in 2011 for purposes of disability and survivors benefits ranged from approximately $1,813 to $2,409. The higher PIA results for workers who are disabled or who die at younger ages.

If a worker is retired or disabled, these benefits are paid to family members. If the worker dies, survivors benefits are as shown. (See the following tables.)

However, the full benefits described above may not be payable because of a limitation imposed on the total benefits that may be paid to a family. This family maximum is again determined by a formula and is usually reached if three or more family members (including a retired or disabled worker) are eligible for benefits.

If the total amount of benefits payable to family members exceeds the family maximum, the worker's benefit (in the case of retirement and disability) is not affected, but the benefits of other family members are reduced proportionately.

Social Security, Medicare, and Medicare Supplements

Table 8-2 Benefits for Family Members of a Disabled or Retired Worker

Family Member	Percentage of Worker's PIA
Spouse at full retirement age	50%
Spouse caring for disabled child or child under 16	50%
Child under 18 or disabled	50% each

Table 8-3 Benefits for Survivors of a Deceased Worker

Family Member	Percentage of Worker's PIA
Spouse at full retirement age	100%
Spouse caring for disabled child or child under 16	75%
Child under 18 or disabled	75% each
Dependent parent	82.5% for one
	75% each for two

EXAMPLE

Sam Malloy died in 2011, leaving a spouse aged 50 and three children who are each eligible for 75 percent of Sam's PIA of $1,200. If the family maximum is ignored, the benefits would total $3,600 ($900 for each family member). However, the Social Security family maximum, using the prescribed formula for 2011 was $2,105. Therefore, each family member has his or her benefit reduced to $526 (rounded to the next lower dollar.)

When the first child loses benefits at age 18, the other family members each have benefits increased to $701 (if any automatic benefit increases, including the family maximum, are ignored).

When a second family member loses eligibility, the remaining two family members each receive the full benefit of $900 because the total benefits received by the family are now less than the $2,105 calculated by the formula.

Other Factors Affecting Benefits

Benefits Taken Early. If a worker elects to receive retirement benefits prior to full retirement age, benefits are permanently reduced by 5/9 of one percent for each of the first 36 months that his early retirement precedes full retirement age and 5/12 of one percent for each month in excess of 36. For example, for a worker who retires 3 years before his full retirement age, the monthly benefit is only 80 percent of that worker's PIA. A spouse who elects retirement benefits prior to full retirement age has benefits reduced by 25/36 of one percent per month, for each of the first 36 months and 5/12 of one percent for each month in excess of 36. A widow or widower has benefits reduced proportionately from 100 percent at full retirement age to 71.5 percent at age 60. If the widow or widower elects benefits prior to age 60 because of disability, there is no further reduction.

EXAMPLE

Walter Davis will be 64 years old on June 9, 2012. He is considering retiring from his full time job in June 2012. Walter's full retirement age is 66. Walter's primary insurance amount (PIA) is $1,500 (at the full retirement age in current dollars). If Walter claims his Social Security retirement benefits in June 2012, his benefit will be $1,300. This represents a 13.3 percent reduction from his PIA of $1,500 calculated as follows: (24 months X 5/9 = 13.33 percent reduction. Then, 86.67 percent of $1,500 equals $1,300.)

Delayed Retirement. Workers who delay applying for benefits until after full retirement age are eligible for an increased benefit. Benefits are increased for each month of late retirement until age 70. The actual percentage increase varies by the year of birth of the worker, but it is generally between 7 and 8 percent per year. To encourage later retirement, the monthly percentage gradually increases. The following table shows the percentage increase for each month of deferral, the percentage increase for each year of deferral, and the maximum percentage increase if retirement is postponed until age 70.

Note that these increases apply to a worker's PIA as determined at the time she applies for retirement benefits. If a person continues to work during the period of delayed retirement and covered wages are sufficiently high, it is possible for a worker's PIA to increase above what it would have been at full retirement age. Therefore, the increased monthly retirement benefit realized from working past full retirement age may be greater than the percentages in the table.

Table 8-4 Increase for Delayed Retirement

Year of Birth	Monthly Percentage Increase	Yearly Percentage Increase	Maximum Percentage Increase
1917–24	1/4	3	15.00
1925–26	7/24	3.5	17.50
1927–28	1/3	4	20
1929–30	9/24	4.5	22.50
1931–32	5/12	5	25.00
1933–34	11/24	5.5	27.50
1935–36	1/2	6	30.00
1937	13/24	6.5	32.50
1938	13/24	6.5	31.42
1939	7/12	7	32.67
1940	7/12	7	31.50
1941	15/24	7.5	32.50
1942	15/24	7.5	31.25
1943–54	2/3	8	32.00
1955	2/3	8	30.67
1956	2/3	8	29.33
1957	2/3	8	28.00
1958	2/3	8	26.67
1959	2/3	8	25.33
1960 and later	2/3	8	24.00

EXAMPLE

Morris was born in 1946 and will reach his full retirement age of 66 in July 2012. His primary insurance amount (PIA) in July 2012 will be $1,500 per month based on his entire work history to date. However, Morris is at his peak salary and has an excellent job in which he makes approximately $100,000 per year. By continuing to work and delaying his Social Security retirement benefits, Morris can achieve at least three favorable results: (1) his actual PIA can increase because he will continue to pay into Social Security based on his high current income; (2) each year he works past age 66, Morris increases his eventual Social Security retirement benefit by 8 percent; and (3) all future cost-of-living-adjustments (COLA) will be based on the higher retirement benefit.

earnings test

Earnings Test. The earnings test is a process to determine whether income benefits of Social Security beneficiaries under full retirement age should be reduced because their earned income exceeds a specified amount. For the earnings test, earned income includes wages and net self-employment income. It does not include interest, dividends, pension income, or annuity income.

In 2012, beneficiaries who are under their full retirement age are allowed to earn up to $14,640 under this *earnings test*, and this figure is subject to annual indexing for later years. If a beneficiary earns more than this amount, his Social Security benefit is reduced by $1 for each $2 of excess earnings. There is one exception to the test: The reduction is $1 for every $3 of earnings in excess of $38,880 (in 2012) in the calendar year a worker attains the full retirement age, for earnings in months prior to such age attainment. Once the beneficiary reaches full retirement age, any amount can be earned without a Social Security reduction.

EXAMPLE

Elizabeth turned 64 years old in July 2010 and began receiving her Social Security retirement benefits. Her full retirement age is 66 and any earned income she makes will be subject to the earnings test until July 2012 when she reaches age 66. For the 2012 calendar year, she could earn up to $38,880 for the months January through June. If she exceeded that amount, her Social Security would be reduced $1 for every $3 of earnings in excess of the $38,800. For example, if Elizabeth earned $44,880 in the first six months of 2012, she would exceed the earnings limit by $6,000. Her Social Security benefits would be reduced by $2,000 (that is $6,000 ÷ 3 equals $2,000). Her Social Security monthly check will be reduced until the full $2,000 is "repaid", after which her normal payment would be restored.

Social Security Earnings Test

- Beneficiaries who have reached full retirement age—no loss of benefits regardless of annual wages
- Beneficiaries who are under full retirement age—$1 of benefits lost for every $2 of annual wages in excess of $14,640 (2012). A more liberal test applies in the calendar year a worker attains the full retirement age.

The reduction in a retired worker's benefits resulting from excess earnings is charged against the entire benefits that are paid to a family and based on the worker's Social Security record. If large enough, this reduction may totally eliminate all benefits otherwise payable to the worker and family members. In contrast, excess earnings of family members are charged against their individual benefits only. For example, a widowed mother who holds a job outside the home may lose her mother's benefit, but any benefits received by her children are unaffected.

<u>cost-of-living adjustment (COLA)</u>

Cost-of-Living Adjustments. Social Security benefits are increased automatically each January as long as there has been an increase in the Consumer Price Index for Urban Wage Earners and Clerical Workers (CPI-W) for the one-year period ending in the third quarter of the prior year. The increase, known as the Social Security *cost-of-living adjustment (COLA)* is the same as the increase in the CPI-W since the last cost-of-living adjustment, rounded to the nearest 0.1 percent. Benefits do not automatically decrease if the CPI-W declines; however, we have recently experienced a year in which there was no COLA.

Offset for Other Benefits. Disabled workers under full retirement age who also receive workers' compensation benefits or disability benefits from certain other federal, state, or local disability programs will have their Social Security benefits reduced if the total benefits received (including family benefits) exceed 80 percent of their average current earnings at the time of disability. In addition, the monthly benefit of a spouse or surviving spouse is reduced by two-thirds of any federal, state, or local government pension that is based on earnings not covered under Social Security on the last day of employment.

> **FOCUS ON ETHICS**
> **Understanding the OASDHI Program**
>
> It is very important that a financial advisor understand government programs available to clients. To complete a comprehensive financial plan for a client, the advisor must be knowledgeable about Social Security and Medicare so the financial plan can build upon the foundation provided by these programs. To ignore these important programs is to ignore that, for most people, their contributions to Social Security and Medicare exceed the combined cost of all other types of insurance purchased directly by them. To a majority of retirees, Social Security benefits represent a major portion of their retirement income. The advisor who does not properly take these programs into account when developing plans for clients is guilty of malpractice at worst and unethical behavior at best.

Requesting Benefit Information

The Social Security Administration used to send an annual *Social Security Statement* to each worker aged 25 or older who has worked in employment covered by Social Security and who is not currently entitled to monthly benefits. In April 2011, the Social Security Administration announced they would cease sending out annual paper statements in a move to save money and drive beneficiaries to the Social Security website. They have also created an online Retirement Estimator (access at socialsecurity.gov/planners/calculators.htm). Beneficiaries can create an account and check their estimated benefits on this website. The Retirement Estimator accesses a worker's employment history through a secure interface. Note that only workers who are permanently insured by Social Security can use the Retirement Estimator.

Eligibility for Medicare

Part A, the hospital portion of Medicare, is available to any person aged 65 or older as long as the person is entitled to monthly retirement benefits under Social Security or the railroad retirement program. Civilian employees of the federal government aged 65 or older are also eligible. It is not necessary for these workers to actually be receiving retirement benefits, but they must be fully insured for purposes of retirement benefits. The following persons are also eligible for Part A of Medicare at no monthly cost:

- persons aged 65 or older who are dependents of fully insured workers aged 62 or older
- survivors aged 65 or older who are eligible for Social Security survivors benefits
- disabled persons at any age who have been eligible to receive Social Security benefits for 2 years because of their disability. This includes workers under age 65, disabled widows and widowers aged 50 or over, and children 18 or older who were disabled prior to age 22.
- workers who are either fully or currently insured and their spouses and dependent children with end-stage renal (kidney) disease who require renal dialysis or kidney transplants. Coverage begins either the first day of the third month after dialysis begins or earlier for admission to a hospital for kidney-transplant surgery.

Most persons age 65 or over who do not meet the previously discussed eligibility requirements may voluntarily enroll in Medicare. However, they must pay a monthly Part A premium and also enroll in Part B. The monthly Part A premium in 2012 is $451 for individuals with fewer than 30 quarters of Medicare-covered employment and $248 for individuals with 30 to 39 quarters. The premium is adjusted annually, and the $451 amount reflects the full cost of the benefits provided.

Any person eligible for Part A of Medicare is also eligible for Part B. However, a monthly premium must be paid for Part B. This premium for most beneficiaries is $99.90 in 2012 and is adjusted annually. For higher income taxpayer/beneficiaries, the Part B premium can be as much as $319.70. Approximately 4 percent of current Part B enrollees are expected to be subject to the higher premiums in 2012. The premiums collected by all Part B enrollees represents only about 25 percent of the cost of the benefits provided. The remaining cost of Medicare Part B is financed from the general revenues of the federal government.

Persons receiving Social Security or railroad retirement benefits are automatically enrolled in Medicare if they are eligible. If they do not want Part B, they must reject it ("opt out") in writing. Other persons eligible for Medicare must apply for benefits. As a general rule, anyone who rejects Part B, or who does not enroll when initially eligible, may apply for benefits later during a general enrollment period that occurs between January 1 and March 31 of each year. However, the monthly premium is increased by 10 percent for each 12-month period during which the person was eligible but failed to enroll.

EXAMPLE

Marilyn Taylor, will be 66 years old in July 2012. She was initially eligible for Medicare Parts A and B in July 2011; however, she opted out of Medicare Part B coverage at that time, without a valid reason. She can enroll during the general enrollment period from January 1 – March 31, 2012, and her coverage will be effective July 1, 2012. Since Marilyn delayed enrollment in Part B for 12 months, her Part B premiums will be increased (permanently) by 10 percent.

Medicare secondary rules make employer-provided medical expense coverage primary over Medicare for certain classes of individuals who are over 65, who are disabled, or who are suffering end-stage renal disease. These persons (and any other Medicare-eligible persons still covered as active employees under their employers' plans) may not wish to elect Medicare because it largely constitutes duplicate coverage. When their employer-provided coverage ends, these persons have a 7-month special enrollment period to elect Part B coverage, and the late enrollment penalty is waived.

Medicare is also secondary to benefits received by persons (1) entitled to veterans' or black lung benefits, (2) covered by workers' compensation laws, or (3) whose medical expenses are paid under no-fault insurance or liability insurance.

Medicare Part A: Hospital Benefits

Part A of Medicare provides benefits for expenses incurred in hospitals, skilled-nursing facilities, and hospices. Some home health care benefits are also covered. For benefits to be paid, the facility or agency providing benefits must participate in the Medicare program. Virtually all U.S. hospitals are participants, as are most other facilities or agencies that meet the requirements of Medicare.

Part A of Medicare, along with Part B, provides a high level of benefits for medical expenses. However, as described below, deductibles and copayments are also high and will, no doubt, become even higher as they are adjusted annually to reflect increasing costs. Moreover, certain benefits previously provided under employer-provided plans may be excluded or limited under Medicare. For this reason, persons without supplemental retiree coverage from prior employment should consider the purchase of a Medicare supplement (Medigap) policy in the individual marketplace.

Hospital Benefits

benefit period

Part A pays for inpatient hospital services for up to 90 days in each benefit period (also referred to as a "spell of illness"). A benefit period begins the first time a Medicare recipient is hospitalized and ends only after the recipient has been out of a hospital or skilled-nursing facility for 60 consecutive days. A subsequent hospitalization then begins a new benefit period.

In each benefit period, covered hospital expenses are paid in full for 60 days, subject to an initial deductible ($1,156 in 2012). This deductible is adjusted annually to reflect increasing hospital costs. Benefits for an additional 30 days of hospitalization are also provided in each benefit period, but the patient must pay a daily co-payment ($289 in 2012) equal to 25 percent of the initial deductible amount. Each recipient also has a lifetime reserve of 60 additional days that may be used if the regular 90 days of benefits have been exhausted. However, once a reserve day is used, it cannot be restored for use in future benefit periods. When using reserve days, patients must pay a daily co-payment ($578 in 2012) equal to 50 percent of the initial deductible amount.

> **EXAMPLE**
>
> Karen Chung, a 75-year-old widow, suffered a small stroke in March 2012. She was admitted to a local hospital through its emergency room and remained in the hospital for six days. Karen did not have any Medicare supplement (Medigap insurance). She must pay a Medicare Part A deductible of $1,156 for the first day of the hospitalization. All other hospital services (semi-private room, nursing services, inpatient medications, and so on) were provided at no additional charge. However, she received care from several doctors during her hospital stay. The charges for the doctors' services were billed through Medicare Part B. Karen must pay 20 percent of the Medicare-approved charges for the doctors' services, after she pays an annual Part B deductible of $140 for 2012. She is responsible for approximately $4,000 of those charges.
>
> Karen recovered sufficiently at home. However, 61 days after she was released from the hospital, she suffered another small stroke and was again admitted to the hospital. Since more than 60 days had expired from her first "spell of illness," a new benefit period starts under Medicare. Thus, Karen must pay another Part A deductible of $1,156, and then Part A will pay all approved hospital charges for up to 60 days. Once again, Karen must pay 20 percent of Medicare-approved physicians' charges under Medicare Part B.

There is no limit on the number of benefit periods a person may have during her lifetime. However, there is a lifetime limit of 190 days of benefits for inpatient treatment in psychiatric hospitals.

Covered inpatient expenses include the following:

- room and board in semiprivate accommodations. Private rooms are covered only if required for medical reasons.
- nursing services (except private-duty nurses)
- use of regular hospital equipment such as oxygen tents or wheelchairs
- drugs and biologicals ordinarily furnished by the hospital
- diagnostic or therapeutic items or services
- operating room costs
- blood transfusions after the first three pints of blood. Patients must pay for the first three pints of blood unless they get donors to replace the blood.

There is no coverage under Part A for the services of physicians or surgeons.

Skilled-Nursing Facility Benefits

In many cases, a patient may no longer require continuous hospital care but may not be well enough to go home. Consequently, Part A provides benefits for care in a skilled-nursing facility if a physician certifies that skilled-nursing care or rehabilitative services are needed for a condition that was treated in a hospital within the last 30 days. In addition, the prior hospitalization must have lasted at least 3 days. Skilled-nursing facility benefits are paid in full for 20 days in each benefit period and for an additional 80 days with a daily co-payment ($144.50 in 2012) that is equal to 12.5 percent of the initial hospital deductible. Covered expenses are the same as those described for hospital benefits.

A skilled-nursing facility may be a separate facility for providing such care or a separate section of a hospital or nursing home. The facility must have at least one full-time registered nurse, and nursing services must be provided at all times. Every patient must be under the supervision of a physician, and a physician must always be available for emergency care.

One very important point should be made about skilled-nursing facility benefits. Custodial care is not provided under any part of the Medicare program unless skilled-nursing or rehabilitative services are also needed and covered.

EXAMPLE

After two small strokes, Karen Chung had a serious stroke in June 2012 which caused paralysis on the right side of her body. After one week in the hospital, her doctor authorized her transfer to a skilled-nursing facility (SNF) for rehabilitation. Since she went directly from the hospital into the SNF, her stay was in the same benefit period (or spell of illness). Thus, she did not have to pay a new Part A deductible. However, if Karen remains longer than 20 days in the SNF, she will have to pay a deductible of $144.50 per day for days 21–100. If she were to stay longer than 100 days (very unlikely!) she would have to pay all costs of her treatment. Additionally, to be approved for continued stay in the SNF, Karen must require "skilled nursing" such as physical rehabilitation or pulmonary therapy. Medicare will not pay for purely "custodial care" which provides assistance for "activities of daily living," such as bathing, dressing, toileting, and so on. In other words, if Karen requires only custodial care, she will be released from the skilled-nursing facility and either go home, enter an assisted-living facility or a nursing home, or make some other arrangements to receive care.

Home Health Care Benefits

skilled nursing services

If a patient can be treated at home for a medical condition, Medicare pays the full cost for an unlimited number of home visits by a Medicare-approved home health agency. To receive these benefits, a person must be confined at home and be treated under a home health plan set up by a physician. The care needed must include *skilled-nursing services,* physical therapy, or speech therapy. Skilled nursing care includes services and care that can only be performed safely and correctly by a licensed nurse or other professional, such as a licensed physical therapist. In addition to these services, Medicare also pays for the cost of part-time home health aides, medical social services, occupational therapy, and medical supplies and equipment provided by the home health agency. The only charge for these benefits is a required 20 percent co-payment for the cost of such durable medical equipment as oxygen tanks and hospital beds. Medicare does not cover home services that primarily assist people in activities of daily living (ADLs) such as transferring (from bed to chair), dressing, bathing, or toileting. It is important for financial advisors to understand that Medicare does not pay for any of the following:

- 24-hour-a-day care at home
- meals delivered to a patient's home
- homemaker services such as shopping, cleaning, and laundry service
- personal care given by home health aides like bathing, dressing, and toileting when this is the only care needed

Understanding the limitations of Medicare-provided services helps you see how long-term care insurance (LTCI) is a critical part of many clients' financial planning. LTCI will pay for long-term care and services, including purely custodial services, that Medicare does not cover.

Hospice Benefits

Hospice benefits are available under Part A of Medicare for beneficiaries who are certified by their doctor and the hospice medical director as being terminally ill with a life expectancy of 6 months or less. While a hospice is thought of as a facility for treating the terminally ill, Medicare also covers benefits provided by a Medicare-approved hospice to patients in their own homes. However, inpatient care can be provided if needed by the patient. In addition to including the types of benefits described for home health care, hospice benefits also include drugs, bereavement counseling, and inpatient respite care when family members need a break from caring for the ill person. Care provided through hospice is meant to help the patient make the most of the last months of life by giving comfort and relief from pain. The focus of hospice is on care, not cure.

To qualify for hospice benefits, a Medicare recipient must elect such coverage in lieu of other Medicare benefits, except for the services of the attending physician or services and benefits that do not pertain to the terminal condition. There are modest co-payments for some services. A beneficiary may cancel the hospice coverage at any time (for example, to pursue chemotherapy treatments) and return to regular Medicare coverage. The beneficiary can elect hospice benefits again but must be recertified as terminally ill.

Exclusions

There are some circumstances under which Part A of Medicare does not pay benefits. In addition, there are times when Medicare acts as the secondary payer of benefits. Exclusions under Part A include the following:

- services outside the United States and its territories or possessions. However, there are a few exceptions to this rule for qualified Mexican and Canadian hospitals.
- elective luxury services such as private rooms or televisions
- hospitalization for services that are not necessary for the treatment of an illness or injury such, as custodial care or elective cosmetic surgery
- services performed in a federal facility such as a veterans' hospital
- services covered under workers' compensation

Under the following circumstances, Medicare is the secondary payer of benefits:

- when primary coverage under an employer-provided medical expense plan is elected by (1) an employee or spouse aged 65 or older or (2) a disabled beneficiary
- when medical care can be paid under any liability policy, including policies providing automobile no-fault benefits
- in the first 30 months for end-stage renal disease when an employer-provided medical expense plan provides coverage. By law, employer plans cannot specifically exclude this coverage during this period.

Medicare pays only if complete coverage is not available from these sources and then only to the extent that benefits are less than would otherwise be payable under Medicare.

Medicare Part B Benefits

Benefits

Part B of Medicare provides benefits for most medical expenses not covered under Part A. These include

- physicians' and surgeons' fees. Under certain circumstances, benefits are also provided for the services of chiropractors, podiatrists, and optometrists.
- diagnostic tests in a hospital or in a physician's office
- physical therapy on an outpatient basis
- drugs and biologicals that cannot be self-administered
- radiation therapy
- medical supplies such as surgical dressings, splints, and casts
- rental of medical equipment such as oxygen tents, hospital beds, and wheelchairs
- prosthetic devices such as artificial heart valves or lenses after a cataract operation
- ambulance service if a patient's condition does not permit the use of other methods of transportation
- mammograms and Pap smears
- diabetes glucose monitoring and education
- colorectal cancer screening
- bone mass measurement
- prostate cancer screening
- pneumococcal vaccinations and flu shots
- dilated eye examinations for beneficiaries at high risk for glaucoma
- home health care services as described for Part A when a person does not have Part A coverage or when Part A benefits are not applicable

Note that the Affordable Care Act of 2010 (health care reform) provides a onetime review of Medicare beneficiaries' health, along with education and counseling about preventive services, certain screenings, shots, and referrals for other care if needed. Medicare will cover this visit if the patient gets it within the first 12 months of his Medicare eligibility, with the patient paying 20 percent of the Medicare-approved amount. After the first visit, Medicare provides "wellness visits" annually to beneficiaries at no cost.

Exclusions

Although the preceding list of benefits may appear to be comprehensive, there are numerous medical products and services not covered by Part B, some of which represent significant expenses for the elderly. These include

- most drugs and biologicals that can be self-administered except drugs that are used for osteoporosis, oral cancer treatment, and immunosuppressive therapy under specified circumstances. However, benefits are available now under Medicare Part D, which is discussed later.
- routine physical, eye, and hearing examinations except those previously mentioned
- routine foot care
- immunizations except pneumococcal vaccinations, flu shots, or immunization required because of an injury or immediate risk of infection
- cosmetic surgery, unless it is needed because of an accidental injury or to improve the function of a malformed part of the body
- dental care, unless it involves jaw or facial bone surgery or the setting of fractures
- custodial care
- eyeglasses, hearing aids, or orthopedic shoes

In addition, benefits are not provided to persons eligible for workers' compensation or to those treated in government hospitals. Benefits are provided only for services received in the United States, except for physicians' services and ambulance services rendered for a hospitalization that is covered in Mexico or Canada under Part A.

Amount of Benefits

The benefits available under Part B are subject to a number of different payment rules. A few charges are paid in full without any cost sharing. These include (1) home health services, (2) pneumococcal vaccine and its administration, (3) certain surgical procedures that are performed on an outpatient basis in lieu of hospitalization, (4) diagnostic preadmission tests performed on an outpatient basis within 7 days prior to hospitalization, (5) mammograms, (6) Pap smears, and (7) the annual "wellness" visits.

For other charges, there is a $140 calendar-year deductible (2012, indexed). When the deductible is satisfied, Part B pays 80 percent of approved charges for most covered medical expenses other than professional charges for mental health care and outpatient services of hospitals and mental health centers. Until 2009, Medicare Part B paid only 50 percent of approved charges for the mental health services of physicians and other mental health professionals. This percentage is gradually increasing to 80 percent by 2014, when the patient will still be subject to 20 percent of approved charges as with other medical services.

The approved charge for doctors' services covered by Medicare is based on a fee schedule issued by the Center for Medicare & Medicaid Services, which administers Medicare. A patient will be reimbursed for only 80 percent of the Medicare- approved charges above the deductible—regardless of the doctor's actual charge. Most doctors and other suppliers of medical services accept an assignment of Medicare benefits and, therefore, are prohibited from charging a patient in excess of the fee schedule. However, doctors can bill the patient for any portion of the approved charges not paid by Medicare because of the annual deductible and/or coinsurance. They can also bill for any services that are not covered by Medicare.

By law, doctors who do not accept assignment of Medicare benefits cannot charge a Medicare patient more than 115 percent of the approved fee for nonparticipating doctors. As a result, some doctors either do not see Medicare participants or limit the number of such patients they treat.

> **EXAMPLE**
>
> Henry Davis is a 70-year-old Medicare recipient who recently was admitted to a hospital for removal of a kidney stone. Henry had no Medigap insurance. The total charges were $20,000 from the three doctors who treated Henry. Medicare approved $12,000 of the doctors' charges under Part B. Medicare reimbursed the doctors $9,600 (that is 80 percent of $12,000). All three doctors accepted Medicare reimbursement and "wrote off" the excess charges. Since Henry had already met his annual deductible, he was responsible for $2,400 (that is 20 percent of the $12,000 in Medicare-approved charges.) Note, if the doctors did not accept assignment, they could legally charge up to 115 percent of the Medicare-approved charges. That would have increased their total charges to $13,800. Medicare would still have paid only $9,600, and Henry would have been charged the remainder of $4,200. Note, this example shows the need for Medicare supplemental insurance (Medigap coverage) to cover the potentially large "gaps" in Medicare, even from routine health care services such as removal of a kidney stone!

The previous limitation on charges does not apply to providers of medical services other than doctors. Although a provider who does not accept assignment can charge any fee, Medicare pays only what it would have paid if the provider accepted assignment. For example, assume the Medicare-approved charge for medical equipment is $100 and the provider charged $190. Medicare will reimburse $80 (.80 × $100) to the provider, and the balance is borne by the Medicare recipient.

Medicare Part C

Medicare Advantage

In 1985, Congress amended the Medicare program to allow a beneficiary to elect coverage under a *health maintenance organization (HMO)* as an alternative to the traditional Medicare (Parts A and B) program.

In 1999, Part C of Medicare (called *Medicare+Choice*) went into effect. It expanded the choices available to most Medicare beneficiaries by allowing them to elect health care benefits through one of several alternatives to the traditional Parts A and B, as long as the providers of these alternatives enter into contracts with the Centers for Medicare & Medicaid Services.

The initial reaction to Medicare + Choice was less than overwhelming. Few new providers of alternative coverage entered the marketplace, and enrollment had decreased after several years of growth. However, the situation changed in 2005 as a result of provisions in the Medicare Prescription Drug, Improvement, and Modernization Act. The act changed the name of Medicare + Choice to *Medicare Advantage*. The act also made many changes to encourage more participation by providers, including larger payments to Medicare Advantage providers than those paid to traditional Medicare providers. Today, about one out of every seven Medicare beneficiaries is enrolled in a Medicare Advantage plan.

Today's Medicare Advantage plans include

- health maintenance organizations (HMOs)
- preferred-provider organizations (PPOs)
- private fee-for-service (PFFS) plans
- Medicare medical savings account (MMSA) plans
- special needs plans (SNPs)

These plans must provide all benefits available under Parts A and B. They may include additional benefits as part of the basic plan or for an additional fee.

The Affordable Care Act of 2010 provided for gradually decreasing Medicare reimbursements to Medicare Advantage plans to align them with costs under traditional Medicare. The law also provides clear incentives for Medicare Advantage plans to improve quality of care and medical outcomes for beneficiaries. Higher performing plans will qualify for payment bonuses beginning in 2012.

Medicare Part D Prescription Drug Plans

Medicare Part D doughnut hole

Along with numerous other changes to Medicare, the Medicare Prescription Drug, Improvement, and Modernization Act added a prescription drug program to Medicare—*Medicare Part D*.

The act also gives employers a financial incentive to provide or continue to provide drug coverage to retirees as an alternative to enrollment in Part D.

Medicare Part D is a voluntary prescription drug benefit available to all Medicare beneficiaries enrolled in either Part A and/or Part B, or enrolled in any of the various Medicare Advantage plans. Each enrollee must pay a monthly premium that averages about $42 in 2012. No one can be denied coverage because of income level or health reasons. Part D benefits are typically referred to as *Medicare prescription drug plans.*

Medicare prescription drug plans are private plans offered by insurance companies, Blue Cross and Blue Shield plans, managed care plans, and other organizations. The sponsors of plans typically contract with pharmacy benefit managers to design plan formularies, or groups of covered drugs. The plans must meet certain consumer standards and be approved by the Department of Health and Human Services (HHS).

There are two basic types of Medicare prescription drug plans. One type is for persons enrolled in most Medicare Advantage plans. When a Medicare Advantage plan has its own prescription drug program, members can obtain coverage only through that plan. The other type of plan, referred to as a *stand-alone plan,* is available to persons enrolled in traditional Medicare or in Medicare Advantage plans that do not have prescription drug programs.

The legislation provides for a standard prescription drug plan but also allows for alternative plans, if certain requirements are met and the plans are at least as generous as the standard plan. Most plans available today do provide broader coverage than the standard plan. The standard prescription drug program has an annual deductible of $320 (2012, as indexed). After the deductible is satisfied, the plan will pay 75 percent of the next $2,930 of prescription drug costs covered by the plan. At that point, the beneficiary reaches the Part D *coverage gap* or *doughnut hole.* Benefits then cease until a beneficiary's total drug costs reach $4,700. Above the $4,700 limit, the beneficiary must pay the greater of (1) 5 percent of the cost of the prescription, or (2) a modest co-pay of $2.60 for a generic drug and $6.50 for a brand name drug. For all but very inexpensive drugs, this means the plan will pay 95 percent of the drug's cost above the "doughnut hole."

Note that all the above limits apply to drug costs covered by the plan. If a beneficiary purchases a drug that is not covered, he must pay the full cost of the drug and cannot apply this amount toward the initial deductible or use it to satisfy previously-mentioned limits.

Each Medicare prescription drug plan has a formulary, which is a list of approved drugs covered by the plan. Formularies do not need to cover every prescription drug. By law, drug plans must include at least two drugs in each of 146 therapeutic classes. Most plans today cover more than the minimum number of drugs.

Very few Medicare prescription drug plans meet the exact design of the standard benefit plan. Some ways in which most plans provide more comprehensive benefits are:

- include more drugs in their formulary than required by law

- reduce the annual calendar-year deductible, and some plans have no deductible
- provide more benefits in the doughnut hole
- use a tiered co-payment schedule with increasingly higher copayments for the most expensive drugs

---

EXAMPLE

Wilma's Medicare prescription drug plan has a three-tiered co-payment structure. Tier I consists of generic drugs and has no co-pay. Tier II is preferred brand name drugs and has a $15 per prescription co-pay. Tier III includes other brand name drugs and has a co-pay of $30 per prescription.

The initial enrollment period for a person who becomes eligible for Medicare prescription drug coverage is the 7-month period that includes the month of eligibility and 3 months before and after that month. This is the same as the Medicare Part B enrollment period. If an individual fails to enroll in a Medicare prescription drug plan upon first becoming eligible, there is a penalty assessed, unless the person had prior *creditable prescription drug coverage*. For coverage to be creditable under other plans, it must be at least as generous as Medicare's. The other plans, such as an employer-provided plan, must certify the actuarial equivalency of their plan's benefits to Medicare. If an individual fails to enroll in a drug plan and has not had prior creditable coverage, there is a penalty added to his premium for Part D coverage. The penalty is equal to one percent of the national base beneficiary premium ($31.08 in 2012), as calculated by the Centers for Medicare & Medicaid Services (CMS), for each month of delayed enrollment. The percentage of the penalty does not change after an individual enrolls, but the dollar amount changes each year as the national base beneficiary premium changes.

EXAMPLE

Ruth decided not to purchase Medicare prescription drug coverage when she was first eligible because she took no medications then. Twenty-four months later, she was taking several medications and decided that drug coverage made sense. If the average base beneficiary premium was then $31.08, her monthly penalty would be 24 percent of that amount, or $7.46. This would be added to the regular premium of any plan she selected. Next year, if the average base beneficiary premium increased to $34, her penalty would be $8.16 per month (that is 0.24 X $34 = $8.16).

It is obvious from our brief discussion that the Medicare prescription drug plan is quite complex. Seniors will need to decide whether to obtain coverage and, if so, what plan to purchase. Some seniors will need assistance to help make their decisions. Information is available on the Medicare website (medicare.gov) and through such consumer groups as AARP (aarp.org).

COVERAGE TO SUPPLEMENT MEDICARE

This section is devoted to explaining the various types of coverages designed to supplement Medicare.

Employer Plans to Supplement Medicare

Some employers still provide retirees with medical expense benefits to supplement Medicare; however, the number of employers doing so is declining due to higher costs of the coverage. Employer plans may take the form of Medicare carve-outs or supplements. These benefits are not always secure. Employers may eliminate benefits for future retirees or raise contributions for coverage paid by retired employees. In addition, some retirees may find these benefits eliminated entirely, as has occurred with increasing frequency in the last few years. Those retired employees, however, can still obtain additional coverage through Medicare supplement policies or Medicare Advantage plans.

Individual Medigap Policies to Supplement Medicare

While Medicare is a program that provides significant benefits to many Americans, it has many limitations that can lead to large out-of-pocket costs for many beneficiaries. Some of the reasons for these costs are the following:

- a significant Part A deductible for each spell of illness ($1,156 in 2012)
- unlimited coinsurance for many Part B expenses
- very limited coverage for treatment outside the United States
- very limited coverage for prescription drugs outside a hospital or skilled-nursing facility. However, this has been helped by the Medicare Part D prescription drug programs.

Estimates indicate that 60 to 70 percent of Medicare beneficiaries have some type of coverage to supplement Medicare. The beneficiaries are split among those with coverage provided by a former employer, those who purchase coverage in the individual marketplace, and those who elect Medicare

Advantage plans. In addition, Medicaid can be a supplement to Medicare for certain persons with limited assets and income.

Medicare supplement insurance purchased in the individual marketplace is frequently referred to as *Medigap insurance*. As the name implies, the objective is to fill some of the gaps left after Medicare benefits have been exhausted. When originally developed, Medigap plans were as diverse as the companies that sold them. This led to great confusion in the marketplace and to questionable sales practices and duplications of coverage. As a result, the federal government investigated and eventually enacted legislation to deal with the structure and marketing of Medigap plans.

In 1990, the Medigap market became directly subject to federal regulation when Congress directed the National Association of Insurance Commissioners (NAIC) to develop a group of standardized Medigap policies. Congress mandated several other features, including a 6-month open enrollment period, limited preexisting-conditions exclusions, prohibition of the sale of duplicate coverage, and guaranteed renewability of Medigap policies.

Basic Benefits

basic benefits — The NAIC initially adopted 10 standard Medigap plans, with all 10 requiring the inclusion of a core of specified *basic benefits*, also known as core benefits. The plans were called A through J, with Plan A being the basic benefit package. Each of the other plans included the basic Plan A package and varying combinations of additional benefits.

The basic benefits that must be included in all Medigap plans consist of the following:

- hospitalization. This is the beneficiary's percentage participation share of Medicare Part A benefits for the 61st through the 90th day of hospitalization and for lifetime reserve days. In addition, full coverage is extended for 365 additional days after Medicare benefits end.
- medical expenses. This is the Part B percentage participation share (usually 20 percent) for Medicare-approved Part B charges for physicians' and medical services.
- blood. This is the payment for the first 3 pints of blood each year.

Changes in Medigap Benefits

There have been numerous changes in the structure of Medigap plans over the years. Four of the original plans (E, H, I, and J) are no longer offered by insurance companies. There are now four additional standard plans (called K, L, M, and N that contain so-called consumer-directed health plan features. States may approve, and insurers may offer, fewer than the 10 standard plans, but all states must permit the basic benefit plan (Plan A) to be sold. Three states (Massachusetts, Minnesota, and Wisconsin) maintain somewhat different standardized plans that were in place prior to the federal legislation. Those plans must still contain the basic benefits available in all other states. The table below shows the current plans generally available.

Additional Medicare Supplement Plan Benefits. Today's Medicare supplement plans include, in addition to the basic benefits, an array of coverage and benefits that are not included in original Medicare. These additions encompass the following:

- paying the hospital inpatient Part A deductible for each benefit period
- paying the Part A percentage participation share for the 21st through the 100th day of skilled-nursing facility care
- paying the annual Part B deductible.
- paying excess charges for physicians' and medical services. These are charges that exceed the Medicare-approved amount because the provider does not accept assignment. The plan pays either 80 percent or 100 percent of these excess charges up to any limitation set by Medicare or the state.
- paying 80 percent of the charges after a $250 deductible for emergency care in a foreign hospital (with several limitations) and a $50,000 lifetime maximum
- paying (up to $40 per day and $1,600 per year) for a care provider to give assistance with activities of daily living (at-home recovery) while a beneficiary qualifies for Medicare home health care benefits (with certain limitations). Note, the Medigap plans that provided at-home recovery benefits are no longer sold; however, individuals who owned the plans can keep them.
- paying for certain preventive care that is not covered by Medicare

Plans H, I, and J were originally designed to pay 50 percent of outpatient prescription drug charges after a $250 deductible up to an annual $1,250 or $3,000 calendar limit. Insurance companies no longer issue these policies to new insureds after June 30, 2010. Persons already insured under these policies have two options. They may continue to renew them with drug benefits included as long as they do not enroll in the Medicare prescription drug program. However, they will then probably be subject to the penalty for late enrollment if they later enroll in the program because the benefits under the Medicare supplement policy will likely not qualify as creditable coverage. Or they may enroll in the Medicare prescription drug program. In this situation, they may keep in force their existing Medicare supplement policies but with the drug benefit eliminated and the premium adjusted accordingly.

The following table indicates which of these other benefits plans B through N provide.

Table 8-5 Benefits Under Medicare Supplement Policies

	A	B	C	D	F	G	K	L	M	N
Basic benefits	X	X	X	X	X	X	X (1)	X(2)	X	X(4)
Skilled-nursing facility (days 21–100)			X	X	X	X	X (1)	X(2)	X	X
Part A deductible		X	X	X	X	X	X(1)	X(2)	X(3)	X
Part B deductible			X		X					
Part B excess charges					100%	80%				
Foreign travel emergency			X	X	X	X			X	X
At-home recovery				X		X			X	
Prescription drugs										
Medicare Part B Preventive Care Coinsurance	X	X	X	X	X	X	X	X	X	X

(1) Plan K pays Basic Benefits at 50% (Part A Deductible, Part B Coinsurance, Blood-First 3 Pints, and Skilled Nursing Facility Coinsurance). Plan K also has a maximum out-of-pocket limit of $4,660 in 2012. (2) Plan L pays Basic Benefits at 75% (Part A Deductible, Part B Coinsurance, Blood-First 3 Pints, and Skilled Nursing Facility Coinsurance). Plan L also has a maximum out-of-pocket limit of $2,330 in 2012. (3) Plan M pays the Part A Deductible at 50%. (4) Plan N requires a co-pay of up to $20 for each doctor's office visit and up to $50 for each emergency room visit, unless the patient is admitted to the hospital as an inpatient.

Eligibility

Persons aged 65 or older may buy any available Medigap policy, regardless of health status, at any time during the 6-month period after initial enrollment for Medicare Part B benefits. Insurance companies are allowed to exclude benefits for no more than 6 months because of preexisting conditions. However, some policies immediately provide benefits for preexisting conditions or have an exclusion period shorter than 6 months. If a person initially elects a managed care option under Medicare Advantage in lieu of regular Medicare benefits, the person will be eligible to purchase a Medigap policy, without evidence of insurability, if he leaves the managed care option during the first 12 months of coverage and returns to regular Medicare benefits. Similarly, a person who drops a Medigap policy and elects a managed care option can regain the Medigap coverage if she decides to drop the managed care option during the first 12 months of coverage.

In addition, a person can obtain a Medigap policy on a guaranteed-issue basis because of the termination of an employer-provided plan that supplements Medicare, or because a Medicare Advantage plan no longer provides coverage, or the person loses eligibility by moving out of the plan's service area.

POSTSCRIPT

Many of the Social Security and Medicare numbers change every year and, consequently, are difficult to learn. It is not as important to memorize these numbers as it is to understand that they do change every year. Both Social Security (www.ssa.gov) and Medicare (www.cms.gov) have websites that display the updated numbers every year when they are available. In addition, these websites also provide a lot of useful information about the programs. They are worth investigating if only to sift through the wealth of information located there.

CHAPTER REVIEW

Key Terms and Concepts are explained in the Glossary. Answers to the Review Questions are found in the back of the book in the Answers to Questions section.

Key Terms and Concepts

old-age, survivors, disability, and health insurance (OASDHI)
quarters of coverage
fully insured
currently insured
disability insured
full retirement age
primary insurance amount (PIA)

earnings test
cost-of-living adjustment (COLA)
benefit period
skilled nursing services
Medicare Advantage
Medicare Part D
doughnut hole
basic benefits

Review Questions

1. How are the Social Security and Medicare programs financed? [1]

2. As of this year, Evelyn Grey, aged 38, had 28 quarters of coverage under Social Security. Twenty-four of these quarters were earned prior to the birth of her first child 11 years ago. Four quarters have been earned since she reentered the labor force one year ago. (a.) Is Grey fully insured? Explain. (b.) Is Grey currently insured? Explain. (c.) Is Grey disability insured? Explain. [2]

3. Explain when a worker is eligible to receive retirement benefits under Social Security. [2]

4. What categories of persons are eligible for Social Security survivors benefits? [2]

5. What is the definition of disability under Social Security? [2]

6. (a.) Explain the relationship between a worker's PIA and the benefits available for dependents and survivors. (b.) What happens if the total benefits for a family exceed the maximum family benefit? [2]

7. Explain how a worker's retirement benefits under Social security will be affected if that person elects early or delayed retirement. [2]

8. Describe the earnings test applicable to the Social Security program. [2]

9. Describe the automatic cost-of-living adjustment provision under Social Security as it relates to benefit amounts. [2]

10. With respect to Part A of Medicare: (a.) Describe the types of benefits that are available. (b.) Explain the extent to which deductibles and copayments are required. (c.) Identify the major exclusions. [3]

11. With respect to Part B of Medicare: (a.) Describe the types of benefits that are available. (b.) Explain the extent to which copayments are required. (c.) Identify the major exclusions. [3]

12. Describe the managed care options available under Part C of Medicare. [4]

13. Explain the basic purpose and structure of Medicare Part D prescription drug coverage. [5]

14. Besides the basic benefits that must be included in all Medigap policies, what other features did Congress mandate for Medigap insurance? [6]

15. What are the eligibility criteria for Medigap insurance? [6]

APPENDIX A: ANSWERS TO QUESTIONS

Chapter 1

Answers to Review Questions

1. The eight steps in the financial planning process and their corresponding activities are as follows:

    a. Establishing and defining the client-planner relationship. Outline the responsibilities of both the planner and client. Disclose the length and scope of the relationship and methods of compensation.

    b. Gathering information necessary to fulfill the engagement. Gather all relevant client information through fact-finder forms, questionnaires, counseling, and examination of documents. Help the client define broad and specific goals and objectives. Ask the client about risk tolerance measures.

    c. Analyzing and evaluating the client's current financial status. Identify the strengths and weaknesses in the client's present financial condition as they affect the ability to achieve the client's goals. Revise goals if necessary.

    d. Developing the recommendations. Design a set of recommended strategies tailored to the client's circumstances and goals, including alternative ways of achieving those goals.

    e. Communicating the recommendation(s). Ensure clients understand what actions are recommended, what the costs in capital and time will be, and the consequences of inaction. The client must approve the plan and agree to proceed to the next steps.

    f. Implementing the recommendation(s). Outlines how implementation will occur. The planner may implement on behalf of the client, or the client may implement his or her own recommendations. Any conflicts of interest must be discussed with the client.

    g. Monitoring the recommendation(s). Agree on monitoring responsibilities, frequency of reviews, and updating as necessary. Evaluate the performance of all implementation vehicles. Review changes in the client's circumstances and the financial environment. Revisit the steps when necessary.

h. Practicing within professional and regulatory standards. Planners must be constantly vigilant within their regulatory environments. Standards of care, due diligence are continuing concerns.

2. Answers:

   a. The single-purpose approach to financial planning involves the sale to a client of a product to implement a recommendation developed according to the financial planning process and approved by the client.

   b. The multiple-purpose approach to financial planning involves solving multiple financial problems with financial products and/or services used to implement the recommendation(s) developed according to the financial planning process and approved by the client.

   c. The comprehensive approach to financial planning considers all of a client's financial needs and objectives by developing a plan according to the financial planning process and approved by the client for fulfilling those needs and objectives.

3. At a minimum, the subjects that should be included in a comprehensive financial plan are

   - financial planning principles
   - insurance planning and risk management
   - employee benefits planning
   - investment planning
   - income tax planning
   - retirement planning
   - estate planning

4. Financial planning is a process that should be ongoing throughout a client's financial life. Life-cycle financial planning occurs when an advisor actually engages in financial planning over a client's entire financial life cycle.

5. Some of the major events in the history of financial planning as a profession are as follows:

   - Financial advisors claiming to be practicing financial planning first appeared in numbers in the late 1960s, a period of rising inflation and interest rates.

- The financial planning movement grew rapidly in the 1970s and prices continued sharply upward.
- In the mid-1980s, more advocates of comprehensive financial planning began to adapt a fee-for-service approach primarily with affluent clients. The maturing of the baby boomers gave a boost to the profession.
- In the 1990s, the financial planning profession gained maturity and stability.
- Today, financial planning is widely accepted and many specialized planning areas have developed such as education planning, divorce planning, and income distribution.

6. The financial planning marketplace presents opportunities for advisors as a result of a(n)
    a. rising median age—This results in more clients needing retirement planning and assistance in planning for their children's college educations.
    b. increasing number of dual-income families—These families typically have higher total incomes, pay higher income and Social Security taxes, and have less time to manage their finances, providing many opportunities for advisors to assist clients.
    c. volatility of financial conditions—With the possible exception of the bull market of the late 1990s when many investors felt they could do it themselves without the benefit of professional advice, volatile economic conditions generally create greater demand for financial planning services. They also emphasize the need for financial advisors to continuously monitor their client's financial circumstances and to adjust the plans as circumstances dictate.
    d. increasing use of sophisticated technology by the financial services industry—The revolution in technology has made possible the creation of many new financial products and has made it easier to tailor these products to individual client needs. Also, the technology has made possible improved analysis of the performance of these products by advisors with the skills to do so.

7. The top 10 reasons why people begin financial planning are
    a. building a retirement fund (83 percent of those surveyed)

b. building an emergency fund (38 percent)
c. home purchase/renovation (35 percent)
d. managing/reducing current debt (34 percent)
e. vacation/travel (32 percent)
f. building a college fund (32 percent)
g. accumulating capital (31 percent)
h. providing insurance protection (30 percent)
i. sheltering income from taxes (28 percent)
j. generating current income (23 percent)

8. Three important obstacles preventing households from gaining control of their own financial destinies are

- the natural human tendency to procrastinate
- the tendency to live up and spend to, or beyond, their current income
- their lack of financial knowledge

Chapter 2

Answers to Review Questions

1. For insurance and financial planning purposes, the term risk means the possibility of financial loss. However, risk is not the same as uncertainty. Risk exists as a state of the world, while uncertainty is a state of mind characterized by doubt. Although risk can give rise to uncertainty, risk is not uncertainty. Moreover, risk is not the probability of loss. While risk may be measurable in terms of probabilities, it need not be measurable to exist. This is the reason risk is defined as the possibility, not the probability, of financial loss.

2. The two categories of risk are

    - pure risk, which involves only the possibility of financial loss or no loss
    - speculative risk, which involves not only the possibility of financial loss, but also the possibility of financial gain

3. The three types of pure risk are

    - personal risks, which involve the possibility of
        a. loss of income-earning ability because of
            (1) premature death
            (2) disability

(3) unemployment

(4) retirement

    b. extra expenses associated with accidental injuries, periods of sickness, or the inability to perform safely some of the activities of daily living

- property risks, which involve the possibility of

  a. direct losses associated with the need to replace or repair damaged or missing property

  b. indirect (consequential) losses, such as additional living expenses that are caused by a direct loss

- liability risks, which involve the possibility of

  a. loss from damage to or destruction of others' property

  b. loss from physical or personal injuries to others

4. The risk management process is used to deal with pure risks involving possible damage or destruction of property or legal liability, while the needs analysis process is used to deal with pure risks involving the loss of income-earning ability due to death, disability, or old age. However, the risk management and needs analysis processes not only contain the same steps as each other, but also involve the same steps as the financial planning process. In other words, all three processes are simply different statements of the same professional approach for helping to identify and solve an individual's financial problem(s).

5. Actual cash value is defined as replacement cost less a reduction resulting from depreciation and obsolescence. This is expressed as: Actual cash value = Replacement cost — Depreciation. Replacement cost is that cost necessary to replace or repair the damaged asset. Depreciation is a function of the age of the asset, its use, its condition at the time of loss, and any other factor causing deterioration.

When used for real property, replacement cost is interpreted to mean the cost to rebuild the same type dwelling on the same site for the same type of occupancy and with materials of like kind and quality. It has become the more practical measure of the maximum possible loss associated with real property in pure-risk situations. Sometimes there is a temptation to use market value as the measurement of loss for real property, but market value is closely linked to supply and demand conditions and should be used with caution.

For insurance purposes, the measurement of loss for personal property such as furniture, clothing, and automobiles has traditionally been the item's actual cash value. However, the maximum possible loss for a particular item is its replacement cost.

6. No perfect method has been developed for measuring the maximum possible dollar loss that individuals can suffer from the liability exposure. An individual can enter into certain contractual arrangements that will limit the extent of liability, but in most cases the liability loss will depend upon the severity of the future accident and the amount the court awards to the injured parties (or the amount of the out-of-court settlement agreement).

7. Two methods of measuring the financial loss associated with premature death are the

- human-life-value method—This approach is based on the calculation of the present value of a given number of years at some assumed interest rate.
- needs analysis method—This approach involves (1) identifying and attaching a dollar amount to the specific financial needs of the survivors, (2) identifying and attaching a dollar amount to the resources currently available to meet those needs, and (3) determining the gaps between the survivors' needs and the resources available to meet them. These gaps must be filled with additional financial resources if the survivors' needs are to be fully met.

8. The two categories of techniques for handling pure risks are

- loss control, which is concerned with reducing the probability that events resulting in financial loss will occur and minimizing the magnitude of those losses that do occur
- loss financing, which is concerned with how to fund the losses that do occur

9. As insurers accept insureds, they pool those insureds with similar loss exposures, and the combination of many similar exposure units permits the operation of the law of large numbers. That is, as

the number of exposure units increases, the deviation of actual experience from expected experience diminishes.

10. Participating (par) policies provide for, but do not guarantee, the payment of dividends to the policyowner. The dividends reflect the insurance company's past experience with respect to mortality, interest, and expenses. Favorable experience—lower mortality, lower expenses, and higher interest than expected—tends to increase the dividend scale, whereas unfavorable experience tends to have the opposite effect. In contrast to par policies, nonparticipating (nonpar) policies do not pay policyowner dividends.

11. The reserves (and, thus, cash values) of traditional whole life policies are invested in the general assets of the insurance company. Moreover, these policies contain a guaranteed interest rate that is the lowest rate with which policy funds can be credited. In contrast, variable life policies permit the policyowner to allocate the funds generated by the policy among a variety of separate accounts. In other words, these policies shift the investment risk to the policyowner and provide no minimum guaranteed rate of return or guaranteed cash value. The rate of return credited to policy funds and, thus, the amount of the cash value depend upon the investment success of the policyowner.

12. Definitions of disability in disability income policies are based on the ability of the insured to perform certain occupational tasks. One definition, typically called the any-occupation definition, states that insureds are considered to be totally disabled when they cannot perform the major duties of any gainful occupation for which they are reasonably suited by education, training, or experience.

A somewhat less restrictive definition is usually referred to as the own-occupation definition. With a pure own-occupation definition, insureds are deemed to be totally disabled when they cannot perform the major duties of their regular occupations. Because this definition would allow an insured to work in some other capacity and still be entitled to benefits, many insurers now use a modified own-occupation definition that also provides that benefits either will not be paid or will be reduced if the insured chooses to work in any other occupation.

Due to adverse claims experience, most companies no longer issue contracts of long benefit duration that have pure own-occupation definitions of disability for the contract duration. Instead, either a modified own-occupation definition or a dual definition of total disability is typically used in long-term disability income policies. With a dual definition, an own-occupation definition applies during the first few policy years after which it is replaced by an any-occupation definition.

13. Answers:

    a. Policies pay benefits in one of two basic ways—reimbursement or per diem. The majority of newer policies pay benefits on a reimbursement basis. These contracts reimburse the insured for actual expenses up to the specified policy limit. Some policies provide benefits on a per diem basis once care is actually being received. This means that benefits are paid regardless of the actual cost of care.

    b. There are two ways that the benefit period is applied in the payment of benefits. Under one approach, benefit payments are made for exactly the benefit period chosen. If the client selects a benefit period of 4 years and collects benefits for 4 years, the benefit payments cease. The other approach, most commonly but not exclusively used with reimbursement policies, uses a pool of money. Under this concept, there is an amount of money that can be used to make benefit payments as long as the pool of money lasts. The client does not select the amount in the pool of money; it is determined by multiplying the daily benefit by the benefit period selected.

    c. Most states require that a long-term care policy offer some type of automatic inflation protection. The client is given the choice to select this option, decline the option, or possibly select an alternative option. The cost of an automatic-increase option is built into the initial premium, and no additional premium is levied at the time of an annual increase. The automatic option found in almost all policies is a 5 percent benefit increase that is compounded annually over the life of the policy. Under such a provision, the amount of a policy's benefits increases by 5 percent each year over the amount of benefits available in the prior year. A common alternative that many insurers make available is based on simple interest, with each annual automatic increase being 5 percent of the original benefit amount. Another alternative offered by some insurers is to allow the policyowner to increase benefits without evidence of insurability on a pay-as-you-go basis at specified intervals, such as every one, 2, or 3 years.

14. Answers:

    a. Coverage A or dwelling coverage requires the selection of a limit or dollar amount of insurance coverage. For HO-2 and HO-3, this is the only part of Section I for which the client must choose a limit of coverage, and it should be chosen with care. If a loss should occur to the dwelling and at the time of loss the amount of insurance carried is equal to 80 percent or more of the full replacement cost of the dwelling, the loss will be settled on a full replacement-cost basis. If the current replacement cost of the dwelling is $200,000, a minimum limit of coverage on the dwelling of $160,000 and a maximum limit of $200,000 should be recommended. In most cases, it would be appropriate to recommend the selection of a limit closer to the top of the range, particularly if the client would need to replace the entire dwelling following a total loss.

    b. Coverage B or coverage for other structures provides insurance on other structures located on the premises that are not attached to the dwelling. These include detached garages or tool-sheds and such things as fences, driveways, and retaining walls. Unless increased by the insured, the amount of coverage is 10 percent of the limit on the dwelling. Losses to these other structures are settled on a replacement-cost basis.

    c. Coverage C or coverage on personal property includes the items normally contained in a dwelling, such as furniture, appliances, and clothing, and property stored in a garage, other structure, or outdoors. Unless increased, the limit of coverage on personal property for HO-2 and HO-3 is 50 percent of the dwelling limit. Personal property coverage is provided worldwide.

15. Coverage D, the loss-of-use coverage, provides insurance protection for certain indirect losses. The primary loss-of-use coverage is for additional living expenses—those increased costs necessary to maintain normal living standards when the insured's dwelling is uninhabitable because of damage caused by a covered cause of loss. The automatic limit for this coverage is a percent of the coverage applicable to the dwelling for HO-2 (30 percent),

HO-3 (30 percent), HO-5 (30 percent), and HO-8 (10 percent), and a percent of the coverage applicable to personal property for HO-4 (30 percent) and HO-6 (50 percent). Payment is limited to the period required to repair or replace the damage or if the insured permanently relocates, to the period required to resettle the household.

16. Answers:

    a. Coverage E, personal liability coverage, provides protection for activities and conditions at the premises where the named insured maintains a covered residence and for personal activities of the named insured and members of his family anywhere in the world. All homeowners forms contain the same liability coverage.

    Coverage E is similar to other liability insurance policies. Protection is provided for legal liability involving bodily injury or property damage, but not for personal injury. The latter includes such injuries as libel, slander, violation of privacy, malicious prosecution, and wrongful entry. These may be added by endorsement or covered under an umbrella liability policy.

    Also, as with other liability policies, the insurer promises to defend the insured at the company's expense even if the suit is groundless, false, or fraudulent. The insurer may investigate and settle any claim that it feels is appropriate. The costs associated with investigating and defending a claim against an insured are paid in addition to the limit of liability.

    Exclusions play an important role in liability insurance coverage, because the insurer is essentially promising to pay any claim involving bodily injury or property damage for which an insured is legally liable unless the particular situation is specifically excluded by the policy. Some of the exclusions found in homeowners policies should be expected, such as war and nuclear exposure. Others should be anticipated because the exposure can be covered with a different policy as in the case of motor vehicle, large and powerful watercraft, aircraft, workers' compensation, and business and professional service exposures. Liability arising out of the transmission of a communicable disease, sexual molestation or abuse, and the use, sale, manufacture, delivery, transfer, or possession of a controlled substance by an insured is also excluded. Finally, losses that are intentionally caused are not covered, nor is bodily injury to an insured.

b. Coverage F, medical payments to others, provides medical benefits to persons, other than the residents of the insured household, who suffer bodily injury at an insured location or who are injured because of an insured's activities away from the insured location. The basic limit for Coverage F is $1,000 per person. This amount is available for all necessary medical expenses incurred within 3 years of the date of the accident. Benefits under this coverage will be paid whether or not the insured is legally liable.

17. An umbrella liability policy provides excess liability limits over underlying liability coverage limits. The insured is required to carry certain underlying liability policies and limits—for example, a homeowners policy with a liability limit of $300,000 and an automobile liability policy with a single limit of $500,000. If the insured has an umbrella liability policy with a limit of $2,000,000, the first $500,000 of any claim arising out of an automobile accident would be payable under the automobile policy, and the balance (up to the policy limit) would be payable under the umbrella policy. Therefore, the insured would have total coverage amounting to $2,500,000.

Chapter 3

Answers to Review Questions

1. The five categories of employee benefits are

   - legally required payments for government programs
   - payments for private insurance and retirement plans
   - payments for time not worked
   - extra cash payments, other than wages and bonuses based on performance
   - cost of services to employees

2. The growth of employee benefits over the last 75 years stems from the following six factors:

- industrialization and urbanization of society
- labor unions ability to negotiate for benefits
- wage controls during World War II and the Korean War
- inflationary pressures on benefit levels
- cost advantages of benefits compared to alternatives
- legislation favorable to benefits

3. The steps in the benefit-planning process for employers are the same as those in the financial planning process. The eight steps are
   a. establish and define the client-planner relationship
   b. gather information necessary to fulfill the engagement
   c. analyze and evaluate the employer's current benefits status
   d. develop recommendations for a new benefits plan
   e. communicate the plan
   f. implement the plan
   g. monitor the plan performance and make changes as needed
   h. practice within professional and regulatory standards

4. Financial advisors should be aware of employee benefits for the following reasons:
   - Employee benefits form the basis for almost all financial plans.
   - Many employees can purchase additional insurance and retirement benefits through employer-sponsored plans.
   - Many executives can negotiate their own compensation packages, including employee benefits.

5. Requirements that employee benefit plans may use to determine who is an eligible person for coverage purposes include
   - covered classifications
   - full-time employment
   - probationary periods
   - evidence of insurability
   - employee premium contributions
   - termination of coverage

6. The five basic characteristics of a true managed care plan are

- controlled access to providers
- comprehensive case management
- preventive care
- risk sharing
- high-quality care

7. PPOs differ from HMOs in the following ways:
    - Preferred providers are generally paid on a fee-for-service basis as their services are used.
    - Employees are not required to use the practitioners or facilities that contract with the PPO.
    - Most PPOs do not use a primary care physician as a gatekeeper; employees do not need referrals to see specialists.

8. The qualifying events for which employees or their dependents can extend medical expense coverage under the provisions of COBRA are the loss of coverage because of
    - the death of the covered employee
    - the termination of the employee for almost any reason except for gross misconduct
    - a reduction in the employee's hours so that the employee or dependent is ineligible for coverage
    - the divorce or legal separation of the covered employee and his or her spouse
    - the employee becoming eligible for Medicare with the spouse and children ceasing to be eligible under the plan
    - a child's ceasing to be an eligible dependent under the plan

9. Benefits under a group life insurance plan are determined by one or more of the following:
    - multiple-of-earnings schedule
    - specified-dollar-amount schedule
    - scheduled reduction in benefits for older employees

10. There are two possible options that an employee may have for the continuation of life insurance coverage if he or she terminates employment.

- Conversion allows an employee to convert to an individual cash value life insurance policy without evidence of insurability at attained-age rates.
- Portability of term coverage allows an employee to continue coverage at group rates in much the same manner as is found in voluntary employee-pay-all plans.

11. The monthly amount that will be reportable by Bruce as taxable income is calculated as follows:

Coverage provided	$100,000
Minus Sec. 70 exclusion	- 50,000
Amount subject to taxation	$ 50,000

Monthly cost - $0.06/$1,000 x $50,000 = $3.00

12. The tax treatment of employees under a noncontributory group long-term disability income insurance plan is that employer contributions result in no taxable income to employees. However, any disability benefits paid to employees are taxable income, but the Code provides for a tax credit to persons of modest means who are permanently and totally disabled.

13. Characteristics of voluntary benefit plans that make them popular with employees are
    - payment through payroll deduction
    - more liberal underwriting than for similar coverage in the individual insurance marketplace
    - lower cost than in the individual marketplace
    - portability of coverage

14. Benefits not considered qualified benefits under Code. Sec. 125 include medical savings accounts, long-term care insurance, scholarships and fellowships, transportation benefits, educational assistance, no-additional-cost services, employee discounts, and de *minimis* fringe benefits.

Chapter 4

Answers to Review Questions

1. The two types of assets that consumers buy are

Appendix A: Answers to Questions   A.15

- personal assets—which are bought primarily for the creature comforts they provide. Examples include homes, cars, and clothes.
- investment assets—which are acquired for investing. Investing is defined as the purchase of an asset with the expectation that it will provide a return commensurate with its risk.

From the above descriptions, it should be obvious that the distinction between personal and investment assets is not always clear. For example, the purchase of an antique car may be for pleasure or it may be for investment purposes or it may be for both. In cases where there is ambiguity, the ultimate distinction is based on the intent of the buyer. The exact same asset may be a personal asset for one person and an investment asset for another person.

[margin note: explain investing vs. speculating →]

2. Investing is based on a reasoned consideration of expected return and the risk associated with that return. Speculating occurs when a person buys an asset in the hopes of receiving some form of return, without consideration or knowledge of the expected return or risk, or both.

[margin note: what is investment risk?]

3. Investment risk is measured by the likelihood that realized returns will differ from those that are expected. An asset with a wide range of possible returns is considered risky, while an asset with a narrow range of possible returns is considered more secure. The range of returns is generally measured in terms of the distance or dispersion from the mean or expected return. Risk refers to the magnitude of the range of possible returns. The greater the range of possible returns, the riskier the investment.

4. The two most basic theorems of investment are as follows:

    - All investors are greedy. Everyone would like a risk-free investment with an incredibly high rate of return.
    - There is no free lunch. This means that there is a well-established relationship in the world of investments between risk and expected return. Low risk investments have low expected returns, and high-risk investments have high expected returns.

5. Asset allocation models are recommended investment portfolios for different levels of financial risk tolerance. These recommended portfolios are based on categories of assets and the percentage to be placed in each category. To properly determine both the

categories and the appropriate percentages for a client, the client's level of risk tolerance needs to be known.

6. Preferred stockholders usually have two privileges that provide them with a preferential position relative to common stockholders. The first privilege is the right to receive dividends before any dividends are paid to the common stockholders. This preference is usually limited to a specified amount per share each year. The second privilege is the right to receive up to a specified amount for each share at the time of liquidation. This liquidation value must be paid in full before anything can be paid to the common stockholders.

7. Price risk results from the fact that any change in market interest rates typically leads to an opposite change in the value of investments. When interest rates rise (fall), the value of an investment declines (increases). This inverse relationship is most pronounced for debt instruments that have a contractually specified rate of interest or return and a specified time to maturity. The longer the time until maturity, the greater will be the resulting change in market price.

8. An asset is said to be liquid if it can be converted to cash (sold) quickly at any time with little or no loss of principal. Marketability is a little different than liquidity, but the two are frequently confused. Marketability refers to the ability to sell an asset quickly. Thus, liquid assets are marketable, but not all marketable assets are liquid. Stock is a classic example of a marketable asset that is not liquid. If a stock is listed on a major exchange, it can be sold in a matter of seconds. However, there is no certainty as to the price at which the stock can be sold.

9. Jack's equivalent fully taxable yield is calculated as follows:

$$\text{equivalent fully taxable yield} = \frac{\text{tax-exempt yields}}{(1 - \text{MRT})}$$

$$\text{equivalent fully taxable yield} = \frac{.03}{1 - .33} = \frac{.03}{.67} = .0448$$

$$\text{equivalent fully taxable yield} = 4.48\%$$

10. Joe's after-tax holding period return would be calculated as follows:

$$\text{after-tax HPR} = \frac{\text{TCI} \times (1 - \text{MRT}) + [\text{TCA} \times (1 - \text{TCG})]}{\text{total initial investment}}$$

where: TCI is Joe's total current income

MRT is his marginal income tax rate

TCA is his total capital appreciation

TCG is his tax rate for capital gains

Under JGTRRA, however, dividends are taxed the same as capital gains, so the formula becomes

$$\text{after-tax HPR} = \frac{TCI \times (1-TCG) + TCA \times (1-TCG)}{\text{total initial investment}}$$

which reduces to

$$\text{after-tax HPR} = \frac{(TCI + TCA) \times (1-TCG)}{\text{total initial investment}}$$

$$\text{after-tax HPR} = \frac{\$14(1-.15)}{\$50} = \frac{\$14 \times .85}{\$50}$$

$$\text{after-tax HPR} = \frac{\$11.9}{\$50} = .238 = 23.8\%$$

11. Sally's after-tax approximate yield for a 5-year holding period would be calculated as follows:

$$\text{before-tax approximate yield} = \frac{\text{annual income} + \frac{\text{future price} - \text{current price}}{\text{number of years}}}{\frac{\text{future price} + \text{current price}}{2}}$$

$$\text{before-tax approximate yield} = \frac{\$5,000 + \frac{\$200,000 - \$100,000}{5}}{\frac{\$200,000 + \$100,000}{2}} = \frac{\$5,000 + \frac{\$100,000}{5}}{\frac{\$300,000}{2}}$$

$$\text{before-tax approximate yield} = \frac{\$5,000 + \$20,000}{\$150,000}$$

To calculate the after-tax approximate yield, multiply each segment of the numerator by one minus Sally's appropriate tax rate where MRT is Sally's marginal income tax rate and TCG is her capital gains tax rate.

$$\text{after-tax approximate yield} = \frac{\$5,000(1-\text{MRT}) + \$20,000(1-\text{TCG})}{\$150,000}$$

$$\text{after-tax approximate yield} = \frac{\$5,000 \times .72 + \$20,000 \times .85}{\$150,000}$$

$$\text{after-tax approximate yield} = \frac{\$3,600 + \$17,000}{\$150,000} = \frac{\$20,600}{\$150,000} = .1373$$

$$\text{after-tax approximate yield} = 13.73\%$$

12. Prior to beginning an investment program, an investor should set aside some funds for emergency purposes. In addition, the investor should also take steps to protect himself or herself from several types of pure risks. This typically is done by purchasing the appropriate kinds of insurance.

13. Dollar-cost averaging requires the investment of a fixed amount of dollars at specified time intervals. Investing a fixed amount of dollars at set intervals in the stock market means that the investor buys more shares when prices are low and fewer shares when prices are high. Unless the market goes into a persistent decline, this approach to investing works fairly well, and it establishes a consistent pattern of investing. Moreover, the overall cost of investing using dollar cost averaging is lower than it would be if a constant number of shares were bought at set intervals.

14. Answers:

    a. Negotiated markets are markets where sellers list their offerings with brokers who then seek to attract buyers through various advertising and other marketing methods. After a buyer has been located, negotiations determine the price. When these transactions involve listed securities, this negotiated market is called the fourth market because the transaction does not take place on the floor of an exchange.

    b. For many securities, one or more dealers make an active market by offering to buy (at a bid price) and sell (at an ask price) as much of a particular security as desired by investors. The difference between the bid and ask price is the dealer's spread, or compensation, for making the market and bearing the risk of holding an inventory of the security. This network of securities dealers is called the over-the-counter market and includes over 30,000 different securities issues.

15. Answers:
    a. The Securities Act of 1933 requires issuers of new securities to file a registration statement with the Securities and Exchange Commission (SEC). The issuing corporation may not sell the security until the SEC verifies that the information contained in the registration statement is complete and is not false or misleading. Once approval is obtained, a prospectus is prepared that contains a summary of information from the registration statement. Then the securities can be sold to the public if a copy of the prospectus is made available to all interested buyers.
    b. The Maloney Act of 1938 permits the establishment of trade associations for the purpose of self-regulation of a segment of the securities industry. The only self-regulating organization that has formed is the National Association of Securities Dealers (NASD), which regulates securities firms, their owners, and stockbrokers. The NASD establishes rules of practice to which members must adhere. Securities firms that are not members of the NASD are regulated by the SEC.

Chapter 5

Answers to Review Questions

1. Gross income for income tax purposes includes every item of value, whether consisting of money or other property, that is either made available to or comes into the possession of the taxpayer. In other words, anything of value is considered to be gross income for income tax purposes unless the Internal Revenue Code contains a specific provision that excludes a particular item from the taypayer's gross income.
2. An exclusion from gross income is an item of value that a taxpayer receives that is not includible in his gross income. A deduction from gross income is an item of expense that reduces the amount of the taxpayer's income that is subject to tax.
3. An above-the-line deduction consists of those deductions that are subtracted from gross income to determine adjusted gross income. A below-the-line deduction consists of those deductions that are subtracted from adjusted gross income to determine taxable income.

4. The standard deduction is a specified amount, indexed annually for inflation, that a taxpayer who does not itemize deductions may claim in calculating taxable income. If the taxpayer is entitled to claim itemized deductions that, when added together, are less than the amount the standard deduction, then the taxpayer will claim the standard deduction. The amount of the standard deduction depends on the taxpayer's filing status.

5. The three basic categories of deductions allowable to individual taxpayers are as follows:

   - The first includes deductions for expenses that are incurred in the course of carrying on a trade or business.
   - The second includes deductions for expenses that are incurred in the course of an activity that is not a trade or business but is engaged in to producing income and making a profit.
   - The third includes deductions for expenses that are simply personal, family, or living expenses. Although the Code provides a general rule that these expenses are nondeductible, there are several important exceptions to the general rule.

6. Medical expenses are deductible only to the extent that they exceed the floor of 7.5 percent of the taxpayer's adjusted gross income (AGI). Therefore, assuming George has medical expenses of $9,500, an AGI of $80,000, and he itemizes, he will be able to deduct $3,500 of his medical expenses, calculated as follows:

   - 7.5 percent x George's $80,000 AGI = $6,000
   - $9,500 of medical expenses − $6,000 = $3,500 of medical expenses that George can deduct

7. The tax rate applicable to each of the six income brackets is called a marginal tax rate. The six marginal tax rates are 10 percent, 15 percent, 25 percent, 28 percent, 33 percent, and 35 percent. Due to the progressive structure of these marginal rates, an additional dollar of income could be taxed at a higher rate than all previous income. An effective tax rate is the rate at which a taxpayer would be taxed if his taxable income were taxed at a constant rate rather than progressively. This rate is computed by dividing the total tax liability by taxable income. Except when a taxpayer is in the lowest marginal tax bracket, his effective tax rate will always be lower than his marginal rate because of the progressive structure of the

income tax system. A taxpayer in the lowest tax bracket has both an effective tax rate and a marginal tax rate equal to 10 percent.

8. A $10,000 tax deduction will reduce the taxpayer's taxable income by $10,000 and the federal income tax payable by $10,000 multiplied by the taxpayer's marginal tax rate. A $10,000 tax credit, on the other hand, will reduce the taxpayer's federal income tax payable by $10,000.

9. The alternative minimum tax (AMT) is a separate and parallel system of income taxation to the regular system. It applies to any taxpayer whose tax liability under the parallel system is greater than the liability for that year under the regular income tax system. In other words, the taxpayer pays the AMT amount if the AMT is greater than the regular tax. The purpose of the AMT is to ensure that the taxpayer who enjoys certain tax benefits will not be permitted to reduce her tax liability below a minimum amount by claiming certain tax deductions.

10. Answers:

    a. The economic benefit doctrine holds that a taxpayer must pay tax whenever an economic benefit has been conferred on the taxpayer, regardless of whether the taxpayer has actually received any cash or property. In other words, any event or transaction that confers an economic benefit on the taxpayer will result in gross income to the taxpayer, as long as the economic benefit is certain and can be measured.

    b. The doctrine of the fruit and tree holds that income is to be taxed to the person who earns it, or to the person who owns the asset that produces it. In other words, for income tax purposes, the fruit comes from the tree that produced it and must be taxed accordingly. The fruits of a person's labor cannot be assigned to another person for tax purposes.

    c. The doctrine of constructive receipt holds that a cash-basis taxpayer is deemed to have received income for tax purposes when it is either credited to the taxpayer's account, set apart for the taxpayer, or otherwise made available to be taken into the taxpayer's possession. However, if there is any condition or restriction that limits the taxpayer's right to receive the income, the doctrine of constructive receipt will not apply.

11. Federal income tax avoidance involves a reasonable interpretation of the tax laws. It is perfectly acceptable (and perhaps even commendable) to use every legal means to avoid the payment of federal income taxes. Tax evasion, on the other hand, happens when the taxpayer either ignores the tax laws or flouts them.

12. The purpose behind income-shifting techniques is to get taxable income into the hands of taxpayers who are in lower tax brackets than the taxpayers who would otherwise have to report the income. The result is that less tax is paid on the income. Deduction shifting, on the other hand, is the converse of income shifting. The purpose behind deduction shifting is to shift deductions to taxpayers who are in higher tax brackets than the taxpayers who would otherwise claim the deductions. The result, again, is greater tax savings.

13. Answers:

    a. For income tax purposes, passive losses are losses that typically are generated by activities in which the taxpayer has an ownership interest but does not participate in the activity of the business.

    b. The basic rule is that tax losses generated by passive activities can be deducted only against income generated by passive activities and not against salary or other income. The rule is intended to prevent taxpayers from investing in activities merely for tax purposes, as distinguished from the actual economics of the investment.

14. The intent of the nonrecognition provisions is merely to defer taxation. However, the deferred gain may never be taxed if the taxpayer does not sell the property received in the exchange at a later date. In other words, there is no assurance that the government will ever get its tax money, particularly if the taxpayer keeps the new property until death when it receives a stepped-up basis in the hands of the beneficiary.

15. The social policy issue surrounding the sale of capital assets has two sides. Those people who believe that the sale of such assets should receive a tax break relative to other kinds of income argue that capital-gain tax relief encourages savings and investment. They also argue that full taxation of capital gain subjects taxpayers to what is really a tax on inflation, rather than one on real economic gains. These views have helped to introduce varying legislative measures over the years that provide relief for the taxation of capital gain. Those people who argue against favorable tax treatment for

capital gain believe that preferential treatment for capital gain favors wealthy taxpayers at the expense of the average citizen because most stocks and other investment assets are owned by the rich.

Chapter 6

Answers to Review Questions

1. A spendthrift lifestyle during a client's active working years makes retirement planning more difficult because it reduces the client's ability to accumulate savings that will produce an adequate income stream to compliment employer pension and Social Security income. In addition, the client becomes accustomed to an unnaturally high standard of living. By living below his means before retirement, the client establishes a lifestyle that is more easily maintained throughout the retirement years.

2. Roadblocks preventing the accumulation of adequate retirement saving include

    a. inadequate insurance coverage. Many Americans remain uninsured or underinsured for life, disability, health, home or auto risks. Because clients cannot always recover economically from such losses, an important element of retirement planning is protection against catastrophic financial loss that would drain existing savings and make future saving impossible. Two frequently overlooked areas are disability insurance and umbrella liability insurance.

    b. divorce. Divorce often leaves one or both parties with little or no accumulation of pension benefits or other private sources of retirement income. These clients may have only a short time to accumulate any retirement assets and may not accrue significant pension or Social Security benefits. If the marriage lasted 10 years or longer, however, divorced persons are eligible for Social Security as early as age 62 based on their former spouse's earnings record. In addition, a spouse may be entitled to a portion of the former spouse's retirement benefits if the divorce decree includes a qualified domestic relations order (QDRO). QDROs are judgments, decrees, or orders issued by state courts that allow a participant's retirement plan assets to be used for marital property rights, child support, or alimony payments to a former spouse or dependent.

c. frequent changes of employer. Workers who have frequently changed employers also may arrive at retirement with little or no pension. Statistics show that employees today are unlikely to remain with one employer for their entire working life and will, typically, hold seven full-time jobs during their career. Generally, these people will not accumulate vested defined-benefit pension benefits because they do not remain with an employer long enough to become vested. Even if they did become vested, they may have received a distribution of their accumulated pension fund upon leaving the job and many have spent this money rather than investing it or rolling it over for retirement.

3. Many of the variables affecting the amount a client will need to save to achieve retirement goals can dramatically change overnight and without warning. The following are examples of how variables could change.

- The client may be planning to retire at age 65 but health considerations, or perhaps a plant shutdown, force retirement at age 62.
- A younger client may be planning on a relatively moderate retirement lifestyle but business success may lead to a higher retirement income expectation.
- Forecasters may predict that long-term inflation will result in an annual 4 percent increase in the cost of living when in reality 6 percent increases occur. (Even a one percentage point disparity can make a significant difference.)
- Clients may hope for an after-tax rate of return of 7 percent when in fact investment returns are adversely affected by a bear market, or the real after-tax rate of return is suppressed by rising tax rates.
- Clients may plan on a short life expectancy and have the "misfortune" of living longer.

4. The replacement ratio method of determining retirement income assumes that the standard of living enjoyed during the years just prior to retirement will determine the standard of living during retirement. The expense method, on the other hand, focuses on the projected expenses that the retiree will have. As with the replacement ratio method, it is much easier to define the potential expenses for those clients who are at or near retirement. However,

if a younger client is involved, more speculative estimates of retirement expenses must be made (and periodically revised).

5. Retirees can assume that a lower percentage of their income will go toward paying taxes in the retirement years because, in many cases, there is an elimination or a reduction of certain taxes they previously had to pay. Tax advantages for the retiree include the elimination of the Social Security tax, an increased standard deduction depending on the retiree's age and filing status, the exclusion of all or part of Social Security benefit from gross income, reductions in state and local income taxes, and an increased ability to use deductible medical expenses.

6. Answers:

    a. Retirees face a variety of changes in spending patterns after retirement, and some of these changes will reduce their living expenses. These reductions often include the elimination of work-related expenses, the elimination of home-mortgage expenses, the elimination of dependent care, that is, child-rearing expenses, the elimination of long-term savings obligations, and a reduction in automotive expenditures.

    b. It is not all good news for retirees, however. Retirees also face several factors that tend to increase the amount of income they will need during the retirement period. These may include increases in long-term inflation, in medical expenses, in travel expenses, and in other retirement-related expenses. On the other hand, it is also true that retirees typically start to spend less later in their retirement when travel and other activities become more difficult to manage.

7. Answers:

    a. A defined-benefit plan provides a fixed predetermined benefit for the employee that has an uncertain cost to the employer. On the other hand, a defined-contribution plan has a predetermined cost to the employer but provides an uncertain benefit for the employee.

    b. Under a pension plan, the employer commits to making annual contributions to the plan, since the main purpose of the plan is to provide a retirement benefit. Under a profit-sharing plan, the employer retains the flexibility and can avoid funding the plan annually, at least for a number of years. Moreover, a profit-sharing plan is not necessarily intended to provide a retirement benefit as much as to provide tax deferral of present compensation. To this end, under certain profit-sharing plans, employees are permitted to withdraw funds after they have been in the plan for at least 2 years.

8. A defined-contribution plan may result in inadequate retirement income for a client if investment results are unfavorable. This is because the employer's obligation begins and ends with making the annual contribution. If plan investments are poor, the employee suffers the loss and may have inadequate retirement resources.

    In addition, a second problem with a defined-contribution plan is that contributions are based on participants' salaries for each year of their careers, rather than on their salaries at retirement as in most defined-benefit plans. Consequently, if inflation increases sharply in the years just prior to retirement, the chances of a participant achieving an adequate income-replacement ratio are diminished because most of the annual contributions would have been based on his salary paid prior to the inflationary spiral.

    Another instance where a defined contribution plan may provide inadequate retirement income occurs when a client joins a plan late in his or her career. In this situation, since the years to retirement are few, the plan may not provide enough time to accumulate an adequate amount of assets.

9. Two important factors should be kept in mind if a client has a profit-sharing plan. First, the advisor should closely monitor the funding of the plan. A common mistake is to assume that the employer is making scheduled payments to the plan when in actuality the employer is not contributing as expected because employer contributions are discretionary. Another common mistake is to assume that the employee is allowing the funds to accumulate for retirement when in actuality the employee is depleting the account by taking withdrawals.

    The second factor concerning profit-sharing plans is that the ability to withdraw funds prior to retirement under some profit-sharing plans opens up some interesting planning possibilities for the client and her advisor. For example, the client may want to gradually take money out while employed (starting after age 59½ to avoid the 10 percent penalty tax) to reposition assets or take advantage of an excellent investment opportunity. In addition, the client may want to prepay any debt that would carry over into retirement, such as prepaying a mortgage or reducing interest expenses on a major capital purchase.

10. Answers:

    a. A unit-benefit formula might read as follows: Each plan participant will receive a monthly pension commencing at the normal retirement age and paid in the form of a life annuity equal to 2 percent of final-average monthly salary multiplied by the participant's years of service. Normal retirement age in this plan is defined as the later of age 65 or 5 years of plan participation. Service is limited to a maximum of 30 years.

    b. A flat-percentage-of-earnings formula might read as follows: Each plan participant will receive a monthly pension commencing at the normal retirement age of 65 and paid in the form of a life annuity equal to 40 percent of the participant's final-average monthly salary. However, to receive the full benefit promised, the participant must have at least 25 years of service. If the participant has less service, the benefit is proportionately reduced.

11. A 401(k) plan allows employees to elect to defer current salary, which is contributed to the plan on a pretax basis. In addition to the salary deferral feature, a 401(k) plan can contain a traditional profit-sharing feature, an employer matching contribution feature, or both. The plan may even allow for employee after-tax contributions. This means the plan can be as simple as a stand-alone plan (salary deferrals only) or as complex as a plan that allows both pretax and after-tax employee contributions, employer matching contributions, and employer profit-sharing contributions. In today's market, many employers, even those that already have defined-benefit or money-purchase pension plans, opt to sponsor 401(k) plans.

12. One trap awaiting clients covered by nonqualified plans is that these plans have somewhat inflexible withdrawal provisions. For instance, distributions cannot be rolled over to an IRA. In addition, the client generally is not given a choice of distribution options at retirement. The options generally are quite limited, and the option desired typically must be selected (to avoid tax problems) at the time participation begins.

    A second trap awaiting clients covered by nonqualified plans is that promised benefits are typically subject to loss for a variety of reasons. For example, a nonqualified plan may contain a forfeiture provision stipulating that benefits will be forfeited if certain conditions are not met. In many circumstances, the client may be either unwilling or unable to meet his or her part of the commitment. A second way nonqualified benefits can be lost is if the employer sponsoring the plan goes bankrupt. Nonqualified plan funds are typically held as corporate assets that are subject to the claims of corporate creditors in bankruptcy.

A final insecurity associated with nonqualified plans is the threat of immediate taxation to the employee that would result in a lower overall retirement accumulation. For example, despite employer contentions to the contrary, some plans are construed by the IRS as providing an immediate economic benefit to the employee, or the employee may be deemed to be in constructive receipt of the income. In either case, the prefunded benefit will be taxable while the client is still employed and the advantages of tax deferral will be lost.

13. Answers:
    a. There are limitations on contributions to a traditional IRA. Any person under age 70½ who receives $5,000 (2012, indexed) in compensation (either salary or self-employment earned income) may make a $5,000 contribution to a traditional IRA. In addition, if a person is married, even if he or she does not work, that person can contribute $5,000 as long as the spouse's salary is at least $10,000 (then each spouse can make a $5,000 contribution).
    b. The contribution to a traditional IRA is only deductible if certain eligibility requirements are satisfied. The contribution will be deductible if neither the taxpayer nor the taxpayer's spouse is an active participant in any employer-maintained retirement plan. If the taxpayer is an active participant, then the contribution is deductible only if his modified adjusted gross income falls below prescribed limits (designed to approximate a middle-class income). If an individual is not an active participant, but his spouse is, then the contribution is deductible for the spouse who is not an active participant if the couple's income is less than a different higher income threshold.

14. Answers:

a. Contributions to a Roth IRA are not deductible.

b. Distributions from a Roth IRA are tax free as long as two requirements are satisfied. First, the distribution must be made more than 5 years after the Roth IRA was established. Second, the distribution must be made after one of the four following events has occurred:

- The participant has attained age 59½.
- The distribution is paid to a beneficiary because of the participant's death.
- The participant has become disabled.
- The withdrawal is made to pay qualified first-time homebuyer expenses.

15. Strategies that can be used to maximize a client's retirement income include the following:

a. trading down to a less expensive home. If a client can be persuaded to sell his or her home and relocate to a smaller, less expensive residence, the money made available from the transaction can be a valuable source of retirement income. This is very desirable from a financial perspective, because it enables retirees to capitalize on what for many of them is their single most important financial asset—their home. In addition, the Internal Revenue Code allows taxpayers to exclude up to $250,000 of gain ($500,000 on a joint return in most situations) from the sale or exchange of their homes if certain conditions are met.

b. obtaining a reverse mortgage. If a client would like to take some equity out of her home, but is reluctant to move to a less expensive one, an alternative that is available is a reverse mortgage. A reverse mortgage is a loan against an individual's home that requires no repayment as long as the individual continues to live in the home. In other words, a reverse mortgage is a strategy that allows a client to live in her home while withdrawing substantial amounts of money from its built-up equity. This money can be used for current needs, and there is no need to repay it. A reverse mortgage is typically available only when all of the owners are aged 62 or older and when the home is the principal residence. Also, the home must either have no debt or only a small debt that can be paid off with part of the reverse mortgage loan.

c. postretirement employment. A part-time job during retirement can be used to provide a client with extra cash. Many clients find that working on a scaled-back basis not only meets their financial needs but also helps them adapt psychologically to the changes that retirement brings. This is especially true for clients whose self-esteem and sense of self-worth were tied to their careers.

Chapter 7

Answers to Review Questions

1. An accurate asset inventory will indicate the composition and magnitude of the client's assets available for distribution. This data will help the client and advisor determine whether the assets are in the appropriate form for distribution and whether their total value is adequate to provide the desired distributions to the client's beneficiaries. Planning to convert the assets into the appropriate form and/or to accumulate additional wealth could follow.

2. An interview by a financial advisor gathering information for a client's estate plan may be an uncomfortable event for the client because he or she may feel uneasy talking about issues associated with death and personal family matters.

3. Answers:

    a. A life estate provides the life tenant with the right to possess and enjoy the property for a time period measured by the life of an individual (typically the life tenant). The life estate gives the life tenant the absolute right to possess, enjoy, and receive current income from the property until the life estate terminates.

    b. An estate for a term of years (or term interest) provides the current tenant with the right to possess, enjoy, and receive income from the property during a specified term. The interest of the current tenant terminates at the end of the specified term.

    c. A future interest in property is the current right to future enjoyment of the property. A future interest in property could either be vested or contingent on the occurrence of some future event. The future interest holder has no immediate right to use and enjoy the property. Two common types of future interest are a remainder interest and a reversionary interest. A remainder interest is an interest that takes effect immediately on the expiration of another interest in the same property, while a reversionary interest occurs when the current property owner transfers current possessory rights to another but retains the right to the return of the property at the end of the possessory term of the transferee.

4. Answers:

   a. A tenancy in common occurs when two or more individuals hold current possessory rights to property without survivorship rights. Such individuals, known as tenants in common, each hold an undivided interest in the property and may transfer their interests during their lifetimes or at their deaths. Both related and unrelated individuals may hold property by tenancy in common.

   b. A joint tenancy with right of survivorship occurs when two or more individuals hold property jointly with their survivors ultimately receiving the entire interest in the property. Both related and unrelated individuals may hold property jointly with rights of survivorship.

   Because this property interest transfers automatically at the death of a joint tenant to his or her surviving tenants, the property is not subject to disposition by a joint tenant at his or her death. Usually, a joint tenant may transfer his or her interest during life without the consent of the other joint tenants. Such a transfer will generally sever the joint tenancy and destroy the survivorship rights of the joint tenants.

   c. A tenancy by the entirety is a property interest restricted solely to spouses. It is joint ownership of the property by the spouses with rights of survivorship. A tenancy by the entirety creates a unique situation with respect to disposition of the property. Property is transferred automatically to the surviving spouse at the death of his or her spouse. Thus, the property is not subject to disposition by will of the deceased spouse. In addition, the property cannot be transferred during the lifetime of the spouses unless both tenants consent. Tenancy by the entirety is severed automatically upon divorce.

5. A general power of appointment gives the holder of the power broad authority to transfer the property subject to the power to virtually any recipient. On the other hand, a special power of

appointment typically limits to whom the holder of the power can transfer the property.

6. Answers:

   a. With some minor exceptions for rare circumstances, the requirements for a valid will are as follows:
      - The will must be in writing.
      - The will must be dated.
      - The testator (maker) of the will must have the legal capacity (that is, in terms of age and mental capacity) to make the will.
      - The testator of the will must sign the will at the end of the document, usually in the presence of witnesses.
      - A number of witnesses (generally two or three) must sign the will after the testator's signature. The witnesses are attesting that the signature of the testator is his or her true signature.

   b. A properly drafted will can accomplish the following objectives:
      - Direct the disposition of the client's probate assets.
      - Nominate the personal representative of the testator, known as the executor, who will handle the administration of the client's estate.
      - Nominate the guardians of any minor children of the testator.
      - Create testamentary trusts that will take effect at the testator's death to hold the property of the testator for the benefit of named beneficiaries.
      - Name the trustee of any trust created under the will.
      - Provide directions to the executor and/or trustees named in the will indicating how these fiduciaries will manage assets contained in the estate or testamentary trust. (The directions could be quite specific or provide broad powers to the fiduciaries.)
      - Provide directions for payment of the estate's taxes and expenses. (Care should be taken in

naming the components of the estate that will be responsible for taxes and expenses. Incorrect designation of the component obligated to pay such expenses could result in increased death taxes or inappropriately diminished shares of specific beneficiaries.)
- Establish the compensation of executors and/or trustees named in the will.

7. A conventional power of attorney authorizes the agent (otherwise known as an attorney-in-fact) to act on behalf of the principal with respect to the powers specifically enumerated in the document. The powers given the agent can be quite limited or very broad. However, no matter how limited or broad the powers, a conventional power becomes inoperative if the principal is incapacitated. A durable power of attorney is similar to a conventional power except that it does not become inoperative if the principal is incapacitated. Instead, it continues to operate during the incapacity of the principal when it is needed most.

8. The probate estate includes all assets passing by will or intestacy. Probate property is owned outright by the deceased and is not transferred by operation of law or contract. Probate technically means the process of proving the validity of the will. It begins when the original will is deposited in the court with jurisdiction over the deceased's estate. The probate court oversees the settlement of the estate, the distribution of probate property, appointment and supervision of fiduciaries, and settlement of disputes concerning the deceased's will. The probate court will ensure that probate property is distributed according to the terms of a valid will after all estate settlement costs are paid.

9. If an individual dies without a valid will, all probate property passes under the laws of intestate succession of the jurisdiction state. The intestate laws are deemed to replace the intent of the deceased individual in the distribution of his or her probate property. Distribution under these laws depends on which relatives survive the deceased. The deceased individual's spouse receives primary consideration and will receive the entire probate estate, if the deceased is not also survived by children or parents. If the deceased is survived by both a spouse and children, the surviving spouse and children will generally each receive 50 percent of the estate. The parents of a deceased individual will generally get a share only if the deceased individual is not also survived by

children. If the deceased individual is not survived by a spouse, children, or parents, the next closest surviving relatives will inherit.

10. Certain transfers are exempt from the gift tax base by statute. First, a transfer of property pursuant to a divorce or property settlement agreement is deemed to be for full and adequate consideration under some circumstances. Second, transfers directly to the provider of education or medical services on behalf of an individual are not taxable gifts to the recipient of the services. Finally, gifts that are disclaimed by the donee in a qualified disclaimer are not treated as taxable gifts.

11. The types of property includible in a deceased's gross estate are as follows:

    - property individually owned by the deceased at the time of death
    - (some portion of) property held jointly by the deceased at the time of death
    - the proceeds of any insurance on the deceased's life if either (1) incidents of ownership are held by the deceased within 3 years of death or (2) the proceeds are deemed payable to the estate
    - pension or IRA payments left to survivors
    - property subject to general powers of appointment held by the deceased at the time of death
    - property transferred by the deceased during his or her lifetime if he or she retained (1) a life interest in the property, (2) a reversionary interest valued greater than 5 percent of the property at the time of death, or (3) rights to revoke the transfer at the time of death

12. Answers:

    a. The GST tax was created to prevent the federal government from losing transfer tax revenue when individuals transfer property to a generation that is more than one generation below their own generation (for example, when grandparents make gifts of property to their grandchildren). In other words, the GST tax is designed to prevent people from finding a transfer tax loophole in the federal gift tax or estate tax.

    b. The GST tax applies to the following three types of transfers:

- It applies to a direct skip, which is an outright transfer during life or at death to a skip person. A skip person is an individual who is two generations or more younger than the transferor.
- It applies to a taxable termination, which occurs when an interest in property held in trust for a skip person is terminated by an individual's death, lapse of time, release of a power, or otherwise and the trust property is either held for or distributed to the skip person.
- It applies to a taxable distribution, which is any distribution from a trust to a skip person that is not a taxable termination or a direct skip.

13. A state inheritance tax is a tax imposed on a beneficiary's right to inherit property from a deceased person's estate, while a state estate tax is imposed on a deceased person's right to transfer or pass property to beneficiaries.

14. Answers:

    a. The nontax advantages from making lifetime gifts are as follows:

    - The donor can provide for the support, education, and welfare of the donee beneficiary.
    - The donor gets the pleasure of seeing the donee beneficiary enjoy the gift.
    - The donor avoids the publicity and administrative costs associated with a probate transfer at death.
    - The donated property is protected from the claims of the donor's creditors.

    b. The tax advantages from making lifetime gifts are as follows:

    - The gift tax annual exclusion for gifts of $13,000 (2012, as indexed for inflation) or less provides a complete loophole from federal transfer taxes. Each year any number of $13,000 gifts can be made by donors ($26,000 if their spouses join with them) to reduce their transfer tax bases.

- The gift tax is imposed on the value of the gift at the time a completed transfer is made. Thus, any posttransfer appreciation in the property avoids all transfer tax.
- The gift tax payable on gifts made more than 3 years prior to the donor's death is excluded from his or her estate tax base.
- The income produced by gifted property is shifted from the donor to the donee beneficiary for income tax purposes. In other words, lifetime gifting may be used to move taxable income from a high-bracket donor to a lower-bracket donee beneficiary. (This advantage is somewhat limited by special tax rules related to unearned income of children under age 18 by the so-called "kiddie tax" rules.)
- Unlimited qualifying transfers can be made between spouses without incurring gift taxes. Spouses can advantageously shift assets between themselves to meet the needs of the estate and financial plan of each spouse.

15. Answers:

   a. The UGMA and UTMA statutes are model laws that have been adopted in various forms in individual states. They permit the transfer of funds to a custodial account for the benefit of a minor. The custodian of a UGMA or a UGMA account manages the property under the rules provided by state law. There are restrictions on the type of property permissible as an investment for these purposes. The original UGMA model law has been expanded in many states to increase the types of permissible investments. In a majority of states, the newer UTMA model law has been adopted, and relatively few restrictions exist in these states on the permissible investments. A UGMA or a UGMA transfer is particularly favorable for smaller gifts because it provides for the protection of the assets without the expense of administering a trust. The provisions for distribution from a UGMA or UTMA are provided under the various state laws. Generally speaking, UGMA or UTMA funds can be accumulated during the minority of the donee beneficiary, but the custodial assets must be distributed to the beneficiary when he or she reaches the age specified in the relevant statute—generally 18 or 21. Some states allow a donor to select ages up to age 25.

b. A donor often wishes to make gifts to a minor in trust for the purpose of accumulation. If the trust provides for accumulation and does not currently benefit the minor beneficiary, the gift tax annual exclusion would normally be forfeited. Provisions of the law, however, permit the annual exclusion if current beneficial rights are given to the beneficiary. These rights, known as Crummey powers, provide the beneficiary with temporary withdrawal rights to the funds contributed to the trust. Under these rules, a gift to a trust will qualify for the annual exclusion if the beneficiary has the noncumulative, temporary (for example, 30 days) right to demand up to the annual exclusion amount from his or her share of the amount contributed to the trust by the donor.

16. Answers:

a. A transfer to a surviving spouse through an estate trust qualifies for the marital deduction. Under this arrangement, a deceased spouse leaves a life estate in trust to the surviving spouse. The surviving spouse's estate is the remainderperson of the trust. Income from the estate trust can either accumulate or be paid to the surviving spouse at the discretion of the trustee. Because the remainder interest is transferred to the surviving spouse's estate, the property will be included in the surviving spouse's gross estate, and a second-death estate tax may be payable at that time.

b. Another common marital-deduction trust is the power-of-appointment trust. This trust is designed to distribute income to the surviving spouse during his or her life and to provide the surviving spouse with a general power of appointment over the trust property. The general power of appointment may be exercisable by the surviving spouse in all events, or it may be exercisable only at the death of the surviving spouse. Because the surviving spouse has a general power of appointment over the trust property, it is included in his or her gross estate for federal tax purposes.

c. A special provision of the tax law provides for a marital deduction if qualifying terminable interest property (QTIP) is left to a surviving spouse. Under these rules, a terminable property interest can be transferred to a surviving spouse with the interest qualifying for the marital deduction. The QTIP deduction is available if the executor of the deceased (first to die) spouse elects QTIP treatment on the estate tax return. The QTIP trust can be funded by probate assets or other types of testamentary dispositions. The surviving spouse must have the right to all income annually from the QTIP trust for life. At the death of the surviving spouse, the QTIP election provides that the trust property will be included in the surviving spouse's gross estate.

17. The typical dispositive scheme for most married couples makes maximum use of the marital deduction. This occurs when all property is left to the surviving spouse either outright or in another manner that qualifies for the marital deduction. Because no estate tax is payable under these circumstances, the applicable credit amount that is available at the first spouse's death is wasted.

   However, the typical dispositive scheme can be altered to make maximum use of each spouse's applicable credit amount while also making optimal use of the marital deduction. This maximum estate tax shelter is accomplished by designing each spouse's estate and financial plan to transfer property to two separate trusts, an A or marital trust and a B or family trust. This two trust arrangement is commonly referred to as an AB trust arrangement. The AB trust arrangement is designed to operate as follows:

   - The A or marital trust is some form of marital-deduction trust. This trust receives assets in a manner that qualifies them for the federal estate tax marital deduction and provides for maximum use of these assets by the surviving spouse. The remainder of the assets transferred by the deceased are placed into the B or family trust.
   - The B or family trust is designed not to qualify for the marital deduction. Instead, the B trust may be funded with transfers valued at approximately the applicable exclusion amount of $5.12 million in 2012 and will be part of the individual's taxable estate since the transfers are not deductible under the marital deduction. However, the $5.12 million transferred to the B or family trust can be

sheltered from estate taxes by the applicable exclusion amount.

The AB trust arrangement makes maximum use of each spouse's applicable credit, and since the A or marital trust qualifies for the marital deduction and B or family trust is sheltered entirely by the applicable credit, no estate tax will be paid at the first spouse's death. Thus, the AB trust arrangement does not change the usual first-death tax results. However, the second-death taxes are reduced since the applicable credit amount is used at the time of the first death. Thus, the surviving spouse's estate is reduced in size by the amount of property transferred to the B or family trust at the first death of the two spouses.

Note that The Tax Relief Act of 2010 (TRA 2010) introduced a new idea into the estate tax system—portability in regard to use of a deceased spouse's unclaimed estate tax exemption. Portability allows a surviving spouse to use a predeceased spouse's unused applicable exclusion amount ($5.12 million in 2012), effectively doubling the amount that a married couple can pass to their beneficiaries free of tax. Thus, this will definitely help married couples who have failed to plan for their estates at all.

18. A charitable remainder trust can be employed to retain the current enjoyment of the property for the life of the donor client (or lives of the donor's family members) while providing income, gift, and estate tax advantages. The charitable remainder trust can be established during the donor client's lifetime or at his or her death. The charitable remainder trust permits the donor client to retain the current income for his or her use or the use of his or her family. The income from the trust's assets will be retained for a time period (usually measured by the life of the donor client or lives of selected family members) with the charitable institution holding the remainder interest. The current charitable deduction is measured by the present value of the remainder interest held by the charity. Thus, the donor client (or possibly members of the client's family) receives not only the current enjoyment of the trust property but also a current tax deduction, while the charity receives outright ownership of the property sometime in the future when the remainder interest is distributed by the trust.

19. Life insurance is generally used for estate enhancement by (1) younger clients, (2) clients with dependent family members, and (3) clients with small to moderate-sized estates. Clients in these

categories generally cite protection as their primary need for life insurance. They want to protect their families from the loss of future earnings needed for support. These clients are either in or are headed toward their peak earning years, and their families are relying on these future earnings to maintain their standard of living, educate the children, and accumulate retirement assets.

The death taxes facing younger clients with small to moderate-sized estates are relatively minor. The applicable credit amount and marital deduction will generally remove the danger of federal estate taxes for these individuals. Thus, estate liquidity is not their primary concern. Nonetheless, it is highly improbable that these clients can accumulate enough wealth to replace their future incomes. This is where life insurance plays a role. It is the perfect estate enhancement tool for replacing some or all of the lost earnings resulting from a client's premature death.

20. A revocable life insurance trust serves no estate tax planning purposes. Because the trust is revocable, the grantor insured is treated as the owner of the policy and the death proceeds will be included in his or her gross estate. The revocable life insurance trust is ordinarily used when a specific, perhaps temporary, protection need exists.

Chapter 8

Answers to Review Questions

1. The Social Security program and Part A of Medicare are financed through a system of payroll and self-employment taxes paid by all persons covered under the programs. In addition, employers of covered persons are also taxed. (These taxes are often referred to as FICA taxes because they are imposed under the Federal Insurance Contributions Act (FICA).)

   In 2012, an employee and his employer pay a tax of 6.2 percent each on the first $110,100 of the employee's wages for Social Security. The employee and employer also pay the Medicare tax rate of 1.45 percent on employee wages. The tax rates are currently scheduled to remain the same after 2012, but the wage base is adjusted annually for changes in the national level of wages.

Part B of Medicare if financed by a combination of monthly premiums paid by persons eligible for benefits and contributions from the federal government.

2. Answers:
    a. Evelyn does not meet the first test, as she has not earned credit for 40 quarters. However, she does qualify as fully insured under the second test. Evelyn is 38 in 2012, so she was born in 1974. She was age 21 in 1995, so would require 15 quarters from 1996 to 2011 to be fully insured, and she has 28 quarters.
    b. Because Evelyn is fully insured, she is also currently insured.
    c. Although Evelyn is fully insured, she is not disability insured because she does not have the minimum number of quarters within a recent time period.

3. A worker who is fully insured under Social Security is eligible to receive monthly retirement benefits as early as age 62. However, the election to receive benefits prior to the full retirement age results in a permanently reduced benefit. Starting with workers born after 1937, the age at which full benefits are payable will increase in gradual steps from age 65 to age 67. Workers born in 1960 or later will wait until age 67 for their full retirement benefits.

4. If the deceased worker was either fully or currently insured at the time of death, the following categories of persons are eligible for survivor benefits:

    - dependent, unmarried children under age 18. This child's benefit will continue until age 19 as long as a child is a full-time student in elementary or secondary school. In addition, disabled children of any age are eligible for benefits as long as they were disabled before reaching age 22.
    - a spouse (including a divorced spouse) of any age if the spouse is caring for at least one child of the deceased worker who is (1) under age 16 or (2) disabled and entitled to a child's benefit.

If the deceased worker was fully insured at the time of death, the following categories of persons are also eligible for survivor benefits:

- a widow or widower aged 60 or older. However, benefits are reduced if taken prior to full retirement age. This benefit is also payable to a divorced spouse if the marriage lasted at least 10 years. The widow's or widower's benefit is payable to a disabled spouse at age 50 as long as the disability commenced no more than 7 years after the (1) worker's death or (2) end of the year in which entitlement to a mother's or father's benefit ceased.
- a parent aged 62 or over who was a dependent of the deceased worker at the time of death

5. The definition of disability requires a mental or physical impairment that prevents the worker from engaging in any substantial gainful employment. The disability must also have lasted (or be expected to last) at least 12 months or be expected to result in death. A more liberal definition of disability applies to blind workers who are aged 55 or older. They are considered disabled if they are unable to perform work that requires skills or abilities comparable to those required by the work they regularly performed before reaching age 55 or becoming blind, if later.

6. Answers:

   a. The primary insurance amount (PIA) is the amount a worker receives if he or she retires at full retirement age or becomes disabled, and it is the amount on which benefits for family members are based. If a worker is retired or disabled, benefits are paid to family members as follows:

    - The spouse at full retirement age, or a spouse at any age caring for a disabled child or a child under 16 receives 50 percent of the worker's PIA.
    - Each child under 18 or disabled receives 50 percent of the worker's PIA.

   If a worker dies, benefits are paid to family members as follows:

    - The spouse at full retirement age receives 100 percent of the worker's PIA.
    - A spouse at any age caring for a disabled child or a child under 16 receives 75 percent of the worker's PIA.
    - Each child under 18 or disabled receives 75 percent of the worker's PIA.

- A sole dependent parent receives 82.5 percent, while two dependent parents receive 75 percent each.

However, the full benefits described above may not be payable because of a limitation imposed on the total benefits that may be paid to a family.

b. If the total amount of benefits payable to family members exceeds the family maximum, the worker's benefit (in the case of retirement and disability) is not affected, but the benefits of other family members are reduced proportionately.

7. If a worker elects to receive retirement benefits prior to full retirement age, benefits are permanently reduced by 5/9 of one percent each of the first 36 months that the early retirement precedes full retirement age and 5/12 of one percent for each month in excess of 36. Workers who delay applying for benefits until after full retirement age are eligible for an increased benefit for each month of late retirement until age 70.

8. Beneficiaries under full retirement age are allowed earnings of up to $14,640 in 2012, and this figure is subject to annual indexing for later years. If a beneficiary earns more than this amount, then her Social Security benefit is reduced by $1 for each $2 of excess earnings. There is one exception to the test: The reduction is $1 for every $3 of earnings in excess of $38,880 (in 2012) in the calendar year a worker attains the full retirement age, for earnings in months prior to such age attainment.

9. Social Security benefits are increased automatically each January if there was an increase in the CPI for the one-year period ending in the third quarter of the prior year. The increase is the same as the increase in the CPI since the last cost-of-living adjustment, rounded to the nearest 0.1 percent.

10. Answers:

    a. Hospital Benefits. Part A pays for inpatient hospital services for up to 90 days in each benefit period (also referred to as a spell of illness). A benefit period begins the first time a Medicare recipient is hospitalized and ends only after the recipient has been out of a hospital or skilled-nursing facility for 60 consecutive days. A subsequent hospitalization then begins a new benefit period.

Skilled-Nursing Facility Benefits. In many cases, a patient may no longer require continuous hospital care but may not be well enough to go home. Consequently, Part A provides benefits for care in a skilled-nursing facility if a physician certifies that skilled-nursing care or rehabilitative services are needed for a condition that was treated in a hospital within the last 30 days. In addition, the prior hospitalization must have lasted at least 3 days. Benefits are paid in full for 20 days in each benefit period and for an additional 80 days with a daily co-payment charge.

Home Health Care Benefits. If a patient can be treated at home for a medical condition, Medicare will pay the full cost for an unlimited number of home visits by a home health agency. To receive these benefits, a person must be confined at home and be treated under a home health plan set up by a physician.

Hospice Benefits. Hospice benefits are available under Part A of Medicare for beneficiaries who are certified as being terminally ill with a life expectancy of 6 months or less.

b. Hospital Benefits. In each benefit period, covered hospital expenses are paid in full for 60 days, subject to an initial deductible ($1,156 in 2012). This deductible is adjusted annually to reflect increasing hospital costs. Benefits for an additional 30 days of hospitalization are also provided in each benefit period, but the patient must pay a daily co-payment ($289 in 2012) equal to 25 percent of the initial deductible amount. Each recipient also has a lifetime reserve of 60 additional days that may be used if the regular 90 days of benefits have been exhausted. However, once a reserve day is used, it cannot be restored for use in future benefit periods. When using reserve days, patients must pay a daily co-payment ($578 in 2012) equal to 50 percent of the initial deductible amount.

Skilled-Nursing Facility Benefits. Benefits are paid in full for 20 days in each benefit period and for an additional

80 days with a daily co-payment ($144.50 in 2012) that is equal to 12.5 percent of the initial hospital deductible.

Home Health Care Benefits. There is no charge for these benefits other than a required 20 percent co-payment for the cost of such durable medical equipment as oxygen tanks and hospital beds.

Hospice Benefits. There are modest co-payments for some services.

c. Exclusions under Part A of Medicare include the following:

- services outside the United States and its territories or possessions. However, there are a few exceptions to this rule for qualified Mexican and Canadian hospitals.
- elective luxury services such as private rooms or televisions
- hospitalization for services not necessary for the treatment of an illness or injury such as custodial care or elective cosmetic surgery
- services performed in a federal facility such as a veterans' hospital
- services covered under workers' compensation

In addition to the exclusions, there are times when Medicare will act as the secondary payer of benefits.

11. Answers:

a. Part B of Medicare provides benefits for most medical expenses not covered under Part A. These can include physicians' and surgeons' fees, diagnostic tests, physical therapy, drugs and biologicals that cannot be self-administered, radiation therapy, medical supplies, rental of medical equipment, prosthetic devices, ambulance service, mammograms and Pap smears, diabetes glucose monitoring and education, colorectal cancer screening, bone mass measurement, prostate cancer screening, pneumococcal vaccine and its administration, dilated eye examinations when at risk for glaucoma, and home health care services as described for Part A when a person does not have Part A coverage or when Part A benefits are not applicable.

b. A few charges are paid in full without any cost sharing. These include (1) home health services, (2) pneumococcal vaccine and its administration, (3) certain surgical procedures that are performed on an outpatient basis in lieu of hospitalization, (4) diagnostic preadmission tests performed on an outpatient basis within 7 days prior to hospitalization, (5) mammograms, and (6) Pap smears.

For other charges, there is a $140 calendar-year deductible (for 2012). When it is satisfied, Part B pays 80 percent of approved charges for most covered medical expenses other than charges for mental health care. Medicare pays only 50 percent of approved charges for mental health care.

c. A list of exclusions includes most drugs and biologicals that can be self-administered, most routine examinations, routine foot care, most immunizations, most cosmetic surgery, most dental care, custodial care, eyeglasses, hearing aids, and orthopedic shoes.

12. Medicare Advantage plans include HMOs as previously allowed, PPOs, PSOs, private fee-for-service plans, private contracts with physicians, and medical savings accounts. These plans must provide all benefits available under Parts A and B. They may include additional benefits as part of the basic plan or for an additional fee.

13. Medicare Part D is a voluntary prescription drug benefit available to all Medicare beneficiaries enrolled in either Part A or Part B, or enrolled in various Medicare Advantage plans. No one can be denied coverage because of their income or health reasons. One type of plan is for persons enrolled in most Medicare Advantage plans. The other type is a stand-alone plan, available to those enrolled in traditional Medicare or in Medicare Advantage plans that do not offer drug coverages. Medicare Part D provides for a standard plan with a deductible and coinsurance levels. Above a certain level, the beneficiary enters a coverage gap ("doughnut hole") in which they pay all costs out-of-pocket. Above the coverage gap, beneficiaries pay either 5 percent of drug costs or small co-payments.

14. Besides basic benefits, Congress mandated several other features for Medigap insurance including a 6-month open enrollment period, limited preexisting-conditions exclusions, prohibition of the

sale of duplicate coverage, increased individual loss ratios, and guaranteed renewability.

15. Persons aged 65 or older may buy any available Medigap policy, regardless of health status, at any time during the 6-month period after initial enrollment for Medicare Part B benefits. If a person initially elects a managed care option in lieu of regular Medicare benefits, the person will be eligible to purchase a Medigap policy, without evidence of insurability, if he or she leaves the managed care option during the first 12 months of coverage and returns to regular Medicare benefits. Similarly, a person who drops a Medigap policy and elects a managed care option can regain the Medigap coverage if he or she decides to drop the managed care option during the first 12 months of coverage. Also, a person can obtain a Medigap policy on a guaranteed-issue basis because an employer-provided plan that supplements Medicare terminates, because a Medicare Advantage plan no longer provides coverage, or because the person loses eligibility by moving out of the plan's service area.

APPENDIX B: BIBLIOGRAPHY

The most recent editions of the following American College texts provide a more in-depth treatment of many of the topics covered in the major planning areas. These books can be purchased online from The American College Website at theamericancollege.edu.

The Financial Planning Process

- *Readings in Financial Planning*
- *Financial Planning Applications*

Insurance Planning and Risk Management

- *Fundamentals of Insurance for Financial Planning*
- *Individual Medical Expense Insurance*
- *Meeting the Financial Need of Long-Term Care*
- *McGill's Life Insurance*
- *McGill's Legal Aspects of Life Insurance*
- *Disability Income Insurance: The Unique Risk*

Employee Benefits Planning

- *Group Benefits: Basic Concepts and Alternatives*
- *Executive Compensation*

Investment Planning

- *Fundamentals of Investments for Financial Planning*
- *Mutual Funds: Analysis, Allocation, and Performance Evaluation*

Income Tax Planning

- *Fundamentals of Income Taxation*

Retirement Planning

- *Planning for Retirement Needs*
- *Financial Decision Making at Retirement*

Estate Planning

- *Fundamentals of Estate Planning*
- *Estate Planning Applications*

APPENDIX C: RISK IDENTIFICATION QUESTIONNAIRE

(Individual Form)

_____
(Name)

_____
(Mailing Address)

_____

_____

_____
(Phone Number)

_____
(E-Mail Address)

Real Property

REAL PROPERTY

Address of principal residence _____
_____

This is a single family dwelling _____ duplex _____ apartment unit _____ condominium _____
other (describe) _____

Address of all additional locations:

Seasonal residence _____
Farm _____
Income property _____
Vacant land _____
Other property interests _____

Property Owned	**Principal Residence**	**Other (identify)**	
Residence—square ft.			
Number of stories			
Type of construction			
Year built			
Original building cost			
Date purchased			
Purchase price			
Actual cash value			
Replacement cost (excl. land value)			
Current mortgage			

Describe detached garage or other buildings on the same premises.
_____

If any of these properties were rented rather than owned, what amount of rent would probably be charged? _____

If any occupied property would become untenantable because of damage or destruction, what monthly expenses over and above current living expenses would be incurred? _____
_____

Provide a copy of the latest appraised value excluding land or property. _____

Appendix C: Risk Identification Questionnaire

C.3

Property Rented

Single family dwelling _____ duplex _____ apartment _____

Monthly rent _____

Lease termination date _____

If premise becomes untenantable because of damage or destruction, does lease require continuation of rent?
_____

Income Property	**Location 1**	**Other**
Number of units		
Type of commercial use		
Rental income—annual		
Monthly rates		

If all leases could be cancelled and rewritten today, what change would there be in annual rental income and rate per unit? _____

Land	**Farm**	**Vacant Land**
Number of acres		

General

Occupation and other business pursuits (describe duties) _____
_____

Amount of largest personal check likely to be drawn _____

Number of credit cards _____ Number of fund transfer cards _____

Number of full-time servants _____ part-time _____

Number of caretakers or other household employees _____

Personal Property

PERSONAL PROPERTY

Estimated Value of	Principal Residence		Secondary Residence	
	Actual Cash Value	Replacement Cost	Actual Cash Value	Replacement Cost
a. Silverware, pewter				
b. Linens (including dining and bedroom)				
c. Clothing (men's, women's, children's)				
d. Rugs (including floor coverings and draperies)				
e. Books				
f. Musical instruments (including pianos)				
g. Television sets, radios, record players, and records				
h. Paintings, etchings, pictures and other objects of art				
i. China, glassware (including bric-a-brac)				
j. Cameras, photographic equipment				
k. Golf, hunting, fishing, and other sports equipment				
l. Refrigerators, washing machines, stoves, electrical appliances, and other kitchen equipment				
m. Bedding (including blankets, comforters, covers, pillows, mattresses, and springs)				
n. Furniture (including tables, chairs, sofas, desks, beds, chests, lamps, mirrors, and clocks)				
o. Business property				
p. All other personal property (including wines, liquors, foodstuffs, garden and lawn tools and equipment; trunks, traveling bags; children's playthings; and miscellaneous articles in basement and attic)				
Total Estimated Value				

Appendix C: Risk Identification Questionnaire

C.5

Special Items

Jewelry and watches:

    a. Describe each item _____

    b. Original cost of each _____

    c. Appraised value (obtain appraisal) _____

    d. Where kept (safe-deposit box) _____

Furs:

    a. Describe each article of fur _____

    b. Original cost of each _____

    c. Appraised value (obtain appraisal) _____

    d. Where stored (limit of liability per receipt) _____

Describe and value other items of unusual value:

    a. Stamp collections _____

    b. Fine arts _____

    c. Paintings _____

    d. Antiques _____

    e. Securities _____

Boats or marine equipment:

    a. Length and type of boat _____

    b. Size of motor _____

Miscellaneous Items

Dogs, saddle horses, and other pets (pedigreed) _____

Contents of barns, sheds, and other outbuildings _____

Value of children's property away at school _____

Airplanes, motorcycles, and motorized scooters _____

Location, nature, and value of property in storage warehouses: furs in storage, sports equipment at clubs, silver in safe-deposit vaults, etc. _____

Cash on hand _____

Automobiles

	#1	#2	#3
Year and make			
Body style/model			
Identification number			
Name of registered owner			
Purchase date (new/used)			
Purchase price			
Actual cash value (current)			
Use of automobile			
Distance to work			
Where garaged (if other than principal residence)			
Trailers—Type			
Weight			
Axles			

Describe all recreational vehicles _____

_____

Do you ever rent an automobile? _____ Length of typical rental period _____

Describe your use of company-owned vehicles _____

_____

Appendix C: Risk Identification Questionnaire

PREMATURE DEATH

	If You Die	If Spouse Dies
Lump-Sum Cash Needs of the Survivor(s)		
Cleanup fund. Includes unpaid last illness expenses, burial costs, federal and state taxes, probate costs, and other unpaid bills or debts	$	$
Mortgage. The remaining balance, (Assumes that preference is to pay off mortgage. If not, mortgage payments should be included in income needs.)	$	$
Education fund. Estimated present value of future costs to educate children	$	$
Emergency fund. Used for unexpected expenses not readily payable from current income	$	$
Other	$	$
Totals	$	$

Income Needs of the Survivor(s)

Level of income desired for each category (based on current purchasing power)

Survivors

	If You Die	If Spouse Dies
Lifetime monthly income to surviving spouse	$	$
Additional monthly income to family during child-raising years (dependency period)	$	$
Monthly income during first 2 years after death (readjustment period)	$	$

DISABILITY INCOME

	You	Spouse
Estimated monthly income needed if disability occurs today	$	$

MEDICAL EXPENSES

	For You and/or Your Family
Estimated cost of major illness requiring extended hospitalization and physician care	$

LONG-TERM CARE EXPENSES

Estimated cost of long-term care expenses	$

RETIREMENT INCOME

Desired monthly income at retirement	$

GLOSSARY

above-the-line deductions • deductions taken from gross income in determining adjusted gross income

accidental death and dismemberment (AD&D) insurance • insurance that pays benefits if an employee dies accidentally or suffers certain types of injuries. Coverage is commonly provided as a rider to a group life insurance contract but may also be provided through a separate group insurance contract.

accrual method • a tax accounting method that C corporations typically use. Under this method, income is accounted for when the right to receive it comes into being, that is, when all the events that determine the right have occurred. It is not the actual receipt but the right to receive that governs.

actual cash value • replacement cost less a reduction for depreciation and/or obsolescence

adjusted gross income (AGI) • for income tax purposes, gross income minus all allowable above-the-line deductions. It is an intermediate calculation that is made in the process of determining an individual's income tax liability for a given year.

advance medical directives • durable power of attorney for health care and living wills

adverse selection • the tendency of persons with a higher-than-average chance of loss to seek insurance at standard (average) rates. Because this is selection against the insurer, it will result in higher-than-expected losses if it is not controlled by underwriting.

agency bonds • bonds issued by federal agencies or organizations, such as the Tennessee Valley Authority. They are not direct obligations of the U.S. Treasury, and thus they provide investors with returns greater than that available on U.S. Treasury bonds, although the difference in return is quite small.

alternative minimum tax (AMT) • a separate and parallel method of calculating income tax liability. The reason for using this method is to prevent the taxpayer from reducing his or her tax liability below reasonable levels through the use of certain tax benefits targeted by the AMT rules.

allocation formula • a formula used to determine the amount of profits distributed to each participant in a profit-sharing plan. Allocation formulas can divide the profit-sharing "pie" to favor employees with higher salaries and longer service.

annual exclusion • see *gift tax annual exclusion*.

applicable credit amount • a credit to which the estate of every individual is entitled, which can be directly applied against the gift or estate tax

applicable exclusion amount • equivalent value of an individual's property offset by the applicable credit amount in estate calculations

approximate yield • a method that provides the investor with a quick approximation of an investment's internal rate of return. It is found by using the following formula:

$$\text{before-tax approximate yield} = \frac{\text{annual income} + \frac{\text{future price} - \text{current price}}{\text{number of years}}}{\text{future price} + \text{current price}}$$

asset allocation • the principal method of portfolio management by financial planners, based on the idea of dividing wealth among different types of assets

asset allocation models • portfolio recommendations developed by financial advisors to divide wealth among different types of assets. The emphasis is on the different categories of assets and the percentage to be placed in each category. A person's level of risk tolerance needs to be known to properly determine both the categories and the appropriate percentages.

asset selection • the step in the investment planning process that follows the development of asset allocation models. This occurs when specific assets are recommended and purchased.

attorney-in-fact • someone who is authorized to act as an agent for another under a power of attorney, which may be general or limited in scope

baby boom generation • the generation of people born between 1946 and 1964

basic benefits • the core of specified benefits that must be included in all Medigap insurance plans. These basic benefits are designed to supplement the Medicare coverage for hospitalization, medical expenses, and blood.

below-the-line deductions • deductions taken from adjusted gross income in determining taxable income

beneficial interest • the right to use, possess or enjoy property and to derive income from the property. Also known as *equitable interest.*

benefit period • in Medicare, also called a "spell of illness;" the benefit period begins upon the first day of a Medicare beneficiary's hospitalization and ends 60 days after release from the hospital or skilled-nursing facility.

blackout period • the period of time from whenever the youngest child of a deceased worker reaches age 16 (or is no longer disabled in certain cases) until the surviving spouse is aged 60. It is called the blackout period because the surviving spouse of a deceased worker is not eligible for monthly benefits during this time.

business (default) risk • risk that is based on the degree to which a firm's performance is subject to all potential risk factors such as a change in consumer preference away from a particular good or service, ineffective management, law change, or foreign competition. Because of the impact of these risk factors, some firms will be unable to repay bond principal or make interest payments on a timely basis. Because every firm has its own set of risk factors and degree of exposure, business risk is unique for each firm.

business expense • for income tax purposes, an expense paid or incurred during the taxable year in carrying on any existing trade or business. This type of expense is allowable as a deduction to an individual taxpayer.

buy-up plan • a benefit plan under which a covered person can purchase additional coverage at his or her own expense

C corporation • a regular corporation that is treated as a separate taxable entity, distinct and apart from the owners of its stock. The result is that a C corporation must compute its own income and deductions, file its own tax return, and pay its own tax at the applicable corporate rates.

cafeteria plans • flexible benefit plans that allow employees to purchase additional benefits on a payroll-deduction basis. Under these plans, employees can design their own benefit packages by purchasing benefits with a prespecified amount of employer dollars from a number of available options.

capital appreciation • one of two main sources of investment returns, it is an increase in the market value of an investment asset. The appreciation is the asset value above the cost basis of the asset.

capital assets • an asset generally owned to contribute to a business's ability to generate profit over a long term, such as property or large items of equipment

capital gain • income that is realized through the sale or exchange of a capital asset. A capital asset is any property the taxpayer holds other than property held for sale, or intellectual or artistic property the taxpayer creates.

cash-balance pension plan • a defined-benefit plan that is designed to look like a defined-contribution plan. As a defined-benefit plan, it has some level of funding flexibility, but the employer is ultimately responsible for making the contributions necessary to pay promised benefits.

cash-basis method • a tax accounting method that reflects income actually received during the taxable year. The one exception is the constructive receipt doctrine that is designed to prevent taxpayers from unilaterally determining the tax year when an item of income is received by them for federal income tax purposes. Almost all individual taxpayers who do not own a trade or business use this method of accounting.

cash equivalents • instruments that either have no specified maturity date or have one that is one year or less in the future. Investments in this category often provide only a modest current income and typically have little or no potential for capital appreciation. They usually are of such high liquidity and safety that they are virtually as good as cash.

certificate of deposit (CD) • deposits for a specified period such as 3, 6, or 12 months that pay a predetermined interest rate. Most are issued by commercial banks and are normally insured up to $250,000 by the Federal Deposit Insurance Corporation (FDIC).

charitable lead trust • a type of trust established to provide a charity with a current term income interest. At the end of the term period, the property either reverts to the donor or passes to a member of the donor's family. The donor gets an immediate income and gift or estate tax deduction for the present value of the lead income interest donated to the charity.

charitable remainder trust • a trust designed to take advantage of the tax benefits provided by charitable contributions while retaining the donor's use or enjoyment of the property. A charitable remainder trust permits the donor to retain the current income for himself or herself or for his or her family. The income will be retained for a time period (measured by the life of the donor or lives of selected family members) with a charitable institution holding the remainder interest. The current charitable deduction is measured by the present value of the remainder interest held by the charity.

closed-end investment company • an investment company that issues a given number of shares at its formation. These shares are traded in the stock markets in exactly the same manner as those of traditional corporations. That is, the forces of demand and supply for the stock determine the share price. Rarely if ever does this type of investment company issue additional shares.

COBRA • the Consolidated Omnibus Budget Reconciliation Act of 1985 (COBRA). This act requires that group health plans allow employees and dependents covered under the plans to elect to have their current health insurance coverage extended at group rates for up to 36 months following a qualifying event that results in a loss of coverage. The act applies only to employers with 20 or more full-time employees.

collision • an automobile insurance term that refers to the upset of an auto or its impact with another vehicle or object

Glossary.4

community property • property acquired during marriage in which both husband and wife have an undivided one-half interest. Not more than one-half can be disposed of by either party individually by will. There are now nine community-property states for federal tax law purposes: AZ, CA, ID, LA, NM, NV, TX, WA, and WI.

compound interest • interest earned on interest as a result of reinvesting one period's income to earn additional income during the next period

comprehensive approach • the approach to financial planning that occurs when an advisor follows the financial planning process to develop a comprehensive financial plan that solves a client's financial problems. The plan considers all aspects of a client's financial position, which typically includes financial problems from all the major planning areas. In addition, the plan usually encompasses several integrated and coordinated planning strategies that can be used to help solve the client's problems and achieve his or her goals.

constructive receipt doctrine • a doctrine stating that a cash-basis taxpayer is deemed to have received income for tax purposes when it is either credited to the taxpayer's account, set apart for the taxpayer, or otherwise made available to be taken into the taxpayer's possession. It is important to know, however, that if there is any condition or restriction that limits the taxpayer's right to receive the income, the doctrine of constructive receipt will not apply.

Consumer Price Index (CPI) • the index that measures the change in consumer prices as determined by a monthly survey of the U.S. Bureau of Labor Statistics. It is also referred to as the cost-of-living index.

conventional power of attorney • a general power of attorney that authorizes another to act on behalf of the principal. However, no matter how limited or broad the power, it becomes inoperative if the principal is incapacitated.

conversion provision • a provision found in term life insurance that allows the policyowner insured to replace the term coverage with (permanent) whole life insurance without having to show evidence of insurability

coordination of benefits (COB) provision • a provision in most group medical expense plans under which priorities are established for the payment of benefits if an individual is covered under more than one plan

cost-of-living adjustment (COLA) • automatic annual increase in Social Security benefits based upon increases in the Consumer Price Index for Urban Wage Earners and Clerical Workers (CPI-W)

credit estate tax • a tax formerly imposed by states to take full advantage of the amount allowed as a credit against the federal estate tax. It is also referred to as a sponge, slack, or gap tax. The credit was phased out and then eliminated in 2005.

Crummey powers • temporary rights granted to the beneficiaries of an irrevocable trust that allow them to demand all or a portion of the grantor's contributions to the trust. With these temporary withdrawal rights given to the beneficiaries, gifts (contributions) to the trust qualify for the gift tax annual exclusion.

current assumption whole life • nonpar whole life policies under which premium rates or cash values are redetermined periodically based on current assumptions as to mortality, interest, and expenses

current yield • perhaps the most widely used method for measuring an investment's return. It is calculated by dividing an investment's current annual income by its current market price. This calculation provides the investor with a before-tax current yield. To calculate an after-tax current yield, the investor's current annual income is reduced by his or her marginal rate of tax. The major shortcoming of the current yield is that it fails to look beyond the present moment.

currently insured • an insured status under Social Security. This status requires a person to have credit for at least six quarters of coverage out of the 13 quarter period ending with the quarter in which death occurs.

deceased spousal unused exclusion amount (DSUEA) • under TRA 2010, a "portability" provision allows a decedent's unused exclusion amount to be utilized by the surviving spouse at his/her death. The DSUEA is the amount of the unused exclusion.

deduction floor • one common way in which the law limits deductions. A taxpayer is allowed to deduct items that are subject to the floor, but only to the extent those items exceed a specified percentage of income (which is, in most cases, adjusted gross income).

deduction • for income tax purposes, an item of expense (not an item of receipt) that reduces the amount of income that is subject to tax

defensive stocks • stocks that are more stable than average and provide a safe return on an investor's money. When the stock market is weak, defensive stocks tend to decline less than the overall market.

deferred annuities • annuities that begin to pay periodic benefits at a specified future time. They can be purchased with a single premium or on an installment premium basis. A deferred life annuity provides a tool for accumulating financial resources before retirement.

defined-benefit plan • a retirement plan that specifies the benefits that each employee receives at retirement. The employer is responsible for making the contributions necessary to pay the promised benefits. In other words, this type of plan provides a fixed predetermined benefit for each of the employees but has an uncertain cost for the employer.

defined-benefit pension plan • a retirement plan that specifies the benefits that each employee receives at retirement, based on a benefit formula. Employers must make minimum funding to this plan annually and employees may be subject to vesting schedules. See *defined-benefit plan*.

defined-contribution medical expense plan • a type of medical expense plan under which an employer makes a fixed contribution with which an employee can purchase his or her own coverage. This practice enables an employer to control costs because the amount of the contribution can remain level from year to year or change at any rate the employer chooses.

defined-contribution plan • a retirement plan in which employer contributions are allocated to the participants' accounts. The participants' benefits are based on their account balances, which consist of the employer's contributions and investment experience. In other words, this type of plan involves a predetermined cost for the employer but provides uncertain benefits for the employees.

dental insurance • insurance that may be limited to specific types of dental expenses or broad enough to cover virtually all dental expenses. In addition, coverage can be obtained from various types of providers, and benefits can be in the form of either services or cash payments.

dependency exemption • an exemption that an individual taxpayer is allowed to claim for his or her support of a dependent. There are strict rules regarding whom a taxpayer may claim as a dependent and under what circumstances. The exemption amount changes annually by way of an inflation adjustment.

dependent life insurance • group life insurance on the lives of eligible dependents of persons covered under a group life plan. Amounts of coverage are usually limited, and the employee is automatically the beneficiary.

depreciation • a function of the age of an asset, its use, its condition at the time of loss, and any other factor causing deterioration. In addition, anything that causes the property to become obsolete is also included. Depreciation as a factor in measuring actual cash value differs from depreciation in an accounting sense.

depreciation deduction • the most important noncash deduction. It permits a taxpayer to recover for tax purposes the cost of certain property by allowing the taxpayer to deduct a specified portion of the cost of the property each year against the taxpayer's income.

direct skip • one of the three different types of transfers that the generation-skipping transfer tax applies to. A direct skip can be an outright transfer during life or at death to a skip person (an individual who is two generations or more younger than the transferor) or a transfer in trust for the benefit of a skip person.

disability income insurance • insurance that partially replaces the income of a person unable to work because of disability resulting from an accident or illness. It is most efficiently used in dealing with the possibility of a person experiencing a long-term, total disability.

disability insured • an insured status under Social Security. This status requires that a worker (1) be fully insured and (2) have a minimum amount of work under Social Security within a recent period.

diversification • the technique of spreading an investment portfolio over different industries, companies, and investment types for the purpose of reducing risk

dollar cost averaging • a method that requires the investment of a fixed amount of dollars at specified time intervals. Investing a fixed amount of dollars at set intervals means that the investor buys more shares when prices are low and fewer shares when prices are high. However, the overall cost of investing using dollar cost averaging is lower than it would be if a constant number of shares were bought at set intervals.

durable power of attorney for health care • a durable power of attorney that gives authority to another to make medical decisions about the principal's care

durable power of attorney • an estate planning tool with which a principal grants powers with respect to his or her property or health to an agent. A durable power of attorney remains valid and operative despite any subsequent incapacity of the principal.

doughnut hole • in Medicare Part D prescription drug programs, the coverage gap in which no drug benefits are provided. Above the doughnut hole. drug plans generally pay approximately 95 percent of the cost of drugs.

earnings test • the process for determining whether income benefits of Social Security beneficiaries who are under full retirement age should be reduced because of wages that exceed a specified level. The earnings threshold at which benefits are reduced changes annually on the basis of changes in national wage levels.

economic benefit doctrine • a doctrine stating that a taxpayer must pay tax whenever an economic benefit has been conferred on him or her regardless of whether the taxpayer has actually received any cash or property

effective marginal tax rate • for an upper income taxpayer this rate depends on the level of his or her adjusted gross income, the amount of his or her itemized deductions, and the number of personal and/or dependency exemptions that he or she can claim. It should be noted that an upper income taxpayer's effective marginal tax rate may be higher than his or her statutory marginal rate. This can happen as a result of the phaseout rules that reduce the taxpayer's itemized deductions and personal and/or dependency exemption amounts as his or her adjusted gross income increases.

effective tax rate • the rate at which the individual would be taxed if his or her taxable income were taxed at a constant rate rather than progressively. This rate is computed by determining what percentage the taxpayer's tax liability is of his or her total taxable income.

elimination (waiting) period • a period of time that a person must be disabled before benefits commence under disability income insurance, Social Security disability benefits, and workers compensation insurance

employee benefits • all benefits and services, other than wages for time worked, that employees receive in whole or in part from their employers. A narrower definition includes only employer-provided benefits for situations involving death, accident, sickness, retirement, or unemployment.

employee stock ownership plan (ESOP) • a variation of a defined-contribution profit-sharing plan. However, unlike a traditional profit-sharing plan, it is required to invest primarily in employer stock, thus providing a market for the stock. It also permits distributions to participants in the form of employer stock. In addition, it allows the plan to borrow to purchase employer stock. The loan is then repaid with employer contributions to the plan.

equitable interest • see *beneficial interest*.

estate for a term of years • a property interest established for a specific duration such as 15 or 20 years. Also known as a *term interest*.

estate trust • a type of trust commonly used to qualify property for the marital deduction. The surviving spouse is given an interest for life, and the remainder is payable to the surviving spouse's estate.

exclusion • for income tax purposes, an item of value that the taxpayer receives that is not includible in his or her gross income under a specific provision of tax law

exempt transfers • transfers of property which incur no gift or transfer taxes. For example, a donor can make unlimited gifts directly to a hospital or certain educational organizations on behalf of a donee without incurring a gift tax.

expected return • the most likely return. It typically is calculated as the arithmetic average of possible returns weighted by their respective likelihoods.

expense for the production of income • for income tax purposes, expenses incurred in the course of an activity that is not a trade or business but is engaged in for the purpose of producing income and making a profit. This type of expense is allowable as a deduction to an individual taxpayer.

expense method • a method of determining retirement income. It focuses on the projected expenses that a retiree will have. A list of expenses that should be considered includes general expenses as well as expenses unique to the particular individual. As with the replacement ratio method, it is much easier to define the potential expenses for individuals who are at or near retirement.

fact-finder form • a form that needs to be completed by a financial advisor engaged in financial planning for a client. It typically includes both quantitative and qualitative information that the advisor needs in order to develop a financial plan for the client.

federal estate tax • an excise tax levied on the right to transfer property at death, imposed upon and measured by the value of the taxable estate left by the decedent.

fee simple estate • the most complete interest in property. The individual who holds such an unlimited interest in property owns all the rights associated with the property. They include the

Glossary.8

current possessory rights and the ability to transfer the property at any point during his or her lifetime or at death.

fiduciary • a person who occupies a legally defined position of trust. Fiduciaries are charged with the responsibility of managing and investing money wisely for beneficiaries. Some examples of fiduciaries are executors of wills and estates, trustees, and those who administer the assets of underage or incompetent beneficiaries.

fiduciary capacity • the position held by a fiduciary. See *fiduciary*.

filing status • the taxpayer's filing selection (that is, single taxpayer, unmarried head of household, married taxpayer filing jointly, or married taxpayer filing separately). The filing status has a significant impact on taxable income. For each filing status, the amount of taxable income subject to each marginal tax rate varies considerably.

financial capacity • a technique insurers rely on to handle the risk that continues to exist after the operation of the law of large numbers. Insurers hold at least minimum amounts of required surplus (net worth) to, among other things, absorb underwriting losses that are not covered by investment gains.

financial life cycle • the five distinct phases in an individual's financial life or career. The five phases are (1) early career, (2) career development, (3) peak accumulation, (4) preretirement, and (5) retirement. Together the five phases span a person's entire financial life. Starting at a relatively young age, a career-minded person typically will pass through four phases en route to phase 5 and his or her retirement.

financial plan • a plan designed to carry a client from his or her present financial position to the attainment of financial goals. Since no two clients are alike, the plan must be designed for the individual, with all the advisor's recommended strategies tailored to each particular client's needs, abilities, and financial goals.

financial planning process • a eight-step process that financial advisors must follow when they are engaged in financial planning. The steps are (1) establishing and defining the client-planner relationship, (2) gathering information necessary to fulfill the engagement, (3) analyzing and evaluating the client's current financial status, (4) developing the recommendations, (5) communicating the recommendations, (6) implementing the recommendations, (7) monitoring the recommendations, (8) practicing within professional and regulatory standards.

financial planning • a process that focuses on ascertaining a client's financial goals and then developing a plan to help the client achieve those goals

financial risk tolerance • a client's psychological attitude toward his or her willingness to expose financial assets to the possibility of loss for the chance to achieve greater financial gain. It is measured along a continuum with individuals who are very risk tolerant at one end and those who are very risk averse at the other.

flat-percentage-of-earnings formula • a benefit formula in which the plan's retirement benefit is directly tied to salary. Because the IRS passed regulations that require this type of formula to have a 25-year minimum period of service in order for the participants to receive the full benefits promised, length of service with the employer is also a factor, albeit an indirect one.

flexible spending account (FSA) • a cafeteria plan in which an employee can elect to fund certain benefits on a before-tax basis by taking a salary reduction to pay the cost of any qualified benefits included in the plan. Benefits are paid from an employee's account as expenses are incurred, but any money remaining in the account is forfeited if not used by the end of the plan year.

401(k) plan • a type of defined-contribution profit-sharing plan that gives participants the option of reducing their taxable salary and contributing the salary reduction on a tax-deferred basis to an individual account for retirement purposes. In addition to the salary deferral feature, a 401(k) plan can contain a traditional profit-sharing feature, an employer-matching contribution feature, or both.

403(b) plan • a retirement plan that can be sold only to tax-exempt organizations and public schools. It is similar to a 401(k) plan in that it allows salary deferral contributions and before-tax employer contributions to be made to the employee's individual account. Employer contributions can be made as matching contributions based on employee elections to defer compensation. Frequently referred to as a tax-sheltered annuity (TSA).

fourth market • a market in which large institutional investors employ brokers to locate buyers or sellers of large blocks of stocks or bonds. When these transactions involve listed securities, this negotiated market is called the fourth market because the transaction does not take place on the floor of an organized exchange.

fruit and tree doctrine • a doctrine stating that income is to be taxed to the person who earns it or to the person who owns the asset that produces it. In other words, the fruits of an individual's labor cannot be assigned to another individual for tax purposes.

full retirement age • the age at which non-reduced Social Security retirement benefits are paid

fully insured • an insured status under Social Security. This status requires one of the following: (1) 40 quarters of coverage or (2) credit for at least as many quarters (but a minimum of six) of coverage as there are years elapsing after 1950 (or after the year in which age 21 is reached, if later) and before the year in which a person dies, becomes disabled, or reaches age 62, whichever occurs first.

future interest • the postponed right of use or enjoyment or income of the property.

gatekeeper • in managed care health plans, a primary care physician, often a general practitioner, who sees patients for all ailments (except emergencies) and directs further treatment by referring patients to specialists. The gatekeeper system is considered a major cost-reduction feature of managed care.

general obligations • state and local government bonds that are backed by the taxing power of the state or local government

general power of appointment • a power over the disposition of property exercisable in favor of any person whom the donee of the power may select including the donee, the donee's estate, the donee's creditors, or the creditors of the donee's estate

gift tax annual exclusion • a gift tax exclusion that a donor is allowed each year for each donee, provided the gift is one of present interest

grantor • the individual who creates a trust. A grantor is also referred to as a *settler*, *creator*, or *trustor*.

gross estate • an amount determined by totaling the value of all assets that a decedent had an interest in, which are required to be included in the estate by the Internal Revenue Code

gross income • for income tax purposes, all income from whatever source derived minus allowable exclusions. In other words, anything of value is considered gross income unless the Internal Revenue Code contains a specific provision that excludes a particular item.

group term life insurance • yearly renewable term life insurance that provides death benefits only and no buildup of cash values. The coverage is bought for and provided to a group instead of an individual.

growth stocks • stocks of corporations that have exhibited faster-than-average gains in earnings over the recent past and are expected to continue to show high levels of profit growth. They also tend to outperform slower-growing stocks but are riskier because they typically have higher price/earnings ratios and pay little or no dividends to stockholders.

guaranteed renewable • a continuance provision in an insurance contract that gives the insured the right to renew the coverage at each policy anniversary date, usually up to a stated age. Under this provision, the coverage cannot be terminated during the policy term, and renewal is guaranteed up to the stated age. However, unlike a noncancelable contract, the insurer has the right to raise the premium rate for broad classes of insureds.

health maintenance organizations (HMOs) • a managed system of health care that provides a comprehensive array of medical services on a prepaid basis to voluntarily enrolled persons living within a specific geographic region. HMOs both finance health care and deliver health services. There is an emphasis on preventive care as well as cost control.

health reimbursement account (HRA) • a type of defined-contribution medical expense plan under which an employer contributes a specified amount each year to an account from which the employee can make withdrawals to pay medical expenses that are not covered because of the plan's deductible. The employee can carry forward any unused amount in the account and add it to the following year's employer contribution to the account. Such a plan gives the employee an immediate incentive to purchase medical care wisely because if the amount in the account is exceeded, the employee will have to pay medical expenses out of his or her own pocket until the plan's deductible is satisfied.

holding-period return • a method most appropriately used for measuring an investment's return over a period of one year. This is because it gives no consideration to the timing of investment returns and therefore to the time value of money. It is calculated by dividing the total amount of current income plus the total amount of capital appreciation by the beginning dollar value of the investment. This calculation provides the investor with a before-tax holding-period return (HPR). An after-tax HPR can also be calculated by reducing each component of the numerator by the investor's appropriate marginal rate of tax.

holistic retirement planning • a way of looking at retirement planning that considers all aspects of the person, not just his or her financial picture

homeowners insurance • insurance that provides a package of coverages for a family's home, personal possessions, and liability that arises out of the many activities of family members. There are several homeowners insurance forms that provide varying degrees of coverage for different types of homeowners and tenants.

human-life-value method • a method for determining the amount of life insurance a person should carry. It is based on the proposition that a person should carry life insurance in an amount equal to the present value of the portion of the person's estimated future earnings that will be used to support his or her dependents.

immediate annuity • an annuity that must be purchased with a single premium because it begins to pay periodic benefits at the end of the first payment period (such as one month) following the purchase date

income tax basis • an amount designed to reflect the taxpayer's capital investment in property for income tax purposes. It is used to determine any gains or losses on disposition of the property.

indenture • the contract a company makes with its bondholders, including a commitment to pay a stated coupon amount (interest) periodically and return the face value (usually $1,000) at maturity

inflation risk • the degree to which one's purchasing power of an investment asset's future cash flows is affected by changes in the general level of prices in the economy. In other words, the risk that one's future assets will purchase less than they would today.

insurance • a risk financing technique that involves the transfer of the financial burden of risk to an insurer, who pools together a large number of similar risks in an effort to make losses more predictable and thus, reduce risk. A technique for handling pure risk must have both of these features—risk transfer and pooling of similar risks—in order to be insurance.

interest rate risk • the risk that changes in interest rates will adversely affect the value of debt securities. In other words if interest rates rise, the value of debt securities, especially long-term ones, will fall.

internal limits • special limits of coverages on certain types of property. Some of these internal limits can be increased for an additional premium.

inter vivos trust • a trust created during the settlor's lifetime. It becomes operative during lifetime as opposed to a trust under will (testamentary trust), which does not become operative until the settlor dies.

intestacy • the state or condition of dying without having made a valid will. The estates of these individuals are distributed according to the state's intestate laws.

intestacy laws • a state's laws that provide for the disposition of a person's probate estate if he or she dies without a valid will. See also *intestacy* and *intestate succession*.

intestate succession • a disposition of probate property that occurs when the deceased has left no will or when the will has been revoked or annulled as irregular

investing • what occurs when a person buys an asset with the expectation that it will provide a return commensurate with its risk. Investing is distinguished from speculating, which occurs when a person buys an asset hoping to receive some form of return without consideration of the expected return or risk or both.

Investment Advisors Act of 1940 • act that requires investment advisors to register with either the SEC or state regulatory authorities, depending on the amount of assets under the advisor's management, and full disclosure to clients.

Investment Company Act of 1940 • established rules and regulations that apply to all investment companies in dealing with shareholders. Provides for adequate disclosure, and refraining from charging excessive advisory, management, or brokerage fees. Later amendments regulated contractual mutual funds purchase.

investment assets • assets acquired for the purpose of investing, which is defined as the purchase of an asset with the expectation that it will provide a return. However, the distinction between investment assets and personal assets is not always clear and is based on the buyer's intent. The exact same asset may be an investment asset for one individual and a personal asset for another.

investment risk • risk measured by the likelihood that realized returns will differ from those that are expected. An asset with a wide range of possible returns is considered risky, while an asset with a narrow range of possible returns is considered more secure.

irrevocable life insurance trust (ILIT) • a trust arrangement in which the trust owns one or more life insurance policies on an insured's life within the trust.

irrevocable trust • a trust created when the grantor permanently transfers property to the trustee and cannot alter, amend, revoke, or terminate the arrangement or reclaim the property

itemized deductions • a limited group of expenditures by individuals that can be deducted from adjusted gross income (in lieu of the standard deduction) in determining taxable income. They typically include interest, taxes, medical expenses, and charitable contributions, subject to certain restrictions and limitations.

joint tenancy with right of survivorship • the holding of property by two or more persons in such a manner that, upon the death of one, the survivor or survivors take the entire property by operation of law

junk bonds • bonds that have weak quality ratings from S&P or Moody's. Junk bonds are risky because the firm either has a large amount of debt outstanding relative to its equity base or has suffered financial reverses and may be headed for serious trouble or bankruptcy. Because the risk is high, the return on them also is high if the issuer does not default.

large cap stocks • stocks with a large capitalization (number of shares outstanding times the price of a share). They typically have at least $5 billion in outstanding market value. There are numerous mutual funds that specialize in these stocks.

law of large numbers • a concept that embodies a mathematical principle stating that as the number of independent trials or events (that is, exposures) increases, the more closely will actual results approach the probable results expected from an infinite number of trials or events (exposures)

legal expense insurance • insurance designed to provide coverage for the legal services sometimes needed by employees. Most plans usually contain a list of covered services, although there may be limited coverage for a service that is not on the list as long as it is not specifically excluded.

liability risks • pure risks that involve the possibility of loss, and being held responsible, for damaging or destroying the property of others or from causing physical or personal injuries to others

life annuities • annuities whose benefit payments continue for the duration of a designated life

life-cycle financial planning • a financial planning process that is ongoing and occurs throughout a client's financial life. The advisor who monitors this type of planning is practicing life-cycle financial planning.

life estate • the title of the interest owned by a life tenant (income beneficiary)

liquidity • the ease with which an investment can be converted to cash with little or no loss of principal. Every portfolio should have some liquidity in it because it allows the investor the flexibility to quickly obtain cash for emergency purposes. There are two ways to obtain liquidity. One is to own liquid assets, and the other is to have readily available opportunities for borrowing money.

living trust • a trust that is created and operates before the death of the grantor. See *inter vivos trust*.

living will • a document in which the principal specifies the types of medical treatment he or she wishes to receive and does not wish to receive. Its existence lets others know of the principal's medical wishes, should he or she become terminally ill and lie in a persistent vegetative state, unable to communicate.

loan provision • a provision in cash value life insurance that allows the policyowner to borrow cash. The amount borrowed is charged interest at either a fixed or variable rate as stated in the policy. A variation of this provision can be used to automatically pay the premium when the policyowner, for whatever reason, fails to pay it.

long-term care insurance • insurance that provides coverage for custodial care, intermediate care, and skilled-nursing care. Benefits may also be available for home health care, adult day care, and assisted living. Benefits are usually limited to a specified dollar amount per day.

long-term debt instruments • debt instruments whose term to maturity is one year or more. Some people, however, refer to bonds with maturities of one to 10 years as being intermediate term.

loss control • one category of techniques available to handle pure risks. Loss control is concerned with activities that reduce both the frequency and severity of losses. Loss control techniques typically available include risk avoidance, loss prevention, and loss reduction.

loss financing • one category of techniques available to handle pure risks. Loss financing is concerned with how to finance the losses that do occur despite ongoing loss control activities. Loss financing techniques commonly used are retention and insurance.

loss prevention • a risk control technique that involves activities designed to reduce the frequency of loss associated with inescapable risks by preventing the occurrence of loss

loss reduction • a risk control technique that involves activities designed to reduce the severity of losses that do occur

major medical plans • a plan in which medical coverage is designed to provide substantial protection against catastrophic medical expenses. There are few exclusions and limitations, but deductibles and coinsurance are commonly used.

managed care plans • a plan that delivers cost-effective health care without sacrificing quality or access. Common characteristics include controlled access to providers, comprehensive case management, preventive care, risk sharing, and high-quality care.

marginal tax rate • the tax rate applicable to each income bracket. In the U.S. progressive income tax system, the marginal tax rate increases as income rises. It is the rate of tax applied to the last dollar of income.

marital deduction • the ability of spouses to pass property to each other with no gift tax or estate tax consequences. The marital deduction is thus unlimited in its scope either while a spouse is alive or at his/her death.

marketability • the ability to sell an asset quickly. Although marketability and liquidity are often confused, they are not the same. Liquid assets are marketable, but not all marketable assets are liquid. Stock is a classic example of a marketable asset that is not liquid. It is important that portfolios have marketable assets, but they are not a substitute for liquidity.

medical expense insurance • insurance that provides protection against financial losses that result from medical bills because of an accident or illness

Medicare Advantage • Part C of Medicare. It expands the choices available to most Medicare beneficiaries by allowing them to elect health care benefits through one of several alternatives (e.g., HMOs, PPOs, POS plans) to traditional Medicare Parts A and B.

Medicare Part A • the part of Medicare that covers hospitalizations, confinement in certified skilled-nursing facilities, home health care, and hospice care under certain circumstances. Also known as *hospital insurance.*

Medicare Part B • the part of Medicare that covers most physicians' services as well as medical items and services not covered under Medicare Part A. Part B premiums are normally deducted from participants' Social Security or railroad retirement benefits.

Medicare Part C • see *Medicare Advantage*

Medicare Part D • the part of Medicare that, as of 2006, makes prescription drug coverage available to Medicare enrollees. See also *Medicare prescription drug plans*.

Medicare prescription drug plans • private prescription drug plans in which Medicare participants can voluntarily enroll. The plans must meet certain standards established by Medicare, and beneficiaries normally pay a monthly premium and/or copayments for covered prescription drugs.

Medicare SELECT policy • one of the 10 standard Medigap policies. It can exclude or limit benefits (except in emergencies) for medical services if they are not received from network providers. Medicare SELECT policies are issued by insurance companies as PPO products and by some HMOs. Under certain circumstances, an insured who has a Medicare SELECT policy has the right to switch to a regular Medigap policy sold by the same company.

Medigap insurance • individual Medicare supplement insurance. As the name implies, its objective is to fill some of the gaps left after Medicare benefits have been exhausted. There currently are 10 standard Medigap plans.

miscellaneous fringe benefits • fringe benefits that do not fall into the broad category of insurance. They typically include education assistance, adoption assistance, dependent care assistance, and family leave.

miscellaneous itemized deductions • a group of deductions that includes employee business expenses, fees for safe deposit boxes, and fees for investment and individual tax advice, to name but a few. All of the taxpayer's deductions that fall within this group are subject to the 2 percent deduction floor. The result is that the taxpayer is permitted to deduct miscellaneous itemized deductions only to the extent they exceed the 2 percent floor.

money market deposit accounts (MMDAs) • a popular cash equivalent. MMDAs are offered by banks and permit virtually any amount to be deposited in the accounts. They usually are insured like savings accounts and CDs and allow withdrawals at the bank window or by check.

money market mutual funds (MMMFs) • a popular cash equivalent. MMMFs frequently require minimum dollar deposits and are not insured. They provide access by check, wire transfer, and in some cases by phone. Because they are mutual funds, investments in them are used to buy shares in the funds.

money-purchase pension plan • a type of defined-contribution pension plan. Under this type of plan, the employer's annual contributions are mandatory and are specified in the plan. Plan benefits for each participant are the amounts that can be provided by the sums contributed to the participant's individual account plus investment earnings.

mother's/father's benefit • the spouse of a person receiving retirement benefits is eligible for monthly benefits regardless of age if he or she is caring for at least one child of the retired worker who is (1) under age 16 or (2) disabled and entitled to a child's benefit. This benefit is also available to the surviving spouse (as well as a divorced spouse) of a deceased worker who was either fully or currently insured at the time of death if the surviving spouse is caring for at least one child of the deceased worker under the same conditions as for the retired worker.

multiple-purpose approach • the approach to financial planning that occurs when an advisor follows the financial planning process to develop a plan that solves two or more financial problems for a client. The plan may focus on solving several problems from one of the major planning areas, or it may focus on problems from two major planning areas.

mutual fund • the approach to financial planning that occurs when an advisor follows the financial planning process to develop a plan that solves two or more financial problems for a client. The plan may focus on solving several problems from one of the major planning areas, or it may focus on problems from two major planning areas.

named-perils approach • a way of insuring property that lists the specific perils for which coverage is provided. If the peril is not listed in the policy, it is not covered.

needs analysis • a process for dealing with pure risks involving the loss of income-earning ability resulting from death, disability, or old age. It involves the same six steps as the financial planning process that is used to identify and solve a client's financial problems. The needs analysis (financial planning) steps are (1) identify the client's needs in the event of death, disability, and/or retirement (establish financial goals); (2) collect information on the client's current financial situation (gather relevant data); (3) subtract the resources currently available from the resources required in order to determine the gaps to be filled by additional resources (analyze the data); (4) develop a plan for filling the resource gaps (develop a plan for achieving goals); (5) buy additional insurance and increase saving (implement the plan); and (6) monitor for changes in the client's needs (monitor the plan).

no-load fund • a mutual fund for which no commission is required for purchase. Some purists maintain that a true no-load fund must have no fees at all, other than the expenses of managing the fund.

nominal rate of return • the current rate of return unadjusted for inflation

noncancelable • a continuance provision in an insurance contract that gives the insured the right to renew the coverage at each policy anniversary date, usually up to a stated age. Under this provision, the coverage cannot be terminated during the policy term, renewal is guaranteed up to the stated age, and the premium rate is guaranteed in the contract.

nonforfeiture option • a set of choices available to a life insurance policyowner regarding the use of the policy's cash value. The choices include surrendering the policy for cash, buying a reduced amount of paid-up whole life insurance, or buying extended term insurance. For long-term care insurance, the most common option is a paid-up policy with a shortened benefit period. Another option is the return of a portion of the premium if the policy had been in force for a specified number of years.

nonparticipating (nonpar) policies • policies that do not pay policyowner dividends

nonqualified contracts • long-term care insurance contracts that do not meet the requirements of the Health Insurance Portability and Accountability Act (HIPAA). They are believed to not be eligible for the tax benefits provided under tax-qualified policies as defined by HIPAA.

nonqualified plan • a flexible retirement plan that is established primarily for executives but is not eligible for the special tax benefits available for qualified or other tax-advantaged retirement plans

nonrecognition transactions • transactions in which taxation is merely deferred rather than eliminated. These transactions involve the sale or exchange of property at a gain realized by the taxpayer. However, because of a provision in the Internal Revenue Code, the realized gain is not currently recognized for tax purposes.

notes • bonds issued with maturities of one to 10 years

OASDHI • the old age, survivors, disability, and health insurance program of the federal government, commonly known as Social Security and Medicare

open-end investment company • an investment company that is popularly called a mutual fund and continually sells and redeems its shares at net asset value. Hence the shares are not traded in the stock market. This type of company acquires a portfolio of securities in which each of the company's shares owns a proportionate interest.

open-perils approach • a way of insuring property that covers all types of losses except those that are specifically excluded by the policy's terms. If the peril is not specifically excluded in the policy, it is covered.

opportunity costs • the implicit cost of an activity or course of conduct based on forgone opportunities. In other words, it is the highest price or rate of return an alternative course of action would provide.

ordinary income • gain from the sale or exchange of property that is neither a capital asset nor a Section 1231 asset. In addition, income other than from actual or constructive sales or exchanges (such as rents or wages) is also generally referred to as ordinary income.

other than collision • (formerly referred to as comprehensive) an automobile insurance term that refers to physical damage to a vehicle that is not caused by collision

over-the-counter market • a market in which securities transactions are conducted through a network connecting dealers in stocks and bonds rather than on the floor of an exchange. This market deals in unlisted securities and off-board trading in listed securities.

paper deductions • allowable deductions even though they represent no corresponding cash outlay. Paper deductions represent or are related to some entry on the books of a taxpayer's business or investment activity, but they are not a cash-flow item.

partial disability • the inability to perform some stated percentage of job duties or to need a longer-than-normal amount of time to complete job duties

participating (par) policies • life insurance policies that provide for, but do not guarantee, the payment of dividends to the policyowner. The dividends reflect the insurer's past experience with respect to mortality, interest, and expenses.

passive losses • tax losses generated by activities in which the taxpayer has an ownership interest but does not participate in the activity of the business. The basic rule with respect to tax losses generated by passive activities is that they can be deducted only against income generated by the taxpayer's passive activities and not against the taxpayer's salary or other income.

pension maximization • a strategy a couple can follow to maximize a retiree's pension benefit by electing a "straight life" payout and using the extra funds to purchase life insurance on the retiree to protect the spouse.

pension plan • qualified pension plans include defined-benefit, cash-balance, money-purchase, and target-benefit plans. Pension plans are subject to mandatory annual funding, a prohibition from distributing assets prior to termination of employment, and a limitation on investments to 10 percent (maximum) of employer stock.

per diem basis • the method of paying long-term care insurance benefits whereby the insured receives a specified daily or weekly benefit amount regardless of the actual cost of care

peril • an event that causes a loss. Examples include fire, earthquake, and flood.

personal assets • assets bought primarily for the creature comforts they provide. They include such items as homes, cars, and clothes. However, the distinction between personal assets and investment assets is not clear and is based on the buyer's intent. The exact same asset may be a personal asset for one individual and an investment asset for another.

personal exemption • an exemption that each individual taxpayer is allowed to claim for himself or herself. The amount of the exemption is subtracted from adjusted gross income in the process of computing taxable income. The exemption amount changes annually by way of an inflation adjustment.

personal expense • for income tax purposes, expenses that are simply personal, family, or living expenses. Although as a general rule the Code provides that these expenses are nondeductible, there are several important exceptions to the general rule. However, many of the personal expenses that are allowable as deductions are subject to limitations as to what and how much can be deducted.

personal risks • pure risks that involve the possibility of loss of income-earning ability because of premature death, disability, unemployment, or retirement. In addition, the extra expenses associated with accidental injuries, periods of sickness, and long-term care are types of personal risks.

planned holding period • the period of time that an investor should plan to own a common stock. Periods shorter than 5 years subject stocks to increased risks and often produce negative total returns. The problem of market timing, or when to buy or sell, and the transactions costs of the purchase and sale combine to make success quite difficult with shorter-term holding periods.

point-of-service (POS) plans • a hybrid arrangement that combines aspects of a traditional medical expense plan with an HMO or a PPO. At the time of medical treatment, a participant can elect whether to receive treatment within the plan's network or outside the network.

pool of money • an indirect method for determining the benefit period under a reimbursement type of long-term care policy. Under this approach, there is a pool of money from which benefit payments are made. When the pool is exhausted, the policy terminates. However, the pool of money may last well beyond the policy's specified benefit period if benefits are paid at a rate that is less than the policy's maximum daily benefit amount.

portfolio effect • a technique insurers rely on to handle the risk that continues to exist after the operation of the law of large numbers. This involves reducing risk by writing different lines of insurance whose financial results vary inversely over time.

pour-over trust • a trust created during the grantor's lifetime simply to receive assets at the grantor's death

power of appointment • a property right created by the donor of the power that enables the donee of the power to designate, within such limits as the donor has prescribed, who will be the transferees of the property

power of appointment trust • a trust that provides for a power of appointment in a beneficiary

power of attorney • an instrument by which one person, the principal, appoints another as his or her agent and confers upon the agent the authority to perform certain specified acts or kinds of acts on behalf of the principal

preemptive right • the right that common stockholders sometimes have to maintain their relative voting power by purchasing shares of any new issues of common stock of the corporation

preexisting condition • an illness or injury for which a covered person received medical care during a specified period of time before becoming eligible for coverage. Usually the condition is no longer considered preexisting after the earlier of a period of 3 consecutive months during which no medical care is received for the condition or 12 months of coverage under the plan by the individual.

preferred-provider organizations (PPOs) • groups of health care providers who contract with employers, insurance companies, union trust funds, third-party administrators, or others to provide medical care services at a reduced fee. PPOs may be organized by the providers themselves or by such organizations as insurance companies, the Blues, or groups of employers.

premium-conversion plan • a cafeteria plan in which an employee can elect a before-tax salary reduction to pay his or her premium contribution to an employer-sponsored health or other welfare benefit plan. As a rule, these plans are established for medical and dental expenses only.

price risk • the risk of a bond's price changing in response to future interest rate changes. If rates increase after a bond is purchased, the bond's price in the secondary market will fall; if rates decrease, the bond's price will rise. Because the direction of future interest rates is unknown, there is uncertainty about the bond's future price.

primary insurance amount (PIA) • the amount a worker will receive under Social Security if he or she retires at full retirement age or becomes disabled. It is also the amount on which all other Social Security income benefits are based.

prime interest rate • the interest rate banks charge their most creditworthy customers. It is a key interest rate because loans to less creditworthy customers are often tied to the prime rate.

probate • the process of proving a will's validity in court and executing its provisions under the guidance of the court. The probate estate encompasses all property that passes under the terms of the will or, if no will, under a state's intestacy laws. See also *probate assets*.

probate assets • assets (property) that is passed under the terms of a will; if no will, it passes under the intestacy laws (for example, individually-held property or one-half of community property). See also *probate*.

profit-sharing plan • both a category and a type of qualified plan. A profit-sharing plan is a defined-contribution plan structured to offer employees participation in company profits that they may use for retirement purposes. Employer contributions are discretionary, but if they are made, the contributions must be allocated according to an allocation formula.

property risks • pure risks that involve the possibility of direct losses associated with the need to replace or repair damaged or missing property, and indirect (consequential) losses such as additional living expenses that are caused by a direct loss

prospectus • a document that all companies offering new securities for public sale must file with the SEC. It spells out in detail the financial position of the offering company, what the new funds will be used for, the qualifications of the corporate officers, risk factors, nature of competition, and other material information.

purchasing power risk • sometimes called inflation risk. Purchasing power risk is based on the degree to which the purchasing power of an investment asset's future cash flows is affected by changes in the general level of prices in the economy.

pure risk • risk that involves the possibility of only financial loss. With pure risk, there is no possibility of financial gain. This type of risk has two outcomes—loss or no loss (that is, no change). With few exceptions, insurance is a technique for dealing with pure risk. Pure risks can be categorized as personal risks, property risks, and liability risks.

qualified dividends • dividends defined by the IRS as those that will be taxed at the lower capital gains rate than at the ordinary income rates. Dividends that are qualified must meet certain organizational provisions (most U.S. companies qualify) and holding periods.

qualified domestic relations order (QDRO) • a court decree under state law that allows a participant's retirement plan assets to be used for marital property rights, child support, or alimony payments

qualified plan • a retirement plan that is rewarded with favorable tax status for meeting Internal Revenue Code Section 401(a) restrictions. There are eight types of qualified plans including defined-benefit pension plans, cash-balance plans, money-purchase pension plans, target-benefit plans, profit-sharing plans, 401(k) plans, stock bonus plans, and ESOPs.

qualified terminal interest property (QTIP) trust • a trust holding property that falls under an exception to the terminal interest rule of the gift and estate tax law by allowing a marital deduction to a transferor spouse (or a transferor spouse's estate) for the total value of a gift or bequest of property for the transferee spouse's life benefit. The transferor must make a QTIP election at the time of the gift (or bequest) to identify the property as being included in the surviving spouse's estate at his/her death.

quarters of coverage • the basis on which eligibility for benefits under Social Security is determined. Credit for up to four quarters of coverage may be earned in any calendar year.

real rate of return • the current or nominal rate of return minus the inflation rate. It provides investors in bonds and other fixed-rate instruments a way to see whether their returns will allow them to keep up with or beat the erosion in dollar values caused by inflation.

reimbursement basis • the method of paying long-term care insurance benefits that reimburses the insured for actual expenses incurred up to the specified benefit amount

reinsurance • a technique insurers rely on to handle the risk that continues to exist after the operation of the law of large numbers. This involves an insurer transferring part of its risk to other insurers (that is, insurance for insurance companies).

reinvestment rate risk • the risk associated with reinvesting interest income at unknown future interest rates. If interest rates fall, the investor will have to be satisfied with reinvesting the interest payments from current bonds at a lower rate of return than anticipated. If interest rates rise, the investor will be able to reinvest the interest payments from current bonds at a higher rate of return than anticipated. Because the direction of future interest rates is unknown, there is uncertainty about the rates at which interest income will be reinvested.

remainder interest • a future interest that comes into existence after the termination of a prior interest. For example, Alexandra (the testator) created a testamentary trust under her will in which the corpus (principal) is to be retained, with income paid to Bill (the lifetime beneficiary) until Bill's death, at which time the corpus (remainder interest) will pass to Carl (the remainderperson).

remainderperson • the person who is entitled to receive the principal (corpus) of an estate upon the termination of the intervening life estate or estates. See *remainder interest*.

renewability provision • a provision frequently found in term life insurance that allows the policyowner insured to renew the policy for another period of protection without having to show evidence of insurability. Most insurers, however, do not permit renewals to carry coverage beyond a certain age.

replacement cost • the cost necessary to replace or repair damaged property using equivalent materials and workmanship. Depreciation is not factored into an asset's replacement cost.

replacement ratio method • a method of determining retirement income. It assumes that the standard of living enjoyed during the years just prior to retirement will be the determining factor for the standard of living during retirement. In general, a 60 to 80 percent replacement ratio of a person's final average salary is used for individual retirement planning purposes.

replacement-cost requirement • a provision that requires the insured to carry insurance equal to a specified percentage of the replacement cost of the dwelling. If the appropriate amount of insurance is carried, losses will be settled on a full replacement-cost basis.

residual disability • the replacement of lost earnings due to less-than-total disability. It is based on a person's reduction in earnings rather than his or her physical condition.

retention • a risk financing technique that involves financing or paying for one's own losses. In cases where retention is consciously practiced, an individual may set aside funds earmarked for a particular risk. However, most retention is practiced informally by covering losses with funds in a savings account, by borrowing, or by paying for the loss on an out-of-pocket basis.

revenue bonds • bonds issued by agencies of a state or local government. They are guaranteed by the revenues earned from such ventures as turnpikes, airports, and sewer and water systems. Without the taxing authority behind them, they are viewed as riskier and pay investors a somewhat higher interest rate than do general obligation bonds.

reverse mortgage • a loan against an individual's home that requires no repayment for as long as the individual continues to live in the house. It is available only when all of the owners are aged 62 or older and when the home is the principal residence.

reversionary interest • a right to future enjoyment by the transferor of property that is now in the possession or enjoyment of another party. For example, Anthony creates a trust under which a parent, Barbara, is to enjoy income for life, with the corpus of the trust to be paid over to Anthony at Barbara's death. Anthony's interest is a reversionary interest.

revocable life insurance trust • an arrangement in which a trust owns one or more life insurance policies on an insured, but which can be revoked by the grantor while he or she remains alive.

revocable trust • a trust in which the grantor reserves the power to alter or revoke the agreement. Thus, the grantor can reclaim the trust assets at any time. It becomes irrevocable only when the grantor modifies the trust to become irrevocable or dies and, therefore, is no longer able to modify the trust.

risk • the possibility of financial loss (for insurance and financial planning purposes). Loss can occur as a result of the reduced value of something that an individual already possesses. Loss can also occur as a result of the reduced value of something that an individual does not possess but expects to receive in the future, such as earning only a 5 percent return on an investment that was expected to yield 10 percent.

risk avoidance • a risk control technique that involves avoiding situations that include certain types of risks

risk-free investment • an investment assumed to be free of the risk of losing one's principal or promised risk. U.S. government issues (bonds, notes, bills) are widely-assumed to be risk-free, since failure to pay promised interest and principal would be tantamount to a default of the U.S. government.

risk management • a process for handling pure risks involving possible damage or destruction of property or legal liability. It involves the same six steps as the financial planning process that is used to identify and solve a client's financial problems. The risk management (financial planning) steps are (1) determine objectives (establish financial goals); (2) identify the risks (includes gathering relevant data); (3) risk analysis (analyze the data); (4) consider alternative risk treatment devices and select the device(s) believed to be best for treating the risk(s) (develop a plan for achieving goals); (5) implement the decision (implement the plan); and (6) monitor the process (monitor periodically).

Roth IRA • an individual retirement account plan in which an individual's contributions are not deductible, but qualifying withdrawals are not subject to income tax. Roth IRAs are subject to certain limitations, the most important of which is the maximum contribution limit. Unlike traditional IRAs, the owner of a Roth IRA can make contributions even after he or she attains age 70 1/2. Moreover, the minimum distribution rules that apply to traditional IRAs do not apply to a

Roth IRA while the owner is alive. The owner of a Roth IRA is not required to take distributions at any age.

S corporation • a corporation that is taxed similarly to a partnership under the provisions of the Internal Revenue Code. Like a partnership, an S corporation is not subject to tax at the entity level. Rather, the owners of the business pay the taxes. An S corporation is often referred to as a pass-through entity because the responsibility for paying its taxes is passed through the entity to the owners of the entity.

sandwiched generation • another name for the baby-boom generation. Many of its members are faced with financing their children's educations and aiding their parents while trying to save for their own retirement.

savings incentive match plan for employees (SIMPLE) • a retirement plan funded with individual retirement accounts. Any type of business entity can establish a SIMPLE, but the business cannot have more than 100 employees. Also the sponsoring employer cannot maintain any other qualified plan, 403(b) plan, or SEP at the same time it maintains the SIMPLE. In addition, all eligible employees are able to make elective salary deferral contributions.

Section 79 • Internal Revenue Code Section that gives favorable tax treatment to life insurance plans that qualify as group term insurance

Securities Exchange Act of 1934 • securities law dealing with existing securities, addressing the filing of periodic reports, regulating exchanges and brokerage firms, ongoing disclosure requirements, and prohibiting unethical practices such as market manipulation and insider trading

Securities Investor Protection Corporation (SIPC) • a federal agency that guarantees the safety of brokerage accounts up to $500,000, no more than $100,000 of which may be in cash. SIPC protects investor funds when the clearing firm becomes insolvent and from unauthorized trading in an investor's account, but not from ordinary market losses.

sick-pay plans • a plan that is typically an uninsured arrangement to replace for a limited period of time lost income because of disability or illness

simplified employee pension (SEP) • a type of retirement plan that uses an individual retirement account (IRA) or an individual retirement annuity (IRA annuity) as the receptacle for contributions. Plan contributions must be allocated to participants in a way that provides a benefit as a level percentage of compensation. The only exception to this rule is that the allocation formula may be integrated with Social Security, providing highly compensated employees with contributions that are slightly larger (as a percentage of pay) than those for the rank-and-file employees.

single limit of liability • a limit used in automobile insurance. It specifies the maximum amount that will be paid under the policy for all damages involving bodily injury and property damage resulting from any one accident.

single-purpose approach • the approach to financial planning that occurs when an advisor follows the financial planning process to develop a plan that solves a single financial problem for a client. The plan may be as simple as selling a single financial product or service to the client in order to solve the problem.

skilled-nursing services • care and support services that must be provided only by licensed nurses or other health care professionals, such as a physical therapist. Skilled-nursing services are typically provided to a patient who is improving after and accident or illness.

small cap stocks • stocks that generally have a market capitalization (number of shares outstanding times the price of a share) of $500 million or less. They usually represent companies that are less well established but in many cases are faster growing than large cap stocks ($5 billion or more). Because they are often less well established, they are usually more volatile than Blue Chips.

Social Security Statement • an annual statement issued by the Social Security Administration that enables an individual to verify his or her contributions to the Social Security and Medicare programs. The statement also contains an estimate of benefits that will be available because of retirement, disability, or death. It is sent to each worker aged 25 or older who has worked in employment covered by Social Security and who is not currently entitled to monthly benefits.

special power of appointment • a power over the disposition of property in which the donor of the power limits the donee's appointment of the property to other than the donee, the donee's estate, or the donee's creditors

speculating • what occurs when a person buys an asset in the hopes of receiving some form of return without consideration or knowledge of the expected return or risk or both. Speculating is distinguished from investing, which occurs when a person buys an asset expecting that it will provide a return commensurate with its risk.

speculative risk • risk that involves not only the possibility of financial loss but also the possibility of financial gain. This type of risk has three possible outcomes— loss, gain, or no loss or gain (that is, no change). Speculative risk is the type of risk that investors face in their investment activities.

split limit of liability • a limit used in automobile insurance that is divided into three components. The first number specifies the maximum amount that will be paid for bodily injury to each person in an accident; the second specifies the maximum for all bodily injury in an accident; and the third specifies the maximum for all property damage in an accident.

springing durable power of attorney • a power of attorney that lies dormant and ineffective until it is needed. A determination that the principal has become incapacitated would trigger the springing power.

Standard & Poor's 500 Index • a broad-based measurement of changes in stock-market conditions based on the average performance of 500 widely held common stocks

standard deduction • a fixed amount that an individual may claim in lieu of claiming itemized deductions. The amount depends on the individual's filing status category.

state estate tax • a tax imposed on a deceased person's right to transfer or pass property to beneficiaries

state inheritance tax • a tax imposed on a beneficiary's right to inherit property from a deceased person's estate. The tax rate is often based on the beneficiary's relationship to the deceased.

stock bonus plan • a variation of a defined-contribution profit-sharing plan. However, unlike a traditional profit-sharing plan, it typically invests a large percentage of the plan's assets in the employer's stock, thus providing a market for the stock. It also permits distributions to participants in the form of employer stock.

Subchapter S corporation • see S corporation

target-benefit pension plan • a type of defined-contribution pension plan that has some of the features associated with a traditional defined-benefit plan. This hybrid plan uses a benefit formula like that of a defined-benefit plan and individual accounts like that of a defined-contribution plan. While the employer hopes to provide a specific benefit (the target) at retirement, the employer does not guarantee that the targeted benefit will be paid.

tax avoidance • a strategy that focuses on paying the least amount of tax possible through legal means. Some tax-avoidance techniques, or loopholes as they are often called, require the knowledge of an experienced tax professional to recommend and implement. Illegal strategies to avoid paying taxes is tax evasion.

tax bracket • the range of taxable income applicable to each marginal tax rate for each filing status

tax credits • a dollar-for-dollar reduction of the actual tax payable. There are several personal tax credits available for individual taxpayers. Each tax credit has its own set of rules for eligibility, availability based on the taxpayer's income level, and credit amounts.

tax evasion • any method of reducing taxes not permitted by law. It carries heavy penalties.

tax minimization • a strategy that focuses on minimizing (or avoiding) tax liability by analyzing the tax implications of various alternatives to find the one that best suits the individual within the context of his or her financial plan

tax preference item • items that are deductible for the regular tax but face different rules under the AMT. They generally produce no benefit to the taxpayer under the AMT system as they would under the regular system.

tax sheltered annuity (TSA) • see 403(b) plan

tax shelters • investments that allow taxpayers to write off tax losses against salary and other types of income. Under current law, however, there are strict limitations on the deductibility of losses generated by tax-shelter investments.

taxable distribution • one of the three different types of transfers that the generation-skipping transfer tax applies to. A taxable distribution is any distribution from a trust to a skip person (an individual who is two generations or more younger than the transferor) that is not a taxable termination or a direct skip.

taxable income • the amount of income that will actually be subject to tax in a given year. For individuals it is equal to adjusted gross income minus the standard or itemized deduction(s) and personal exemptions.

taxable termination • one of the three different types of transfers that the generation-skipping transfer tax applies to. A taxable termination occurs when an interest in property held in trust for a skip person (an individual who is two generations or more younger than the transferor) is terminated by an individual's death, lapse of time, release of a power or otherwise, and the trust property is either held for or distributed to the skip person.

taxable year • the annual accounting period during which taxable income or loss is determined for the taxpayer. For most individuals, it is simply the calendar year.

tax-qualified contracts • long-term care insurance contracts that meet the requirements of the Health Insurance Portability and Accountability Act and therefore are eligible for favorable tax treatment

tenancy by the entirety • the holding of property by a husband or wife in such a manner that, except with the consent of each, neither husband nor wife has a disposable interest in the property during the lifetime of the other. Upon the death of either, the property goes to the surviving spouse.

tenancy in common • the holding of property by two or more persons in such a manner that each has an undivided interest, which can be sold or gifted at any time, and upon the death of one is passed to the person(s) designated in the deceased tenant's will (or by intestacy) and does not pass automatically to the surviving tenants in common.

term interest • see *estate for a term of years*

term life insurance • a type of life insurance under which the death proceeds are payable if the insured dies during a specified period. If the insured survives to the end of the period, nothing is paid by the insurer.

testamentary trust • a trust created by the terms of a will. It does not receive property until the testator dies and the executor transfers the property to the trust.

testator • a person who leaves a will in force at death

total disability • the condition of an insured person who is unable to work. One definition, typically called the any-occupation definition, states that the insured is totally disabled when he or she cannot perform the major duties of any gainful occupation for which he or she is reasonably suited by education, training, or experience. A less restrictive definition deems the insured to be totally disabled when he or she cannot perform the major duties of his or her regular occupation.

Totten trust • a revocable transfer in which a donor makes a deposit in a bank savings account for a donee. The donor acts as trustee of the account, and no gift occurs until the donee makes a withdrawal.

traditional IRA • an individual retirement account plan that allows an individual's contributions to be made with pretax dollars (if the taxpayer is eligible) and earnings to be tax deferred until retirement, at which time all withdrawals are taxable. Traditional IRAs are subject to certain limitations, the most important of which is the maximum contribution limit. In addition, contributions may not be made during or after the year in which the individual reaches age 70 1/2, and no loans may be taken from IRA accounts.

U.S. Treasury bills (T-bills) • a popular cash equivalent. T-bills are short-term obligations of the U.S. government issued with a term of one year or less. In addition, they are backed by the full taxing authority of the government and consequently are the safest investment available. Because of their safety, they pay investors the lowest interest rate of the various money market instruments.

trust • a fiduciary arrangement whereby the legal title of property is held, and the property is managed, by someone for the benefit of another

trustee • the holder of legal title to property for the use or benefit or another. See also *trust*.

Uniform Gifts to Minors Act (UGMA) • state laws that authorize the transfer of property to a custodian who holds the property for a minor and distributes all property and income to the minor when he or she reaches adulthood under local (state) laws. See also *Uniform Transfers to Minors Act (UTMA)*.

Uniform Transfers to Minors Act (UTMA) • state laws that authorize the transfer of property to a custodian who holds the property for a minor and distributes all property and income to the minor when he or she reaches adulthood under local (state) laws. See also *Uniform Gifts to Minors Act (UGMA)*.

unit-benefit formula • a benefit formula that directly accounts for both the participant's service with the employer and his or her salary in determining the plan's retirement benefit

universal life insurance • a type of whole life insurance with flexible premiums and adjustable death benefits that enables the policyowner to see how premiums are allocated to the protection and cash value elements of the policy

value stocks • stocks that typically have below average price/earnings ratios and regularly pay dividends to stockholders

variable life insurance • a whole life policy that permits the policyowner to allocate the funds generated by the policy among a variety of separate accounts. These policies shift the investment risk to the policyowner and provide no minimum guaranteed rate of return or guaranteed cash value. The rate of return credited to policy funds and thus the amount of the cash value depend on the investment success of the policyowner.

variable universal life • life insurance that is identical to universal life except that the cash value is invested by the policyowner in a variety of separate accounts rather than in the general assets of the insurer. In other words, it combines the premium flexibility features of universal life with the policyowner-directed investment aspects of variable life.

vision benefit plan • a plan that covers vision care expenses that usually are not covered under other medical expense plans. Benefits are provided for the cost of eye examinations and eyeglasses and/or contact lenses.

voluntary benefit plans • an arrangement in which the employer does not share in the cost of the benefit, but merely makes it available to an employee who pays the entire cost of coverage if he or she elects the benefit. The premiums are paid through payroll deductions by the employer.

whole life insurance • a type of life insurance under which the death proceeds are payable in the event of the insured's death regardless of when that occurs, provided the policy has been kept in force by the policyowner

INDEX

401(k) plan, 6.35
403(b) plan, 6.40

A

above-the-line deductions, 5.5
accidental death and dismemberment (AD&D), 3.30
accrual method, 5.17
active participant, 6.44
actual cash value, 2.13
adjusted gross income, 5.4
advance medical directive, 7.20
agency bonds, 4.13
allocation formula, 6.34
alternative minimum tax, 5.15
American Depositary Receipts (ADRs), 4.16
analyzing and evaluating the client's current financial status, 1.4
any-occupation, 2.42
applicable exclusion amount, 7.35
approximate yield, 4.34
asset allocation, 4.9
asset allocation model, 4.9
assignment of income doctrine, 5.19

B

baby boom generation, 1.33
basic benefits, 8.31
below-the-line deductions, 5.5
beneficial interest, 7.11
benefit period, 2.44
business (default) risk, 4.24
business expense, 5.7
buy-up plan, 3.8

C

C corporation, 5.32
cafeteria plans, 3.50
capital appreciation, 4.31
capital assets, 4.29
capital gain, 5.28
cash equivalent, 4.10
cash-balance pension plan, 6.32
cash-basis method, 5.17
certificate of deposit (CD), 4.11
charitable deduction, 7.33
charitable lead trust, 7.53
charitable remainder trust, 7.52

closed-end investment company, 4.17
COBRA, 3.24
collision, 2.60
communicating the recommendations, 1.5
community property, 7.10
compound interest, 4.40
comprehensive approach, 1.24
comprehensive dental plans, 3.40
constructive receipt doctrine, 5.19
contributory plan, 3.38
conversion, 3.26
conversion provision, 2.32
coordination-of-benefits (COB) provision, 3.21
cost basis, 4.29, 5.26
cost recovery deductions, 5.9
cost-of-living adjustment (COLA), 8.15
coverage gap, 8.28
credit estate tax, 7.39
creditable prescription drug coverage, 8.29
critical illness insurance, 3.44
Crummey powers, 7.45
current assumption whole life, 2.36
current yield, 4.31
currently insured, 8.4

D

de minimis, 3.34
deceased spousal unused exclusion amount (DSUEA), 7.50
deduction, 5.3
deduction floor, 5.22
deferred annuity, 2.38
defined-benefit pension plan, 6.30
defined-benefit plan, 6.26
defined-contribution medical expense plan, 3.22
defined-contribution plan, 6.26
dental insurance, 3.38
dependency exemption, 5.11
dependent life insurance, 3.31
depreciation, 2.13
depreciation deduction, 5.9
developing the recommendations, 1.5
direct loss, 2.5
direct skip, 7.36
disability income insurance, 2.41
disability insured, 8.5
disease management, 3.14
diversification, 4.30
dividends, 2.35
dollar-cost averaging, 4.39
domains of financial planning, 1.4

Index.2

doughnut hole, 8.28
durable power of attorney, 7.18
durable power of attorney for health care, 7.20

E

earnings test, 8.14
economic benefit doctrine, 5.18
effective tax rate, 5.13
elimination (waiting) period), 2.42
elimination period, 2.43
employee benefits, 3.2
employee stock ownership plan (ESOP), 6.37
establishing and defining the client-planner relationship, 1.4
estate for a term of years, 7.6
estate trust, 7.48
exclusion, 5.3
expected return, 4.3
expense for the production of income, 5.8
expense method, 6.19

F

face amount, 2.32
fact-finder form., 1.12
federal estate tax, 7.34
fee simple estate, 7.5
fee-for-service, 3.17
fiduciaries, 7.12
fiduciary capacity, 7.14
filing status, 5.12
financial goals, 1.9
financial life cycle, 1.28
financial plan, 1.16
financial planning, 1.3
financial planning domains, 1.4
financial planning process, 1.4
financial risk tolerance, 1.11
fiscal year, 5.16
flat-percentage-of-earnings formula, 6.31
flexible spending account (FSA), 3.52
fourth market, 4.43
fruit and tree doctrine, 5.18
full retirement age, 8.5
fully insured, 8.4
future interest, 7.7

G

gatekeeper, 3.16
gatekeepers, 3.14
gathering information necessary to fulfill the engagement, 1.4
general obligations (GOs), 4.13

general power of appointment, 7.12
grantor, 7.14
gross estate, 7.34
gross income, 5.2
group term life insurance, 3.27
guaranteed renewable, 2.45

H

health maintenance organization (HMO), 8.26
health maintenance organization (HMO), 3.15
health reimbursement account (HRA), 3.23
holding-period return (HPR), 4.33
holistic retirement planning, 6.3
homeowners insurance, 2.52
hospital indemnity insurance, 3.44
human-life-value method, 2.16

I

immediate annuity, 2.38
implementing the recommendation(s), 1.5
income tax basis, 5.10
indenture, 4.14
index funds, 4.19
indirect loss, 2.5
inflation risk, 4.22
insurance, 2.20
inter vivos trust, 7.15
interest rate risk, 4.23
intestacy, 7.13
intestacy laws, 7.23
Investment Advisors Act of 1940, 4.46
investment assets, 4.1
Investment Company Act of 1940, 4.46
investment risk, 4.5
irrevocable life insurance trust (ILIT), 7.56
irrevocable trust, 7.16

J

joint tenancy with right of survivorship, 7.8

K

Keogh plan, 6.26

L

law of large numbers, 2.23
legal expense insurance, 3.43
liability risk, 2.4
life annuity, 2.38
life estate, 7.6

life-cycle financial planning, 1.30
liquidity, 4.25
living trust, 7.15
living will, 7.20
loan provision, 2.34
long-term care insurance, 2.41
loss financing, 2.19
loss prevention, 2.20
loss reduction, 2.20

M

major medical plans, 3.12
managed care plan, 3.14
marginal tax rate, 5.12
marital deduction, 7.33
marketability, 4.27
mass, 2.24
medical expense insurance, 2.41
Medicare Advantage, 8.26
Medicare carve-out, 3.26
Medicare Part D, 8.27
Medicare prescription drug plans, 8.27
miscellaneous fringe benefits, 3.45
miscellaneous itemized deductions, 5.22
money market deposit account, 4.11
money market mutual fund (MMMF), 4.11
money-purchase pension plan, 6.33
monitoring the recommendation(s), 1.5
mother's/father's benefit, 8.6
multiple-purpose approach, 1.23
mutual fund, 4.17

N

named-perils approach, 2.54
needs analysis, 2.6
net amount at risk, 2.34
net asset value (NAV), 4.17
no-load fund, 4.18
noncancelable, 2.45
noncontributory plan, 3.38
nonforfeiture options, 2.35
nonparticipating (nonpar) policy, 2.36
nonqualified LTCI contract, 2.49
nonqualified plan, 6.24, 6.40
nonrecognition transactions, 5.25

O

old-age, survivors, disability, and health insurance (OASDHI), 8.1
open-end investment company, 4.17
open-perils approach, 2.54
opportunity costs, 4.26

opportunity loss, 4.4
ordinary income, 5.28
other than collision, 2.60
over-the-counter (OTC) market, 4.44
own-occupation, 2.43

P

paper deductions, 5.8
partial disability, 2.42
participating (par) policy, 2.35
passive losses, 5.24
pay-on-death (POD), 7.25
pension maximization, 6.52
pension plan, 6.29
per diem basis, 2.48
peril, 2.3
personal exemption, 5.11
personal expense, 5.8
personal risk, 2.4
personal umbrella liability policy, 2.61
planned holding period, 4.38
point-of-service (POS) plan, 3.15
policy reserve, 2.34
pool of money, 2.48
pour-over trust, 7.16
power of appointment, 7.12
power of appointment trust, 7.48
power of attorney, 7.12
practicing within professional and regulatory standards, 1.5
preemptive right, 4.15
preexisting condition, 3.20
preferred-provider organization (PPO), 3.15
price risk, 4.23
primary insurance amount (PIA), 8.10
pro forma statements, 1.32
probate assets, 7.13
profit-sharing, 6.29
property risk, 2.4
prospectus, 4.18
purchasing power risk, 4.22
pure risk, 2.2

Q

qualified dividends, 4.28
qualified domestic relations order (QDRO), 6.15
qualified plans, 6.24
quarters of coverage, 8.4

R

real estate investment trust (REIT), 4.21
real rate of return, 4.22

reimbursement basis, 2.48
reinvestment rate risk, 4.24
remainder interest, 7.7
renewability provision, 2.31
replacement cost, 2.13
replacement ratio method, 6.19
replacement-cost requirement, 2.54
residual disability, 2.42
retention, 2.20
revenue bonds, 4.13
reverse mortgage, 6.49
reversionary interest, 7.7
revocable life insurance trust, 7.55
revocable trust, 7.16
risk, 2.2
risk avoidance, 2.20
risk management, 2.6
risk pooling, 2.22
risk transfer, 2.22
risk-free investment, 4.12
Roth IRA, 6.46

S

sandwiched generation, 1.39
savings incentive match plan for employees (SIMPLE), 6.38
Sec. 2503(b) trust, 7.44
Sec. 2503(c) trust, 7.44
sector fund, 4.20
Securities Exchange Act of 1934, 4.45
Securities Investor Protection Act of 1970, 4.46
Securities Investor Protection Corporation (SIPC), 4.46
simple cafeteria plan, 3.53
simplified employee pension (SEP), 6.38
single-purpose approach, 1.23
skilled-nursing services, 8.21
Social Security statement, 8.16
special power of appointment, 7.12
specified (dread) disease insurance, 3.44
speculating, 4.2
speculative risk, 2.2, 4.2
spread, 4.44
springing durable power of attorney, 7.18
standard deduction, 5.5
state estate tax, 7.39
state inheritance tax, 7.39
stock bonus plan, 6.37
stop-loss limit, 3.13
structuring, 1.7
Subchapter S corporation, 5.32

T

target-benefit pension plan, 6.33
tax bracket, 5.12
tax credit, 5.14
tax evasion, 5.21
tax preference items, 5.16
tax shelters, 5.24
tax-qualified LTCI contract, 2.49
tax-sheltered annuity (TSA), 6.40
taxable distribution, 7.37
taxable income, 5.4–5.5
taxable termination, 7.37
taxable wage base (TWB), 8.3
taxable year, 5.17
tenancy by the entirety, 7.9
tenancy in common, 7.8
testamentary, 7.3
testamentary trust, 7.17
testator, 7.13, 7.17
total disability, 2.42
Totten trust, 7.25
traditional IRA, 6.43
trust, 7.14
trustee, 7.14

U

U.S. Treasury bills (T-bills), 4.12
Uniform Gifts to Minors Act (UGMA), 7.43
Uniform Transfers to Minors Act (UTMA), 7.43
unit-benefit formula, 6.30

V

variable life insurance, 2.36
variable universal life (VUL), 2.37
vision benefit plan, 3.41
voluntary benefits, 3.8

W

waiting period, 2.43